A DIAL IN YOUR POKE

A BOOK OF PORTABLE SUNDIALS

BY

Mike Cowham

He drew a dial from his poke,
and looking on it with lack-lustre eye,
says very wisely, "It is 10 o'clock:"

Shakespeare's 'As You Like It'
(Act 2, Scene 7)

Second Edition, Revised and Extended
Cambridge 2011

FIRST PUBLISHED IN GREAT BRITAIN BY M. J. COWHAM

PO Box 970, Haslingfield, Cambridge CB23 1FL, England.

CAMBRIDGE 2004

Second Edition

CAMBRIDGE 2011

All Rights Reserved. No part of this publication may be reproduced, stored in a retrieval system, or transmitted in any form or by any means, electronic, mechanical, photocopying, recording or otherwise, without prior permission in writing of the publisher, nor otherwise be circulated in any form of binding or cover other than that in which it is published and without a similar condition including this condition being imposed on the subsequent purchaser.

The rights of Mike Cowham to be identified as the author of this work have been asserted by him in accordance with the Copyright, Designs and Patents Act 1988.

PRINTED BY

Henry Ling Limited
The Dorset Press
Dorchester
Dorset
DT1 1HD

COPYRIGHT © 2004 & 2011, M. J. COWHAM

ISBN 978-0-9551155-2-3

CONTENTS

		Pages
	Acknowledgements	IV
	The Author	V
Preface	How I Became Interested in Portable Dials	VI - VIII
	Introduction	1 - 5
Chapter 1	The First Portable Dials	6 - 9
Chapter 2	Altitude Dials	10 - 19
Chapter 3	Simple Ring Dials	20 - 23
Chapter 4	Equinoctial Ring Dials	24 - 30
Chapter 5	Quadrants	31 - 39
Chapter 6	Ivory Diptych Dials	40 - 50
Chapter 7	French Ivory Dials	51 - 58
Chapter 8	French Dials	59 - 64
Chapter 9	French Butterfield Dials	65 - 77
Chapter 10	Other Butterfield Dials	78 - 85
Chapter 11	English Dials	86 - 96
Chapter 12	Universal Equinoctial Dials	97 - 101
Chapter 13	Vertical Dials	102 - 104
Chapter 14	Polar Dials	105 - 106
Chapter 15	Augsburg Dials	107 - 113
Chapter 16	Inclining Dials	114 - 118
Chapter 17	Scaphe Dials	119 - 121
Chapter 18	Analemmatic Dials	122 - 124
Chapter 19	Magnetic Compass Dials	125 - 128
Chapter 20	String Gnomon Dials	129 - 134
Chapter 21	Towards Precision	135 - 140
Chapter 22	Miscellaneous Dials	141 - 142
Chapter 23	The Compendium	143 - 146
Chapter 24	Nocturnals	147 - 151
Chapter 25	Perpetual Calendars	152 - 160
Chapter 26	Caring for a Collection	161 - 168
Chapter 27	Reproduction & Modern Dials	169 - 174
Chapter 28	A Final Glance	175 - 179
Appendix 1	Numerals, Letters & Sigils	180 - 181
Appendix 2	Saints Days	182 - 186
Appendix 3	Bibliography	187 - 190
Appendix 4	Magnetic Declination	191
Appendix 5	Zodiac & Equation of Time	192 - 193
Appendix 6	Sundial Collections	194 - 198
Appendix 7	Signatures on Dials	199 - 202
	Index	203 - 207

To reduce references in the text to a minimum, all notes taken from a book listed in Appendix 3 - Bibliography, will be noted in the following style: - [Bion 1758 - Plate XX]. This reference therefore reads: -

BION, N. (translated by STONE)
'The Construction and Principal Uses of Mathematical Instruments'. (1758) - Plate XX.

ACKNOWLEDGEMENTS

The act of writing a book of this nature with its copious illustrations is only possible if the dials themselves are available for first hand study. I must therefore thank all of those kind friends, acquaintances, dealers, museum curators and auctioneers who have allowed me to study the dials in their possession and in many cases to photograph them. Most of these people wish to remain anonymous but their considerable help and knowledge has been invaluable. Thank you all.

I wish to thank certain individuals who have given me help or inspiration, either directly or indirectly over the years. Without them I would probably be still looking at my first dial. I list a few of these friends below and can only apologise for those whom I may have omitted.

Jacques van Damme, Robert van Gent, Gilbert Meurgue, Stuart Talbot, Anthony Turner, Gerard L'E Turner, Trevor Waterman and Harriet Wynter.

I would also like to thank my wife Val for her encouragement and suggestions. She has been a keen proof reader and has corrected, in particular, my poor grammar and punctuation and has found alternatives for my frequent

Abraham about to sacrifice Isaac, illustrated on the lid of a Flemish Perpetual Calendar

tortology. She has been very patient throughout the writing when I have spent days glued to my computer keyboard when I should have been doing something around the house or garden.

For all errors and omissions remaining I will take the full blame, as they are all mine.

Stylised English rose engraved on underside of a dial's compass bowl

THE AUTHOR

I was born in 1942 in Rugby, a Midlands engineering town, then dominated by one employer, The British Thompson-Houston Co. Ltd. My education at the local grammar school helped me to get an apprenticeship at BTH where I served my time as a Technician Apprentice. Initially I worked in various large machine departments, showing more interest in electrical rather than mechanical subjects. At the end of my apprenticeship I was working in their Electrical Laboratory repairing electronic test and measuring instruments.

After leaving BTH, then part of AEI, I worked on automotive fuel injection systems research before moving to the Cambridge area where I was involved with image analysis. In the process I was required to make the first interface of an Image Analyser to a Scanning Electron Microscope. SEMs became my life and I eventually started my own company manufacturing accessories for them, selling these throughout most of the World to both manufacturers and end users. The most important product became a Backscattered Electron Detector using a large custom-built semiconductor diode as its detector element. This product was eagerly accepted by the market.

After 25 years in harness, in 1999, I sold the business and 'retired' so that I could follow my interests of research into early scientific instruments, particularly sundials.

According to my wife I am now 'unemployable' and keep myself amused in instrument research.

Although this is my first book I have contributed articles to several magazines, mostly on the subjects of dialling, scientific instruments and horology.

The Author with a modern replica of a Universal Equinoctial Ring Dial

PREFACE

HOW I BECAME INTERESTED IN PORTABLE DIALS

I am often asked how I became interested in Portable Dials. It is not a subject that immediately goes to the top of a hobbies list for the average person, but having carefully studied the various types made I have acquired a deep love for them and a profound respect for their makers.

My first encounter with a portable dial was some 20 or more years ago when I entered an antique scientific instrument shop in Brighton where the dealer had several for sale. After closer inspection of one, I realised how similar it was in so many respects to eighteenth century clocks with which I was more familiar. My interest in clocks had been forged many years ago, encouraged by my Father. He had been trained as a watch and clock repairer and he passed on to me his enthusiasm for horology. When I saw this dial it was then obvious to me how the history of the portable dial, the clock and the pocket watch were so inseparably bound together. My 'new discovery' made in Brighton was a dial from Augsburg by Lorenz Grassl like the one illustrated. It was one of many that were made in Augsburg in the middle of the eighteenth century. Its engraving was, to me, just like that on the dials of early clocks and watches. It was complete with its little leather case and an original instruction leaflet in three languages. I was soon hooked.

After that my interest widened to the whole range of solar and stellar time-telling devices and other scientific instruments. To further my knowledge I joined the Scientific Instrument Society and later the newly formed British Sundial Society. Both societies have many members with similar interests to mine.

I now look carefully through each auction catalogue, each book on scientific instruments, frequent antique shops, museums and instrument fairs looking for portable dials, all the time hoping to come across something a little different. So far I have seen very few dials alike. They were mostly made individually or perhaps in small batches, so the chance of finding two that are identical is quite remote - but I still keep looking and cataloguing their makers. Each dial is a work of art, just like any fine painting, porcelain vase or piece of furniture. The craftsman who worked perhaps four centuries ago has lovingly made his work of art and it deserves our love and attention even if it does not at first glance seem to function quite as we expect it to.

A typical Augsburg Equinoctial Dial by Lorenz Grassl

4.9 × 5.1 CM

I have an enquiring mind, needing to know exactly how each dial operates and what each of its markings can tell me. The meanings of the scales and tables on some of these dials have been quite elusive, but finally I think that I have cracked virtually all and hope to be able to share with you my interpretations throughout this book.

As you will by now realise I am absolutely besotted by these fine works of art and spend much of my spare time in researching the subject and looking for new makers. So far I have found around 1000 individual makers of portable dials. Geographically they are spread over most of Europe with merely a few from other continents, but Europe was really their home for much of the last 500 or more years.

I hope that when you read through the following chapters, you will feel some of the same excitement and enthusiasm that I do from these dials, be they humbly made for the peasant or richly decorated for kings and queens.

Mike Cowham
Cambridge 2004

PREFACE TO THE SECOND EDITION

This Second Edition of *A Dial in Your Poke* has been changed from landscape to portrait format allowing a better presentation of the illustrations, many of which have now been increased in size. New photographs too have been used, where available, and several additional types of Portable Dial have been added to make this history of them more complete. At the request of some readers I have added basic dimensions for many of the dials to give an idea of their real sizes.

Further research has been done in the years since 2004 and some of this has, where appropriate, been added. In particular, a study of Altitude Dials was done and published by the British Sundial Society in 2008. [Cowham 2008] Some of the findings from this have been incorporated in 'A Dial in Your Poke' but for their full story the reader is advised to purchase this other volume.

Since the First Edition, more replica dials have become available. These are affordable copies of some of the World's finest dial types. They give the user an insight into the way that our forefathers found the correct time, directly from the Sun and are recommended for the newcomer to get a feel for this subject.

In the original version a few mistakes have been found, together with a few omissions and these, I hope, have been corrected. There may still be errors and I would ask the reader to bear with these and, if a subsequent edition is ever published, I hope that these too will be corrected. Portable Dials have still remained my passion and I still search out unusual types, for those giving the highest accuracies and for those that offer simplicity of use. There have been many fine designs made over the years, some of which are quite difficult to use correctly, some do not even give an accurate reading of the time, and there are those dials that have other functions, often in astronomy and surveying where the ability to tell the time is an additional and not always a simple to use, feature.

I hope that what I have written will encourage others to follow and produce their own research notes, either as a book or as articles. The British Sundial Society and its sister organisations all over the World are helping to promote the study of Sundials. I would advise the reader to join one of these societies, if he/she has not already done so, for the wealth of information and knowledge that they have available.

Much is also available in books from yesteryear. Their archaic language is sometimes quite hard to follow, but they contain much useful information and often excellent illustrations. That below is from Bion's fine book [Bion 1758 - Plate XXII] and I make no apologies for including some of his fine drawings in the various chapters of this book.

Mike Cowham
Cambridge 2011

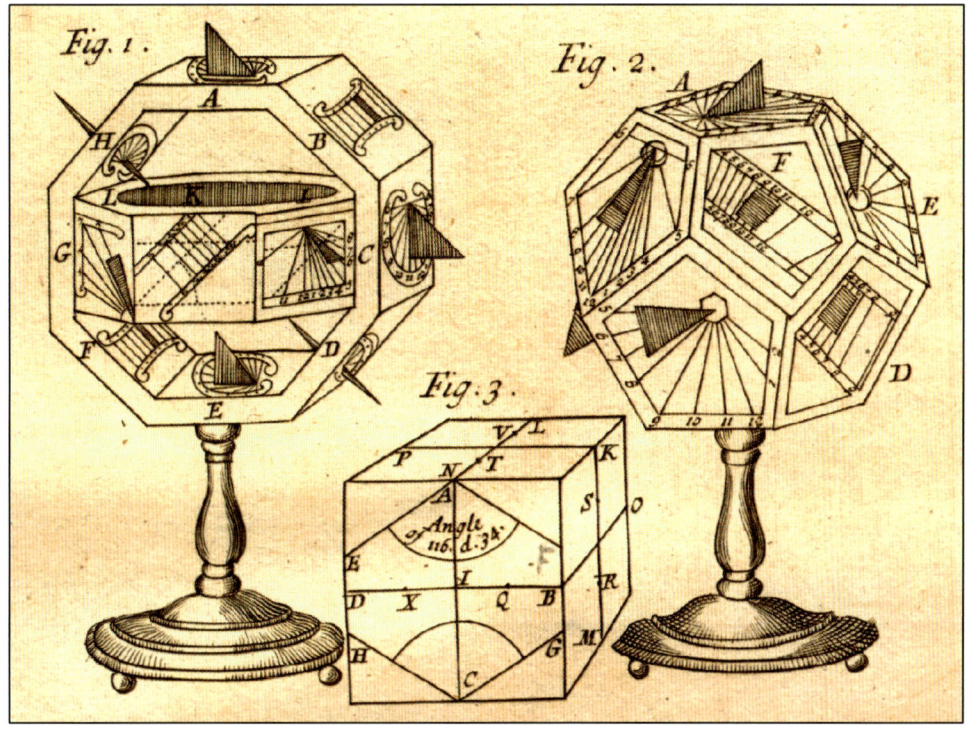

Preface

INTRODUCTION

Most people will have first seen portable sundials during visits to museums where there are many fine examples to be found. They are often placed alongside collections of other horological instruments such as clocks and watches or with scientific instruments. Where there are large collections of dials, they are sometimes given their own individual area.

The sundial itself came long before the mechanical clock, which did not generally appear until the fourteenth century. Even after the introduction of the clock, the sundial still retained its importance. It was an essential tool for finding

An oval silver Butterfield Dial signed 'BVTTERFIELD A PARIS'

the correct time to which the clock should be set and remained so until the advent of the electrical telegraph in the mid nineteenth century. Portable dials, although theoretically suitable for setting a clock, were generally intended for the traveller. A gentleman's dial would need to fit easily into his pocket in a similar way to the more familiar pocket watch of later centuries. This does not mean to say that watches were not available at this period. They were available but at prices considerably higher than the simpler pocket sundial and their timekeeping properties were hardly adequate for recording more than short durations of time. The portable dial was a prized possession and it was often highly decorated, frequently being made of precious metals such as silver and gold. The best surface on which to distinguish a shadow is white and a chemically silvered dial closely approaches this colour. Most dials made from solid silver were usually highly polished and, although this looked very attractive,

it did not have an ideal surface on which to observe the shadow cast by a small gnomon.

Portable dials have been made in a wide range of styles and designs, the variety only being limited by human imagination and ingenuity. Like their big brother, the garden dial, these could only be used when the Sun was shining. For this reason they were most popular in the sunnier countries of Europe.

Portable dials were not just made for the travelling gentleman. Some were made for surveyors, who used them for finding true bearings of buildings or pieces of land. Some were

A typical list of towns on the underside of the oval Butterfield Dial

used by sailors, who had a need to know the exact time, particularly for navigational purposes. Other forms of portable dial were designed to be used in the home in a more or less permanent position, such as just inside a south facing window. Some would be used simply to record the time at noon, an ideal time for setting a clock. Others were large and elaborate and can best be described as transportable rather than portable. They would certainly not fit into the pocket. Due to the size and weight of these larger dials they would probably be permanently mounted in such a place as a gentleman's private observatory.

INTRODUCTION

The majority of portable dials were made for the traveller, and to this end many were made 'universal'. This means that they could be adjusted to function universally, over an extended range of latitudes. Most were finely engraved or stamped with lists of towns with their corresponding latitudes. This figure would enable its owner to ensure that his dial was correctly set for his current location. Lists of towns found on these dials usually cover a wide geographical area and are indicative of the various places that the gentleman may have been expected to travel. Some dials were made specifically for a gentleman who may have intended to go on the 'Grand Tour'. Most dials have lists of cities and their latitudes engraved upon them. These usually include places such as London, Paris and Rome, being popular destinations for the gentleman traveller, in addition to towns in the owner's local area.

With the simpler dials, accuracy at best could only be expected to the nearest half-hour, but as the art of dial making progressed, accuracy gradually improved. Some of the later dials were even engraved with corrections for the Equation of Time (Appendix 5) in order to achieve the most precise readings, necessary when setting the time on the then 'new' and more accurate pendulum clock. A small number of dials were made which could be read to the nearest minute, often by employing mechanical methods to expand their scales.

Various means were used to correctly align portable dials to achieve the best accuracy. Some had spirit levels or plumb bobs to set them precisely horizontal, sometimes with the aid of three levelling screws. Others were self-aligning with the gnomon and hour scale mounted on a floating compass card. The commonest and most important alignment aid, used by the majority of portable dials, was the magnetic compass. It enabled the dial to be set so that its gnomon was directly on a North - South line. Due to the fact that Magnetic North is seldom the same as True North the compass would generally be marked with a line showing the current position for Magnetic North. However this varies from year to year and also differs with location, so that even with a well-calibrated compass the alignment accuracy could still in doubt. A few dials had adjustable compass scales so that their owners could keep their dials correctly aligned with the gradually changing Magnetic North or for when they were travelling to areas of different magnetic declination. Historical records of magnetic declination are available for several locations. (Appendix 4.) In London, for instance, Magnetic North was exactly the same as True North in about 1660, moving slowly towards the West until about 1815 when it was displaced by as much as 24½°. A reversal of drift then took place with the deviation slowly reducing back towards zero. It is expected to pass through zero again, in

The compass bowl from an Augsburg Dial by Andreas Vogler with an arrow showing a magnetic declination of around 16°W

London, some time around 2030 before swinging to an easterly direction. The figures given for deviation in Magnetic North over the years are a useful aid for confirming the dates of dials and compasses. It is simply a matter of checking the variation as marked in the compass bowl with historical records for the appropriate city. With care, a very accurate date check can be achieved but, be warned, this method of dating a dial or compass is not infallible. For this reason it should only be used to *confirm* and not to *establish* a date for the instrument.

The compass in a portable dial was usually quite small and was seldom allowed to take up much of the space on the dial. Its size was generally a compromise between size and accuracy. It was therefore much smaller than many pocket compasses or those used for nautical or surveying purposes. Their needles were small, often no more than ¾" (20 mm) long, and these had to be magnetised by the dialmakers. The normal process was to stroke the iron needle with a

An early brass bound Lodestone

A small silver mounted Lodestone

A black fish skin carrying case decorated with silver clusters, for housing a silver Universal Equinoctial Ring Dial

lodestone, a naturally magnetised ore of iron. The needles were so small that special lodestones were made to suit their size. These lodestones were mounted with two iron poles attached and were then encased in a non-magnetic shell, usually of brass or silver. A few of these have survived and are generally well made and decorated.

The portable sundial was generally intended to fit into the pocket. To achieve this it would be made such that when not in use, its various parts, such as the gnomon, the chapter ring, the latitude arc, etc., would fold as flat as possible. To protect these relatively fragile parts when in the pocket or in a traveller's luggage the dial would have been provided with a custom designed carrying case. Most cases were made of leather or fish skin and were lined with velvet. Some of the cases were elaborately decorated, often with gold tooling, with silver hinges and catches to suit their owner's wishes. Dials such as the Ivory Diptych did not really need a protective case because once the two halves were folded together and safely latched they were generally self-protecting.

The majority of dials with which we are familiar were made in one of just five places. Details of each will be discussed in later chapters. These five centres are listed on the following page with indications of numbers of makers, materials and peak dates for their production of portable dials. Portable dials were obviously made in many other parts of Europe, and occasionally further afield but generally the outputs from these areas were relatively small in comparison to those listed.

INTRODUCTION

THE MAIN PLACES FOR THE PRODUCTION OF PORTABLE DIALS

AUGSBURG   A small number of workshops turned out large quantities of a distinctive style of Equinoctial (or Equatorial) Dial. Most were in brass with just a few by the better makers in silver, occasionally with gilding. The main production period was between 1700 and 1800.

DIEPPE   Dials were made by a small number of makers, mainly in ivory. Two or three standard patterns were produced but the majority were Magnetic Azimuth Dials, a style normally attributed to Charles Bloud. They were produced from around 1650 to 1700.

LONDON   A wide variety of designs were produced by numerous makers. London produced high quality and accurate dials, often with minimal decoration. The predominant material was brass, usually with silvered scales. They were manufactured over a wide time span, typically 1600 to 1850.

NUREMBERG   A relatively large number of workshops concentrated on making Ivory Diptych Dials. These dials were particularly attractive and of good quality. Size and decoration differed widely. The main production period was from 1580 to 1700.

PARIS   The majority of dials were in the so-called 'Butterfield' style. This design proved very popular and they were made by quite a large number of workers. They were mostly well decorated and usually made from silver with lesser numbers in brass. Most of these dials were produced between 1680 and 1790.

INTRODUCTION

THE MAIN PARTS OF A PORTABLE DIAL

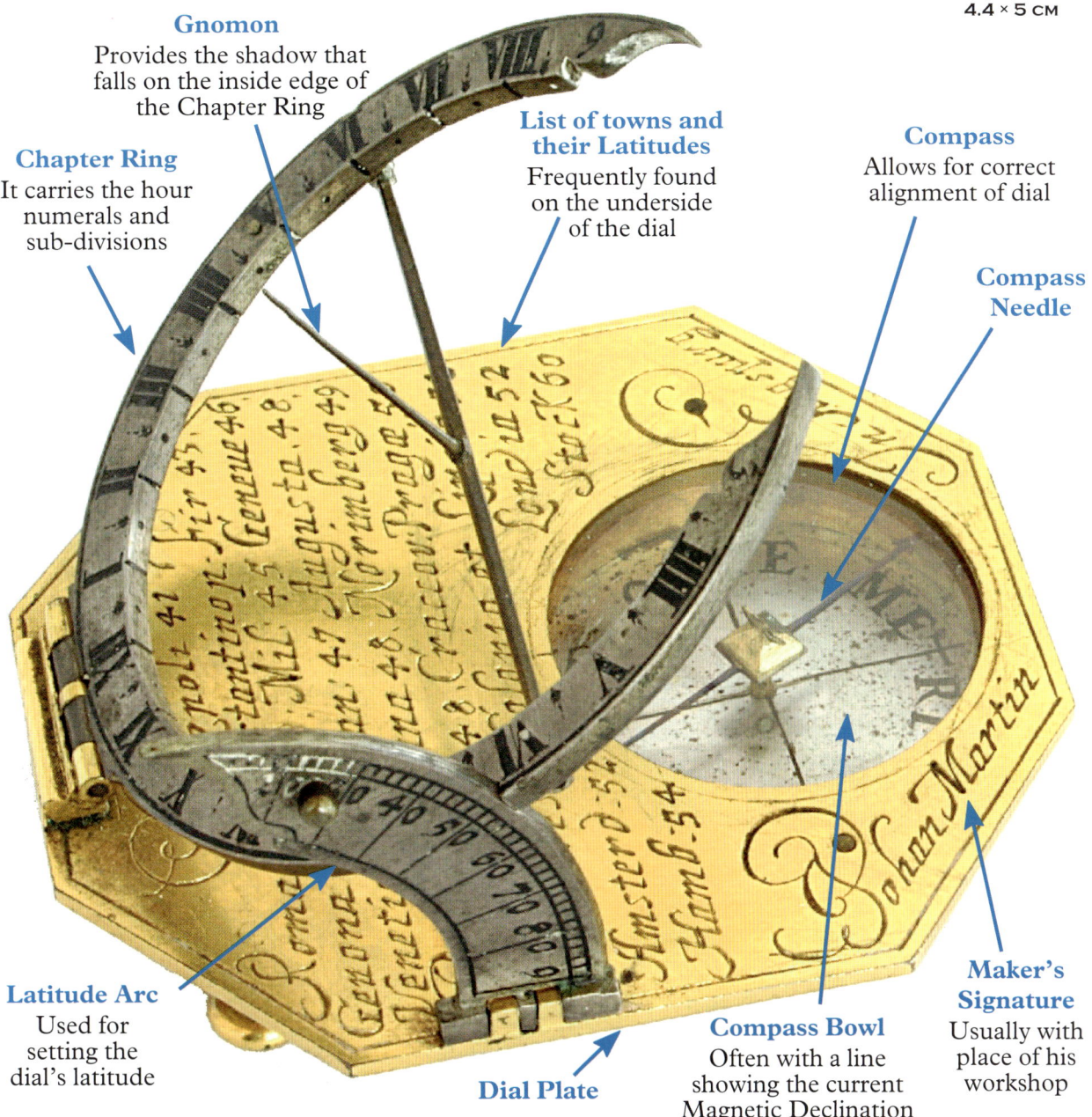

Equatorial Dial by Johan Martin of Augsburg, ca. 1700

This dial is presented to show some of the commoner parts of many Portable Dials. However, there are other parts not exhibited by this dial that will be included in the descriptions of dials shown in the relevant chapters of this book.

Dimensions are shown on many of the pictures in this book. These are generally located in one of the top corners. They just give the basic sizes to enable the reader to get a true feel of the size of these dials. The dimensions, as given for this dial, 4.4 × 5 cm, simply refer to the size of the dial plate. In cases where dials fold together, such as Diptych Dials, the dimensions shown refer to their closed size.

CHAPTER 1 THE FIRST PORTABLE DIALS

It is not known for certain when the first portable dials appeared. Man would have noticed the rising and falling of the Sun in the heavens and would have seen shadows of trees, rocks or dwellings move throughout the day. Initially he would have estimated the proportion of the day that had elapsed from the altitude of the Sun if he was travelling or perhaps its direction in the sky when at home. One of the earliest portable dials recorded is the use of a man's shadow to tell the time by its length. Monks knew when to say their prayers even when they were away from their monasteries. They would simply measure the length of their shadow with their feet and compare this to tables for the appropriate season. The shadow from any object could tell a man how much of the day was remaining for the job that he was doing in the fields or, if travelling, how much daylight was remaining before the onset of night, a time when danger from wild beasts or his fellow man could be lurking in any of the shadows.

At some stage later, the day would have been divided into portions between sunrise and sunset. The length of these portions would therefore change between summer and winter, but such unequal divisions would have been more than adequate for his needs at that time.

It is believed that the Babylonians were the first to divide the daytime into 12 divisions or hours. They would also have divided the night-time into a similar number, again using a system of unequal hours. This was less of a problem at the lower latitudes of Babylon than it would be in Northern Europe where hour lengths can vary by as much as 2 to 1 between the two solstices.

Little is known of the early dials that they must have used and we can only surmise from evidence gathered from later periods. A type of dial in the form of a shadow stick has been discovered in an Egyptian tomb with unequal hour markings. This

A Monk telling the time from the length of his shadow, by measuring it with his feet

type of dial was a great advance on a simple stick placed in the ground or a man's shadow. It was far from accurate but was an early attempt at time reckoning. It was a simple dial and it was only necessary to turn it to point towards the Sun and an immediate reading could be taken against the scale. They had already realised that the height of the Sun in the sky was different for each season of the year, and had learned to make the necessary adjustments. This Shadow Stick can only work satisfactorily if the vertical gnomon height is adjusted seasonally, but this part of the dial did not survive. There is also evidence that a plumb line may have been fitted to keep the dial level. They will also have learned how to record the elapse of time, particularly at night, by the duration of the burning of an oil lamp. The filling or emptying of a bowl with water (a clepsydra) would also have provided a similar function. They even worked out the correct taper on the sides of a water vessel to give an almost linear outflow of water.

Time reckoning had changed little by the days of the Roman Empire. They still divided the daylight into 12 hours and in the relatively sunny climes of the Mediterranean would have devised several types of dial. One of those was the Hemicyclium, a form of the Scaphe Dial. Similar dials have also been found in Greece. The Scaphe Dial is basically a hemispherical hollow in a piece of stone with an added pin gnomon, either

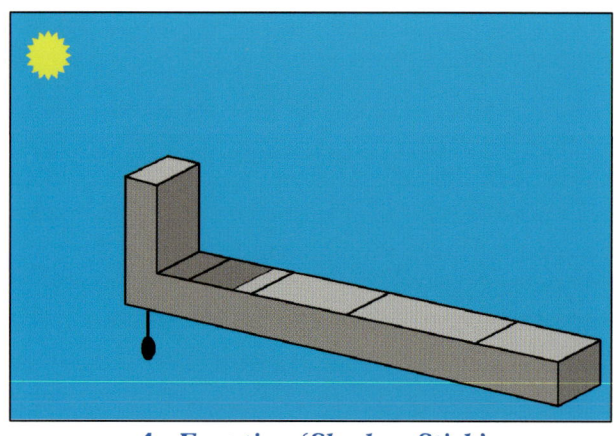

An Egyptian 'Shadow Stick'

Chapter 1 The First Portable Dials

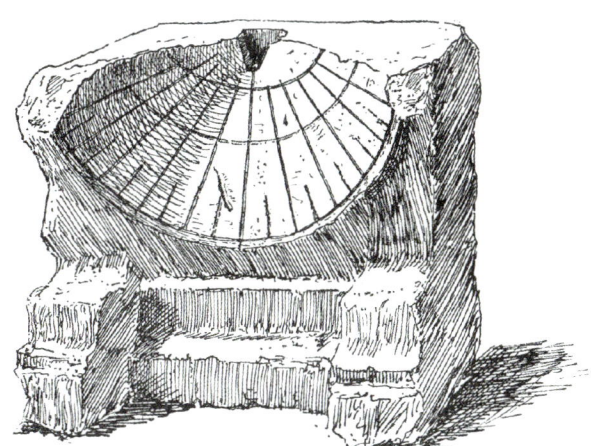
Roman Hemicyclium

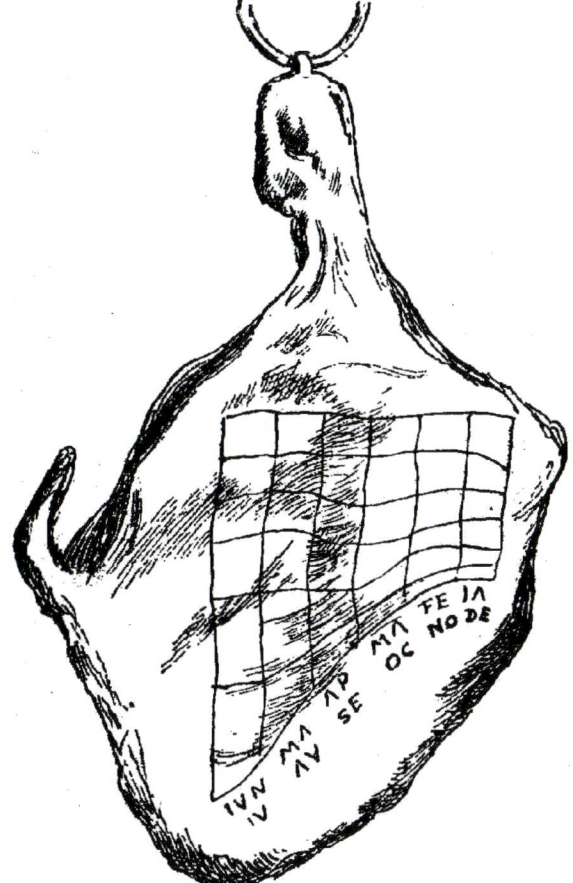
A Roman 'Ham' Dial

horizontal or vertical - it was only the shadow of its tip that really mattered. It is most unlikely that this type of dial was ever made small enough by the Romans or the Greeks to be used as a portable dial. To correctly use a portable version of this dial it would need to be set to face due South and to achieve this it would need to have its own compass, a device that did not reach Europe from China until about 1260. Some much later portable Scaphe Dials are to be found that were intended for keeping in the pocket, but these all have their own built-in compass for correct alignment.

The Romans did however develop very effective portable dials utilising the Sun's altitude. They produced the Pillar Dial which was very similar in design and concept to those produced later, some as late as the end of the nineteenth century. Another dial of theirs is generally known as a 'Ham' Dial due to its shape being like a leg of ham. It was a simple Altitude Dial with a fixed gnomon. On its face was a scale similar to that of a Pillar Dial but laid out flat.

Some writers have shown how the human hand can be used as a dial but it is not known if it was ever really used in this fashion. It is more likely to be a relatively modern idea for time estimation by soldiers or explorers - perhaps ideal for Boy Scouts.

The first truly portable dials probably originated somewhere in the Middle East. It is known that by the tenth century the Arabs had developed the Astrolabe. This had grown into a type of astronomical/scientific computer, capable of showing and calculating many practical things. In particular the Arabs had to be able to navigate across vast tracts of desert with only the Sun and stars as their reference. Their religion also meant that they had to offer prayers towards Mecca at certain fixed times of day and to do this they needed to know its direction from any place to which they may have travelled. The Astrolabe

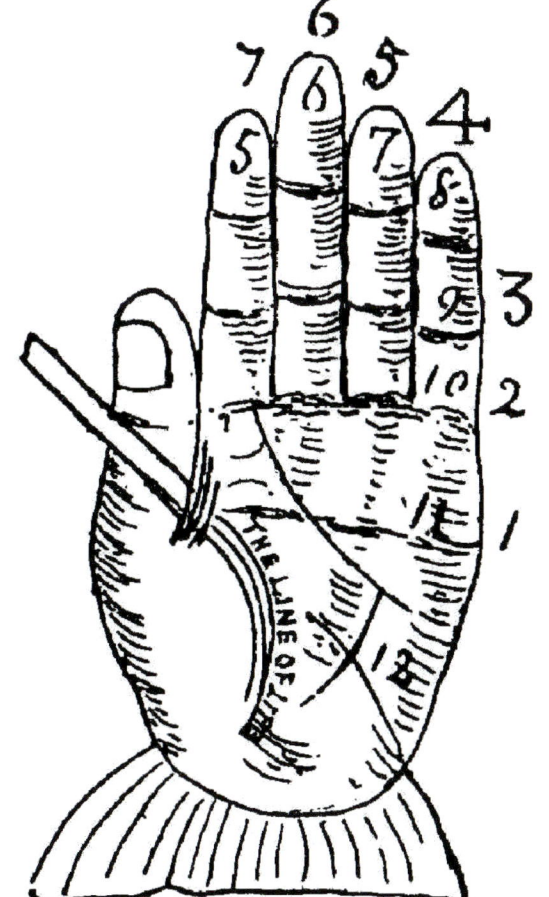
A human hand used as a primitive sundial

Chapter 1 The First Portable Dials

APPROX. 7 CM HIGH

Anglo-Saxon portable sundial

solved all of these problems and many more. It was a rather complex instrument and expensive to make, and therefore not within everyone's means. It is likely that they also had simpler devices for time reckoning. At later times they developed the Quibla Indicator, a type of sundial designed specifically for locating the direction of Mecca.

In Europe, little happened after the Romans left and it was not until perhaps the fourteenth century that any major interest was shown in time reckoning. The earliest European dials were probably made in and for use by ecclesiastical establishments. It was in these communities that most learning had been accumulated. Books from the period show their great interest in astronomy. Timekeeping became an essential part of these studies and later would have become a new science in its own right. Knowledge of the time, both day and night, was essential for regulating the time of prayer. Once established their timekeeping was shared with local villagers, perhaps through the ringing of the monastery bell.

Most, if not all, of the earlier dials were Altitude Dials, relying mainly on the length of a shadow (or height of the Sun) rather than its position. This was clearly a very informative phenomenon in that it could be used to show not only time but seasonal information as well.

One portable dial was found at Canterbury of Saxon origin.[1] This is a very simple Altitude Dial where the peg is moved into the hole at the top of

The Anglo-Saxon sundial at Kirkdale Priory in Yorkshire

8

the column for the appropriate month (the Summer months are on one side and Winter on the other) and the length of its shadow records noon (the lower mark) or mid morning/afternoon (the higher mark). These marks would correspond to the time-reckoning system of Saxon Tides. This system of 'tides' divided the whole day and night period into eight equal divisions. Fixed Anglo-Saxon dials are still to be found on the walls of some churches throughout England with similar dials in Ireland and throughout Europe. The most famous is probably that at Kirkdale in Yorkshire. This dial has been well preserved from the weather having had a porch built over it many years ago. There is also an inscription on two stones either side of the dial through which we are able to date it quite precisely.

Other portable dials have been found like that turned up by the plough in 1816 at Cleobury Mortimer, Shropshire, as illustrated by Haigh[2]. This dial, carved into stone, resembles the dials carved on churches in the Middle Ages with the addition of holes which Haigh believes to be star positions to enable the dial to be used at night. He also believes that it was to be worn around the neck of the user suspended by a cord.

Most portable dials before 1500 would have been Altitude Dials such as Pillar Dials, Quadrants or Regiomontanus types.

Later, perhaps around 1550, a gnomon aligned to

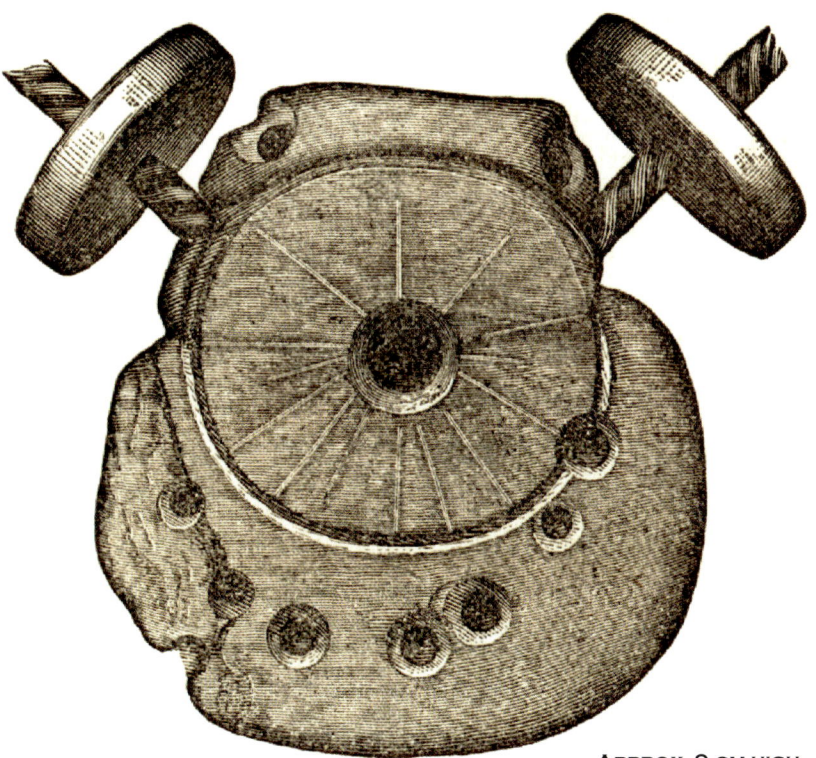

APPROX. 9 CM HIGH

An early portable dial found at Cleobury Mortimer

the Earth's axis would first have been used for portable dials. As this required a knowledge of direction, i.e., north/south, then a compass would have been a necessity. Very quickly the compass would have become part of the dial, and the majority of dials produced since that time have been Compass Dials. Some of the earliest evidence of these dials has been found in excavations of historical sites and in particular from a number found on Henry VIII's flagship, the 'Mary Rose', sunk in 1545, and recovered from the sea bed in 1982[3]. These dials probably originated in Nuremberg and may be identified as the forerunners of the ivory dials for which the city became famous. See Chapter 6 - Ivory Diptych Dials.

REFERENCES

1. A. A. Mills: 'The Canterbury Pendant: A Saxon Seasonal-Hour Altitude Dial' *Bull. BSS.* 95.2, 39-44 (1995).
2. D. H. Haigh: 'Yorkshire Dials' *Yorkshire Archaeological Journal* (1878).
3. Julie Gardiner and Mike Cowham: 'Timepieces' *Before the Mast - Life and Death Aboard the Mary Rose.* Mary Rose Trust (2005).

APPROX. 4 CM DIA.

One of the Mary Rose sundials.

CHAPTER 2 ALTITUDE DIALS

Many of the earlier forms of sundial used the Sun's altitude to record the passage of time and season. For a fixed dial, on a public building or in a garden, an Altitude Dial was unnecessary, the Sun's position giving the most convenient read-out on a clock-like dial. It was when dials started to travel that Altitude Dials became most important. One of the main problems in the use of most portable dials is the requirement to align them correctly to face South (or North in the Southern Hemisphere). Many were fitted with a magnetic compass to achieve this aim, but this was not always the most convenient device to use or keep in good order. In the pocket it had to be protected from damage by a glass or mica cover and was therefore somewhat fragile and likely to sustain damage at some time. Its residual

ship would already have a compass, permanently mounted in such a way they it was unlikely to sustain damage from the movement of the waves. The earlier compass used a dry card; i.e., it was a simple card sitting on top of a pivot point. Later, the compass was totally sealed with a liquid filling. This damped out many of the short-term movements and was much more stable on a moving ship. For navigational purposes various forms of dial were produced over the centuries including the Cross Staff, the Backstaff (or Jacobstaff), the Quadrant, the Mariners Astrolabe and the more complex Planispheric Astrolabe, plus Octants, Quintants and Sextants. Many of these instruments were used basically for

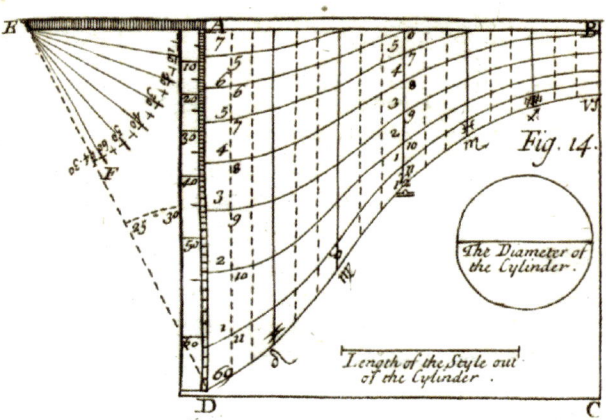

Expanded scale of a Pillar Dial

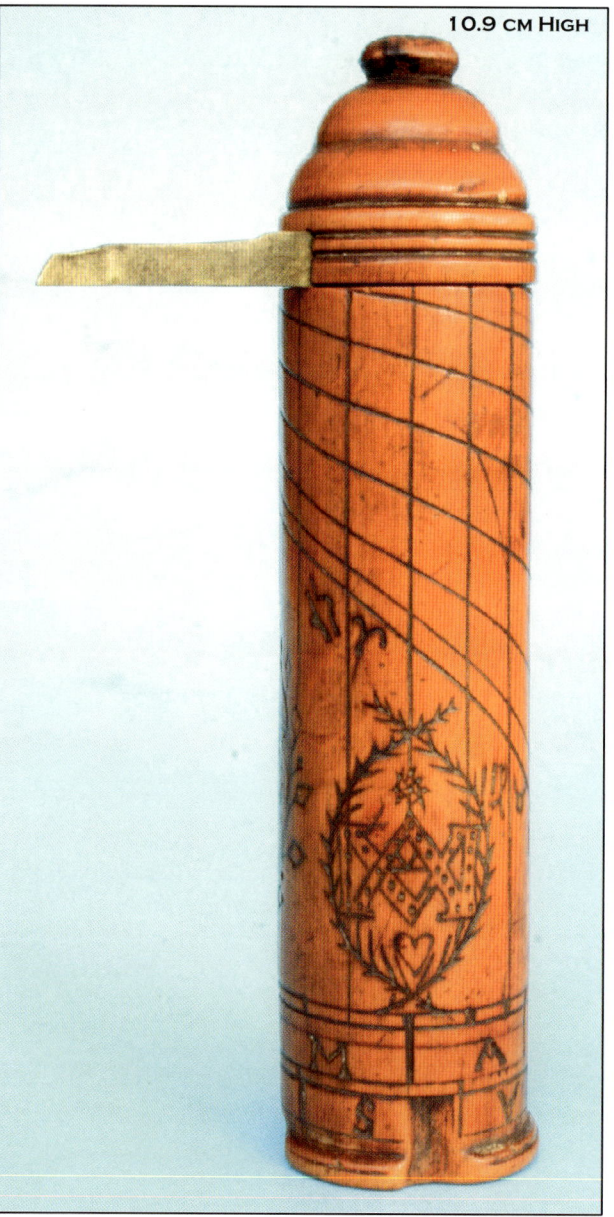

French boxwood Pillar Dial

magnetic field could decay and the pivot point could easily be damaged due to constant vibration during travel. With the Altitude Dial, the direction of South was unimportant. For some types it was generally a matter of pointing the dial's gnomon towards the Sun to obtain a time reading. It could therefore be made much more robust and was relatively simple to use. The original calibrations, however, were somewhat more difficult requiring not only hour lines but also date lines crossing them. The main problem for most Altitude Dials is that they were normally only made for one fixed latitude. This made them less suitable for long distance travel.

The Pillar Dial (often known as a Shepherd's Dial) was perhaps the earliest portable dial to be found, and examples go back to Roman times. For use on board ship and for navigation an Altitude Dial was often preferred as it could also give the latitude of the observation, usually taken when the Sun was at its zenith (due South). The

measuring angles but that angle, once found, could be readily converted into time by reference to the appropriate tables.

THE PILLAR DIAL

This was a compact, robust and easily carried portable dial. It was not designed to travel over great distances, being made for one specific latitude.

The illustration on the previous page shows a simple French Pillar Dial in boxwood made around 1700. A typical Pillar Dial has a thin brass folding gnomon, hinged so that when not required it could be safely stored inside the dial's hollow cylindrical body. Sometimes, there were two gnomons, one long and the other short, provided for Winter and Summer hours respectively. To use the Pillar Dial, the top cap is pulled off and the gnomon is hinged out. Some Pillar Dials were designed to be placed on a flat surface but others were intended to be suspended from the top by a cord. To operate correctly, the gnomon must be positioned vertically above the current date, usually inscribed around its base and extended by vertical lines. The dial would then be rotated until the gnomon's shadow was vertical, the correct time being indicated by the lowest point of that shadow. As with all Altitude Dials, it is not possible to distinguish between the readings in the morning or the afternoon and another reference is necessary to determine this fact. Two consecutive readings taken some minutes apart could be used to determine if the Sun was still climbing (morning) or if it was descending (afternoon). At the times when the shadow was very close to noon it would be more difficult to make a sensible observation. In addition to the hour lines (these are the sloping lines) the vertical lines that project from the calendar scale (often at 10 day intervals) allow a fairly precise setting

11.2 CM HIGH

Attractively decorated German Pillar Dial by Gottfried Reiff

11

Chapter 2   Altitude Dials

Silver Vertical Disc Dial from Germany, ca. 1700, on the back is a Perpetual Calendar

Vertical Disc Dial with painting of an Italian town

of date to be made. Once the Summer Solstice was reached, the months would retrace the path of the first half of the year as a mirror image. Additionally, symbols are given for the signs of the Zodiac corresponding to the calendar scale. A further vertical scale was frequently provided to show the Sun's altitude in degrees. In the first example it reads from 0° to 65°. With suitable calculations or tables, this could also give the time at noon for any latitude.

Pillar Dials were made from a wide range of materials but most commonly were made from wood, ivory or metal. Some of the finest to be found are in ivory with silver or silver gilt attachments. The design is not unique to any particular country, examples being found throughout Europe. They were made over a long period of time, even into the twentieth century. Henry Robert of Paris is known to have been producing quantities of these dials in boxwood with paper scales towards the end of the nineteenth century.

THE VERTICAL DISC DIAL

This type of dial was produced in small quantities from quite early times and was developed from the earlier Ham Dial. To find the time, the dial is held by its suspension ring, with its sharp pin gnomon folded out at right angles. The rotatable arm supporting the gnomon is set against the current date on the left-hand scale and the dial is carefully turned until the gnomon's shadow can be seen to pass across the hour scales on the right. The silver dial shown has a Lunar Volvelle with simple representations of the Moon's four phases. On its reverse is a simple Perpetual Calendar.

The other dial illustrated is silver gilt with a wonderful painting of an Italian town. This would have been made for a particularly rich client. These dials were not very accurate but will usually give the time to within 30 minutes.

The 'Heliochron' is a modern replica of an improved disc dial where the hour numerals are no longer in a circle but follow

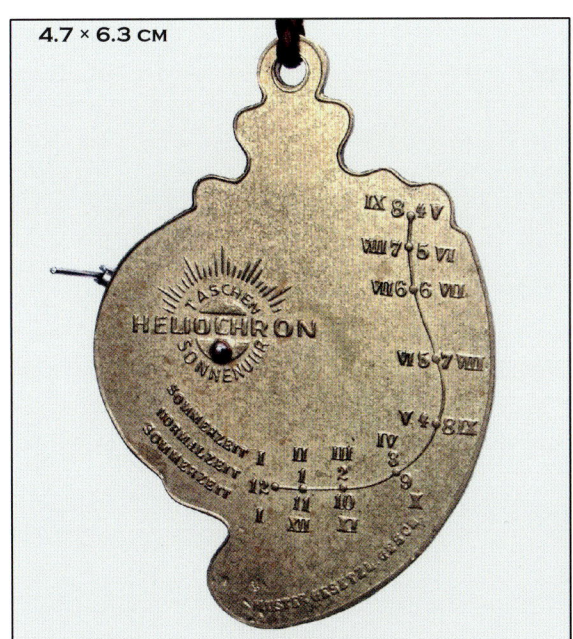
Modern 'Heliochron' Pocket Sundial

a curve which accurately aligns with the shadow at all times throughout the year.

VERTICAL PLATE DIALS

Several versions of these dials have been noted, each type having subtle differences. The Habermel Plate Dial differs from the others in that its gnomon shadow is no longer vertical. In this model the dial has to be turned so that the end of the shadow falls onto the correct date line and the time is then read from the radial hour lines.

On its reverse are a further two plots for alternative latitudes. These are 50° and 51°30' (London) and are placed side by side. In this case the hours for both morning and afternoon must be read from the appropriate side of the plate, reversing at noon, unlike the main side for 48°30' where the hours go right around the disc.

The Vertical Plate Dial shown on the next page has its pin gnomon at the top by the suspension loop. In use it faces the Sun and the shadow falls vertically across the plate pointing at the correct hour line on a heart-shaped pattern. The circular plate must be turned so that the gnomon is positioned exactly above the correct date, the disc being pivoted in the centre. Other versions of this dial have the pin gnomon at the centre, resulting again in a heart-shaped pattern of lines. Another version has the gnomon situated about one third of the radius down from the suspension and by careful

Photographs of the two Vertical Plate Dials were taken with the kind permission of Peter Kalchthaler. These dials are in the collection of the Augustinermuseum, Freiburg im Breizgau, Germany.

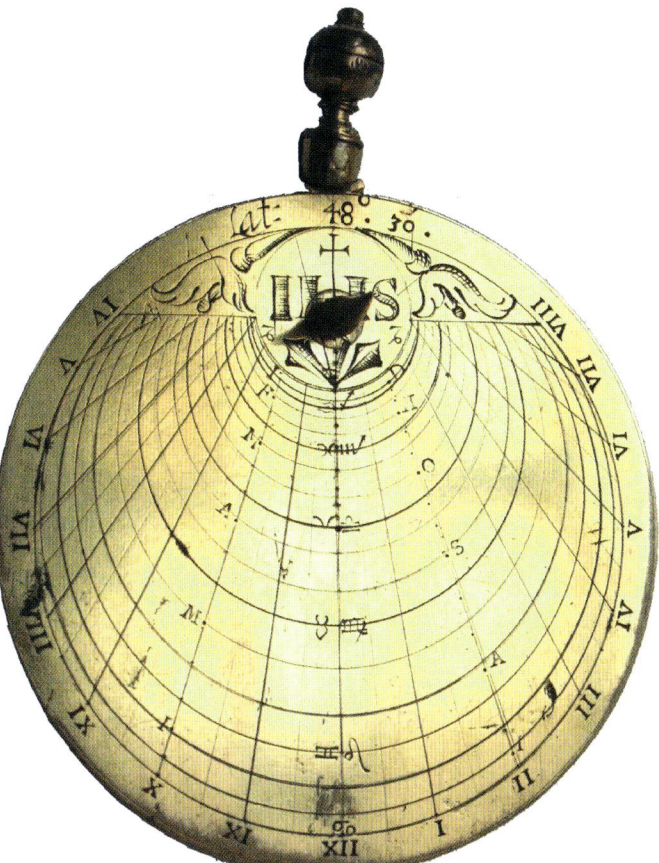
Vertical Plate Dial by Habermel
Augustinermuseum, Freiburg im Breizgau

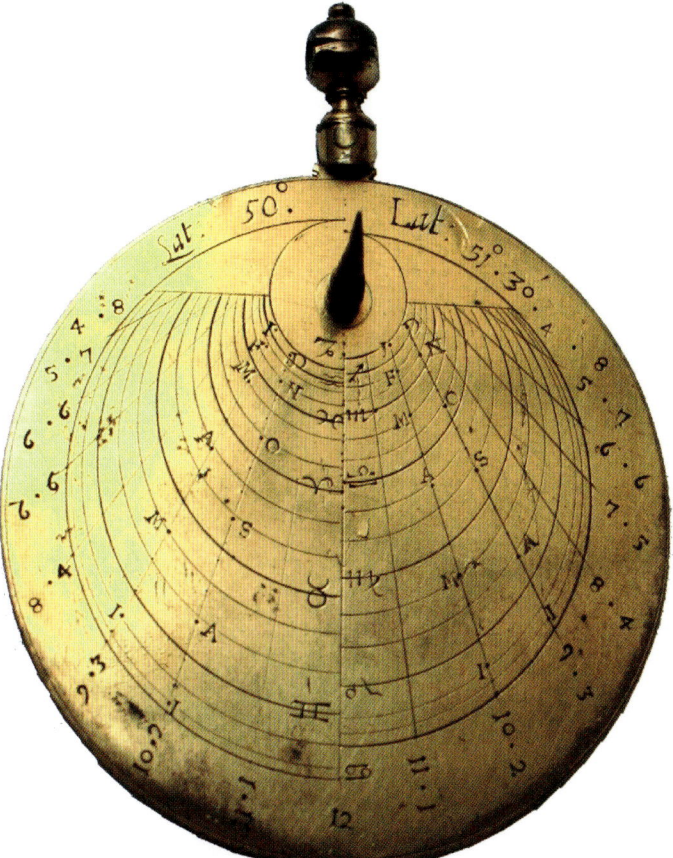
Reverse of the Vertical Plate Dial by Habermel
Augustinermuseum, Freiburg im Breizgau

Chapter 2   Altitude Dials

Vertical Plate Dial
Augustinermuseum, Freiburg im Breizgau

An unsigned Regiomontanus Dial, probably German, ca. 1700

French Regiomontanus Dial, signed 'Roch Blondeau a Paris', ca. 1720. This dial is in the same case as a Butterfield Dial. See page 73

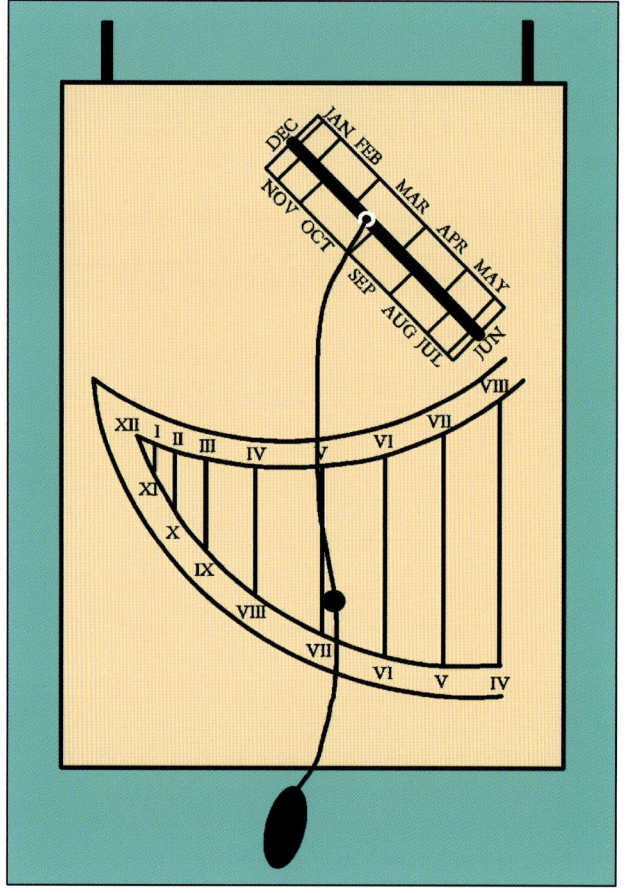

Capuchin Dial, so called because its scale is shaped like to hood of the Capuchin monks

adjustment of the date lines the whole surface of the disc can be used over the course of the year giving a more accurate result.

Further versions of these three types are sometimes found where only half of the year is placed around the edge resulting in a spiral type layout of hour lines. As the Sun traces the same path in the second half of the year, each date line will apply to both halves.

RING & POKE DIALS

These are also forms of Altitude Dials and are described in detail in Chapters 3 & 4.

THE REGIOMONTANUS DIAL

This rather complicated dial is occasionally found but, due to its apparent complexity, it probably did not gain great popularity. Most extant examples come from Italy or Central Europe. Bion [Bion1758 - Plate XXIII] shows this dial and describes its construction and its use. A dial made around 1700, probably in Germany, is illustrated at the top right of the previous page. Its triple jointed arm or Brachiolus, is pivoted at the top of the dial plate, with its plumb line hanging vertically. It is a universal dial, capable of being used from the Equator to 65° North. In use, the tip of the arm to which the line is fastened is positioned on the upper vee shaped section to coincide with the current date at the correct latitude. The bead is then adjusted by being set to the appropriate place on one of the Zodiac scales that are placed either side of the main scale. On many dials these scales are not separated but are placed to one side, as on the Roch Blondeau dial shown. The dial is now ready for use. The two sights on the top edge are used to line up with the Sun, and the point where the bead hangs against the main scale will show the time. This dial has Quadrant markings against the right and lower edges so that an altitude angle may also be measured. To achieve this, the Brachiolus is positioned at the point crossed by both the 0° and 90° lines of the Quadrant on the upper left hand side. Additionally the dial carries a Shadow Square on its left and lower edges with a 0 - 100 unit scaling. The use of a Shadow Square will be described later in Chapter 5.

THE CAPUCHIN DIAL

This is a simpler version of the Regiomontanus Dial and is designed to be used for just a single latitude. This dial has the cord suspended from an anchor point in an angular sliding slot, with its position calibrated for date. The bead hangs across an hour scale that is attractively curved from a point on the left at midday to widely spread lines at sunrise and sunset on the right. The outline produced is similar

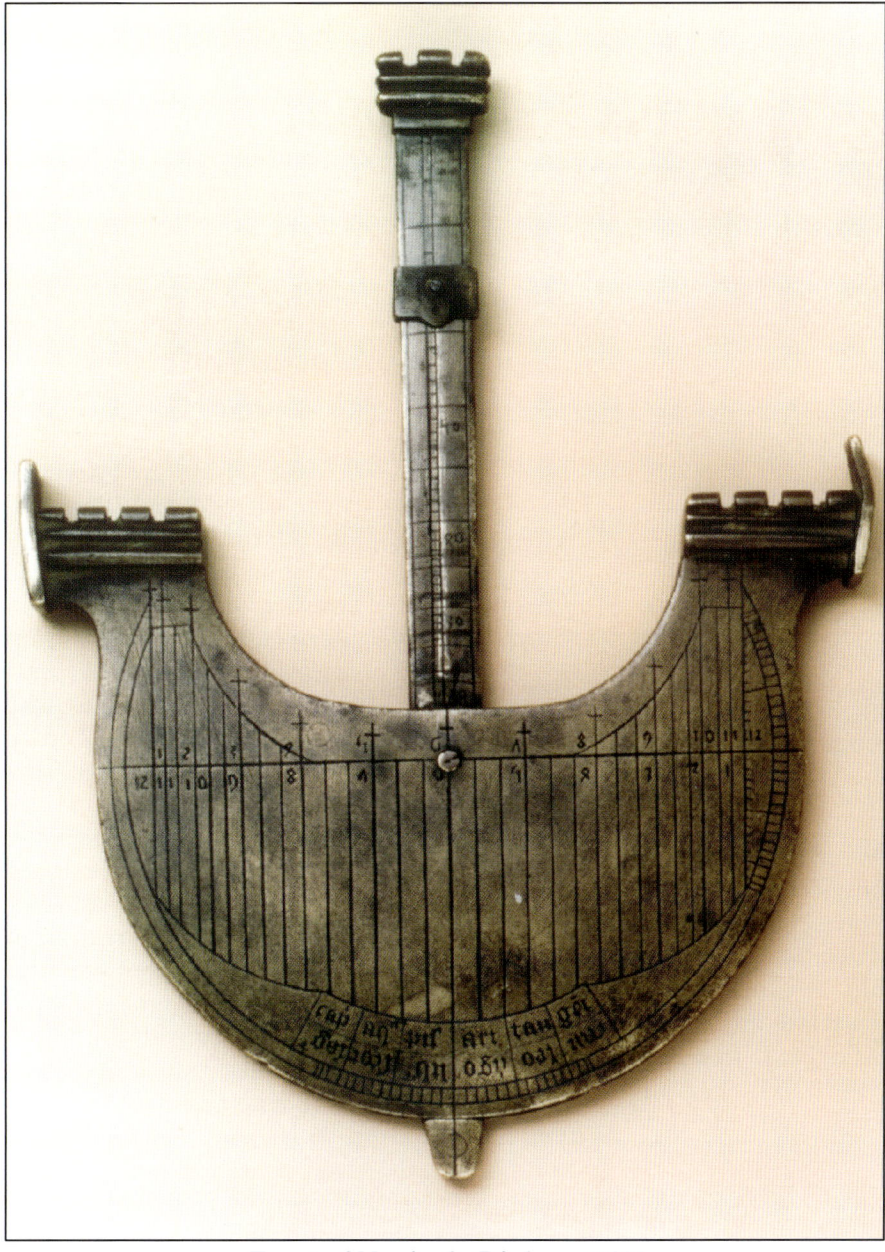

Front of Navicula Dial, ca. 1400
Photo: Trevor Philip & Sons Ltd

CHAPTER 2   ALTITUDE DIALS

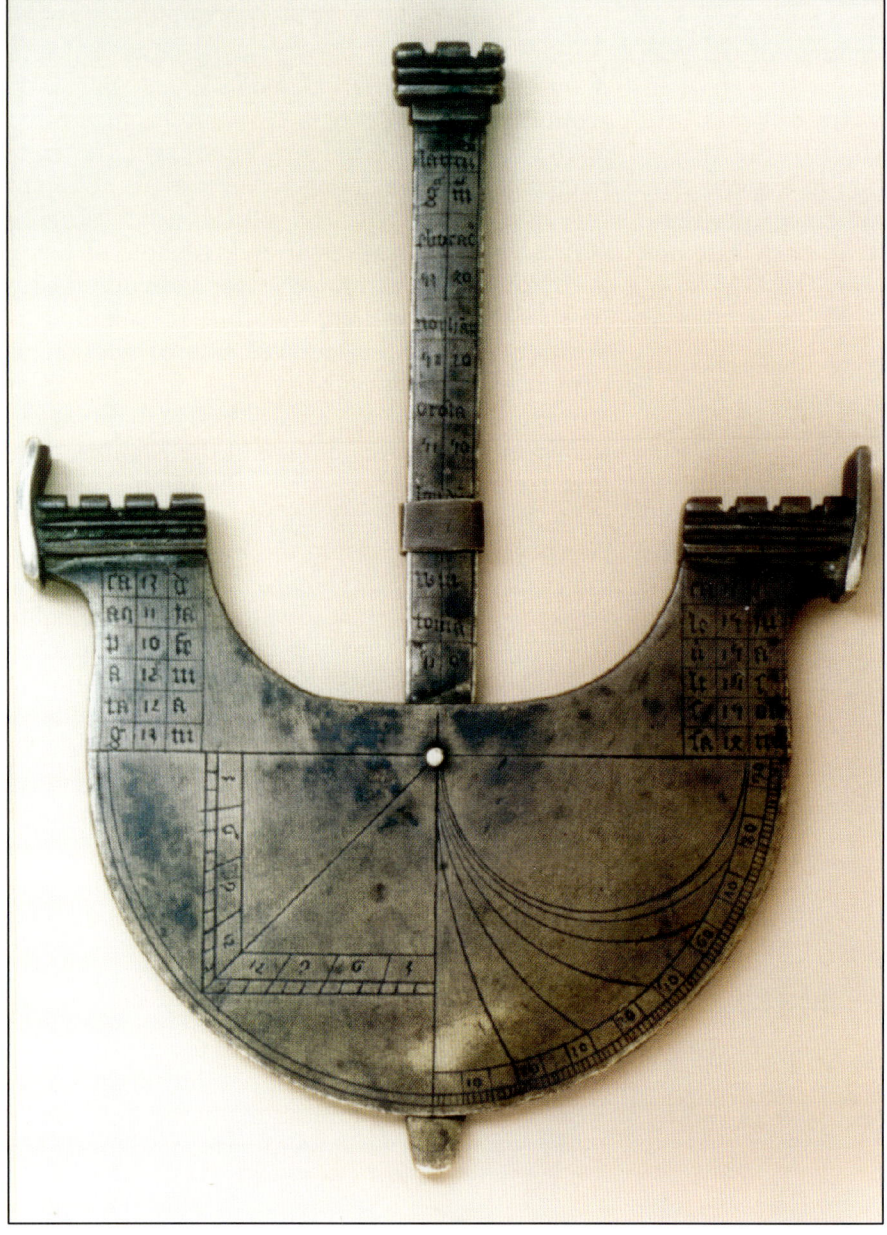

Reverse of Navicula Dial, ca. 1400
Photo: Trevor Philip & Sons Ltd

to the head covering of a Capuchin monk, thereby giving the dial its popular name.

THE NAVICULA
This dial is also known as a Navicula de Venetii or Little Ship of Venice, on account of its shape.
These dials are particularly rare, with only a handful being known.[1] Their style of construction in the form of a sailing ship is particularly attractive. They were made in late medieval times, possibly exclusively in England; the one illustrated between 1400 and 1450. The curved dial plate has been extended to support the two sights. With the central arm vertical, the general shape is that of a ship, and their makers have added typical poop and forecastle ornamentation to complete the effect. These dials are very similar in construction and use to the Regiomontanus Dial already described. The mast of the ship is pivoted and the keel end is set against a date scale along the lower edge of the hull. The mast has a scale of latitude and the sliding suspension point for the line and plummet is set at the correct value. The bead on the line would then be set to the date scale (or the declination) on the right side of the hull. The Sun would then be sighted and the position of the bead would give the time on the appropriate vertical hour line. This particular dial is marked on the reverse of the mast with five English towns and their Latitudes, from 'wintonia' 51 0, (now called Winchester) to 'eborac', 53 20 (now called York). On the reverse of this dial is a shadow square (left) and curved lines of Planetary Hours (right).

QUADRANTS
These are described in Chapter 5 but the attractive heart shaped dial, Page 17, is related to these. It is obviously designed to be worn around the neck on a cord and is only 56mm across. At one time it may have been gilt. On the Summer side the Zodiac lines are drawn as arcs from ♈ - ♋ - ♎ with the straight hour lines across these. In use, a pin, normally held in a small hole drilled into the bottom of the heart, is fitted into the hole at the top right. The dial is then turned so that its shadow crosses the face and the time is read from the point where it crosses the appropriate date line. Note that the Summer Sun goes slightly higher than the scale allows, being 61.5° at 52° North, so will be off the scale for a short period around the Solstice. The reverse side covers the Winter months from ♎ - ♑ - ♈ and the pin gnomon is inserted into the hole at the top left. A further scale of altitude is provided. To use this, the pin is placed in the top right hole and a direct altitude of the Sun may be found. This may be of

16

CHAPTER 2   ALTITUDE DIALS

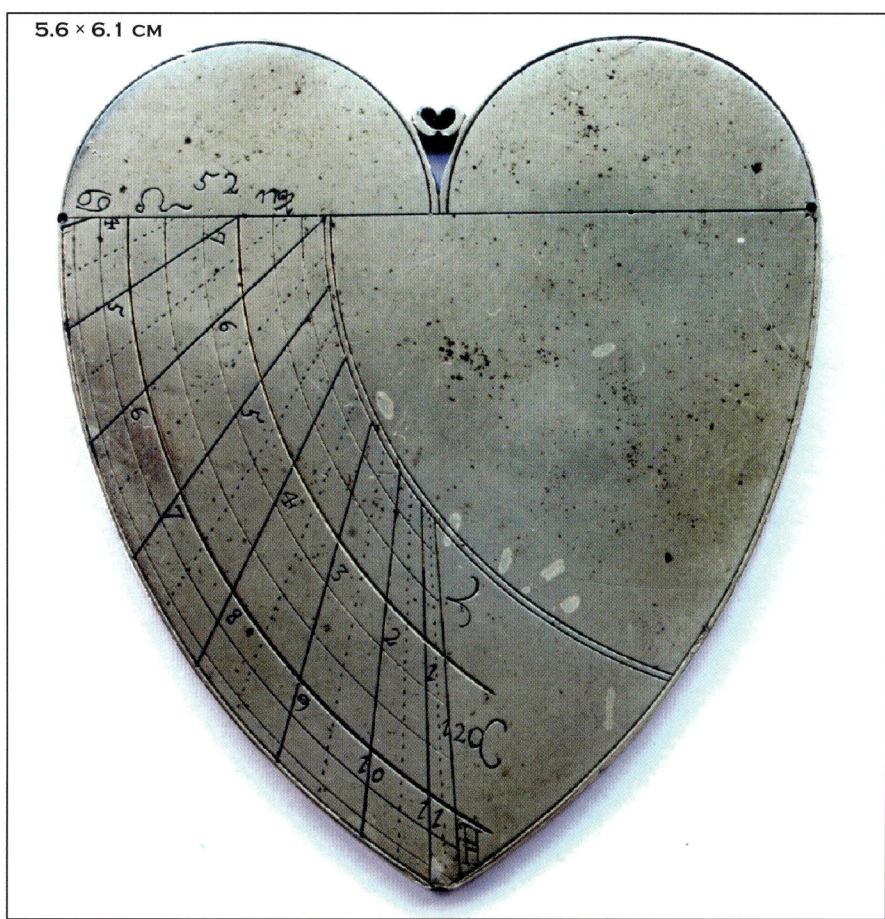
Heart shaped Quadrant - Summer side

Heart shaped Quadrant - Winter side plus an altitude scale

use at different latitudes where the altitude may be compared with tables to give the correct time.

SCAPHE DIALS

The Scaphe or Cup Dial is seldom found in its portable form. Its general design dates from early Greek times. A few Ivory Diptych Dials were produced with small Scaphe Dials on them and a few eighteenth and nineteenth century dials from Japan utilise the Scaphe form, but these are direction dials and are fitted with a magnetic compass. See Chapter 17 where Scaphe Dials are described. Some beautiful Cup Dials are known, made of precious metals, and these are frequently formed like a chalice. In order for the shadow of the rim to indicate the time at the Summer Solstice, the bowl needs to be rather deep. The slope of its sides must be greater than the Sun's height at all times. The problem becomes more acute as dials are made for use further south. One way to overcome this problem was for some dials to be made to function only whilst the cup is filled with water (or wine). For this reason they are sometimes referred to as the 'Dial of Ahaz'. In the Bible, King Ahaz is said to have 'turned back the shadow' on his dial, presumably by filling a Scaphe Dial with water. The shadow of the cup edge is thereby bent by refraction of the liquid giving a reading higher up the opposite edge of the cup. A further version of the dial has a vertical pin gnomon in its centre which allows a wider bowl to be used making it easier to read the time, especially at noon, but then it is rather dangerous as a drinking vessel! The Chalice Dial illustrated is of this type but its central pin gnomon is missing in this sketch.

NAVIGATIONAL INSTRUMENTS

The Cross Staff, Backstaff and Mariners Astrolabe are all mariners' instruments and were not normally used directly for time telling. They allowed not only the altitude of the Sun to be taken on the rolling deck of a sailing ship but also altitudes of stars. They could even be used horizontally for taking angular measurements. Time could be found from their readings, normally by reference to astronomical tables.

PLANISPHERIC ASTROLABE

The Astrolabe is beyond the scope of this book but one has been included here as an example of an Altitude Dial. The Astrolabe is undoubtedly the most attractive and yet most mysterious instrument ever produced. Some of the earliest Astrolabes date from before 1000 A.D. Their manufacture was continued in Europe into the seventeenth century and in India and Arab countries until the end of the eighteenth century.

Chalice Dial

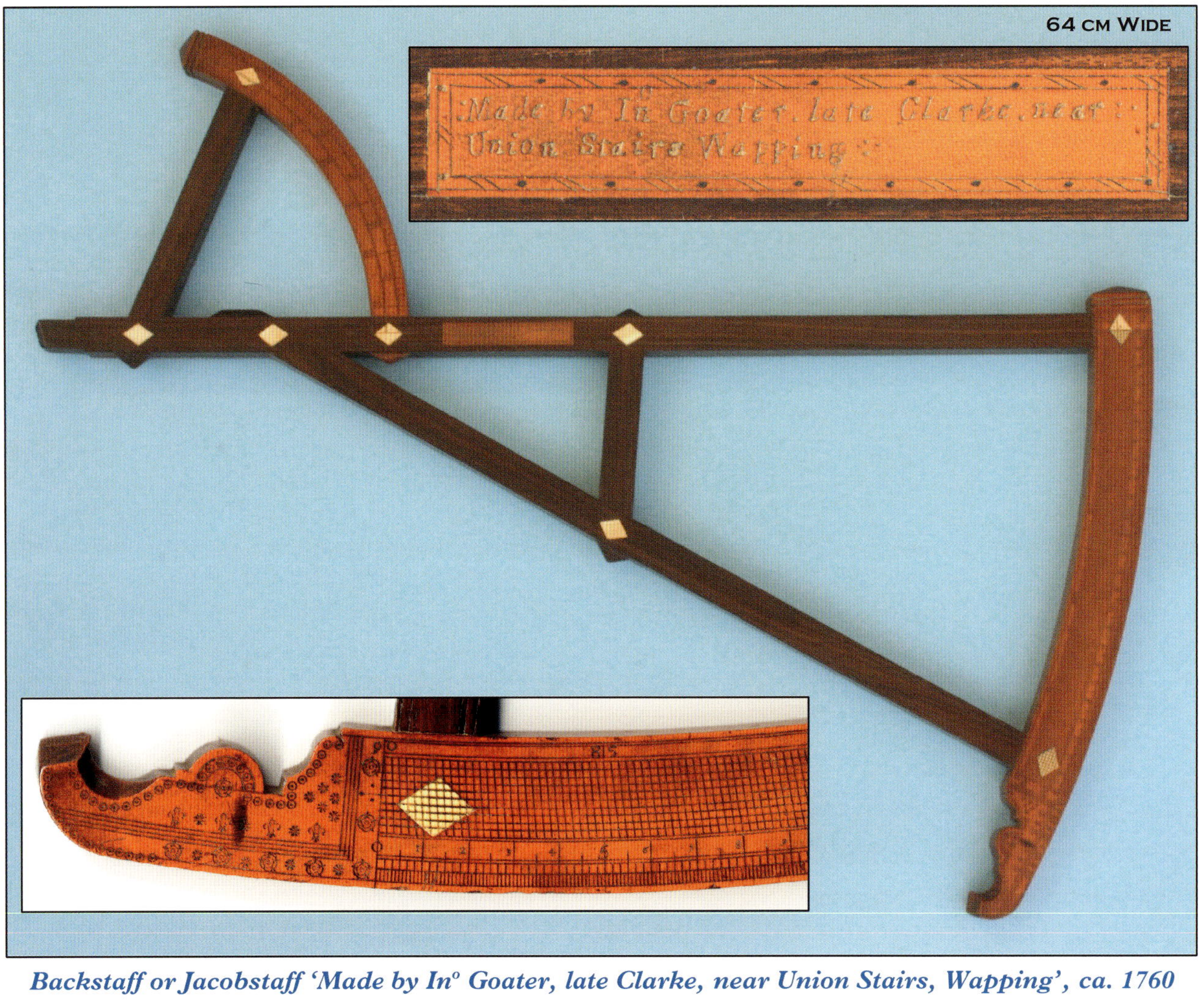

Backstaff or Jacobstaff 'Made by Inº Goater, late Clarke, near Union Stairs, Wapping', ca. 1760

Chapter 2 Altitude Dials

The Astrolabe is a very complex calculating instrument giving time measurements, altitudes, times of sunrise, sunset, twilight, day length and much more. Its great advantage was that it could be used both day and night to obtain exact time information. Astrolabes, especially those from Arab countries, were frequently used to provide astrological information. This was most important, especially for determination of religious festivals.

The illustration shows a medieval brass Astrolabe made in Europe ca. 1300.

Modern copies of Astrolabes are quite common, especially from India, and a good knowledge of them is essential to avoid spending a lot of money on what may turn out to be no more than a decorative piece of brass.

REFERENCE
1. Navicula dials can be seen in the following museums: -
Whipple Museum, Cambridge; Museum of the History of Science, Oxford; National Maritime Museum, Old Royal Observatory, Greenwich; Museum of Science, Geneva.

FURTHER READING
Mike Cowham: *A Study of Altitude Dials*, BSS Monograph, Crowthorne, 2008.

26 CM DIA.

10 inch diameter Medieval European Astrolabe, ca. 1300

CHAPTER 3   SIMPLE RING DIALS

THE POKE DIAL

This dial, perhaps more correctly called an 'Altitude Ring' Dial, is frequently referred to as a 'Poke' Dial because it was carried in the poke or pocket. In Shakespeare's play 'As You Like It' a Fool *'drew a dial from his poke, and looking on it with lack-lustre eye, says very wisely, "It is 10 o'clock:"'* (Act 2, Scene 7). In Germany this dial is known as a Bauernring or Farmers Ring. It is the simplest form of Ring Dial and was relatively cheap to make. It was probably one of the few types of dial that could be afforded by the average man. It appears from the small numbers several European countries most extant dials appear to be of English or German origin.

In its commonest form, it consists of a plain flat ring of metal having a diameter of about 2 inches (50 mm) and a width of about 0.4 inches (10 mm). The hour scales are inscribed on its inner surface. The gnomon is a pinhole that is cut through a thin sliding band that fits into a groove around its outside diameter. The band slides around the circumference enabling it to be set against a calendar scale in order to adjust the gnomon aperture for the Sun's seasonal change in altitude. On some dials there are two pinhole gnomons,

A simple 'Poke' Dial by TW

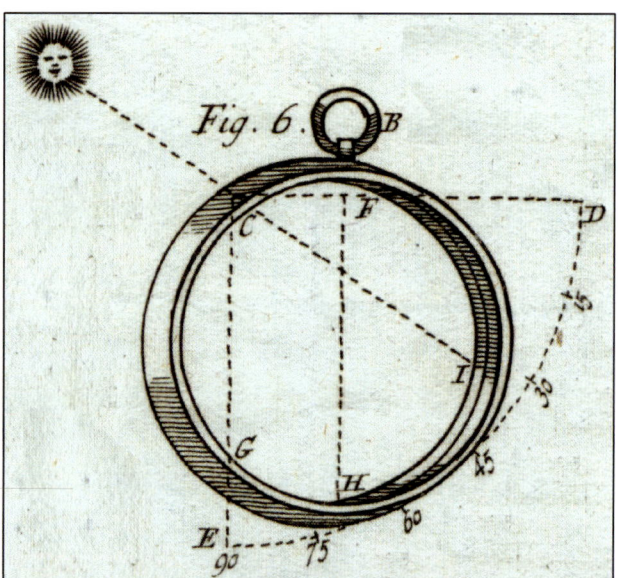

The Poke Dial as illustrated by Bion
[Bion 1758 - Plate XX]

each on opposite sides of the ring, one for Summer and the other for Winter. Correspondingly there are two internal sets of hour scales set on opposite sides of the ring.

In use, the dial is held by the hand, suspended by a cord or ribbon, which is attached to a lug on one edge. Gravity holds it vertical while the dial is rotated to allow the Sun's rays to pass through the appropriate gnomon aperture and fall on the correct scale on the ring's inner surface. As with all Altitude Dials there are no means for the user to know from its reading whether the time is before noon or after noon. Knowledge of the position of North would be of help, but the user would probably rely on his body clock, or stomach, for this information. Otherwise it would be necessary to take two readings separated by several minutes to determine if the Sun was still rising or now falling. At the date of the manufacture of these dials

extant that it perhaps did not gain the great popularity that would have been expected. Another reason for this could be that these simple copper or brass dials were discarded, perhaps when clocks and watches became more widely available, whereas gold and silver dials would be kept for their intrinsic metal value. These dials are sometimes found by users of metal detectors, supporting the theory that they were just discarded as having no value. Although apparently made in

Chapter 3   Simple Ring Dials

Interior calibration of the TW Poke Dial showing the A, B and C scales

A, B and C settings next to the joining link and the maker's initials, TW

Each of the hour scales on some dials are divided into three marked A, B, and C. The hour calibrations are not straight across the inside of the ring but are at an angle (except at noon). On the outside of the dial, next to the joining link in the sliding gnomon band, the same three letters are to be found. It is therefore necessary to use that part of the scale indicated by the appropriate letter. Reference to the ray diagram below will show how the lines for each hour at different seasons converge. By making the lines sloping it is possible to get the hours to fall in their correct positions.

The dial in the diagram is the Stepped Poke Dial and this overcomes the sloping hour line problem by trying to place the hour scale at the correct convergence points, which it does quite successfully.

The first Poke Dial illustrated is signed simply '**TW**'. Several virtually identical dials are known by this, as yet, unidentified maker and a comparison between them reveals some interesting facts. The calibration marks are applied quite crudely with punches and details, such as misalignment of particular letters or numbers, (such as A, B and C) are identical on all **TW** dials so far examined. This leads to the conclusion that the markings were applied in groups and not individually as may first

(around 1700) the need to know the precise time was of little importance to the average farmer or even gentleman. All that he needed was an indication of the time, perhaps to the nearest hour or so. Our society now is geared so much to time that it is difficult for us to appreciate how these simple folk lived. Even today, in parts of the World, certain societies who do not worship time like we do, still do not make their appointments for a certain hour but just specify the day. This is near enough for them but we find it particularly frustrating when we visit these countries.

The Altitude Ring or Poke Dial was not intended for travel and only functions correctly at its own designed latitude. However, one Poke Dial is known where the suspension point can be slid around the periphery to give any latitude. Unfortunately, this solution does not work and would only be of use to someone moving a few degrees from his home.

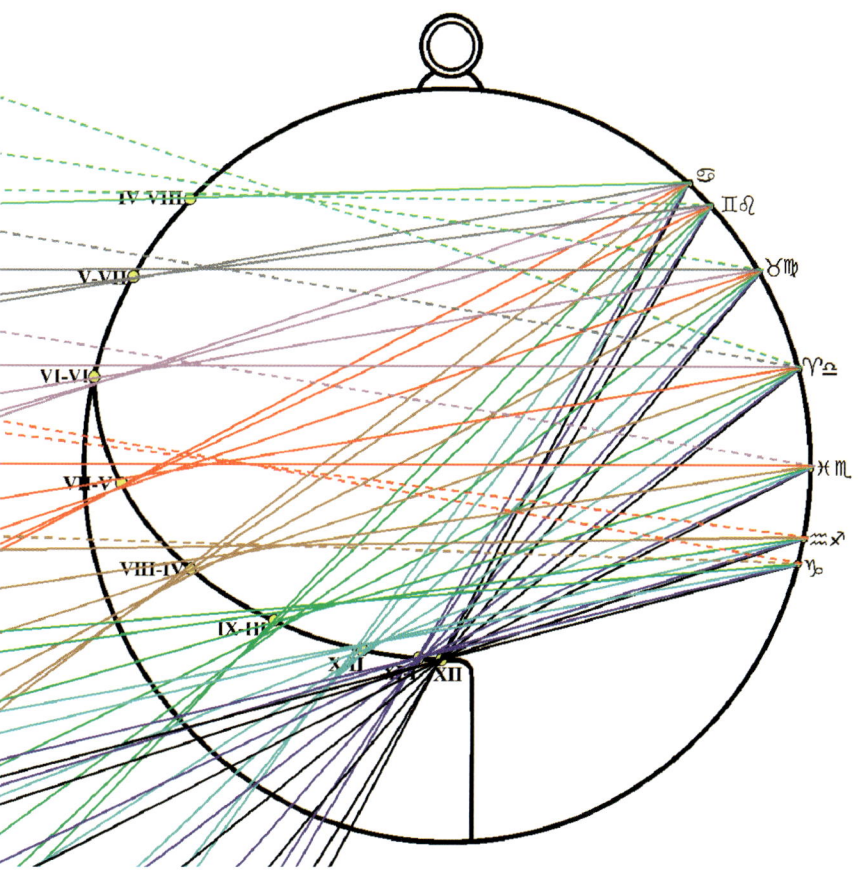

Diagram showing how the Sun's rays converge for each Zodiac Sign

be expected. It is difficult to imagine how a multiple character punch could be made. However, it is quite possible that these dials were produced on some type of rolling machine where the brass ring was pushed against a set of fixed punches; if so, this was probably an early form of mass production. Naturally the scales and calibration marks were applied to a flat strip of metal that was later rolled. It was subsequently joined by brazing close to the suspension loop. Careful inspection shows that when the dials were hooped, the bending is a bit greater at the points where its calibration lines have thinned and weakened the metal.

A very similar dial was found in Cambridgeshire with a metal detector. Although it is somewhat corroded its markings can be plainly seen. This dial does not have hour lines, just the numerals, so this would be less accurate than dials with the sloping hour lines.

Many forms of Poke Dial are known of sizes varying from less than one inch to three inches or more in diameter. Those from the better makers are usually engraved rather than punched. Some only have one pin hole gnomon with a subsequently more complicated hour scale. Others have the stepped internal scale that helps to correct for the small errors caused by the hour lines being on a perfect circle.

A substantially made, and potentially accurate, version of a Poke Dial signed '**I. A. M.**' is also illustrated. Several others are known to have been made by this maker. It differs only slightly from those already described.

An interesting variation on the Poke Dial is the Finger Ring Dial, which was worn on the finger as an ordinary ring. When removed it would be stood on its flat face and was then aligned so that the Sun's rays would pass through a hole in its edge onto the hour scale engraved on its inside. Owing

Stepped Poke Dial in sunlight reading 10:10 am or 1:50 pm

Poke Dial found with metal detector. It has no hour lines, just the numerals

to their very small size, and lack of moveable gnomon hole, the accuracy of these dials would have been particularly poor.

Most Poke Dials were made of brass or bronze, but dials intended to be worn on the finger were often made from gold.

A well-made Poke Dial signed 'I. A. M.'

CHAPTER 4   EQUINOCTIAL RING DIALS

There are three different types of Equinoctial Ring Dial that are normally encountered.
a) The Universal Equinoctial Ring Dial.
b) The Standing Universal Equinoctial Ring Dial.
c) The Astronomical Ring Dial.
In use they are self-aligning, not requiring the aid of a compass to determine the direction of North or South. The gnomon is generally a pinhole through which a small spot of light passes onto the hour scale on the inside of the chapter ring.

Universal Equinoctial Ring Dial in silver signed by Henry Wynne

The Rev. William Oughtred from a late eighteenth century print

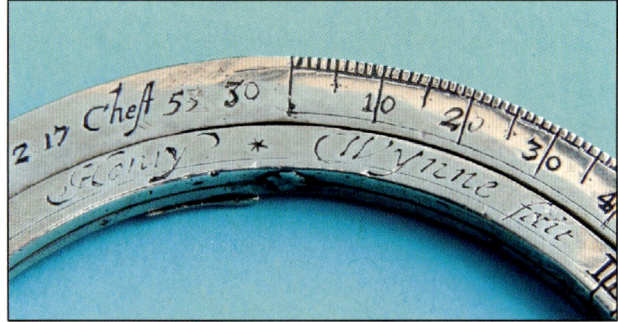

Signature on Henry Wynne dial

UNIVERSAL EQUINOCTIAL RING DIAL

This is the traditional Ring Dial that most of us associate with the name. Gemma Frisius, in 1557, originally developed it from the Armilliary Sphere and the Astronomical Ring, but its final form was only arrived at when the Reverend William Oughtred published a description of it in 1652. Many instrument makers turned their hands to this design, at first in London and later on the Continent. One of the better known exponents of the style was Henry Wynne who published 'The Description and Uses of the General Horological-Ring Dial' [Wynne 1682] in which he describes the dial in detail and explains how it would be used. The dial illustrated, made from silver by Henry Wynne, conforms almost exactly to the details of construction given in his booklet.

This type of dial is also 'universal'. This means that it can be used at any latitude, 0° to 90°, in the Northern Hemisphere.

A Universal Equinoctial Ring Dial by 'John Naish 1707' is shown. The scale on the left of the outer ring is for setting its latitude (the point where the suspension ring will be set) and, unlike many of the earlier dials, covers both hemispheres from pole to pole.

To find the time with this type of dial the

Chapter 4 Equinoctial Ring Dials

Universal Equinoctial Ring Dial (folded flat) by John Naish, dated 1707, made for both hemispheres

poles at either end. It is necessary to set the pinhole in the position that corresponds to the Sun's seasonal altitude. To facilitate this, a calendar scale is engraved on one side and on the reverse is usually an alternative Zodiac scale. A further scale showing the Sun's angular declination appears on many of these dials, calibrated ±23½°. Wynne also describes another scale across the bridge, this time not universal, but for London only, showing the times of sunrise and sunset throughout the year. (See sketch) This scale is seldom seen on Ring Dials.

When suspended in the open position, the Sun's rays will pass through the small pinhole gnomon. The dial should be carefully rotated until the small spot of light falls on the line inscribed around the inside edge of the chapter ring. In theory this is quite easy, but in practice it requires a steady hand. These dials were made with thin rings to reduce the effects of wind but when used outside they will obviously sway in the wind, so a sheltered spot (preferably inside a window) should be sought before attempting to take a reading. A dial used on the deck of a sailing vessel, as many were, would be even more difficult to use due to the continual rolling motion of the deck. The spot of light is very small and can sometimes be quite difficult to see on the inside of the ring.

suspension ring is first set for the user's latitude (in the Naish illustration about 62° North). The inner of the two rings is folded out so that it is at 90° to the outer ring. It carries the hour scale, which is divided into 24 equal parts numbered **I** - **XII** twice. This 24-hour calibration makes the Ring Dial truly 'universal', but many dials made solely for use in the Northern Hemisphere often have a small gap around midnight. This is because their makers did not expect them to be used anywhere north of the Arctic Circle.

Across the centre of the inner ring is a bridge supporting the sliding pinhole gnomon. This bridge may be said to represent the Earth's axis with the two

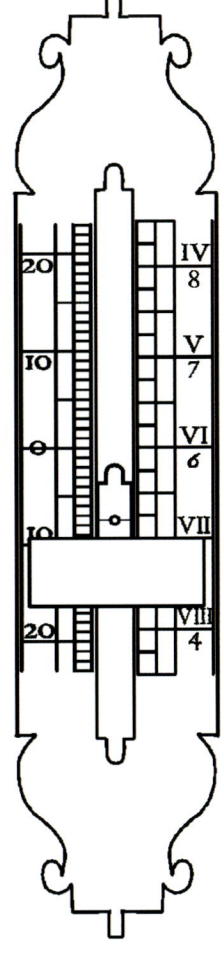

Bridge showing the times of sunrise and sunset (right) as described by Wynne

A useful guide to the dating of British made dials is from the date of the First Point of Aries (the Vernal Equinox) the time when the Sun's declination is 0°. If the gnomon is set at this point, the reverse side of the bridge will indicate a date on the calendar scale. On the Naish dial this shows as the 10th March. The modern Gregorian Calendar gives the Equinox as the 21st March confirming Naish's 1707 date, showing that it was made when the older Julian Calendar was in use. The new calendar was adopted in Britain as late as 1752 but considerably earlier in some parts of the Continent. This method of checking the date on dials must be used with care and does not apply to Continental made instruments. Each country made the calendar change at different dates. See Chapter 25.

On the reverse side of the outer ring there is often a simple Nautical Quadrant calibrated from 0° to

25

Chapter 4   Equinoctial Ring Dials

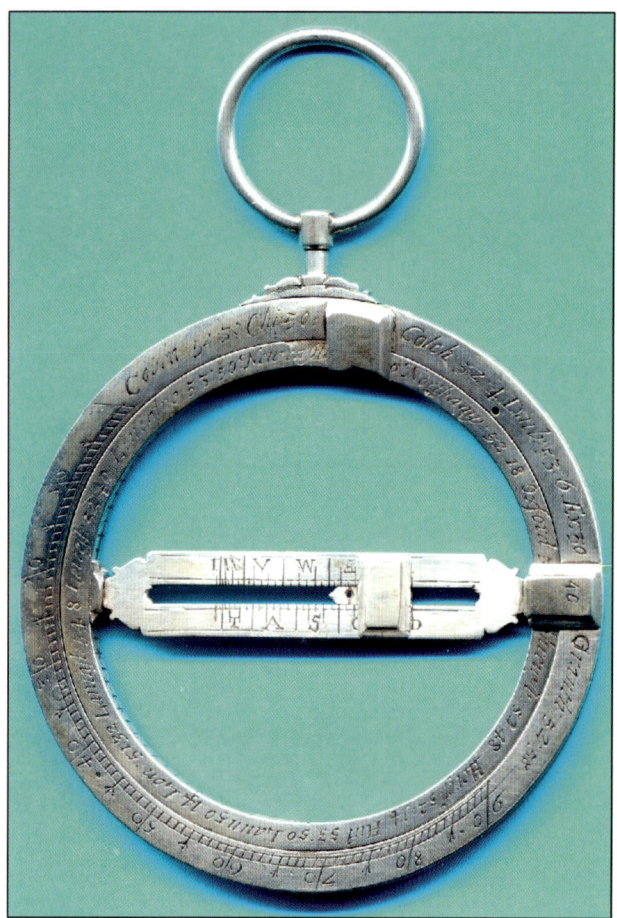

Nautical Quadrant on the left side of the outer ring of the silver dial by Henry Wynne

90°. This is used by inserting a pin in the hole at the top right. With the suspension ring set at 0°, the shadow of the pin will then fall on the quadrant scale, lower left, giving the measure of the Sun's altitude. This reading would enable the user to determine the latitude of his location by reference to the tables of the Sun's altitude.

The Equinoctial Ring Dial is basically an Altitude Dial but has no direct means of indicating morning or afternoon. At noon the outer vertical ring obscures the Sun for about 15 minutes either side of the hour. This is not too much of a problem as the Sun's altitude around noon is hardly changing and unless the dial had been set in a fixed position earlier in the day, the reading taken could be considerably in error. Similarly, at the two Equinoxes the horizontal ring obscures the Sun completely. This ring is, of course, representing the Equator and is in exactly the same place as the Sun at this time. This makes this type of dial unusable for a few days either side of each Equinox. The only real solution is to change the latitude setting by a few degrees, ignoring the small error that would result from this.

These dials were universal and therefore intended for use by travellers. Most are engraved with the names of various towns and cities throughout Europe (sometimes further afield) and their latitudes. There is relatively little space on their

English Ring Dial engraved with the latitudes of many provincial towns

Ring Dial by 'STAMMER - SACROW', outer ring gilt, inner ring silvered

26

slender rings to provide comprehensive lists, but their makers were inventive and used any available space. With some of the longer town names they would frequently resort to abbreviations. The dial by Henry Wynne actually uses the outside edge of the chapter ring to squeeze in the details for seven extra towns. Some makers managed to place the shorter names onto the hinge blocks and occasionally added others to the bridge itself.

Studies of Ring Dials show little variation in style. They were eventually made over most of Europe, mainly between the years of 1680 and 1800. Those that are unsigned can sometimes be attributed to particular countries from their list of towns. The style of engraving can also offer a clue. The design almost certainly started in England following the description of it by William Oughtred and it was soon followed by makers on the Continent. Examples are found from many countries but in particular England, France and Germany.

These dials were predominantly made of brass or bronze but some very beautiful ones are made of solid silver. Occasionally the brass may have been silvered or gilt. Sometimes the main chapter ring would be silvered and the outer ring gilt making a pleasing and useful contrast and also making the spot of light easier to see, as on the dial by

Ring Dial by Pierre Sevin, Paris. This dial includes a latitude scale at the lower edge of the dial, possibly so that it could be used as a Standing Ring Dial

A small gilt Ring Dial in its case

CHAPTER 4 EQUINOCTIAL RING DIALS

15.2 CM DIA.

A six inch diameter Universal Equinoctial Ring Dial by Edmund Culpeper, ca. 1700

Stammer of Sacrow (near Potsdam).

These dials would probably all have had individual carrying cases made to protect them, and a few of these still exist. Some were made as part of a set of surveying instruments and would fit into a much larger communal case.

The dial by Edmund Culpeper is a good example of its kind. Note that it covers both hemispheres, so is truly 'universal'. On its bridge will be seen an unusual set of numerals. These are numbers between 6 and 11 and they are situated above each of the zodiac sigils. These numbers are to be added to the date of the month (seen just below the sigils), to get the number of degrees in that zodiac sign for the date chosen. If the final number exceeds 30, then 30 should be deducted

Chapter 4 Equinoctial Ring Dials

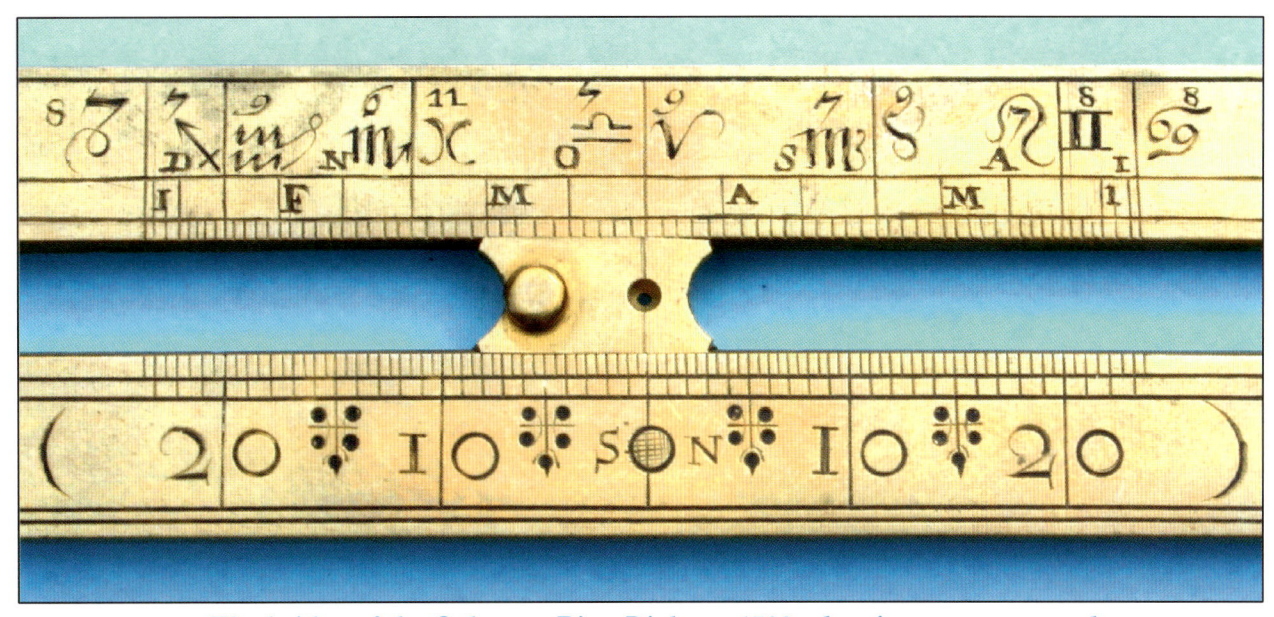

The bridge of the Culpeper Ring Dial, ca. 1700, showing some unusual numbers placed next to each of the zodiac sigils

Detail of the number 7 in the loop of ♌

Detail of suspension on the Stammer dial

from the total. For example, for the 26th April we find that we are in Taurus, ♉, which has number 9 given to it. Adding 26 and 9 we get 35, then deducting 30 this gives Taurus 5. Note also the artistic way that Culpeper has arranged these numerals, in particular the way that 7 fits inside the loop of Leo, ♌. Another point to notice is that the calendar used here is Gregorian (or New Style), where March 20th and September 20th are set for the two equinoxes. However, this dial was made at the time that Britain was still using the Julian (or Old Style) calendar. In fact, on the reverse of this bridge, it is still marked with the Julian calendar, so the dial may be set for either. Another dial in this book (an Analemmatic Dial in Chapter 18) also uses the Gregorian calendar at a time when the Julian calendar was still in use. We can only surmise that their makers either anticipated the calendar change by about 50 years or that they made these instruments for Catholic owners who may already have been using the New Style calendar.

Most Ring Dials are around 4 inches (100mm) in diameter, but examples are known from less than two inches to twelve inches or more, their accuracy increasing with their size.

Their suspension systems are worthy of study in their own right. The author has noted at least ten different methods of attaching the sliding suspension loop to the outer ring.

STANDING RING DIAL

The Universal Equinoctial Ring Dial is potentially very accurate and some large ones were made complete with a stand. Such dials that have lost their stands can possibly be identified by

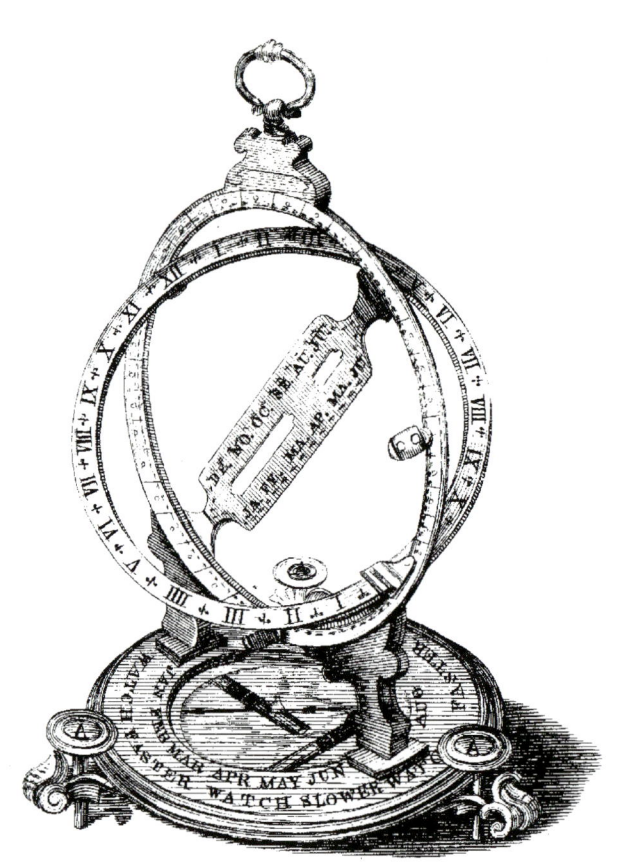

Chapter 4   Equinoctial Ring Dials

Standing Ring Dial

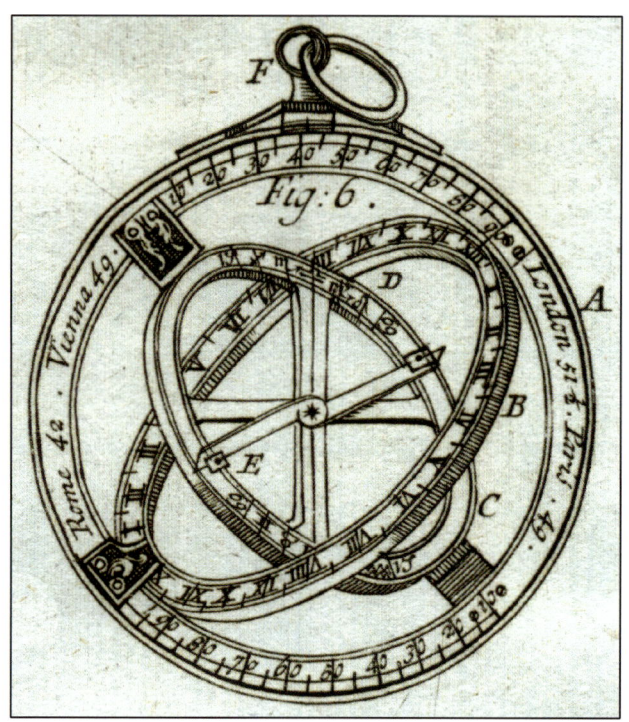

Astronomical Ring Dial

the fact that the outer ring is engraved with a dual latitude scale, as may possibly be the case with the Sevin dial. The extra scale is added at the lower edge where the latitude setting would be read from a line on the stand rather than from the suspension loop. These dials would sit on a solid surface, possibly just inside a window, and could be accurately levelled with three screw feet and the aid of built in bubble levels or plummet. Some stands also included a magnetic compass so that the dial could be correctly and semi-permanently set. Alternatively the dial could be used to check the local magnetic declination or for surveying purposes. Many of the stands were constructed so that the dial could be detached and used separately as any other portable dial. This feature added the flexibility of inside or outside use.

ASTRONOMICAL RING DIAL

This dial is similar in general appearance to the Universal Equinoctial Ring Dial but with the addition of one further ring plus an alidade. These dials are not very common but their method of construction overcame the disadvantage of the loss of time readings at noon and at the Equinox. The time is read from the point where the inner ring crosses the main chapter ring. The inner ring has a rotating alidade. This essentially gives two pinhole sights, one at each end of an arm. Firstly, the latitude is set, then the alidade is rotated to the current date. The dial is held so that the sunlight passes through the upper pinnule to fall exactly on the centre the lower one. This means that it is necessary to rotate the inner ring, quite difficult when suspended from its shackle. However, this was a very accurate method of taking observations and was used on many astronomical instruments. It also saved the observers eyesight making it unnecessary to directly look towards the Sun. The alidade was built on the side of the inner ring and this offset helped to prevent the eclipse of the shadow at noon.

To overcome the difficulties of adjusting the inner ring this dial was often set up on a stand, its accurate measurements warranting the extra stability thereby provided.

For further information on the Ring Dial, its construction and use, the reader is directed to the well known book by Bion. [Bion 1758 - Book VIII] It has several pages devoted to sundials, which are described in detail. The booklet by Wynne [Wynne 1682] also contains much useful information.

CHAPTER 5   QUADRANTS

"**QUADRANT**, quadrans, in geometry, an arch of a circle, containing 90°, or the fourth part of the entire periphery."

"**QUADRANT** also denotes a mathematical instrument, of great use in astronomy and navigation, for taking the altitudes of the Sun and stars, as also for taking angles in surveying, &c."

This is how an eighteenth century Encyclopaedia[1] describes the Quadrant.

The Quadrant comes in many forms and will often carry a great deal of information. In its simplest form it is only a 90° segment of a circle marked with a scale of degrees from 0° to 90° around its circumference. A plumb bob is suspended from its apex so that when it is held with one edge aligned to a distant feature, viewed through the two pinhole sights, the line hangs across the angle scale around its lower edge.

Time is found using a Quadrant by measuring the altitude of the Sun (or by using stars).

QUADRANS NOVUS

The Quadrans Novus, as its name suggests, was preceded by the Quadrans Vetus. This was a much simpler device but had many of the features of the new instrument. This Quadrant was first described by Jacob ben Machir ibn Tibbon of Montpellier around 1300. The Quadrant illustrated comes from fourteenth century and was found in excavations in Canterbury. It is a rather complicated looking instrument supplying much information and giving the time primarily in 'Temporary' or 'Planetary Hours'. A cord would have been suspended from its apex with a plummet hanging below the lower edge and a small sliding bead in between. The process of telling the time was not simple but may be done as follows. Firstly, it is necessary to find the altitude of the Sun at noon on the particular day in question. If this is not known it can be found as follows. The bead should to be set to the position given by the zodiac scale written across the central part of the Quadrant and adjusted to the exact number of degrees for that sign on the inner limb scale beneath. The plumb line is then moved to the left edge where the Sun's declination may be read from the scale (±23½°), positive for Summer months and negative for Winter months. The co-latitude (90° - latitude) of the place then needs to be added to this figure. Next the cord is positioned such that it crosses this number of degrees on the outer scale and the bead is slid to agree with the noon line. This is the arc originating at the apex and passing through the centre (where the rivet is). In Planetary Hours, noon is 6 hours from dawn at the left edge and 6 hours to sunset, also on the left edge. The Sun is then sighted and the bead should position itself on the correct hour for that date and latitude. Luckily, the Sun's altitude setting will not need to be adjusted for

Medieval Qudrans Novus
Reproduced by courtesy of Trevor Philip & Sons

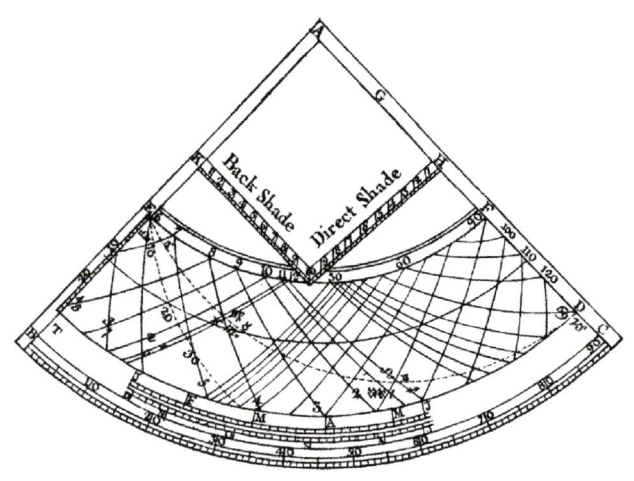

Drawing of Quadrant¹

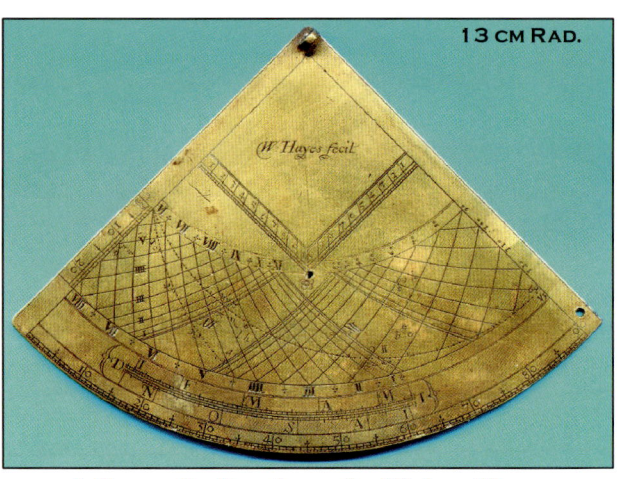

A Gunter's Quadrant by Walter Hayes

several days, so further readings of the hour may be made quite readily.

GUNTER'S QUADRANT

This is also known as the 'Horary Quadrant' and is the one type most often found and of greatest interest to most horologists. It carries an hour scale and a flat representation of the night sky with certain prominent stars marked upon it. Many Quadrants show the same 5 stars and their positions, often with their Right Ascensions.

    PW = Pegasus Wing
    Arc = Arcturus
    Lh = Lions Heart
    Be = Bulls Eye
    Vh = Vultures Heart

This Quadrant is in effect similar to an Astrolabe but with the whole night sky folded into just one 90° segment. The illustration, below, shows a typical English boxwood Quadrant made soon after 1752. It is virtually identical to earlier Quadrants, such as that by Walter Hayes of ca. 1690. Around its outer edge is the degree scale and on the right edge are two pin hole sights for the accurate sighting of an object. It could therefore be used for measuring the altitudes of stars, the Sun or even buildings, mountains and canyons. To find the time, a small sliding bead is moved on the plumb line to the position for the current date by setting it to the correct declination, either from the scale of ±23½° at the left or from the arc originating from the top left corner and ending at the lower right corner. This arc represents the Ecliptic and is normally calibrated with just the Zodiac signs. Each degree is marked along it allowing an accurate setting to be made. Even with the small pinhole sights used, the act of looking directly at the Sun is a dangerous task with the risk of permanent eye damage. Therefore, when taking the elevation of the Sun the Quadrant was used in the hand so that the Sun's rays would pass through the upper sight and project a small spot of light onto the lower one. With a steady hand the Sun's spot could be adjusted to fall exactly into the hole of the lower sight. At this moment the thumb would be used to press the plumb line against the scale to record the exact time from the position of the sliding bead. As with all Altitude Dials it will not immediately tell us the information about whether it is morning or

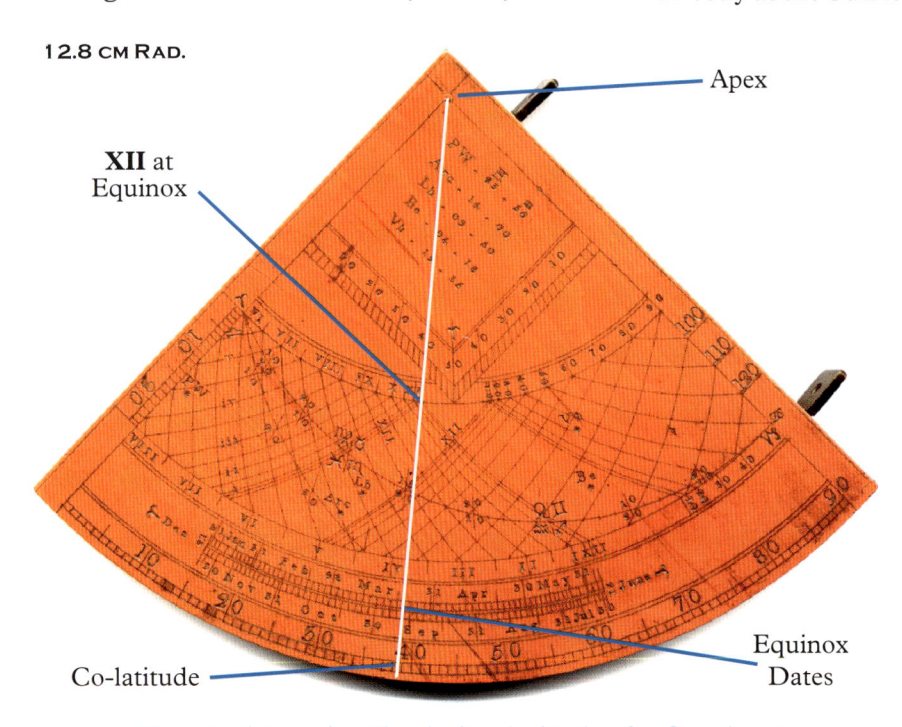

How to determine the design latitude of a Quadrant

CHAPTER 5   QUADRANTS

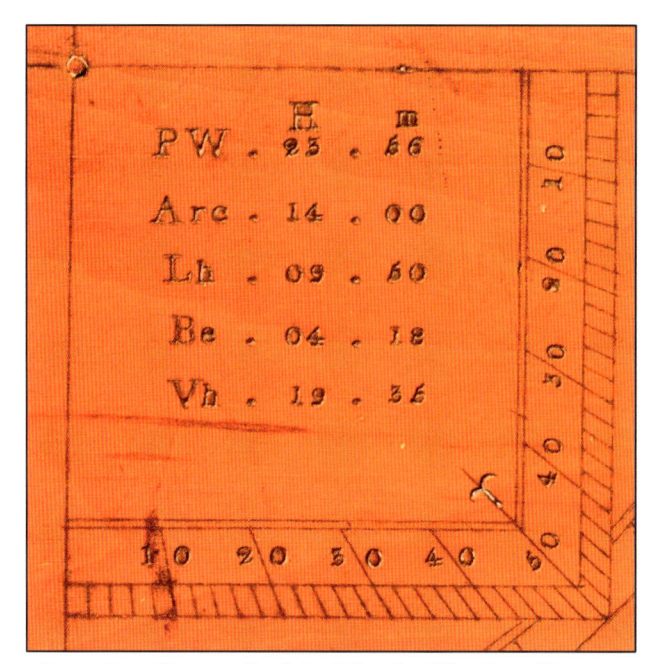

Star details marked inside the Shadow Square showing their Right Ascensions (H and m)

If it had been the earlier Julian Calendar both dates would have been 10 to 11 days earlier, although some small variations on these dates may be found. It also tells us that this Quadrant was probably made for the latitude of a place just north of London. This is found by drawing a radial line from the Equinox at 21st March to the degree scale along its outer edge. This gives around 38° 15', being the colatitude of 51° 45'. The same line also cuts through the noon hour line at the Equinox.

Another interesting scale often shown on Quadrants is the Shadow Square or Quadrat. This is the square nearest the apex, in this case

32 CM RAD.

afternoon, and this needs to be deduced in the ways already discussed.

The information carried on the main scale seems at first sight rather complicated. This is a representation of the sky around the Ecliptic, being the portion of the sky through which the Sun travels throughout the year (±23.5° either side of the Equator). It may be a little confusing at first because the whole 360° circle of the heavens has been folded into just 90°. The curved line from the top left to the bottom right is the Sun's Summer path across the sky. It travels from the Vernal Equinox (the first point of Aries) ♈ through to Midsummer at the right edge and back to the Autumnal Equinox at Libra ♎, then tracing the same path again for the Winter months. Along the lengths of this arc are marked the appropriate Zodiac signs. The plumb line from the apex point, missing in this example, is used for all measurements, either against its sliding bead or directly on the angular scale. When the Quadrant was used, the position of this bead would give the time by tracing its position along the nearest hour line to the Roman hour numerals marked at each end of it.

A further scale is given just inside the degree scale. This is a calendar scale and could be used to check the altitude of the Sun at noon. It tells us a lot about this boxwood Quadrant. It gives us an idea of its date by telling us that it conforms to the new Gregorian Calendar that was adopted in Britain in 1752. On its calendar scale, the Vernal Equinox is on 21st March and this is exactly opposite to the date of the Autumnal Equinox of September 23rd.

Large boxwood Quadrant

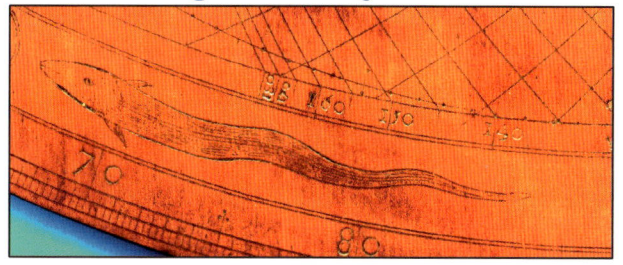

Eel engraved on the large boxwood Quadrant

Interesting pattern on large boxwood Quadrant

Chapter 5   Quadrants

calibrated from 0 to 50 in both directions. On others the calibration may be 0-10, 0-12, 0-100 or any other convenient figure. Similar Shadow Squares will be found on a wide range of scientific instruments. It is used for finding the height of buildings, of mountains, depths of wells or valleys etc. It works on the principle of triangles of proportion (tangents). Basically, if the reading obtained on the horizontal scale was 40, the height of the object would be in proportion to 40/50 of the distance from it. Similarly, a reading of 20 on the vertical

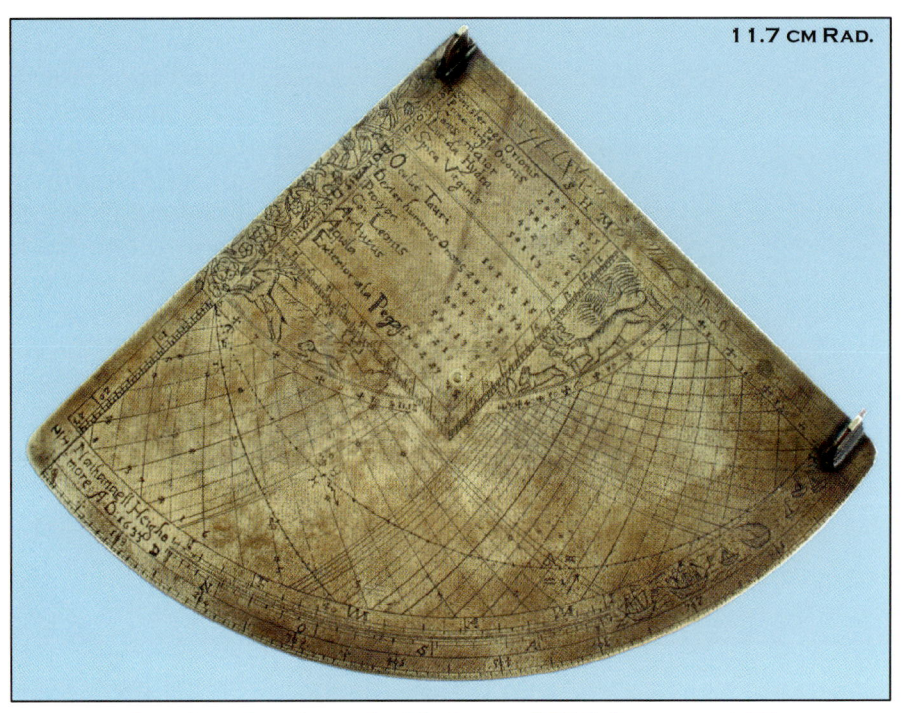

Gunther Quadrant by Nathanaell Heighemore, 1633

Sundial volvelle on the large boxwood Quadrant

scale would give a height of 50/20 times the distance measured to it. Allowance must usually be made for the height of the user in these calculations.

Most boxwood Quadrants are quite small, having a radius of around 5" (120 mm). Larger Quadrants are sometimes to be found in observatories up to several feet in diameter but these are often fixed and are used for more precise astronomical observations. A particularly large boxwood Quadrant from the late seventeenth century has a radius of 12½" (318 mm). This is a most unusual Quadrant, being engraved not only with the usual scales and stars but also some ornate patterns and a beautiful image of a fish or eel in the bottom right hand corner. As with most other Quadrants, it is unsigned, but from its quality, it is made by one of the best instrument makers of its day. On its reverse is a volvelle engraved with a Horizontal Dial.

The inclusion of drawings and patterns as on this

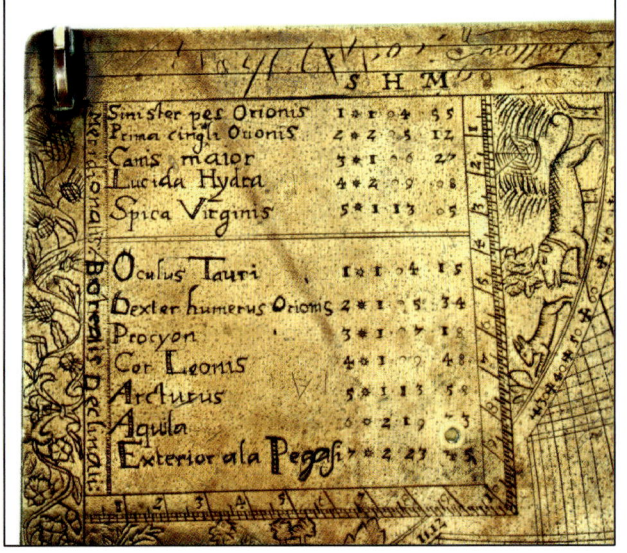

Star chart inside the Shadow Square on the Heighemore Quadrant

Engraving of a deer hunt with a dog on the Heighemore Quadrant

Quadrant is not unique and many such are found on a wide range of Quadrants. The Quadrant by

34

Chapter 5 Quadrants

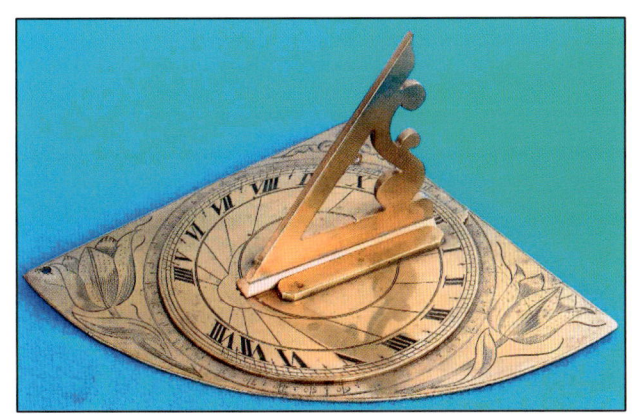

*Sundial on reverse of a Quadrant by Hayes
(The gnomon is a restoration)*

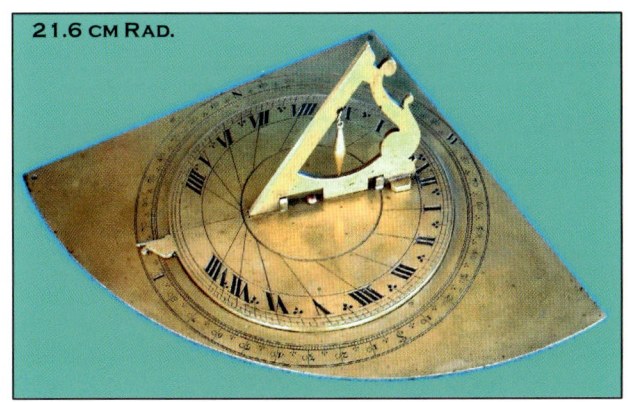

21.6 CM RAD.

*Large brass Gunther Quadrant with a Sundial
on its reverse, ca. 1700*

Heighemore is another good example, and possibly tells us that it was made provincially.

The inclusion of a sundial on the reverse of a Quadrant is not uncommon. Another example is shown by Walter Hayes, ca. 1690. The sundial may be rotated within a 360° scale. This type of

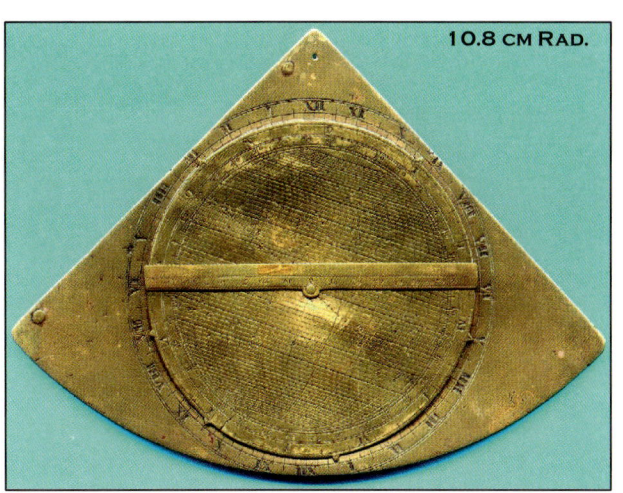

10.8 CM RAD.

*An unsigned brass Quadrant, ca. 1700, with an
Organum Ptolomei on its reverse*

dial was probably used for surveying. Once the time was known from the Quadrant on its reverse, this same time could be set on the shadow from the Horizontal Dial. With one edge of the Quadrant lined up with perhaps the edge of a building or a boundary of a piece of land, it could give its precise angle with reference to true North. It could also be used for checking the angle of a building for setting up a Vertical Sundial. Many of these dials had a plummet suspended from near the gnomon apex with a degree scale below to allow the dial to be set horizontally. It also allowed the dial to be used for a range of nearby latitudes. Many Quadrants are plain on their reverse, but in addition to the occasional Horizontal Dial there is sometimes a volvelle with further astronomical information such as that with the Organum Ptolomei (or Rojas Projection) of the heavens on its reverse side.

The Quadrant above right is unsigned, but it is English and is very similar to Quadrants made by John Prujean of Oxford in the last years of the seventeenth century. On this Quadrant (and on Prujeans) the stars depicted have been joined up to form the shapes of their constellations and may be used as a Planispheric Nocturnal. See Chapter 24 for more details. The Heighemore Quadrant also has the Organum Ptolomei on its reverse. In the photograph it has been removed to show some of Heighemore's construction lines.

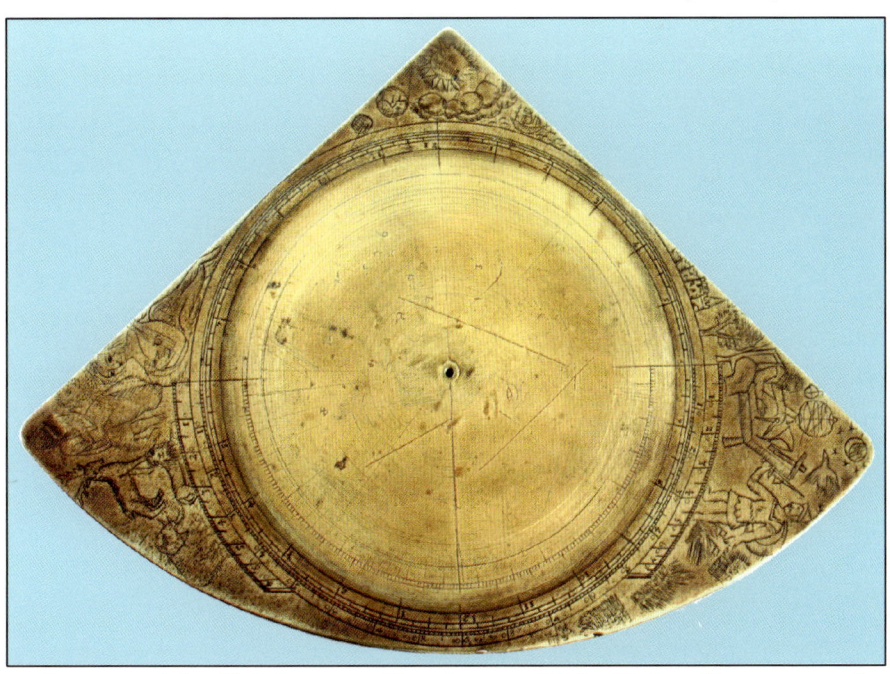

*Reverse of the Heighemore Quadrant with its Rojas disc removed
showing some of his construction lines*

35

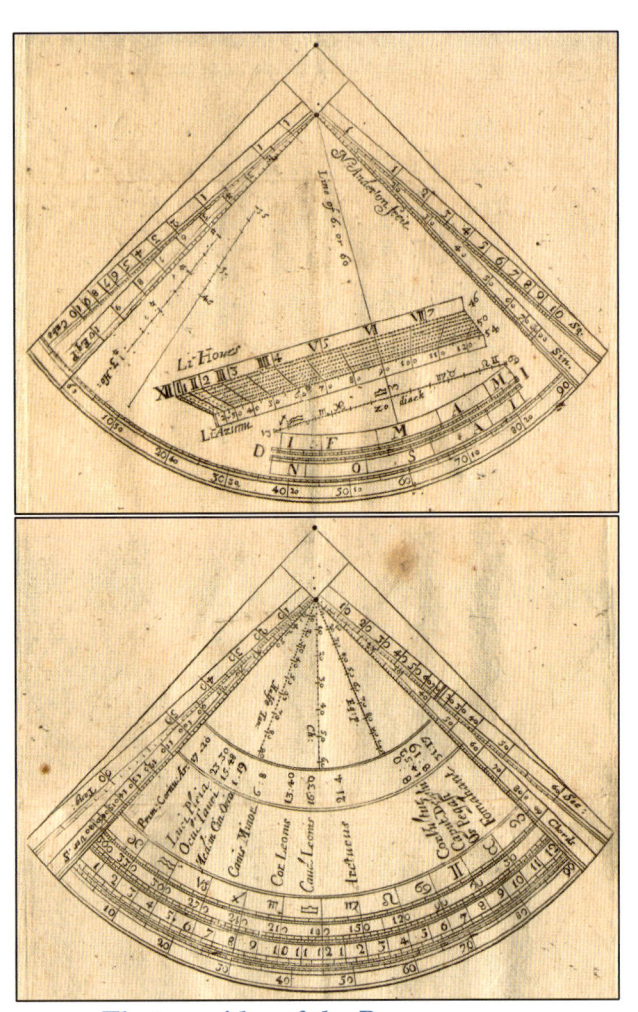

CHAPTER 5   QUADRANTS

The two sides of the Panorganon as illustrated in the book by Leybourn

good idea of the various applications for which this instrument may be used.

For direct time telling, this can be achieved by finding the altitude of the Sun, taking this figure from the scale of sines on the right hand limb with a pair of dividers, applying this at right angles to the thread when laid across the current date to the straight hour scale. It is not really a first choice for a time telling instrument.

The instrument made by Iofeph Wells is similar to the Panorganon although made for a single latitude. It differs in several ways from Leybourn's model, but it will be noted that it is dated nine years before his book was published. The reverse side of Leybourn's Quadrant has star and zodiac information, much of which is also incorporated on the front of the Wells Quadrant.

HORODICTICAL QUADRANT

This version of the Quadrant actually comes from an earlier date than the Gunter's Quadrant and is relatively uncommon. The shape of its hour lines depend on how its calendar scale has been drawn. It is normally as illustrated but sometimes a linear date version is preferred to avoid cramping around the Solstices. When the calendar scale is linear the main curves become 'S' shaped rather than circular. On some Quadrants the Zodiac divisions may be extended as arcs right across the face to cross the hour lines. There is no reason why the calendar scale should have any particular linearity as the equinoctial hour lines can be modified to suit.

In use, the bead on the thread is set to the correct date on the calendar scale and the altitude of the Sun is observed through the sight vanes as with the Gunter's Quadrant. The time may now be read

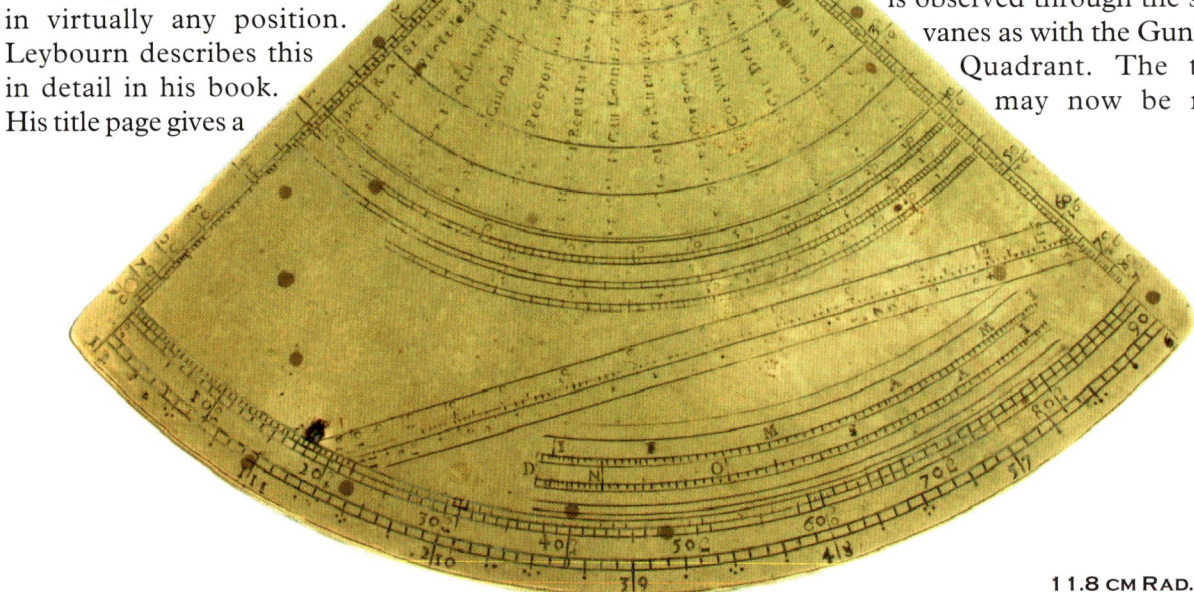

THE PANORGANON

This is a type of Quadrant first described by William Leybourn. [Leybourn 1672] It is not primarily an instrument for time telling but it has many uses including that of making dials in virtually any position. Leybourn describes this in detail in his book. His title page gives a

11.8 CM RAD.

Panorganon type Quadrant made by 'Ioseph Wells' and dated 1663

36

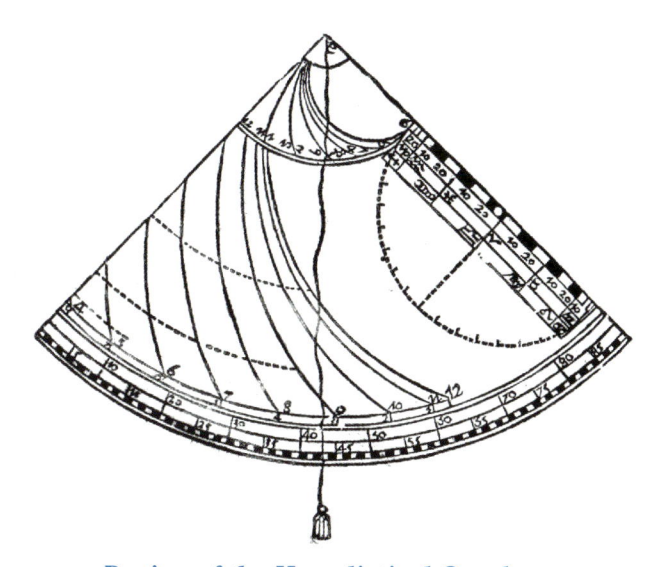

CHAPTER 5 QUADRANTS

Design of the Horodictical Quadrant

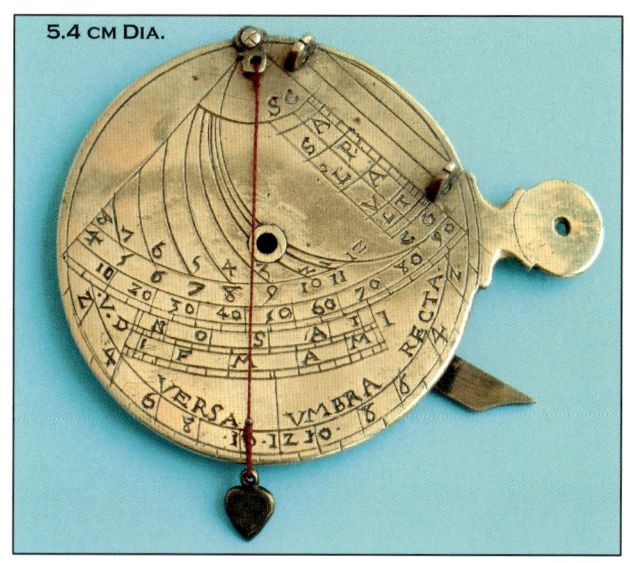

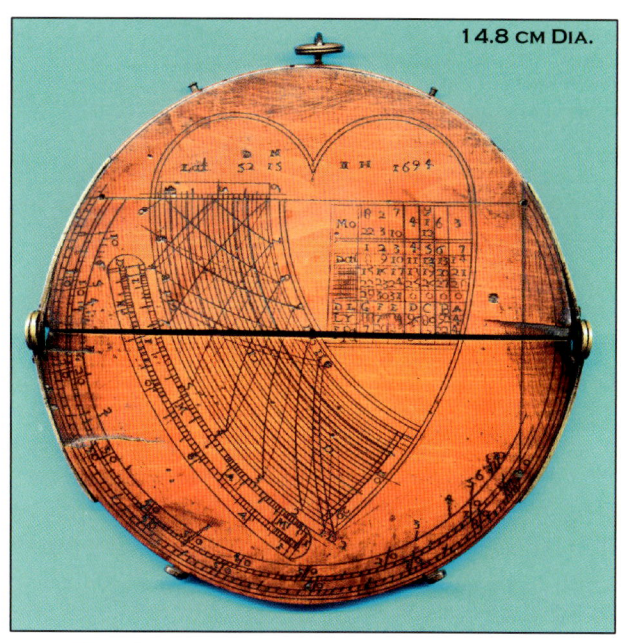

Folding Quadrant by N.H., dated 1694

Horodictical Quadrant on the back of a Nocturnal

Carved Horodictical Quadrant with linear date scale, 'FAIT LE 12 AVRIL MDCCXXV PAR P I MAYNADIE'

from the position of the bead from the hour lines. The times of sunrise and sunset are simply found by moving the thread to the left-hand edge and by reading time from the bead.

In some Quadrants of this type unequal hour lines are also marked. These can be readily identified by having a common origin at the Quadrant's apex with the noon line extending to the right hand edge. (See the small scale at the apex of the Quadrant drawing shown top left.) The time in unequal or 'Planetary' hours may be obtained as follows: - Set the bead to the correct date and then set it on the 12 hour equinoctial line. Move the bead so that it lies exactly over the 6 hour or noon line (the right hand curve). Take a reading from the Sun as normal and the bead will record the time in unequal hours. Sometimes two beads may be used to take simultaneous readings.

An example of an early Horodictical Quadrant on the reverse of a brass Nocturnal is also shown. This Nocturnal/Quadrant, is probably German and dates from around 1600.

The boxwood Quadrant with the finely sculpted angel is dated 1725 and possibly comes from Switzerland. Note that this uses a linear date scale, resulting in 'S' shaped hour lines.

SUTTON'S QUADRANT

The Sutton's Quadrant is a stereographic projection of one quarter of the sphere between the tropics on the plane of the ecliptic. The lines originating from its right edge are parallels of altitude. The lines crossing them at right angles are azimuths. The smaller circle of radius at the top represents the Tropic of Capricorn and the larger circle around the limb, the Tropic of Cancer. Two ecliptic arcs are drawn, one each for Summer and Winter seasons. The two horizons also originate from this same point. The limb is divided into 90° for angular measurement. It has a further scale calibrated each 15° marked with hours. Each hour is usually subdivided into individual minutes for accurate time recording.

Time telling by this Quadrant is a little more complex than the others, but once mastered is capable of giving accurate results. The first step is to set the thread so that it crosses the current date. Then adjust the bead so that it lies exactly on the appropriate ecliptic line (Summer = lower or Winter = upper). If the degrees of Zodiac are already known, then the bead may be set directly to that figure in the ecliptic scale. Once set, the Sun's altitude reading may be obtained as before. Then move the thread so that the bead now lies on the parallel of altitude corresponding to the reading taken and read the time from where the thread now crosses the hour scale on the limb.

Henry Sutton (working 1649, died 1665) [Clifton 1995] was a well known and respected Instrument Maker from London. He produced quantities of these 10" Quadrants around 1658. To enable him to make the quantity required he engraved a printing plate producing the Quadrants on paper,

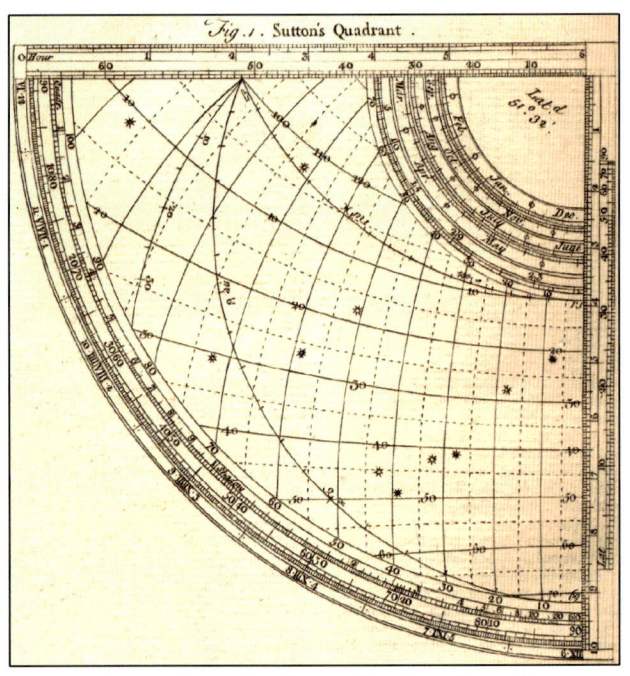

Drawing of a Sutton's Quadrant[1]

which were then pasted onto oak bases. Most of those extant are dated, the different dates showing that he was continually updating his printing plates. On the reverse side are often seen other scales including sines, arcsines, tangents etc. Due to their cheap and relatively fragile method of construction very few of these have survived.

27.5 CM RAD.

Sutton's Quadrant, dated 1658. It consists of paper scales pasted onto an oak board

Reverse of the Sutton's Quadrant showing various trigonometrical scales

Signature and date on the Quadrant by Sutton

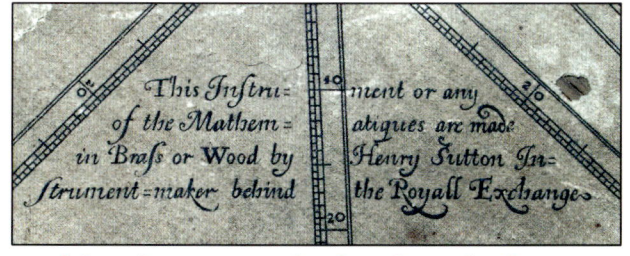

Advertisement on the Quadrant by Sutton

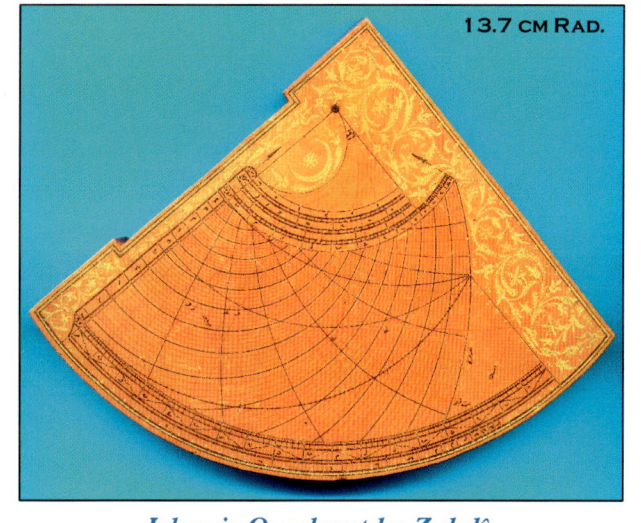

Islamic Quadrant by Zuhdî, A.H. 1294 (1877/8 A. D.)

THE ISLAMIC QUADRANT

The Quadrant (also known as a Prophatius Quadrant) was also made in other countries for time telling and astronomical purposes. In particular the Arabs were very interested in astronomy and are known to have made many very fine instruments. The Quadrant shown is of Arabic origin and was made by Zuhdî in the year AH 1294 (AD 1877/8). It is similar in many ways to the standard European Quadrant apart from its ornate gold decoration and of course the Arabic inscriptions. On its reverse is a scale of sines and cosines.

REFERENCES

1. Society of Gentlemen. *Dictionary of Arts and Sciences.* London 1754.

CHAPTER 6   IVORY DIPTYCH DIALS

The Diptych Dial was probably first made in the fifteenth century and early examples are found from makers such as Georg Hartmann, working in Nuremberg in the first half of the sixteenth century.

As its name suggests, it consisted of two 'tablets', usually of ivory, hinged together, with a Horizontal Dial on the lower tablet and usually with a Vertical Dial on the hinged upper one. The two dials would generally share a common string gnomon. The two dials would therefore conveniently fold together and fit comfortably into a pocket or bag.

Similar dials were also made in other countries throughout Europe and are found in various forms. See Chapter 7 for details of French Ivory Dials and Chapter 20 for String Gnomon Dials.

Other Diptych Dials made from wood came from Southern Germany at a much later date, ca. 1750 - 1850.

Nuremberg was, and still is, a large and prosperous town in Southern Germany. It was home to many workers employed making ivory dials. These workers, however, came from just a few families and between them they turned out large numbers of Ivory Diptych Dials between 1550 and 1650.

The subject of Nuremberg Dials and their makers has been superbly covered [Gouk 1988] and it is not proposed to repeat this information except as required for completeness.

Other areas in Europe also made the Ivory Diptych Dial, such as Dieppe in France. Examples are known from other parts of France, from Spain and from Italy.

The word diptych comes from both Latin and Greek. The Greek word *diptukha* is from *di*, meaning two and *ptakhos*, to fold. In English a diptych is generally an ancient two leaved writing tablet or a religious painting with two leaves that close like a book.

Diptych Dials also consist of two leaves and when folded and latched may be carried safely in the pocket without risk of damage. Original protective cases for these early dials are unknown but a later English model and some wooden examples do have them. It is probable that most of the metal Diptych Dials had cases. These were important to protect their engraving and gilding.

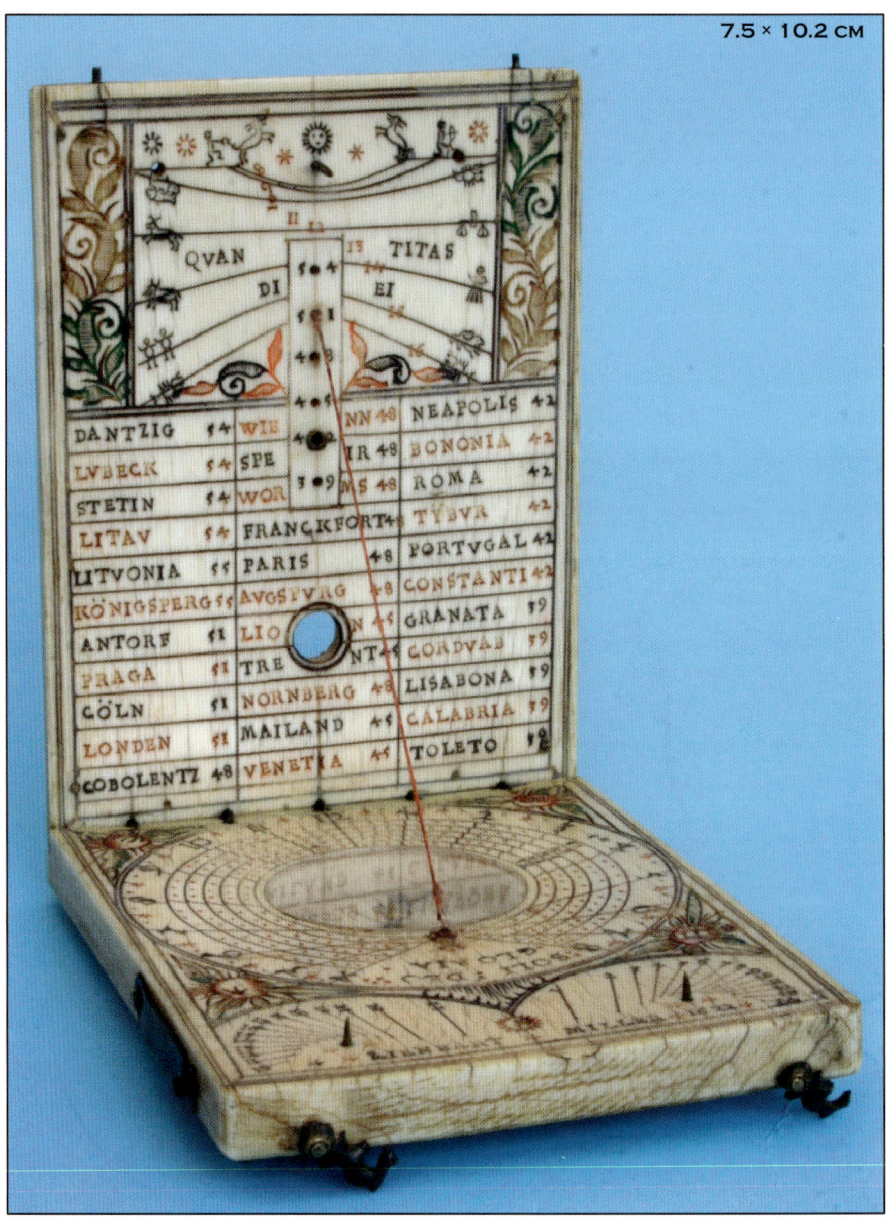

7.5 × 10.2 CM

Fine ivory Diptych Dial by Lienhart Miller, dated 1622

The case would also protect the pocket from their sharp metal edges.

All Diptych Dials have a built-in compass for correct orientation. The compass is often a good aid to fairly precise dating of these dials from the magnetic declination that is usually marked in the bowl. See Appendix 4.

Ivory is a very durable material, which can easily be sawn, cut to shape and polished. However, in time it dries out and over the 300 to 400 years since these dials were made many cracks have appeared along the grain. In some cases they have completely split, usually across the compass bowl and these require expert restoration. Their calibration lines were incised into the ivory with a sharp tool or graver, but in virtually all cases, the numerals and letters were applied with metal punches. Each instrument maker would make his own set, or sets, of punches, probably during his apprenticeship. This was a slow and painstaking process and would have occupied him for a considerable time. These punches would then stay with each maker throughout his working life and would only be replaced when a punch was damaged or worn. It is interesting to make comparisons of one particular maker's set of punch marks over a period of years as it is often possible to see these changes as the damaged punches are replaced.

It is believed that secret formulas were developed for softening the ivory to take the punch marks without it splitting. Marking by punches was probably the only successful way of annotating these dials as ivory is relatively brittle and could be expected to chip when deeply cut with a graver. If its fibres are severed, flaking is inevitable whereas punch marking merely crushes the fibres.

Most dials have scales on all four of their faces and for convenience these will be referred to as Face A, Face B, Face C and Face D starting on the outside top face.

The Nuremberg Diptych Dials in their simplest form were only calibrated internally on Faces B & C. These were usually standard Vertical and Horizontal Dials operating from the shadow formed by the string gnomon, which is set at a fixed angle, i.e., one particular latitude. Some dials have alternative anchoring holes for the top of the string gnomon so that they may be used at several latitudes. These can not have the vertical dial face and the horizontal hour lines are usually cut for several latitudes in concentric circles. When this type of dial is correctly aligned North - South with the aid of its built-in compass and placed on a horizontal surface, a quick and reasonably accurate reading may be obtained. The main errors are as outlined above and also due to the small size of the compass and possibly its out-of-date magnetic declination setting. The contrast obtained on the white ivory surface from the gnomon's shadow gives a crisp and clear line, unlike many metal dials where the shiny surface can obscure its image.

The dial by **HANS TVCHER 1583**, is quite unusual, in that it shows only Italian Hours, from **10** to **24**. It is made for a latitude of 42°, the figure for Rome. This type of dial operates from two pin gnomons (the one on the vertical face is missing) and it shows the same time on both faces, B & C. Faces A and D are unused.

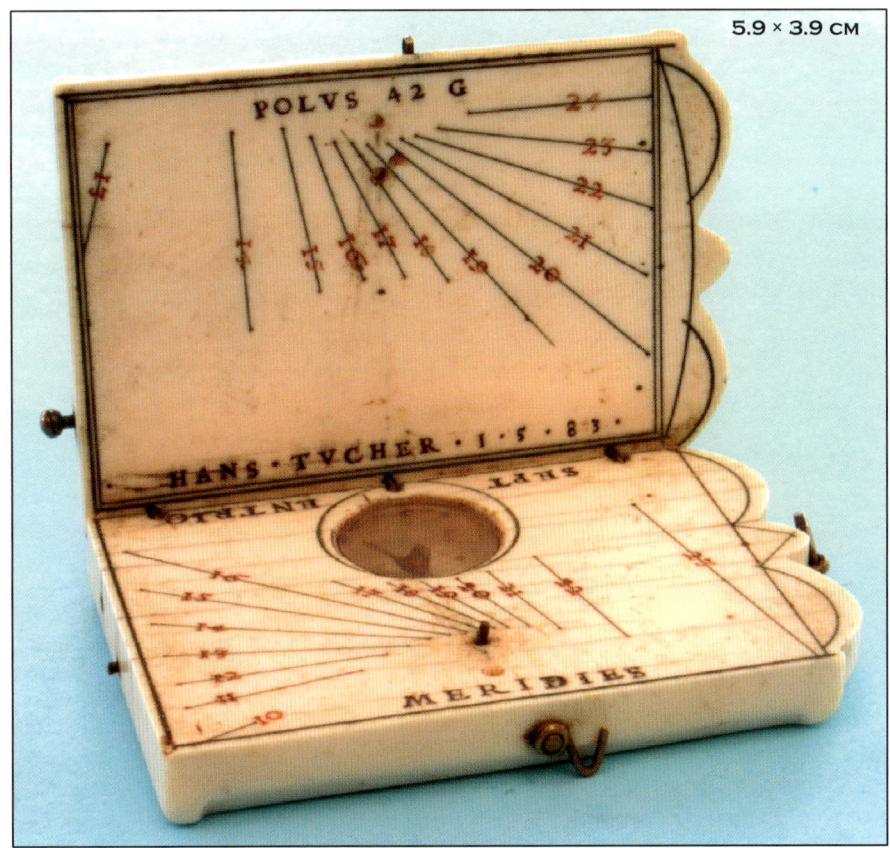

An early ivory Diptych Dial by Hans Tucher, dated 1583

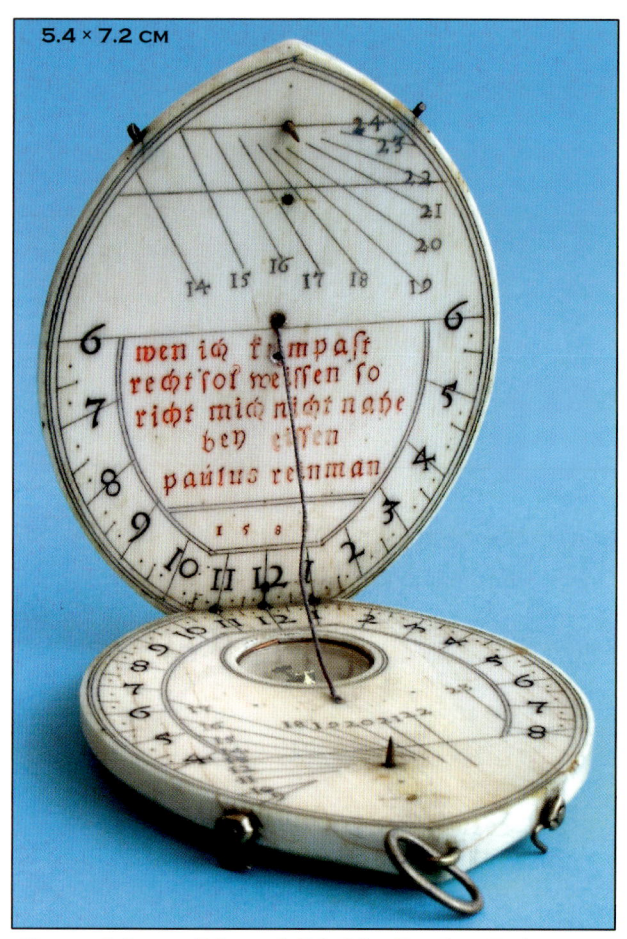

CHAPTER 6 IVORY DIPTYCH DIALS

An oval ivory Diptych Dial by Paulus Reinman, Nuremberg, dated 1588

This dial is of the rare book form. When closed it looks like a small book. It also has a suspension ring at the top and would probably have been worn hanging around the neck by a cord.

The ivory dial by Paul Reinman, dated 1588 is of an unusual oval form. It too has the dials for Italian Hours, operated by pin gnomons but also has equinoctial hours that are read from the shadow of a string gnomon. Like most early dials it has a very small compass. Face A has a simple lunar volvelle but Face D is blank. Its inscription on Face B tells the user "If I shall show the right direction, do not place me near iron."

The more typical Nuremberg Diptych Dials were somewhat more complex, often with a Wind Rose on Face A and with some form of Perpetual Calendar on Face D. Other scales on faces B and C would possibly show day length, astrological signs as well as Babylonian and Italian Hours.

The dial by Lienhart Miller of 1622, illustrated on Page 40, is a particularly good example and has been used to explain the various scales. Refer to the photographs here and on the next page.

Face A. This is the Wind Rose. A small Wind Vane that is normally stored in a side pocket of the dial is fitted in its centre. The dial is lined up with North by viewing the compass needle through the small round window through Face A. The dial may still be used without a Wind Vane by assessing the wind's direction by observing the motion of the clouds, some smoke, bending trees,

Lunar volvelle on the oval Reinman dial

Wind vane on face A of the 1622 Miller dial

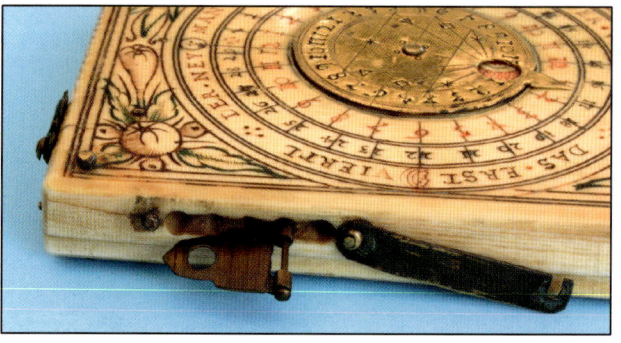

Storage compartment for the wind vane

42

CHAPTER 6   IVORY DIPTYCH DIALS

Face A. Upper surface with wind directions. The wind vane will be fitted in the centre.

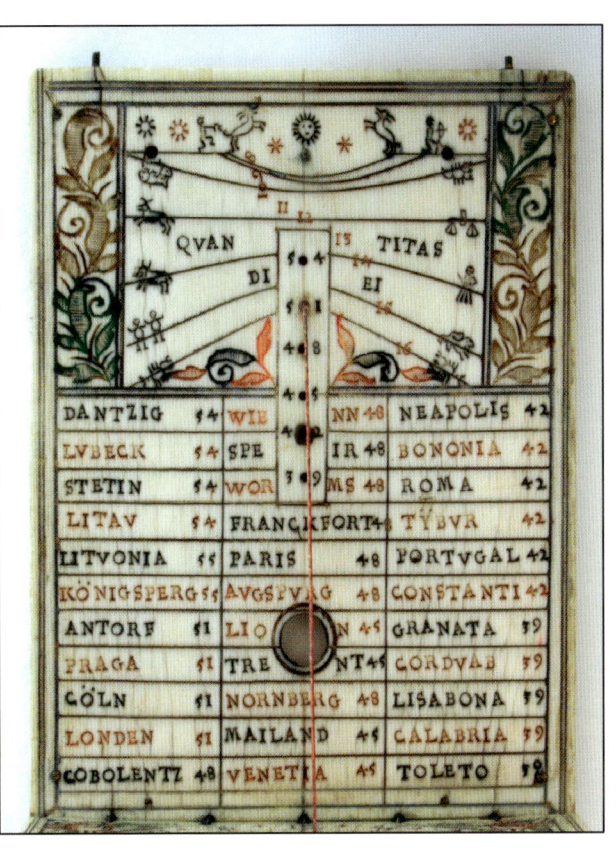

Face B. Vertical face with day length dial, latitude settings and gazetteer. Unusually, this face does not have a Vertical Dial.

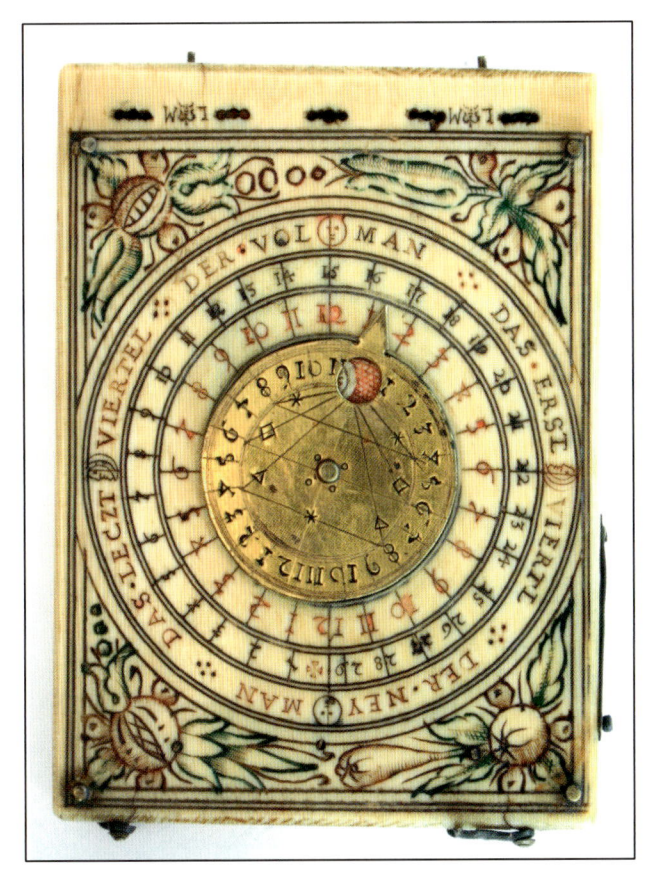

Face D. Underside with lunar calendar and the aspects.

Face C. Horizontal Dials for 39° to 54°, and Pin Gnomon Dials for Italian Hours and Babylonian Hours

43

Crown mark and initials of Lienhart Miller

grasses or even ripples on water. Observations of wind directions and their changes are a good guide to weather forecasting and would have been a useful feature to our forefathers. Once a reading is established, the gilt pointer may be set as a reference until a later reading is required. It must have been an inaccurate device, especially when held in the hand, or anywhere close to the observer's body due to the local disturbance to the airflow.

Note the names of the winds around the outside and the 32 points of the compass starting at East. Little faces in the corners are puffing the winds from a starry sky.

Face B. At the top is a small pin gnomon dial that may be used to give the day length. It has the signs of the zodiac and the hours in red for each line. Astrological information was of much greater importance in earlier times, being used daily and its consequences often completely ruled the everyday actions of people.

In the centre is a panel with six anchoring holes for the string gnomon for latitudes from 39° to 54°. Below this is a list of 33 towns and their latitudes.

Face C. This is the main Horizontal Dial with equinoctial hours from 4 am to 8 pm. Six concentric rings give the hour angles for the six different gnomon latitudes. At the end of the scales is the motto:

SOLI : DEO : GLORIA

(The Sun is the Glory of God)

Above the signature are dials for Italian Hours, ending at sunset and Babylonian Hours, starting at sunrise, both operating from small pin gnomons.

The compass in the centre is marked with a declination line in black with a later one in red. It has four more cherubs blowing towards the centre and Lienhart Miller's mark of a crown.

Face D. Underneath is a Lunar Volvelle showing the Moon's quarters, individual days 1 - 29½ and a 24 hour scale.

This volvelle enables the dial to be used at night if there is enough moonlight. In practice this is only possible for a few days either side of the Full Moon, but as long as the Moon is visible it should be possible to make a reasonable guess as to where its shadow would fall on the dial. The String Gnomon Dial on Face C would be operated as for the Sun's shadow and the Moon's time would be found. If there was insufficient light to set the compass correctly, then the Pole Star could be used and the dial aligned with it. It must be stressed that lunar time measurements without complicated corrections are at best only approximate.[1] This is due mainly to the Moon's cycle over a period of years, during which its altitude changes.

The time reading taken from the Moon should now be converted via the lunar volvelle into solar hours. Firstly the central gilt brass disc is set to the age of the Moon. The Moon's age starts with zero at New Moon and the relevant scale is the middle of the three outer ones. In this example the 16th day has been set. (Full Moon is 14¾ days into the lunar cycle.) In the days after Full Moon, the Moon rises after 6pm and therefore would be in the East in the evening and South after Midnight. If, for example, the time reading was 10 pm lunar, this figure would be read from the brass disc and converted by the adjoining scale which is about 11 pm solar time.

At the centre of the gilt lunar volvelle are shown the astrological Aspects consisting of a triangle, a square and a hexagon. The Aspects are angles formed between two or more celestial bodies as seen from the Earth. Certain combinations of planets at particular angles have different and important astrological significance. The basic aspects are Conjunction 0°, Sextile 60° (separated by two Zodiac signs), Square 90°, Trine 120°, and Opposite 180°.[2]

Opposite, Square and Sextile Aspects were associated with bad luck and the Trine, good luck.

A later dial of 1628 by Lienhart Miller is also illustrated, this time with a fixed latitude gnomon and a Vertical Dial on Face B. The two dials for Italian and Babylonian Hours have now been combined on Face C.

A similar dial by Hans Troschel is illustrated.

CHAPTER 6   IVORY DIPTYCH DIALS

Ivory Diptych Dial by Lienhart Miller, Nuremberg, dated 1628

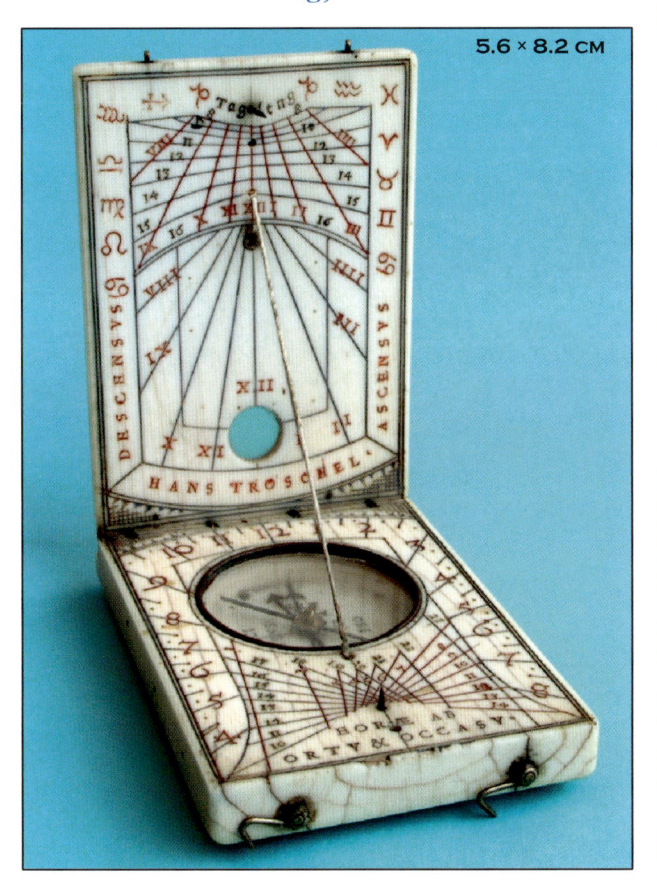

5.6 × 9.1 CM

Dial by Hans Troschel

5.6 × 8.2 CM

Wind rose from the Troschel dial

Around the edge of the Wind rose on Face A is the Latin inscription:

PERGE SECVRVS ✲ MONSTRO VIAM

(Proceed Safely, I Show The Way)

On Face B the Day's Length scale has the addition of hours, also read from its pin gnomon.

On Face C is another Pin Gnomon Dial with the caption in Latin:

HORAE AB ORTV & OCCASV

(Hours from sunset and occasional hours)

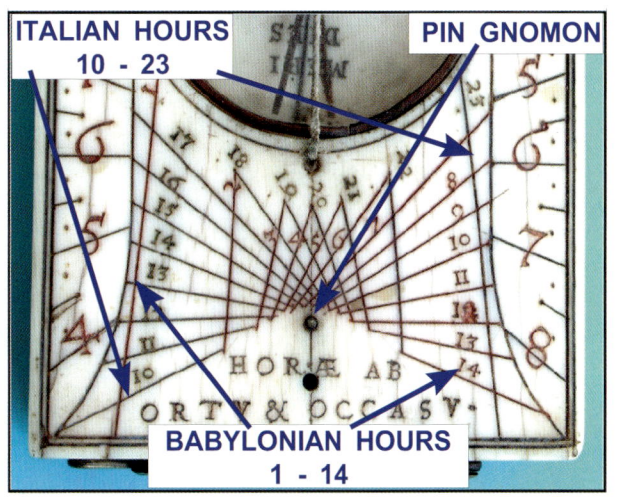

Italian and Babylonian Hours on the ivory dial by Hans Troschel

45

Chapter 6 Ivory Diptych Dials

Lunar Volvelle on the Troschel dial

At first sight this scale seems somewhat confused but it is actually two dials in one, each mirroring the other. Ascending clockwise from **10** through to **23** are the hours reckoned from Sunset. These are known as Italian, Bohemian or 'Welsch' (or foreign) Hours. This form of time reckoning was also used by the Ancient Greeks, Jews, Silesians and the Chinese. The other scale starting at **1** in the top left corner and finishing at **14** on the right shows Babylonian or Greek Hours that begin at Sunrise. When the shadow of the pin gnomon is vertical, i.e., pointing North, it is midday. At the Equinox, Sunrise and Sunset are at 6am and 6pm respectively when reckoned in modern hours. This means that midday will be 18 hours after Sunset, Italian, and 6 hours after Sunrise, Babylonian. Close observation will show that at a short distance North of the gnomon, these two lines for **18** and **6** cross. At the Winter Solstice we know that the Sun rises at 8am and sets at 4pm in Northern Europe. Therefore midday is only 4 hours before sunset, i.e., 20 hours after sunset and 4 hours after sunrise. These two lines join at a point furthest North of the gnomon. At the Summer Solstice when the Sun is much higher in the sky the shadow of the gnomon tip is much closer to the gnomon giving **16** and **8** hours for noon. These scales are completely obsolete by modern standards and therefore are seldom understood.

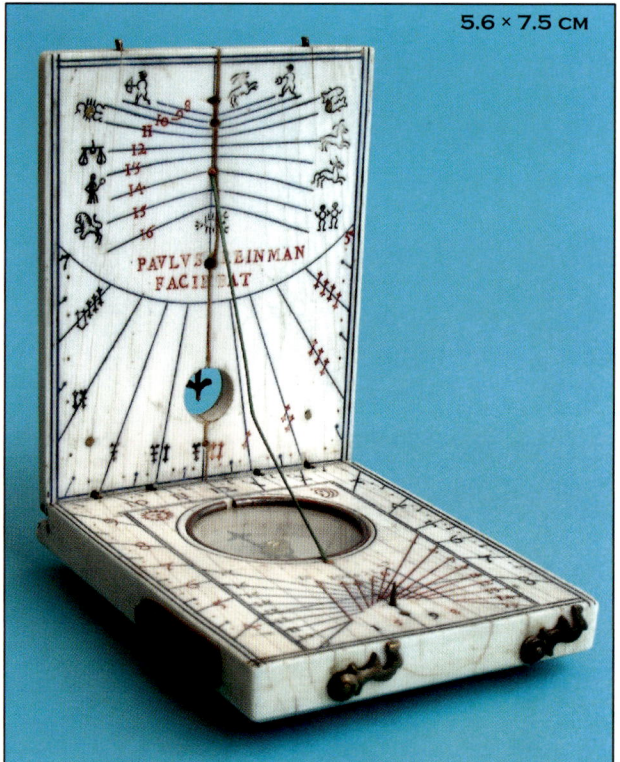

Standard ivory Diptych Dial by Paul Reinman, dated 1598

Hans Troschel's trade mark; a thrush

Crown mark of Paul Reinman and the 'n' quality symbol for Nuremberg

46

Chapter 6 Ivory Diptych Dials

Lunar volvelle on dial by Paul Reinman, 1598

Book-form Diptych Dial by Paul Reinman

It is worth noting on this dial the use of the thrush symbol in three places. This is the trade mark of Hans Troschel whose name translates as 'thrush' in English. Also at the top between **ÆTAS** and **LVNÆ** is the Nuremberg '𝑛' symbol that was applied to dials to denote a quality product. [Gouk 1988]

An alternative lunar volvelle is shown on the dial by **PAVLVS REINMAN**. Note his crown symbol and again the '𝑛' quality mark. Its lunar conversion scale is virtually identical to the Troschel dial.

However, two further scales are added:

EPACTA IVLIA ANNO 1598
and
EPACTA GREGO ANNO 1598.

These are scales for the Epacts starting in the year of 1598 (which is when this particular dial was made) for both Julian and Gregorian calendars. For further details of these calendars and how to use them, see Chapter 25.

Another dial in book form is shown by Paul Reinman. This dial is considerably larger and is decorated more interestingly. Its outside is 'bound' just like a book with triangular brass corners, and metal clasps to hold it shut. Even the 'spine' of the book has been replicated in the carving of the ivory. Its interior, faces B & C, have both Vertical and Horizontal Dials respectively. Its compass is somewhat larger than most and its scales are bold and clear. On face B is a standard Lunar Volvelle to enable the owner to convert lunar reading to regular hours. The areas around the dial and compass are nicely decorated with patterns made by punches.

The small dial by Karner, identified only by his 'hand' symbol, is made from thin plates of ivory, or more probably bone, attached to a boxwood base. This dial is obviously one of the cheaper models that were available. Several dials of almost identical appearance are known and each is signed simply with the punch marked 'hand' symbol. This symbol is believed to be the trademark of Albrecht Karner.

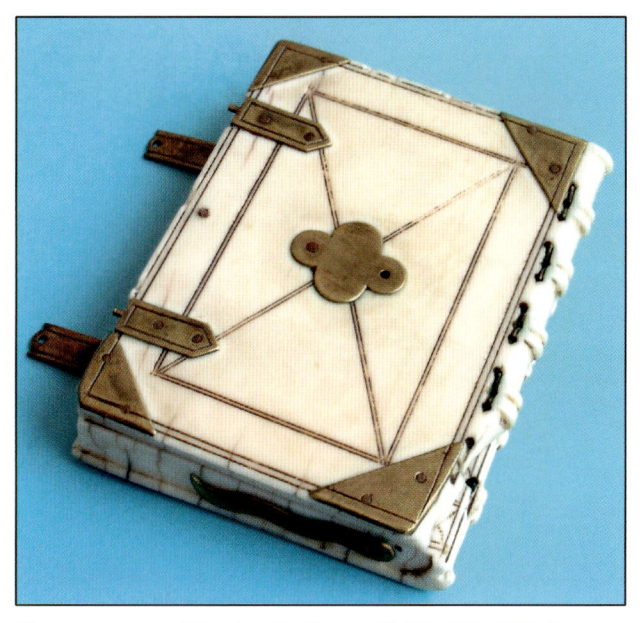

Outer cover of the book-form dial by Paul Reinman

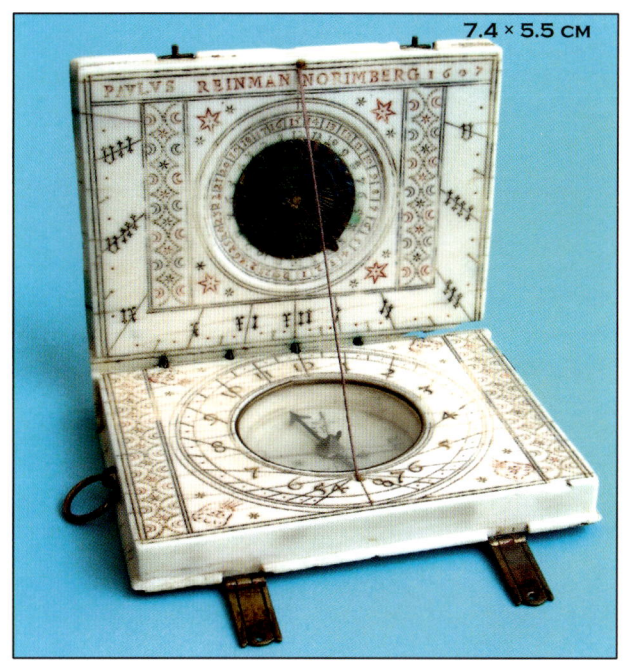

Chapter 6   Ivory Diptych Dials

3.2 × 4.7 cm

Small Diptych Dial by Karner with thin bone plates glued to a wooden base

A hand symbol punched onto underside of the bone and wood dial. It is believed to be the mark of Albrecht Karner

2.6 × 4.3 cm

3.1 × 4.5 cm   2.9 × 4.6 cm

Three ivory Diptych Dials, probably from Nuremberg, with attractive flower decoration

48

CHAPTER 6 IVORY DIPTYCH DIALS

The lids of the three ivory Diptych Dials from the previous page

Some very small dials, probably originating from Nuremberg, are beautifully decorated with flowers on their lids and on Face B. Unusually, their numerals are engraved rather than punched but with no sign of cracking. Their compass declination of 12.5°W suggests a date of ca. 1720 but stylistically these dials belong to the seventeenth century. We tend to assume that most dials were made for the gentleman, but in this case these dials could have been made for the ladies. They are small enough to fit into any pocket or bag and their flowers, filled attractively with red and green wax were surely placed there for a lady.

One dial does not have the flower lid but is engraved with the image of an antelope. A total of 15 of these dials have been seen by the Author in various museums and collections but none carry any signature. An analysis of their hour lines gives an average latitude of 46.6° which suggests that they may have been made for Swiss or Austrian users.

OTHER DIPTYCH DIALS

Ivory Diptych Dials are occasionally found from other countries, usually France, Spain or Italy. (Those from France, Dieppe in particular, are the subjects of the next chapter.) Unfortunately many dials were seldom signed and their origins can only be attributed to a particular country by general styling or language. A dial, which is probably of Spanish origin, is illustrated. Its

Decoration on the lid of an ivory Diptych Dial, possibly of Spanish origin

CHAPTER 6 IVORY DIPTYCH DIALS

4.4 × 7.4 CM

Ivory Diptych Dial, possibly Spanish

Ivory Diptych Dial by R & J Beck, ca. 1880, made for use in the Southern Hemisphere
Photo: Stuart Talbot

decoration differs substantially from both French and German dials and its engraved lines are beautifully coloured with red and green in addition to the basic black calibrations.

Its lid is also well decorated in a more Southern European style. Face B has an additional dial giving Babylonian hours **12 - 10**, (**12** = sunrise). In face C is a Scaphe Dial operating from a pin gnomon with scales of Italian Hours from **9 - 24** (**24** = sunset).

More recent Diptych Dials are sometimes found, but one that is particularly unusual is by R & J Beck of London, ca. 1880. This is complete with its travelling case. A particularly interesting feature of this example is that the dial was made for use in the Southern Hemisphere. Southern dials are particularly uncommon and an Ivory Dial of this period also uncommon. Inside the lid are instructions for use and a table showing the Equation of Time.

FAKES AND FORGERIES

Many goods made from ivory and bone have been replicated in recent years. This is particularly evident from the masses of fake scrimshaw work that may now be found. These goods are often made from resins with mineral fillers, such as chalk, to make them white and dense. It is even possible to replicate cracks and discoloured areas and it is often quite difficult, even for an expert, to tell the difference. However there is one simple test which may be performed, preferably out of sight of its owner. A pin or needle may be heated in a match flame and then pushed into the ivory. If it is resin or plastic it will melt and sink in. If it is real ivory or bone it should withstand this test without damage. However in doing this there is a risk of discolouring or scorching the ivory so a hidden area should be carefully chosen.

The Japanese have recently developed a method of making ivory from the shells of hens' eggs. This is an attempt to slow the trade in illegal ivory. The results that they have achieved are virtually indistinguishable from real ivory except that the moulded blocks of material do not contain any grain markings that would be found in natural ivory.

REFERENCES

1. Fantoni.G: 'Moondials' *Bull. BSS.* 92.1, 11-15 (1992)
2. Sakoian. F. & Acker. L.S. *The Astrologers Handbook.* Harper & Row, New York, 1989.

CHAPTER 7   FRENCH IVORY DIALS

DIEPPE IVORY DIALS

Large quantities of sundials, mostly in ivory, were made in Dieppe in the late seventeenth century. These were mainly of the Diptych and Magnetic Azimuth types with two ivory leaves hinged together. In many ways they were similar to the dials of Nuremberg but Dieppe's own speciality was the Magnetic Azimuth Dial.

Ivory dials were also made in other parts of France, particularly in Paris, but as these were seldom signed some may have been wrongly attributed to Dieppe.

An ivory Diptych Dial, probably from Dieppe

A quite simple ivory dial is shown. It is unsigned, but another almost identical dial in the Science Museum, London, is signed by Charles Bloud, the best known of Dieppe's makers. This is simply a fixed latitude Horizontal Dial operating from a string gnomon. Note the addition of the simple plummet on the vertical face as an aid to levelling. This dial is quite unusual in that most of its markings are engraved on the ivory rather than being punched. The most difficult characters to engrave are those with small enclosed centres such as **A**, **a**, **B**, **b**, **d**, **e**, **4**, **8**, etc., as these small enclosed areas will tend to flake off. Its maker has overcome this problem by avoiding such letters and numerals and has engraved the main scale with Roman Numerals, keeping the engraving relatively shallow.

The compass sunk into Face C is particularly small and severely limits the accuracy of setting. The compass card is of printed paper and is aligned exactly with the body of the dial i.e., zero magnetic declination, suggesting a manufacturing date of close to 1660 when declination was around zero in France and England.

Another French Diptych Dial, again probably from Dieppe, is of a more usual design, with a string gnomon Horizontal Dial inside and a relatively large compass. Inside the compass bowl is a paper dial to show compass direction, again showing zero compass declination. In its centre is a table showing 24 towns and their latitudes in ascending order from 'Malaca, 2°' to 'Nordcap, 72°'.

The vertical face, B, has a simple Lunar Volvelle to enable the dial to be used at night.

On its lid, Face A, is an Equatorial Dial. This is used with a pin gnomon that is stored in a small pocket on the left side of the lower plate. Very few of these original pin gnomons have survived. The

Another ivory Diptych Dial, probably from Dieppe

CHAPTER 7 FRENCH IVORY DIALS

Compass with list of towns and latitudes

Dial set for use as an Equatorial Dial

Horizontal Dial around the compass bowl, similar to the last dial described. However, the Magnetic Azimuth Dial functions differently, and with North and South reversed compared to the Horizontal Dial. On the base of the dial, Face D, is a calendar volvelle, which must be set to the appropriate date against the hand pointer. This moves the silver chapter ring inside the compass bowl slightly North or South to the correct position for that date through a simple cam linkage. In the centre of the calendar ring is a

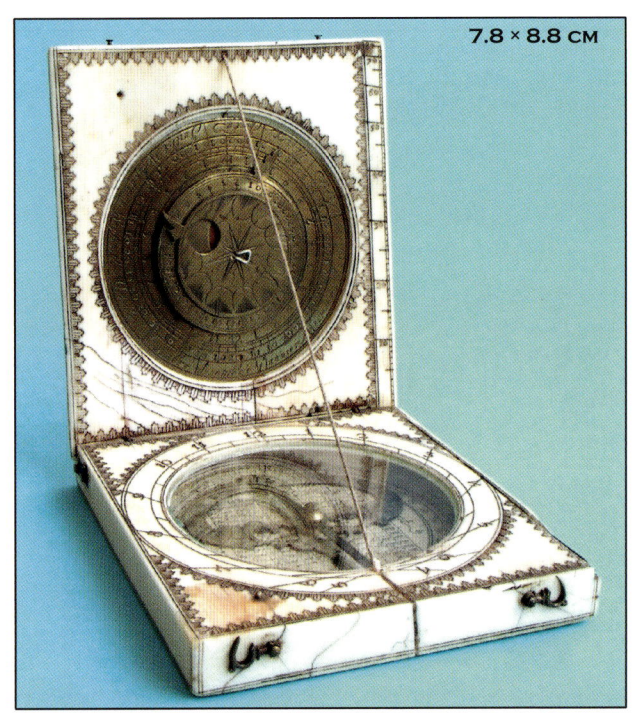

7.8 × 8.8 CM

Magnetic Azimuth Dial by Jacques Senecal, Dieppe, ca. 1660

dial is used by inserting the gnomon, then the lid is raised to the correct latitude, being supported by a small metal arm set against a latitude scale at the edge of Face B. This dial may be used at any latitude during the Summer months. In the Winter period, the gnomon may be inserted to protrude from Face B and the time may be read from the scale around the Lunar Volvelle. For lower latitudes, where the gnomon could clash with the lower tablet or the compass glass, the gnomon could possibly be inserted from Face A to protrude only slightly into Face B.

MAGNETIC AZIMUTH DIAL

The commonest dial from Dieppe, and that for which the town is most famous, is the Magnetic Azimuth Dial. The best known maker of this type of dial was Charles Bloud. The design was also made by a small number of other makers. A Magnetic Azimuth Dial by Jacques Senecal is illustrated. It has a conventional String Gnomon

Calendar volvelle on face D of the Senecal dial

52

Chapter 7   French Ivory Dials

Senecal dial compass bowl with silver chapter ring and gazetteer beneath

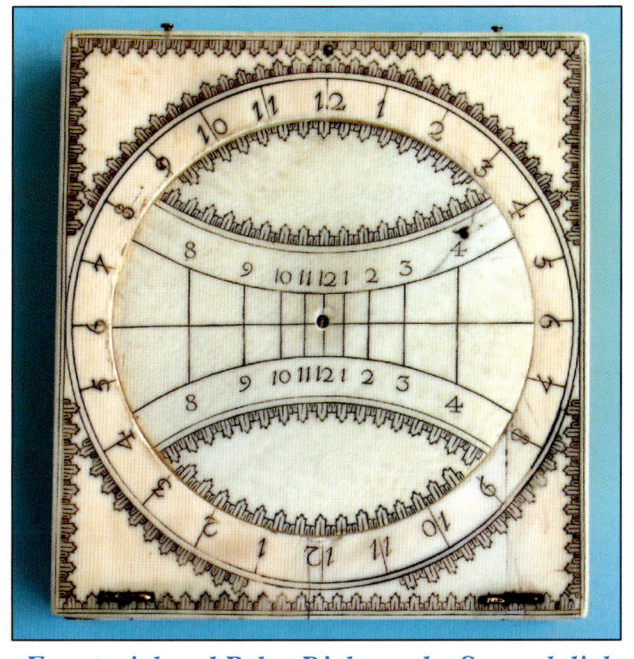

Lunar Calendar Scales on the Senecal dial

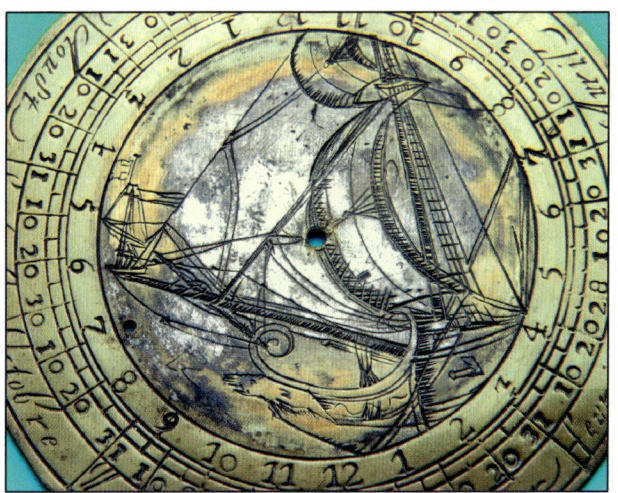

Equatorial and Polar Dials on the Senecal dial

Hidden engraving of ship on the Senecal dial

Perpetual Calendar square. (Details of this type of Calendar are given in Chapter 25.) The dial is then turned with the Sun behind its lid such that the lid's shadow falls exactly in line with the base and the time is read from the place on the chapter ring where the compass needle crosses it. Naturally, this dial can only be used in places of zero magnetic declination, as was the case in much of Western Europe around 1660. These dials are therefore dateable to quite a short period around 1660. It is also a dial for a fixed latitude. To overcome this problem and to make it universal two further dials, a Polar Dial and an Equatorial Dial, are placed on its lid, Face A.

These dials are used with a pin gnomon, normally stored in a small pocket in the base. The lid is held at the correct angle by a small support lever set against a latitude scale on Face B. The addition of these two dials makes it a truly universal sundial. The Equatorial Dial may be used at any northern latitude in the Summer months as in the previous example and the Polar Dial throughout the year.

Face B, has a Lunar Volvelle in its centre. It has a round cut-out representing the appearance of the Moon. It would normally be used in reverse to compare the Moon's form with its likeness on the volvelle and show the actual day of its cycle. Around the edge of this dial is an annual calendar showing the number of days in each month.

This dial was taken apart for restoration of its cracked ivory and beneath the lunar volvelle was found an image of a sailing ship. Metal was expensive so makers would often test their

53

CHAPTER 7   FRENCH IVORY DIALS

Unusual form of Magnetic Azimuth Dial by Charles Bloud

engraving skills on areas that would not be seen. See also the Quadrant by Walter Hayes, Page 87. Another feature sometimes found on these dials is the Gazetteer. This is printed on the paper in the compass bowl. It is partly obscured by the hour scale but as this can be moved everything can be read. The table in this dial lists 18 French towns and their latitudes. In addition, it gives a further 9 columns of information concerning market days, churches and other attributes for each town.

The Magnetic Azimuth Dial does not always have a string gnomon and Chapter Ring. It is unnecessary, only repeating the information produced by the main dial.

French Magnetic Azimuth Dials normally have the Chapter Ring (in silver) that moves inside the compass bowl but an alternative method is illustrated on a dial by Charles Bloud of Dieppe. This is similar in form to the English Magnetic Azimuth Dial by Walter Hayes shown on page 89 which has the curved hour lines read from where they are crossed by the compass needle. A most interesting feature is that the dial has a dotted line across the compass card aligned with the dial but the Magnetic Azimuth lines are skewed about 3° towards the East. This gives it a date of around 1652, making it possibly one of Bloud's earliest dials and therefore pre-dating his better known Magnetic Azimuth Dials. The lid has the usual Equatorial Dial and is held at the correct angle by the support arm stored in the slot on the right. Another unusual feature of this dial is inside the lid where a conversion chart gives times in hours and minutes to add to the time for each day of the Moon's cycle, at the rate of approximately 48.8 minutes per day. This makes the dial useable by the Moon's light during much of its 29½ day cycle.

The mottled effect on the ivory is probably produced by acid, the white spots being produced by some form of 'resist', possibly wax, applied before etching. This is a rare feature, shown on this dial and the next one by Nicholas Crucefix. There are

The Magnetic Azimuth scale

54

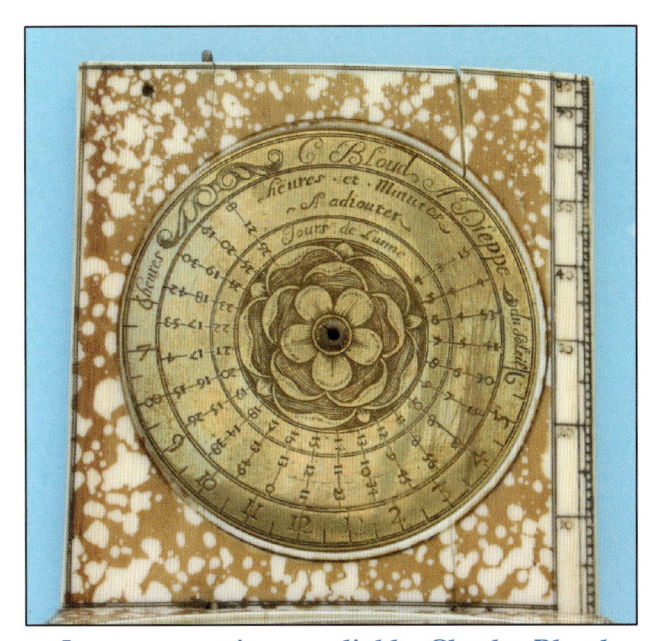

Chapter 7   French Ivory Dials

Lunar corrections on dial by Charles Bloud

from a pin gnomon normally stored in a small pocket in the base. In its compass bowl is a list of towns and their latitudes to enable the Equatorial Dial to be set at the correct angle from the latitude scale on Face B. In the Winter months the gnomon can be reversed and a reading taken from the chapter ring on Face B.

On Face D is a Calendar Volvelle which is rotated against the engraved hand pointer. Once the correct date is set this adjusts the hour scale as previously described. In the centre of the volvelle is a Perpetual Calendar square surrounded by the three further dials like this known in the Museum of the History of Science in Oxford.

The dial by Nicolas Crucefix is a particularly attractive dial. It is the only dial by this maker known to the author but he is recorded as a Dieppe ivory workman. It too has the unusual mottled appearance shown on the last dial. The darker areas are red-brown and are slightly sunk into the surface of the ivory.

This dial has the armorial of its first owner on its lid, surmounted by an image of what is probably 'The Green Man'. Around this is an Equatorial Dial, similar to those already described operating

Crucefix dial set for equatorial use

4.8 × 5.9 CM

Magnetic Azimuth Dial by Nicolas Crucefix, Dieppe, ca. 1680

Armorial in the centre of the Equatorial Dial

55

CHAPTER 7   FRENCH IVORY DIALS

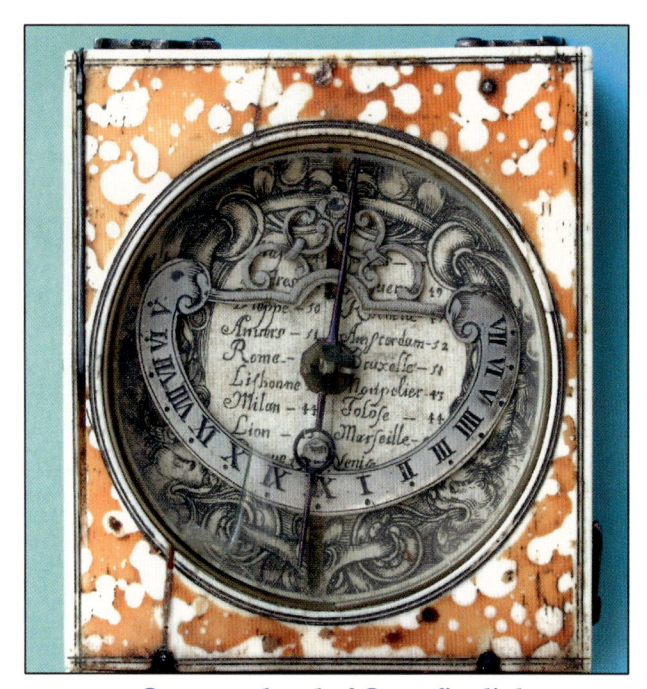

Compass bowl of Crucefix dial

Calendar scale for setting hour scale

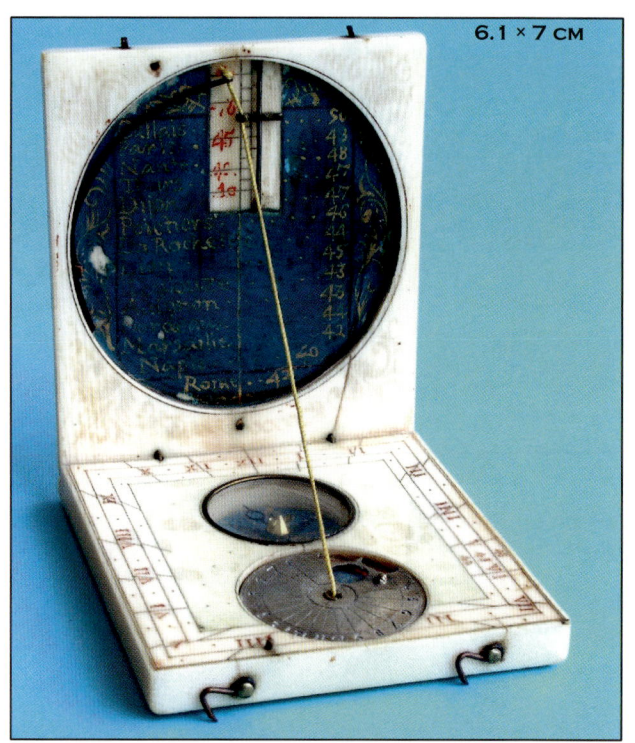

French Diptych Dial, ca. 1620
6.1 × 7 cm

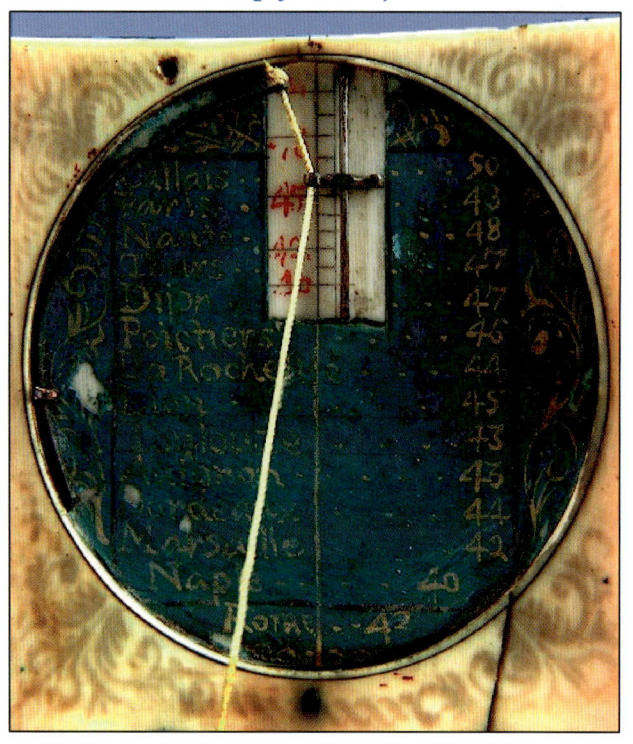

Enhanced picture to show details of former painting on the French Diptych Dial

maker's signature, '**Nicolas Crucefix ADieppe Fecit**'. For full details of this type of calendar refer to Chapter 25.

OTHER FRENCH DIALS
Ivory Diptych dials are occasionally found from other parts of France but they are rarely signed and are therefore frequently thought to have been made in Paris although there is some evidence of other dial workshops in Normandy. An ivory Diptych Dial, typically French, is illustrated. It differs considerably from the dials of Dieppe, its main feature being the painted surface. Note also its delicately painted compass bowl. At one time the whole of its interior would probably have been covered with paint and just its outside left in bare ivory. Paints adhere quite poorly to ivory and as a consequence the flat surfaces have lost their decoration. However, by enhancing the picture of the vertical face, some slight stains can still be seen, evidence of its former rich decorations. This dial also has a direct scale for lunar readings set

56

Method of adjusting the string gnomon for different latitudes

The 'RF' dial lid with a gilt Nocturnal arm

Lunar volvelle on face B of the 'RF' dial

around the root of its gnomon. This is a silver dial identically delineated to the Horizontal Dial but rotatable around its central axis against a lunar scale from 1 to 29½ days.

Its list of towns and their latitudes is painted inside the lid in gold on a dark blue background giving the dial a very attractive appearance.

An interesting feature of this dial is the way in which the string gnomon can be changed to suit different latitudes. A scale running from 40° to 50° is placed alongside a metal rod which has a slider to move along it. This slider supports the top end of the string gnomon. The effective string length needs to be altered as latitude is changed so its top end is attached to a single leaf spring that fits snugly into the circumference of the panel cut-out.

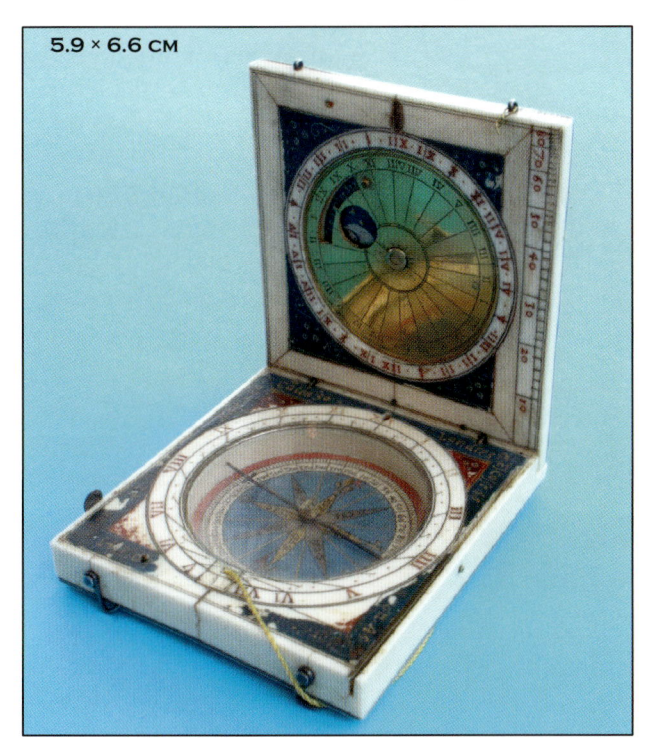

Another dial, clearly by this same maker or workshop, is illustrated. This dial is more complex but shares many of the same features. On its lid is a Nocturnal (part of the arm missing)

Another dial by the same maker, this time stamped with initials 'RF'

57

'RF' and maker's mark on the dial

5.6 × 7.9 cm

An oval ivory Diptych Dial, believed to be by the same unknown maker

with a calendar and inside the lid, Face B, is a fine gilt Lunar Volvelle showing the days and phases of the Moon. Its underside is blank except for a simple panelled border, some later scratch engraving, initials **'RF'**, thought to be the initials of its maker and a mark like a man, or possibly dividers, surmounted by a crown.

Also illustrated is an oval dial, again clearly from the same workshop.

Dials of a similar style are to be found in various collections, notably those found in the National Maritime Museum, in Greenwich, one at Oxford and some in the Collection at Harvard University. All of these dials appear to come from the same unidentified workshop. The dials at Harvard and at Oxford have the initials **'RF'** with the man or dividers mark below a crown on their undersides.

A dial showing similar characteristics to these is to be found in the Musée de la Renaissance at Château d'Ecouen, north of Paris. It is signed by Pierre du Jardin, Paris, 1627. However, this dial is much larger and certainly more complex than those discussed above, but there is a possibility that these could be by du Jardin or from his workshop.

[Chapiro, Meslin-Perrier, Turner, 1989]

CHAPTER 8 — FRENCH DIALS

When most people think of French dials they generally think of the attractive 'Butterfield Dial' that appeared some time before 1700. It is interesting to trace the probable development of this type of dial, as its roots go back somewhat further.

Portable dials were produced in France well before 1700 but few early ones have survived apart from some made in ivory. These probably came from Paris, and others from Dieppe around 1660. Of those that have survived, very few were signed until around 1650 when some very attractive specimens began to appear, often made by provincial makers. The majority were quite small dials and frequently in silver with finely gilt gnomons. They were octagonal or oval and were made for a fixed latitude - normally that of Paris. Their makers were generally watchmakers, already well-known for their fine watches. Their background can be identified from their highly intricate gnomons that are similar to the finely pierced and engraved balance cocks commonly used in their watches.

French Butterfield Dials are the subject of Chapter 9, but many similarities to them will be seen on the dials included here.

BEFORE 1700

The two dials illustrated by Lemaindre of Blois and Nourry of Lyon are good examples of the fine workmanship being turned out by provincial French watchmakers. Their gnomons are particularly attractive and are miniature works of art in their own rights. The dials themselves were made of silver and well engraved with simple hour lines and Roman numerals. The Nourry dial still retains its original silver box and it may be used in the box without removing it.

Nicolas Lemaindre worked in Blois and Paris making fine watches. He died in 1652. (However, this dial could possibly have been the work of his nephew.[1])

Makers of the name Nourry were working in Lyon and Gisors in the seventeenth century. The maker of this dial from Lyon was probably Jean, son of Pierre who had died in 1672.[1]

Dial by Nicolas Lemaindre, Blois

Dial by 'Nourry a Lion', dated 1674

Finely pierced Gnomon on the dial by Nicolas Lemaindre, Blois

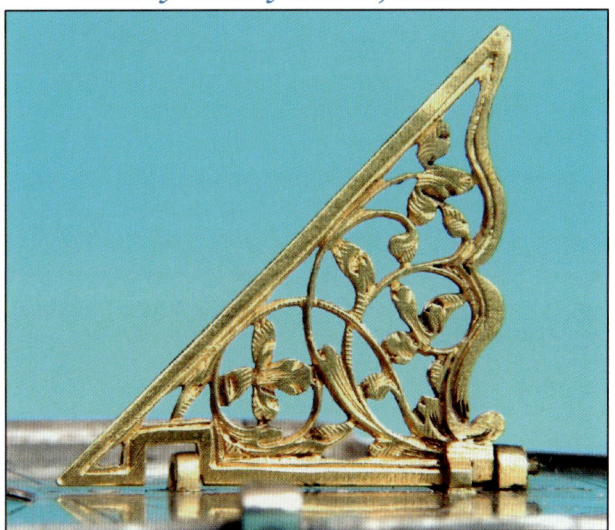

Finely pierced Gnomon on the dial by 'Nourry a Lion', dated 1674

CHAPTER 8   FRENCH DIALS

2.6 × 3.4 CM

Unsigned late seventeenth century silver dial, now lacking its gnomon, fitted into an oval case

Reverse of the unsigned dial

4.1 × 5.5 CM

Silver dial by Pierre Ceuin, (Sevin), Paris, late seventeenth century

Underside of the oval dial by Pierre Sevin

Gnomon of the dial by Pierre Sevin

An unsigned dial, now sadly lacking its gnomon comes from the same period. It too is fitted into its own oval silver box. This time, it is permanently fixed to its box by a hinge. Some of its engraving is a little naive and on its underside there are division marks showing where its maker has laid out the hour lines and then perhaps changed his mind, continuing on the reverse, now its top plate. Note the fine engraving on the underside of the compass bowl and the delicate gilt brass springs designed to keep its gnomon erect.

An oval dial by Pierre Ceuin (more commonly spelt Sevin) of Paris dates from a little later, perhaps 1680. He was one of a group of fine instrument makers working in Paris at this time. [Daumas 1972] He made instruments for the observatory in collaboration with Chapotot, *ingénieur du Roi*. [Marcelin 2004] This dial is particularly well made with an attractive signature underneath and a fine solid silver gnomon decorated with leaves and scrolls.

60

Chapter 8   French Dials

5.1 × 7.7 cm

hinged like the gnomons on Butterfield Dials his are somewhat different. He does not use the bird's beak pointer but a small pointer on the straight sloping edge of the gnomon is set against a degree arc. These dials were all made of silver with finely gilt gnomons. The gnomon also supports a plummet for levelling purposes, partially missing in the example illustrated. An attractive feature was his extension of the hour scale at noon where the figure **XII**, usually obscured by the gnomon hinge, is kept well clear and is certainly prominent.

Universal Dial by Timothée Collet, dated 1663

Universal Dial by Timothée Collet. Note the extension of XII numeral

Universal Gnomon of the dial by Timothée Collet

On the underside of these dials are some wonderfully engraved springs for supporting the gnomon and a Lunar Volvelle to enable the dial to be used at night by converting lunar readings to solar time.

Michael Butterfield was a well known instrument maker, working in Paris around 1700. Although best known for his dials, he made a wide range of scientific instruments. The next two dials illustrated are similar to his regular 'Butterfield Dials' but they are not universal, having fixed gnomons. The first dial is quite large, being 98 mm long and has been fitted with two brackets, presumably to fix it to another instrument, perhaps a surveying instrument like a Plane Table. The dial is set for 48° 30', possibly Chartres or Strasbourg rather than Paris. The magnetic declination may be set inside the compass bowl by a small adjustable brass pointer. All features suggest that it was made to a higher precision than was usual for a French dial.

Underside of the dial by Timothée Collet showing beautifully engraved springs and lunar volvelle

Another maker of this period producing some exceptional dials was Timothée Collet. Little is known about him but he probably came from Rouen to work in Paris.[1] He is known for about four dials, all virtually identical in design, these being universal over a small range of latitudes. Although

Note its particularly florid signature. Its gnomon

61

Chapter 8 French Dials

8.8 × 9.8 cm

Fixed latitude Compass Dial by Michael Butterfield, ca. 1700

6.6 × 7.8 cm

Another fixed latitude Compass Dial in silver made by Butterfield for the latitude of Paris

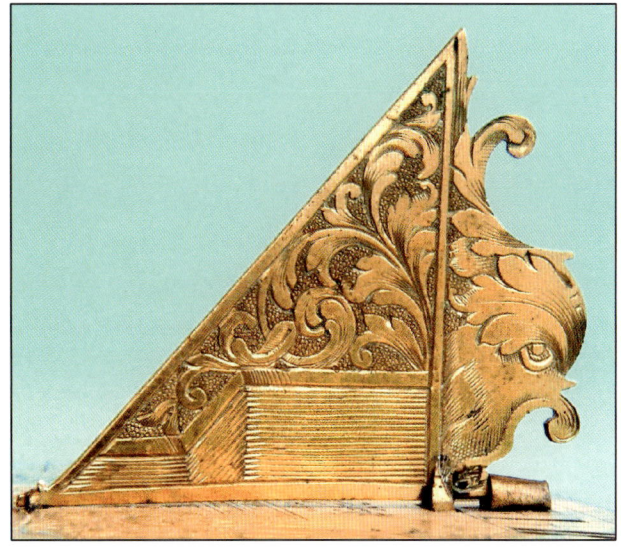

Different engraving to be seen on each side of the gnomon of the brass dial by Butterfield

Underside of the brass dial by Butterfield showing its fine engraving and its unusual fixing feet

too, is unusual, in that it is differently engraved on each side.

The second dial, this time in silver, is made for the latitude of Paris 48° 51'. Although undated, its age can be determined from one of its three poinçon marks which is for Paris 1704 - 1712. It also has similar decoration to its gnomon. Note that its numeral XII is missing at noon.

AFTER 1700

French dials continued to be made in quantity for most of the 1700s. The 'Butterfield' type was the most popular and most makers copied this. For further details of these dials refer to Chapter 9.

The early eighteenth century was a time when the French were active in exploration and founding colonies. Dials were needed for their military

CHAPTER 8   FRENCH DIALS

Octagonal silver Compass Dial by Canivet made for Martinique (Pour · 14 · degres · 45 · Minutes)

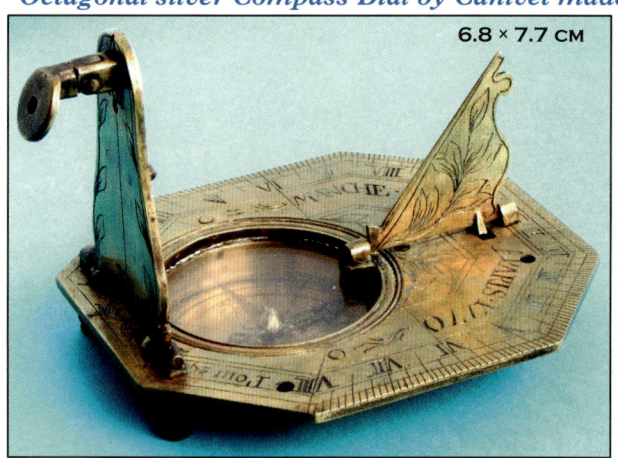

Octagonal brass dial by Manche, Paris, dated 1770

Noon Mark or Meridian on octagonal brass dial by Manche, Paris

personnel in these places as well as in France. Canivet, who succeeded Langlois as chief engineer at the Académie des Sciences in Paris was a particularly fine instrument maker. One of his dials, made in 1764, is signed '**Canivet à La Sphére à Paris**' and is made for the low latitude of 14° 45'. Note its particularly low angle gnomon to suit this latitude, that of Martinique, a French colony since 1635. In 1762 the British were annexing other French colonies in this area and this dial would probably have belonged to a French soldier, sent out to defend Martinique.

A rather unusual brass dial signed '**MANCHE FECIT APARIS 1770**' has a Noon Mark or Meridian attached to its Southern end. He is a little known maker but is believed to have worked at *'au soleil d'or'* in Paris. When the Meridian is erected it can shield the normal gnomon from the Sun, especially around noon. The Meridian has just the **XII** line marked and a round pinhole gnomon. On its reverse, a simple plummet for setting the dial level is now missing. With the Meridian folded down over the compass, the dial acts as a standard fixed latitude dial for 49°; that of Paris. This dial also has an adjustable pointer in the compass bowl for setting the current magnetic declination against a scale of ±30°.

REFERENCES
1 Baillie, G.H: *Watchmakers and Clockmakers of the World*, N.A.G Press, London, 1929.

CHAPTER 9   FRENCH BUTTERFIELD DIALS

The Butterfield Dial is perhaps the best known of all portable dials. It has been named, rightly or wrongly, after Michael Butterfield of Paris, whose workshop turned out large quantities of these attractive dials in the years around 1700. This dial design was very popular and many contemporary workers copied it, trying to cash-in on his success. It is believed that several of these workers have even signed their dials 'Butterfield *A* Paris' because his dial was at the time the 'brand leader'. It is even debatable whether this style of dial was originated by Butterfield himself and it is more than possible that the idea of the design came from London some years before. An almost Butterfield type dial by Roch Blondeau in the Whipple Museum, Cambridge is dated as early as 1673 [Bryden 1988 - No 123] and a similar dial by Timothée Collet dated 1663 was described in Chapter 8. Butterfield himself was English but moved to Paris when still young. He may have taken the idea with him, but it is more likely that he would have returned home at least once and may have seen a similar dial being made by an English maker.

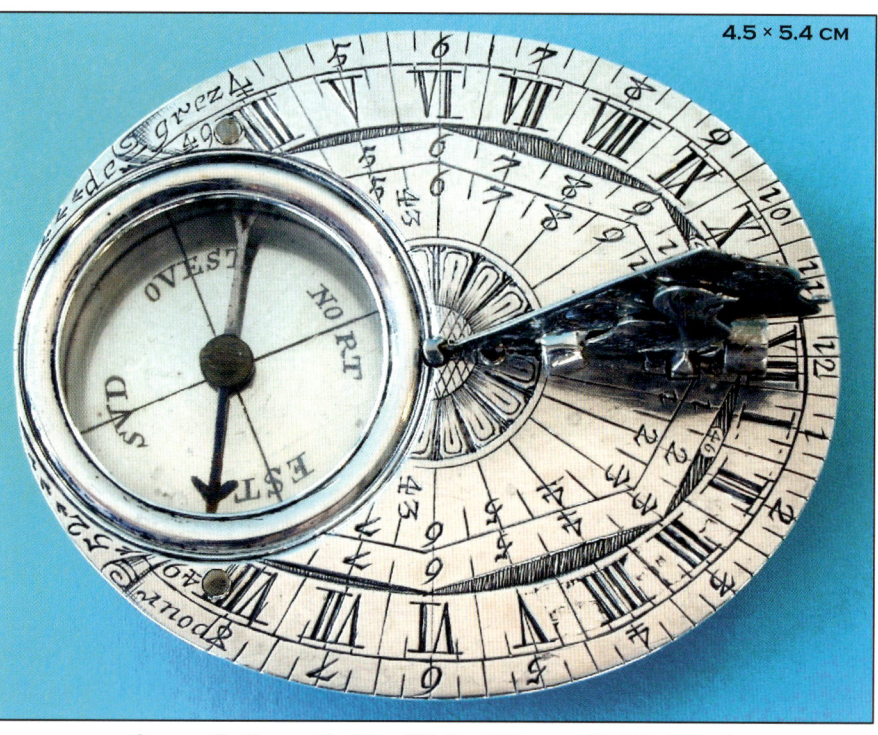

An oval silver dial by Michael Butterfield of Paris

4.5 × 5.4 cm

Before discussing the various details and variations of this attractive design it is important to establish what a typical Butterfield Dial looks like. The majority had an eight sided dial plate, usually with three or four concentric chapter rings

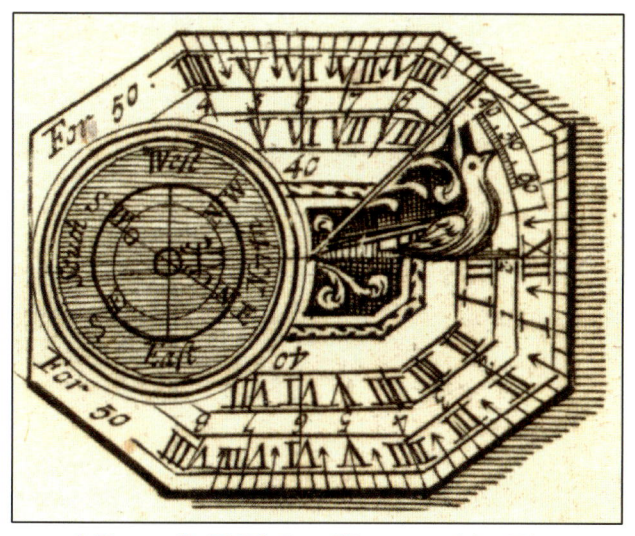

A Butterfield Dial as illustrated by Bion
[Bion 1758 - Plate 24]

Underside of oval dial. The lines over the latitude figures appear to signify an extra ½°

CHAPTER 9   FRENCH BUTTERFIELD DIALS

4.9 × 6 CM

A gilt oval Butterfield Dial by Francois De Laistre

These earlier dials usually had fixed gnomons but often had eight sided or elliptical dial plates and always had a built-in compass. They were usually of silver but generally smaller than the average Butterfield Dial. They were usually made by watch and clockmakers, frequently from outside Paris.

Michael Butterfield was active in Paris between 1674 and 1722 and he was well known as a maker of high quality scientific instruments. English maker Richard Whitehead made a small number of Butterfield Dials. (See Chapter 10) He flourished in London between 1663 and 1693 and it is quite possible that he originated the design, perhaps using the earlier fixed latitude French dials as his model. However he did not manufacture the large quantities such as are found from Butterfield and Bion. Nicholas Bion, another well-known French instrument maker, was working in Paris between 1652 and 1723 and he could equally well have been the originator of the design.

(each one for a different latitude) and a built-in compass. A small bird, using its beak to point to the angle on the latitude scale nearly always supported the gnomon. French Butterfield Dials were more usually made from silver and English ones of brass. Most dials carried a list of towns and their latitudes engraved on their underside. In practice there are many variations on the basic design and two identical dials have yet to be found by the author. Some of the variations produced have given some exceptionally interesting dials. A selection of these are described and illustrated in the following pages.

HISTORY OF THE BUTTERFIELD DESIGN

As has already been mentioned it is possible that the basic idea originated in England but some of its features are evident in the fine dials produced in France some years earlier. (See Chapter 8.)

3.9 × 4.8 CM

A rectangular Butterfield Dial by Bion but with the more standard eight sided layout

List of towns on the underside of the Bion dial

66

Chapter 9 French Butterfield Dials

Brass Butterfield Dial by Le Febvre

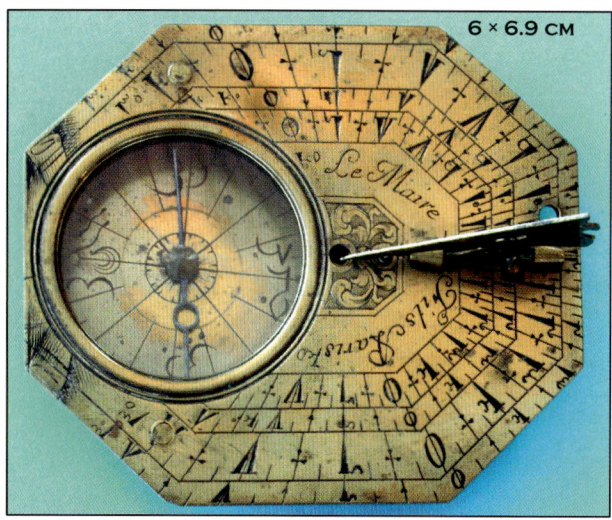

Arabic engraving on a dial by Le Maire

As the eighteenth century progressed, more and more workers turned their hand to this model which continued to be popular well into the nineteenth century.

The author has to date noted over 50 different signatures on Butterfield Dials and new ones are regularly being discovered. Of these, the majority came from Paris or London (see also Chapter 10). Most makers were well known for their instruments and the demand for portable or pocket sundials in pre-revolutionary France seems to have been quite high. Some makers signatures on these dials are merely names with no further details being traced. It is quite possible that some of these are merely retailers who insisted on having their own names on the instruments that they sold.

Of the French makers several were outstanding, producing superior quality dials and often other scientific instruments. The better known ones are Jacques Baradelle, Nicolas Bion, Roch Blondeau, Michael Butterfield, Jacques Canivet, Jean Chapotot, Thomas Haye, Claude Langlois and Jacques Le Maire. These all produced the highest quality dials and several held royal appointments as instrument makers.

HOW TO USE THE BUTTERFIELD DIAL

Its design is relatively simple and could be relied upon to give a reasonable indication of the time of day over a fairly wide geographical area. Firstly the latitude of the location must be determined. A list of towns was usually engraved on the back of the dial with their latitudes. The gnomon, normally folded flat for housing in its case, is erected and adjusted such that the bird's beak points at the correct latitude figure on the scale engraved on one side. The dial is then placed on a horizontal surface or is held carefully with a steady hand. It is then rotated until the compass needle points to Magnetic North. At the time of manufacture this was just a few degrees west of North and was usually marked as a line in the compass bowl. The dial plate is then inspected as it usually has three, four or even five separate chapter rings, each for a different latitude. The nearest one to the user's latitude is selected for the time reading (or by taking an average between the two nearest ones) and a reasonable time can be arrived at from the shadow of the gnomon on the dial plate. Most dials were made from silver but, because of its highly reflective surface, it is often difficult to see the shadow falling upon it. The reflection of the gnomon would be prominent and no doubt this was often confused with the shadow. If the silver dials were allowed to tarnish then they could be read much more easily but would any self respecting gentleman carry such a 'dirty' dial? The inset compass is also very small and as such is subject to quite large errors. The writer Dom Francois Bedos de Celles in his work 'Gnomonique Practique' of 1760 is most critical of Butterfield's dials *'with their considerable faults that do not put them in the class of good portable sundials. His compass is too small to be able to read with any precision. Even when one measures the divisions of the circle on the floor of the compass they are not sensible enough because of its too small diameter. The three or four dials which are marked on the horizontal plane for different latitudes renders the surface confused. It is difficult to distinguish the hour. We are therefore to be concerned that this is a bad dial and it should not be counted to see the hour but imperfectly'*. We therefore have this damning criticism from this Benedictine doctor in his great treatise on gnomonics. However, in fairness, Butterfield's dials had been around for some 50

CHAPTER 9 FRENCH BUTTERFIELD DIALS

6.3 × 6.8 CM

Gilt dial by Butterfield with a large compass

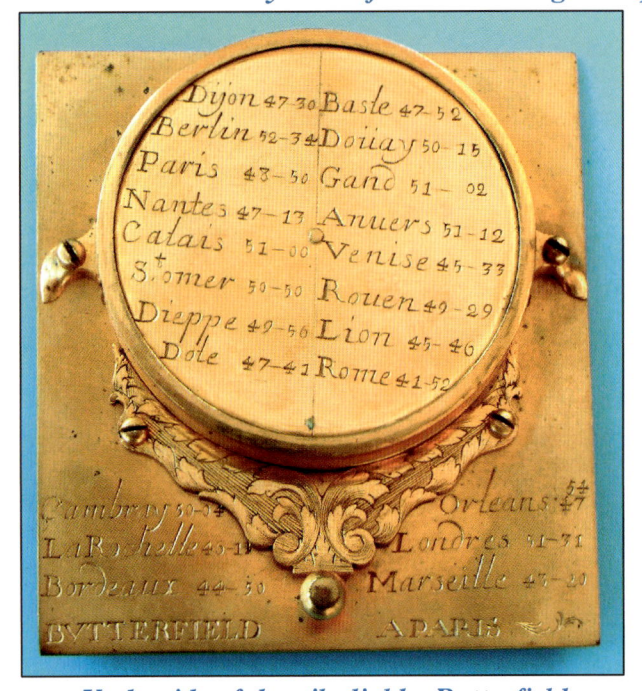

Underside of the gilt dial by Butterfield

instruments. They were intended for rich collectors rather than for being for precision measurement. Dom Bedos' main complaint is of the compass that is too small. The later Butterfield Dials of the nineteenth century were usually made with a large compass with the consequent improvement in accuracy. However, only a few of these later examples are known of Butterfield's work where he had obviously tried to overcome the small compass problem by making this dial with an exceptionally large compass bowl. Compromises had to be made with this improved design and the compass is partly obscured by the dial plate and the gnomon. This means that the North end of the needle can no longer be seen and Butterfield has used the other end to point to the South instead. He has achieved his aim and has not sacrificed his style, which is as good as ever. The dial illustrated is

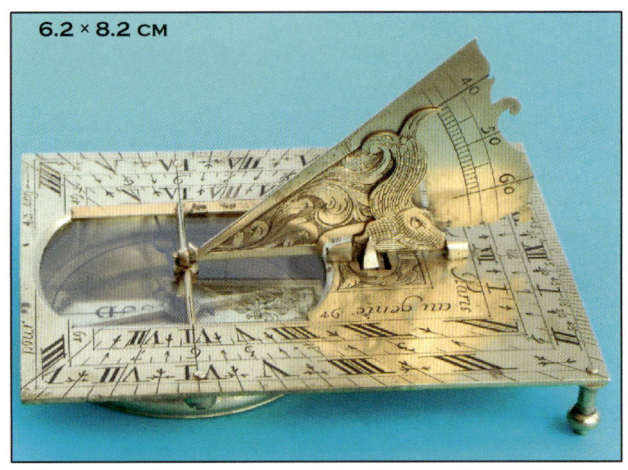

6.2 × 8.2 CM

Rectangular version of the Butterfield Dial by Le Maire, also with a large compass

An unusually detailed Compass fitted to a dial by Butterfield

to 100 years by the time this book was published and by then great improvements had been made to portable dials generally. Despite these comments, the Butterfield Dial was still being made by later workers and it continued to be made for many more years. The Butterfield Dial remained popular due to its fine appearance and we should not look too seriously on it as a precision instrument. It was really a decorative object to be carried in the pocket, perhaps more as a status symbol. The vast majority of Parisian instrument makers produced a wide range of highly decorative instruments to grace the drawing room, fashionable salon or cabinet of

Chubby bird gnomon support on a dial by Butterfield

Lion gnomon supporter on a dial by Bizot

Slim bird gnomon supporter on a Arabic dial by Le Maire

Pheasant gnomon supporter on a dial signed Sautout Choizy

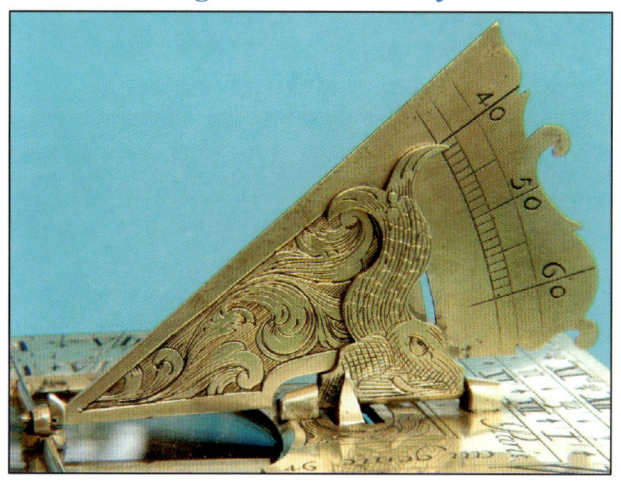

Swan gnomon supporter on a dial by Le Febvre

Grumpy looking dolphin supporter on a dial by Le Maire, using his tail as the pointer

even gilt and so was obviously made for an important customer. Another dial with a large compass is by Le Maire and features a dolphin supporter for its gnomon.

DIAL DETAILS

One of the most charming features of these dials is the bird which normally supports the gnomon and whose beak is used to indicate the latitude. The bird tends to be fairly standard, but several

CHAPTER 9   FRENCH BUTTERFIELD DIALS

'Premier Cadran' details engraved on the underside of a compass bowl

6.4 × 7.4 CM

Brass Butterfield Dial by Cadot showing the extra clarity achieved by using alternate oval and eight sided scales

small variations do occur, some being particularly chubby, some slim and in one case the bird is a swan. The eye of the bird is used as the pin, which rivets both halves together and slides in the cutout arc in the gnomon. On a silver dial this eye pin is often gold or gilt brass giving a pleasing contrast. Occasionally some other gnomon support and accompanying pointer is used such as a lion, a hand or a dolphin (using his tail as the pointer).

The dial plates themselves vary considerably in shape and size. The eight sided shape is commonest, followed closely by the elliptical. Other dials with rectangular and round outlines are occasionally found. The scales on the plates generally consist of three or four chapter rings. These are usually numbered alternately with Roman and Arabic numerals in order to make them more prominent. The outer scale is usually the prime scale and hence has the greatest accuracy. This is often referred to in the list of latitudes as the **'Premier Cadran'**. On most French dials this prime scale is marked for 49°, i.e., the latitude of Paris. The other scales often include 40°, 45° and 52° (London).

One major problem with the Butterfield Dial is that it is not fully universal. Its latitudes can only be adjusted through a range of about 20° to 30° and then only for the Northern Hemisphere. However at least one Southern Hemisphere Butterfield Dial is known.

On most Butterfield Dials the scale follows the outer profile of the dial plate; oval or eight sided. An interesting variation is found which uses two shapes, eight sided and elliptical, which are used alternately. This produces a pleasing effect and helps to remove some of the clutter complained of by Dom Bedos. Although this design was used by many of the makers, some such as Cadot, used it almost exclusively.

THE UNDERSIDE

In virtually every case the underside of the dial is engraved with a list of towns and their latitudes. It is interesting to look at the list and see where the dial was expected to be used. Usually they were made for the international traveller but generally towns in one's own country would feature most prominently.

Two dials are shown where the owner's location can almost certainly be determined. The dial by Bizot shows the small town of *Chastillon sur Seine*. Enquiries there have so far failed to produce a likely owner as there were two or three

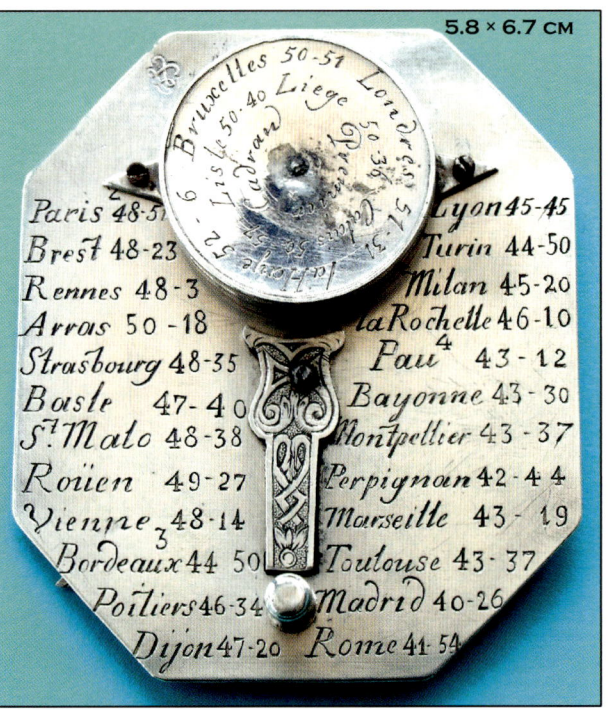

5.8 × 6.7 CM

Underside of dial signed Butterfield, 'Premier Cadran' on the compass, and numbers '2', '3' and '4' to indicate which chapter ring to use

70

Chapter 9 French Butterfield Dials

Dial by Bizot with a lion supporter for its gnomon

Underside of the dial by Bizot showing the small town of Cha(s)tillon sur Seine

The dial by Bizot has several less usual features. Its gnomon supporter is a lion, its chapter rings are laid out differently, its gnomon spring is different and its compass bowl is held onto the dial plate with three, rather than two, screws.

The back of the compass bowl was often used as extra space for the gazetteer. It was frequently used for the list of towns utilising the 'Premier Cadran'. In other cases it was engraved with an attractive floral or foliate pattern. On some dials the towns were grouped into sets of a similar latitude and were identified by the number of the chapter ring, as on the dial by Butterfield shown on page 70.

An interesting silver dial by Pierre Le Maire, made ca. 1740, has been produced for use at Northern European latitudes. Its chapter rings are for 50°, 55°, 60° and 65° and its gnomon will adjust over the range of 45° to 75°. The list of rich families there at that period. The other dial by Haye has the words *Grande Chartreuse 45* placed right across both tables of latitudes. On the underside of its compass bowl is an engraving showing a monk kneeling in prayer. This was almost certainly made for the Abbot of Grande Chartreuse, the monastery now best known for its liqueur. It is situated on a steep rock just north-east of Grenoble and was the main monastery of the Carthusians.

Underside of the dial by Haye showing the latitude of Grande Chartreuse

Chapter 9   French Butterfield Dials

4.5 × 5.9 CM

The dial by Haye is engraved with a castle and stream running nearby

Dial by Pierre Le Maire made for a wider than usual range of European latitudes

towns on its reverse have several that are unexpected. They include **Moscou 55° 30'** and, at the top next to the compass bowl **Torno 65° 47'**. Tornio is a town at the northern tip of the Baltic Sea very close to the Arctic Circle. However, perhaps the most interesting town

5.9 × 6.7 CM

Towns listed on the dial by Pierre Le Maire

listed is **Uranisbourg 55° 54'**. Uraniborg is the place that Tycho Brahe, famous Danish astronomer, set up his observatory on the island of Hven, in the narrow channel between Denmark and Sweden. However, by the time that this dial was produced, the observatory had been abandoned, so its inclusion was presumably just a gesture to the memory of it. Note on the dial the unusual spellings of **Oxfort**, **DunKerque**, **Edenbourg**, **StoKolm** and **Lipsic** (Leipzig). It is also interesting to see the address used by Le Maire. The dial plate is signed *P. le Maire A Paris A La Pierre d'Aiman*. He was famous for his range of instruments and called his workshop Pierre d'Aimant, the French name for the Lodestone.

CARRYING CASES

Many of the dials extant retain their original cases. These were usually made of fish-skin, coloured black or green, and were lined with red or green velvet. The quality of the individual cases is usually comparable to the quality of the dial contained within. Often the case can tell us much about the quality of the dial that it contains, so when studying a dial an examination of its case should be one's first priority.

THE PRINCIPLE MAKERS AND THEIR WORKPLACES

The most famous maker was, of course, Michael Butterfield. It is not certain when he went to Paris from England but it was probably before 1663. Little is known of his early life, but he went to school in Paris. He was appointed Engineer, or Instrument Maker, to Louis XIV and looked after his mathematical instruments. He made many

Chapter 9 French Butterfield Dials

Case of a silver dial signed 'Butterfield'

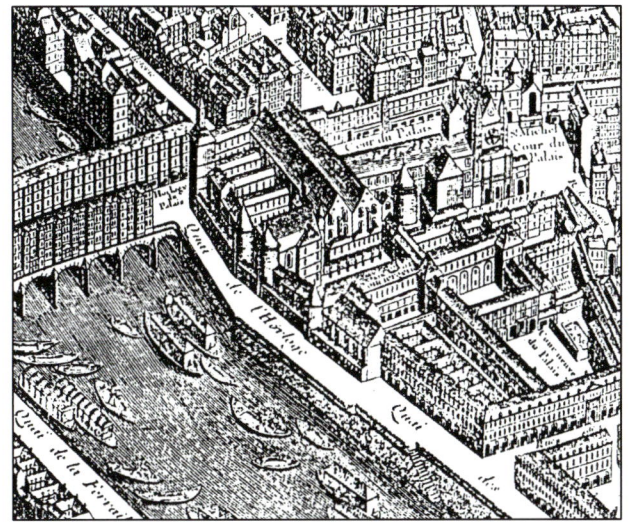

Case holding a Butterfield Dial and a Regiomontanus Dial

View of Paris showing the area around Quai de l'Horloge by Louis Bretez, ca. 1739

Butterfield and Regiomontanus Dials fitted in a common case

types of instruments including graphometers, sectors, compasses of proportion etc. In 1677 he invented a new type of level, and in 1681 he perfected his odometer. His death is recorded as 28th May, 1724.

The second most prolific maker was Nicolas Bion. He again was an accomplished instrument maker. In 1709 he published his famous book 'La Construction et l'Usage des instruments de Mathematique' which ran to five editions by 1752. Edmund Stone translated the book into English in 1723, with a revised edition in 1758. [Bion 1758] It is a rich reference book covering many types of instrument, describing each in detail and explaining how it was to be used. Facsimile editions have been printed in recent years allowing his work to be known more widely. His illustrations show various types of sundial that were in use at the time, including one of the 'Butterfield' type. Several of the illustrations from Stone's book have been reproduced in this book. Bion was also appointed Engineer to the King for mathematical instruments.

It is interesting that most of the instrument makers of Paris were clustered together in one small area. In this case it was around the Quai de l'Horloge on the Ile de la Cité. This was also the

An unusual dual Butterfield and Equatorial Dial, unsigned

Chapter 9 French Butterfield Dials

area of the clock and watch makers and it is thought that several of the instrument makers were also involved in the clock trade. There was not such a strict division of crafts as in Britain, where the various guilds of the City of London carefully regulated and censored the work of their members.

UNUSUAL DIALS

A few dials should be mentioned which clearly fall outside the usual patterns so far described. The first is a late round dial of about 1820. (Not illustrated). It has the hour scale running anti-clockwise and a shallow, but variable, angle of gnomon. This dial was obviously made for the Southern Hemisphere. It is unsigned, but is, almost certainly, of French manufacture - possibly from Lyon. Studying the range of latitudes on the gnomon has not given any clue to its intended region of use, but most probably it would be one of the French colonies. A similar dial has been seen that was made for the Northern Hemisphere, probably for somewhere in North Africa.

Dual Butterfield and Equatorial Dial

Illustrated, page 73, is a silver dial by Butterfield in a dual case. In the rear section is a Regiomontanus Dial by Blondeau. These two dials are both housed in one case and were obviously a special commission. Were they put together by Butterfield, Blondeau or a third party?

A most unusual version of the Butterfield Dial is one that is made as a dual dial, incorporating inside an Equatorial Dial similar to those made in Augsburg around 1720. This dial was probably made as a special commission and has its owners fine armorials engraved right across its underside. The interior is also finely engraved.

Engraving on the underside of the dual Butterfield and Equatorial Dial with armorial motto 'CANDOR ET ODOR'

CHAPTER 9   FRENCH BUTTERFIELD DIALS

5.7 × 7.3 CM

A silver dial by Michael Butterfield fitted with an unusually large plummet

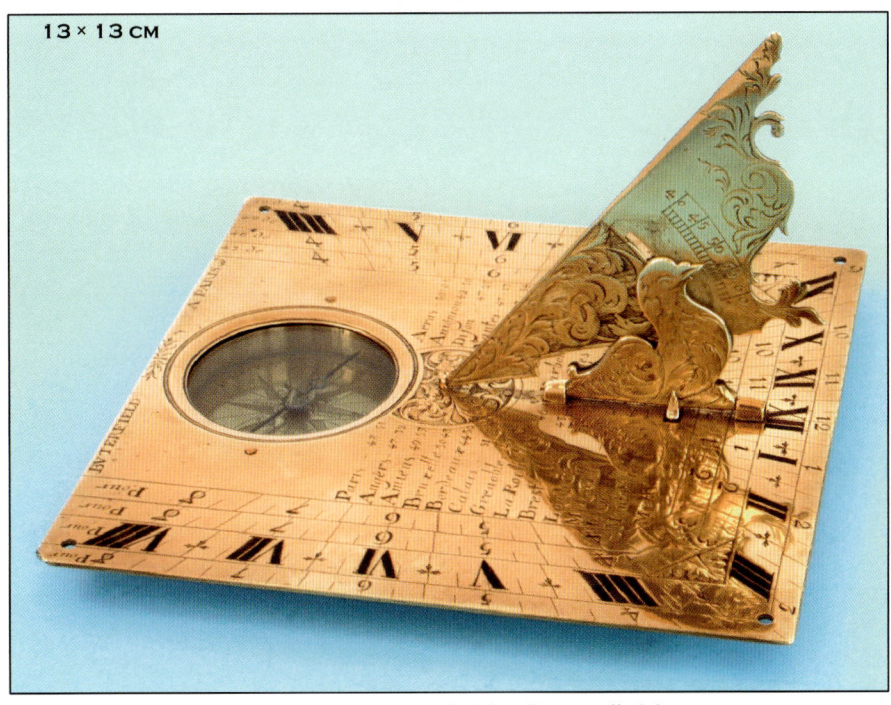

13 × 13 CM

A brass Table Dial by Butterfield

The silver Butterfield Dial above has been fitted with a large upstanding plummet for precise levelling. It looks a little out of proportion but is clearly original to the dial.

An occasional Table Dial in the Butterfield style may be found. The one illustrated is in brass and measures 13 cm × 13 cm. It has all the usual Butterfield features and is signed near to its compass, **BVTERFIELD A PARIS**, strangely with only one **T** in his name. Unlike most of his dials, this one is square rather than being eight sided or oval. It has four Chapter Rings for 43°, 46°, 49° and 52°. On the top plate is a list of 28 towns with their latitudes. Its underside is plain except for his delicately engraved gnomon support spring. The four threaded holes in its corners may have been for some levelling screws, but these may not have been original to this dial.

One interesting feature of this dial is that it has its Magnetic Declination faintly inscribed on the ring around its compass. This is for about 5° West. Taking the zero declination for Paris as being the year 1666 this mark will therefore correspond to a date 25 years later, or about 1690.

THE DECLINE OF THE BUTTERFIELD DIAL

The Butterfield type of dial remained quite popular throughout much of the eighteenth century and it is not difficult to understand why. It is still a most attractive object, which many collectors would like to own. It was made for the nobility who could afford to pay for such a fine and decorative device. However the French Revolution of 1789 soon removed the potential market for such items and for a time production must have stopped. No doubt there

75

CHAPTER 9   FRENCH BUTTERFIELD DIALS

The compass of the Table Dial has faint declination marks on rim of about 5° West

no longer over-decorative but much more utilitarian. Most dials of this period were round with a large compass bowl and were usually of brass, which was then silvered. Many kept the bird design for supporting the gnomon but this was a most thin and uninteresting fowl compared with a century earlier.

FAKES AND FORGERIES

The Butterfield Dial has always been popular and much in demand by collectors. For this reason it is the most copied dial to be found. Today several models are being made as reproductions, often being sold in museum shops or nautical 'antique' shops. These are easy to tell from the originals, mostly from the techniques used in their manufacture. They are still decorative and relatively cheap and as such are quite popular with collectors. The Butterfield Dial has been copied almost since it was first introduced. The copies were often made by the less competent craftsmen and to make them more saleable they were signed with a well-known name, usually that of Butterfield. These copies are more difficult to separate from the originals except to the trained eye. They are, however, interesting in their own right and are worthy of study.

One silver dial signed **Butterfield AParis** in a beautiful shagreen case is possibly not from his workshop, but from that of another contemporary maker. Close examination shows that the engraving is not of the quality to be expected from Butterfield and, if such were produced in his workshop, it would not have been allowed to be sold. There are also some interesting mistakes in the dial's calibration. The **VIII** and **IX** marks are displaced by two quarters on all four chapter rings. There is also some confusion around **III** and **IV** with the wrong number of quarter divisions in certain hours. This dial is, however, contemporary with Butterfield and unusually carries a Paris poinçon, or hallmark, of the period.

Engraving on compass bowl and gnomon support spring of the Table Dial

Bird supporting the Gnomon of the Table Dial

were many of these dials flooding the diminishing market. Many of them would have been taken by the revolutionaries and those of silver must frequently have been melted down. When production was revived in the early nineteenth century the style had changed somewhat. It was

Chapter 9   French Butterfield Dials

5.8 × 6.7 cm

Silver dial signed Butterfield but of slightly inferior quality, possibly a contemporary forgery

Mistakes in engraving are not particularly unusual, but often they are discovered and attempts made to correct them. On this dial the quantity of mistakes is most unusual and it is probably the work of an inferior craftsman trying to cash in on Butterfield's popularity and reputation. More modern fakes are not unknown but thankfully are quite rare. It really comes down to basic economics. Is it really worthwhile to try to make a copy to fool someone into parting with their cash? When one considers the amount of time required to make one and the skill needed to engrave it, complete with correct calibration and division, such that it will pass reasonable scrutiny, it is most unlikely that it would prove lucrative. It seems unlikely that this type of deliberate forgery would be worthwhile. However, some genuine 'Butterfield' dials are found with gnomons or compass bowls missing. A skilled craftsman can restore these items and some of these are most difficult to spot. Once the dial is restored it is obviously more collectable and the monetary gain in this case is worth the effort.

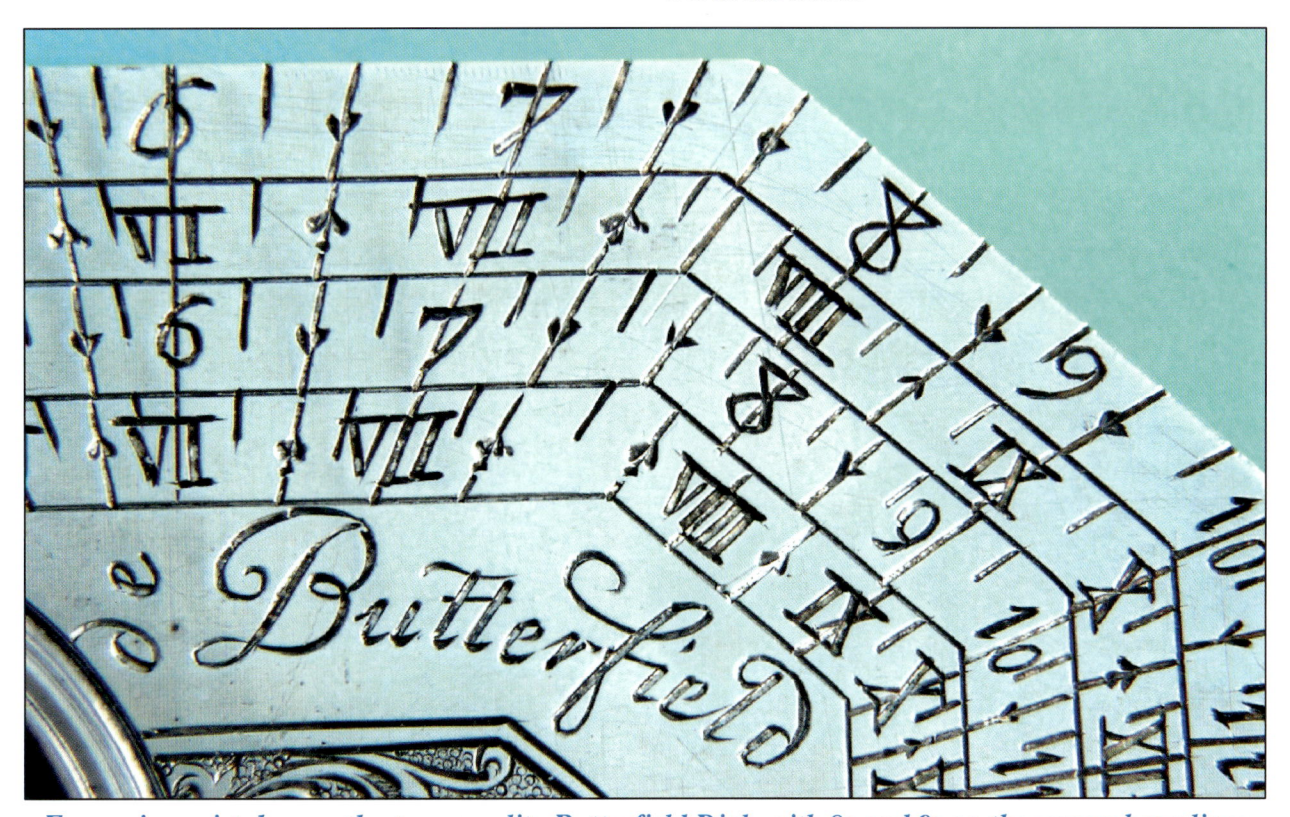

Engraving mistakes on the poor quality Butterfield Dial, with 8s and 9s on the wrong hour lines

77

CHAPTER 10 OTHER BUTTERFIELD DIALS

The Butterfield Dial has been attributed to Michael Butterfield, working in Paris between 1674 and 1722. He was a prolific worker and his workshop must have turned out several thousand of them. For further details of French Butterfield Dials refer to Chapter 9. It is most unlikely that Butterfield produced the first of this attractive design but it is now impossible to say who did make the first one. It was certainly a popular concept and was soon being made in both France and England in large quantities by many instrument makers. One contender for introducing the design must be Richard Whitehead, working in London from around 1683 to 1693. He had been apprenticed to the famous dial and instrument maker Henry Wynne. Whitehead worked in Gunpowder Alley, half-way up Shoe Lane, Fleet Street. [Clifton 1995 - p296] At least two silver Butterfield Dials by him are known. These are well made dials and the one illustrated has an exceptional case, lined with boxwood, sculpted to take the dial as a snug fit. His bird, used for gnomon support, is certainly much chubbier than those used by other makers. Perhaps he has depicted the English garden robin?

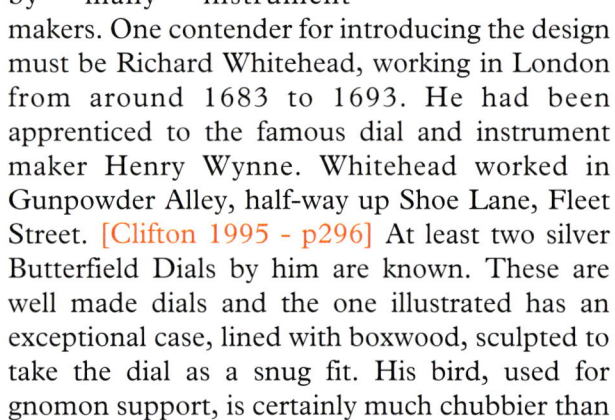

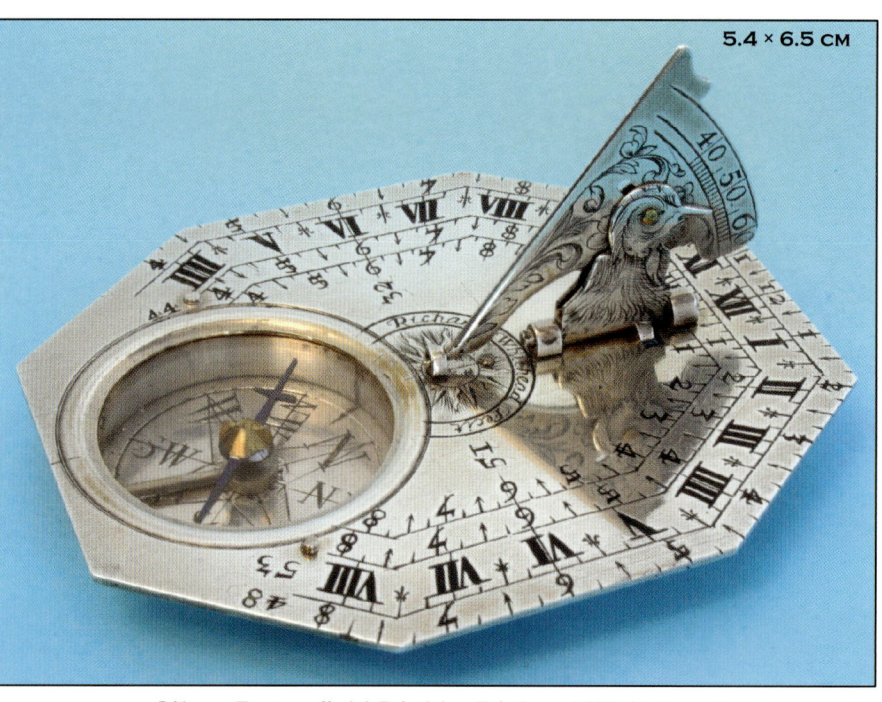

Silver Butterfield Dial by Richard Whitehead

The occasional Butterfield Dial is found that was apparently made by a French Hugenot. The Hugenots, suffering religious persecution in France, travelled to nearby countries setting up their trades. They brought with them their French flair for appearance but were eventually constrained by English tastes. One of these dials is the work of Cheualier (sic). Chevalier is otherwise unrecorded but a man of this name was known to have worked in Guernsey. This dial is

Gnomon supporter for the Whitehead dial

Travelling Case for the Whitehead dial

CHAPTER 10 OTHER BUTTERFIELD DIALS

Gilt brass Butterfield Dial by Chevalier

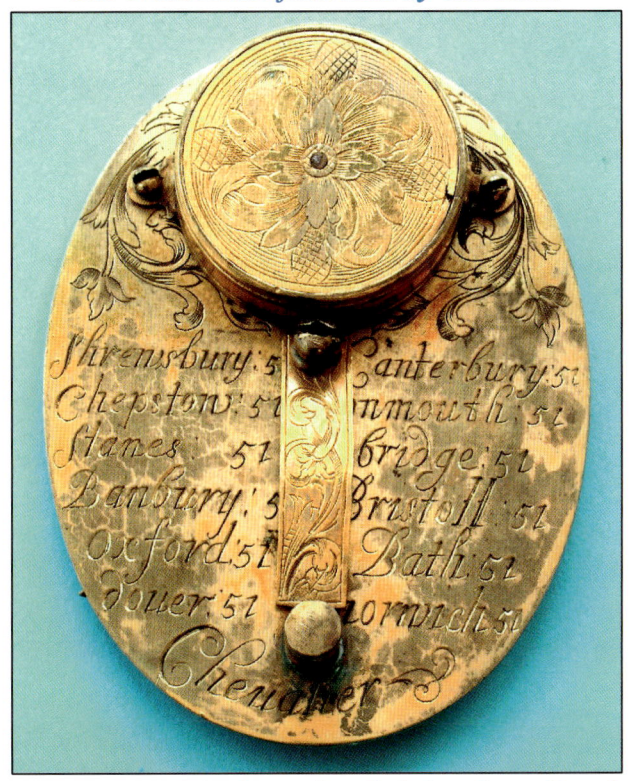

Leaf gnomon supporter of the Chevalier dial

Underside of the Chevalier dial showing a list of English provincial towns and their latitudes

an attractive oval shape with eight sided and elliptical chapter rings. It is of gilt brass and instead of the usual bird gnomon support he uses the top edge of a leaf. On the underside of the dial the list of places are all English, with many provincial towns included. The dial is certainly attractive and shows all the signs of French workmanship and its quality of engraving is reminiscent of the work of Edmund Culpeper.

THE LONDON MAKERS

Other English makers, besides Richard Whitehead who are known to have made the 'Butterfield' design include Thomas Heath, John Rowley, John Coggs and later James Simons. These London instrument makers were mostly producing precision instruments that must be considered as purely functional and not too decorative.

Thomas Heath is known to have made several Butterfield Dials. They were usually quite plain with little decoration. An elliptical dial by him in brass, but once silvered, has its prime scale engraved for 50° 20' which most probably is for Plymouth. It is interesting to note that a second and similar dial by Heath is known, also with this unusual latitude marked. It seems likely that both dials may have been made for sailors who operated from Plymouth. Portable sundials of all sorts, particularly those that are universal, were most popular with seafarers. A further dial by Heath has the main dial engraved for 51° 32', this time London. Another interesting feature of these Heath dials is that the magnetic declination of the compass can be adjusted by means of a sliding button on the outside of the compass bowl against a finely divided declination scale of ±20°. When these dials were made around 1730 the magnetic declination was only about 12° West. Heath was in no position to predict that the maximum

An elliptical brass dial by Thomas Heath made for a latitude of 50° 20', probably Plymouth

79

CHAPTER 10   OTHER BUTTERFIELD DIALS

5.7 × 8.5 CM

A most unusual dial by Thomas Heath in the shape of a figure '8'

declination would eventually exceed his 20° figure. (The declination for London reached as high as 24°W in about 1820 and somewhat less for Paris. See Appendix 4.) This addition of the adjustable declination mark made the dials of Heath much more universal and were ideal for the travelling gentleman. Thomas Heath advertised his dials saying that he was prepared to make out individual itineraries for his customers. *'If any Gentleman about to travel, is pleased to*

Moveable declination marker in compass bowl of the Heath figure '8' dial

Underside of the figure '8' shaped dial

80

Chapter 10   Other Butterfield Dials

Oval silver dial by John Rowley, London, ca. 1710

communicate the Tour he designs to take, he may have a Catalogue of the Towns in his way and their Latitudes, From Mr Heath, with the instrument (the universal dial) in order to ease him of the Trouble of Searching Maps, Globes or Geographical Books.'

The products of the English dialmakers differed in several respects from their French contemporaries. Thomas Heath was no exception and one dial by him uses a most unusual figure-of-eight design. This style also overcomes the problem of the rather small inaccurate compass, giving both compass and the dial their own parts of the plate, thus avoiding possible conflict. The engraving is filled with coloured wax instead of the normal black making it easier to use and particularly attractive.

Its underside has a gazetteer of important towns with foreign towns in the left column and English on the right.

John Rowley is also recorded as having made Butterfield Dials. His are particularly well executed. The dial shown is typical of his work giving the Equation of Time on its underside and '$Latti^d$ of $places$' with English towns on the left and foreign towns on the right.

Travelling Case for the dial by John Rowley, London, c1710

Bird Gnomon of the Rowley dial

CHAPTER 10   OTHER BUTTERFIELD DIALS

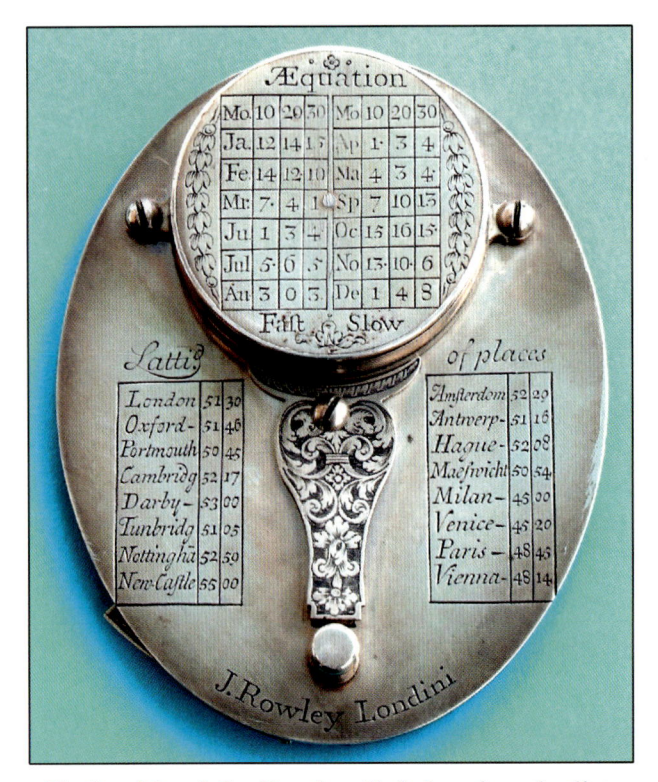

Underside of the Rowley dial showing the lists of towns and their latitudes, English in the left column and foreign towns in the right column

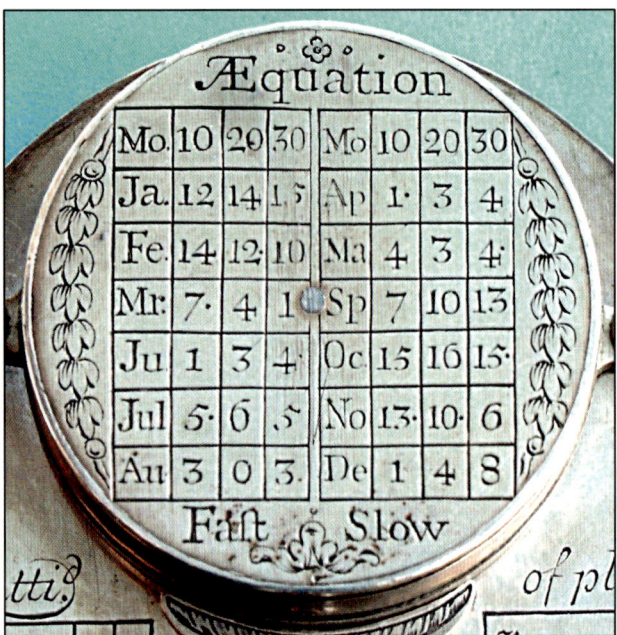

Equation of Time table engraved under the compass bowl of the dial by John Rowley

Several English Butterfield Dials have been noted that are unsigned and appear to have been manufactured provincially. They are all in brass and share various features. The same features are also shared by two Inclining Dials in Chapter 16.

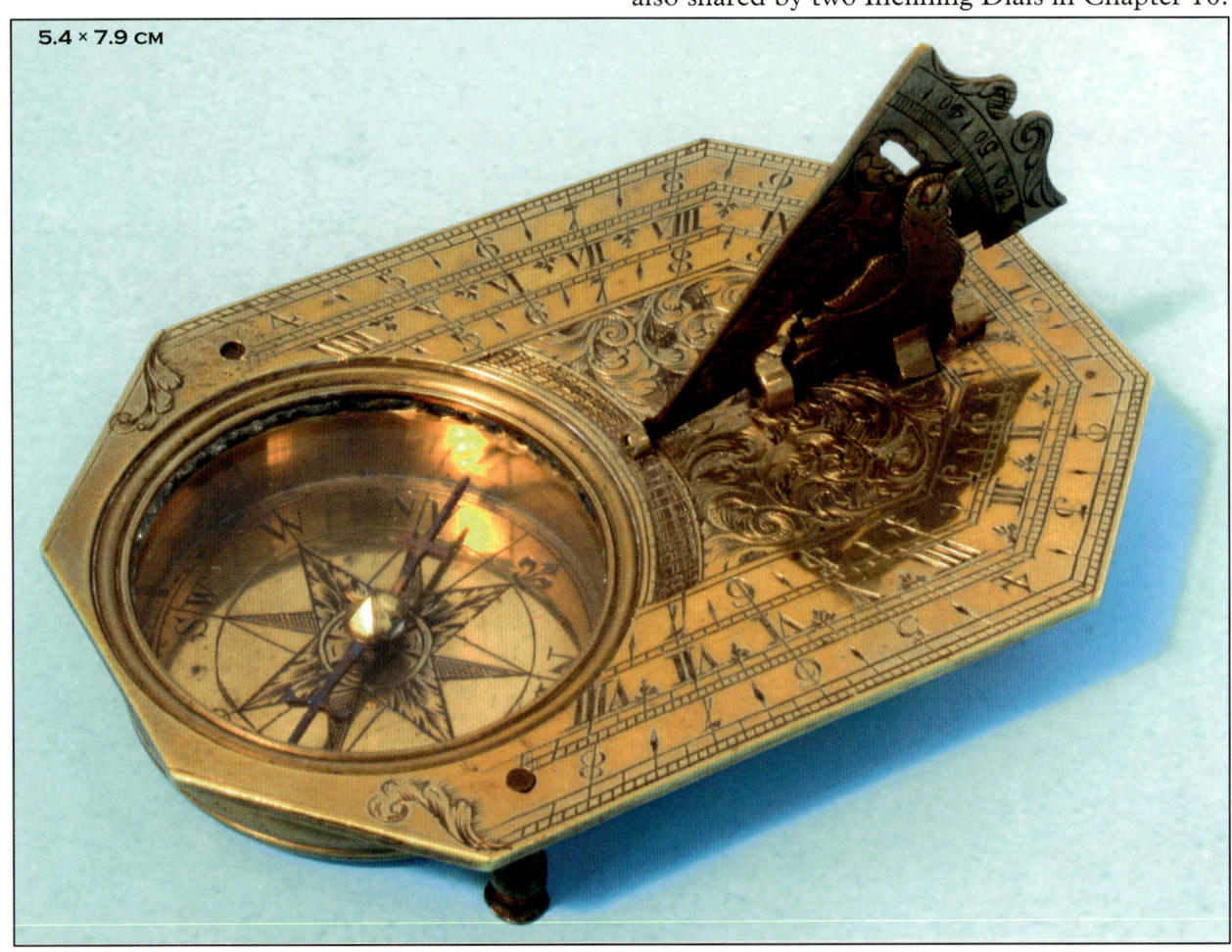

5.4 × 7.9 CM

Eight sided dial by unknown English maker.
Note what appears to be an erased maker's name in the arc next to the gnomon root

Chapter 10 Other Butterfield Dials

5.7 × 6.9 CM

*An oval dial by unknown English maker.
Note the fine quality engraving, its bird with a crest and an English rose in the compass bowl*

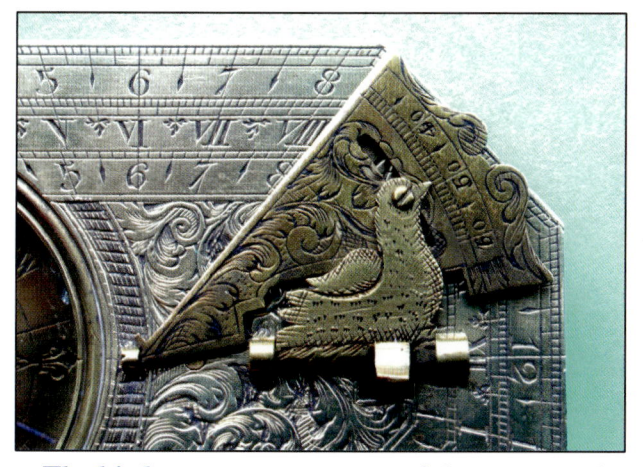

The bird gnomon supporter of the octagonal dial with the erased signature

The main common features are certain details of the engraving. The bird has feather marks made by the jab of a burin. The engraving on the gnomon spring is also very similar and the fleur-de-lys marks for the half hours tend to be virtually identical. A particular feature of interest is on the octagonal dial where there was probably a maker's name between the gnomon root and the compass but this has been erased by rather crude scratch marks. This may mean that the dial was made by a man who was not a member of the appropriate livery company and his name was therefore erased.

Engraving detail on the gnomon springs from the two unsigned dials, oval above and eight sided below. The pattern at the centre of the top spring may also be found on an Inclining Dial (Chapter 16) that is almost certainly by the same maker.

83

CHAPTER 10   OTHER BUTTERFIELD DIALS

5.1 × 6.3 CM

A Russian Butterfield Dial signed by Samoilov, Izhora

Note how most of the dials by English makers have a crested bird, possibly a lark, for the gnomon support.

OTHER MAKERS

Butterfield Dials were rarely made outside of France and England. However, the appetite for these dials must have been substantial and one Russian dial in fine silver is known signed '**при Ижор Заводахъ Самоиловъ**', (Samoilov, Instrument Maker at Izhora Works). Izhora is near to Odessa. Its scales are for 45° and 60° and it has a list of towns and their latitudes engraved on the underside starting with St. Peter(sburg) at 59° 56' and ending with Odessa at 46° 28'. The dial is of the highest quality and its case is tastefully covered with red Morocco leather and is lined with green velvet. All inscriptions are in cyrillic with the exception of the eight direction markings in its compass bowl. Its compass needle has a jewelled bearing and to prevent damage in transit a lever can be used to lift the needle off its mount. In addition the magnetic declination can be adjusted over the range ±15°.

Underside of the dial by Samoilov with towns listed in Cyrillic script

84

CHAPTER 10   OTHER BUTTERFIELD DIALS

DIAL CASES

The quality of the cases provided with French Butterfield Dials have been discussed. Cases for their English and Russian counterparts are no less interesting. A selection of these are shown here. The case below was provided by Thomas Heath for his Figure '8' dial. It is covered in black fish skin lined with red velvet. Its hinge is at the right side allowing the lid to fully open so that the dial may be used without removing it from its case.

The red Morocco leather case, lower left, is for the Samoilov dial. Internally is a recess for the dial lined with green velvet. The black octagonal case, lower right, is for the dial by Richard Whitehead. It was shown opened on page 78. It is covered in black fish skin and is decorated with silver. Its interior is lined with boxwood with green velvet in the lid.

The dial by Samoilov in its red Morocco leather case lined with green velvet

Three cases for Butterfield Dials, Heath (figure '8'), Samoilov and Whitehead

85

CHAPTER 11 ENGLISH DIALS

The tradition of portable dialmaking in England covers a wide period of time with a large number of makers. The majority of dials were made in London with provincial makers almost unheard of until the nineteenth century. Most of the London dialmakers were primarily instrument makers and produced not only sundials but often a wide range of scientific and mathematical instruments. The various craftsmen in London formed themselves into guilds and laid down strict rules for obtaining and for maintaining their memberships. It was one way of keeping out inferior or undesirable members, including those from the provinces seeking employment in London, its rules imposing strict quality controls on their workmanship. Any piece not meeting the required standards could be confiscated and destroyed by guild officials. In general, the guild system did much to enhance the overall standards of tradesmen in all crafts, making London instruments much prized both in Britain and abroad.

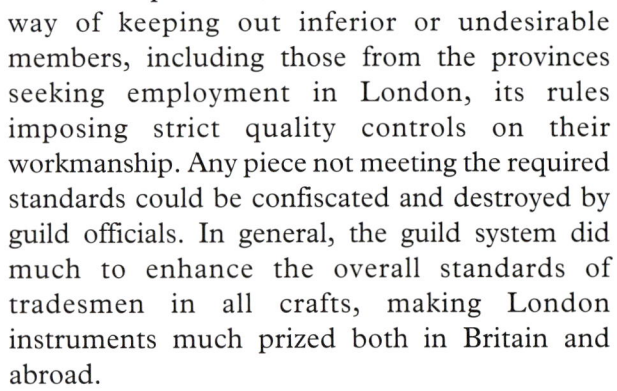

There was no Scientific Instrument Makers Company until relatively recent times (1964), so the instrument makers were to be found in various other companies such as the Clockmakers Company, Spectacle Makers Company and rather surprisingly to us today, the Grocers Company. In fact, the Grocers Company was the main guild for instrument makers at that time. [Brown 1979]

THE SIXTEENTH CENTURY

Portable sundials were known prior to the sixteenth century but extant examples and the names of their makers are mostly unknown. Those that were produced were made individually, probably in workshops of universities or even monasteries by learned men and were not generally made as commercial items. Some portable dials are known, particularly the simple compass dials salvaged from wreck of the Mary Rose, although these were most probably made in Nuremberg. Many of these early dials were made of wood and consequently few have survived. It was not until the time of Elizabeth I, 1558-1603, that instrument making really began to flourish in Britain. [G Turner 2000]

Compendium by Charles Whitwell, dated 1608

It is the three famous instrument makers of this period, Humphrey Cole, James Kynvyn and Charles Whitwell that we know best as makers of sundials.

The Compendium shown above by Charles Whitwell is described in detail in Chapter 23.

Humfrey Cole was the most famous and examples of his work are to be found in several museums. The fine quality and execution of his works show that he was an accomplished instrument maker.

THE SEVENTEENTH CENTURY

It was the early years of the seventeenth century that saw the first instrument makers producing portable sundials in any quantity. Their dials were of high quality, being finely made and were generally accurate in their time recording.

The best known makers of the period were Elias Allen, Edmund Culpeper I, his son Edmund II, Walter Hayes, Henry Sutton, Thomas Tompion, John Worgan, and Henry Wynne. Joyce Brown in her book [Brown 1979] shows the close relationships that existed between many of these

Chapter 11   English Dials

13 cm Rad.

Hidden engraving on a brass Quadrant by Walter Hayes

makers. A line of descent through apprenticeship may be traced from Charles Whitwell, through Elias Allen, Walter Hayes, John Worgan and the two Edmund Culpepers in turn. Further famous makers followed this lineage into the eighteenth century.

In the Whipple Museum in Cambridge is an Horary Quadrant by Edmund Culpeper with a sundial on its reverse. [Brown 1979 - Plate11b] During restoration, the volvelle supporting the gnomon was removed and trial engravings were found beneath it including the name of Culpeper. A similar quadrant by Walter Hayes has been found and this too has hidden engraving beneath the volvelle. It is interesting to surmise whether Culpeper engraved this Quadrant during his apprenticeship to Hayes or if Hayes passed on his habit to the young Culpeper. As the trial engraving on the Quadrant is fairly crude, it may be that one of his apprentices was responsible for it. Note how he has tried to copy the tulips and has drawn a bird.

Henry Sutton is perhaps the best known maker from the seventeenth century. His work covered a wide range of instruments but in dialling he is best known for his Horary Quadrants and his Ring Dials. A Quadrant by him is illustrated in Chapter 5.

Thomas Tompion was the famous 'father of clockmaking', working around the end of the seventeenth century and into the eighteenth. His main output was in clocks and watches but a few sundials signed by him are known to exist. The best known is a superb Garden Dial at Hampton Court. It shows clearly the wonderful quality of his workmanship for which he is justly famous. Portable dials by him are rare but the British Museum in London has two virtually identical examples, one in gold and the other in silver. [Ward 1981 - p29-30 & Plate 5] However, there is a distinct possibility that Tompion did not actually make these dials in his own workshop and may have had them made to order.

John Worgan was another fine instrument maker producing portable sundials and Garden Dials of the highest quality. One interesting feature of his work that appears on virtually every instrument that he made is a beautifully engraved English Tudor Rose. Other makers of the period, including Edmund Culpeper, also used a similar symbol but not so exclusively as Worgan.

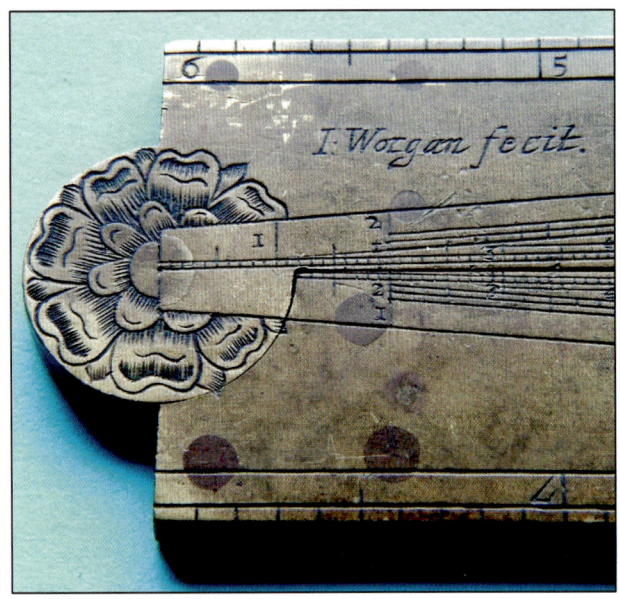

Chapter 11   English Dials

Typical Tudor Rose engraving on a bronze Sector by John Worgan

Signature of Edmund Culpeper on an Inclining Dial

Advertisement.

THis Inftrument, or any other Mathematical Inftrument, is exactly made either in Silver, Brafs, or Wood, by Mr. *Walter Hayes*, at the Crofs-Daggers in *Moore-Fields*, next Door to the *Popes Head* Tavern; where they may have all forts of Maps, Globes, Sea-Plats, Carpenters Rules, Poft and Pocket-Dials for any Latitude, Steel Letters, Figures, Sines, Planets, or Afpects, at reafonable Rates.

An extract from Leybourn's book 'The Panorganon' advertising the work of Mr. Walter Hayes

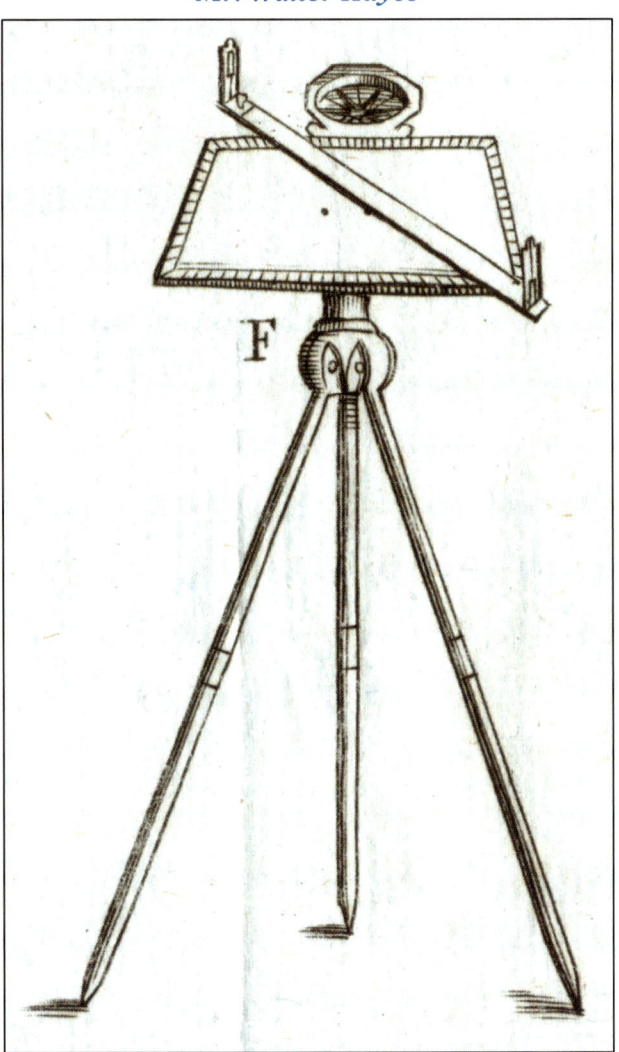

Henry Wynne is well known for his Universal Equinoctial Ring Dials and he produced a small book entitled 'The Horological Ring' to explain how to use them. [Wynn 1682] Further details have already been given of Equinoctial Ring Dials in Chapter 4 where a fine silver example of his work is described.

Another type of dial occasionally found is the Magnetic Azimuth Dial. This is similar in function to those from Dieppe but looks completely different. These dials were usually associated with surveying equipment and are normally found as part of the compass of a Plane Table (or Plain Table). The Plane Table was a rather simple surveying device requiring little in the way of trigonometrical or mathematical skills. It consisted of a flat board mounted on a tripod.

Magnetic Azimuth Dial by Walter Hayes

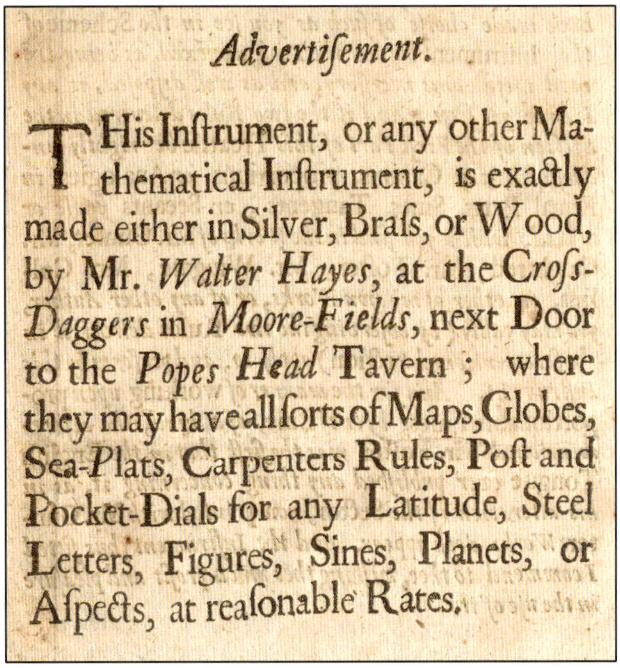

Plane Table with its compass fitted at the far side
[Bion 1758 - Plate XII]

88

Chapter 11 English Dials

Magnetic Azimuth Dial as part of a Plane Table Compass by Walter Hayes, dated 1663

In use it would be aligned by its compass to be precisely North - South. Across the centre of the board would be an alidade. A sheet of paper was attached to the board and the surveyor would sight through the alidade, perhaps along the border of a piece of land and with a pencil draw a line on the paper along the edge of the alidade which would then be exactly parallel to that side of the land. He would continue for each boundary or section until an exact scale replica of the property was drawn, using a surveying chain to measure distances. The compass would sometimes include a Magnetic Azimuth Dial.

The various scales printed on the compass card at first look quite complicated but are relatively simple. The outer scale is for surveying purposes and gives an angular reading from North or South. The next scale is simply a 0° - 360° scale, also used for surveying with a scale just inside this dividing the circle into 240 parts.

The next scale is for the Sundial. Look first at the inner scale which has a Calendar, starting on the left with the Vernal Equinox ♈ at March 10th. This shows every second day of the year and corresponding Zodiac degrees, in 2° steps. This clearly shows that it is using the older Julian Calendar which was not abandoned in Britain until 1752.

The Magnetic Azimuth Dial was only popular for a few years around 1660, which was when the Magnetic North was almost the same as True North. (See Appendix 4.) The compass needle therefore could be relied upon to show True North and no corrections were necessary. To use it, the dial or the Plane Table is set so that it is aligned with the Sun, possibly by using the

89

Comparison of the signatures of Sutton and Hayes on two Magnetic Azimuth Dials showing remnants of Sutton's name beneath that of Hayes (which is dated ten years later)
The Sutton print is courtesy Trevor Philip & Sons

alidade. The needle will cross the scales on both halves of the dial. Firstly, if we assume that the date is 10 April (Old Style), this corresponds to the first day of the Zodiac sign Taurus shown by its sigil of a bull's head with two horns ♉ (refer to the calendar scale). We can find this same sigil on the dial scale to the left, between **VII** and **VI** on the outer hour scale, referring to the circle about mid-way between both sets of numerals. It is then only necessary to find where the compass needle crosses this circle in the top half of the dial to be able to read the correct time in hours and the subdivided half-hours. For other dates we would use different concentric circles as appropriate. Note that the hours are indicated from **IIII - XII - VIII** in Roman Numerals. These are the Summer hours on the dial.

If we now take a Winter date, say 11 November, this is indicated as the arrow of Sagittarius, ♐, which may be seen on the dial scale at the lower right near to numeral **IIII**. This concentric ring is near to the outside edge of the dial. Again we look for where the compass needle crosses this ring and read out the time, but this time on the lower section of the scale against the Arabic Numerals.

We believe that these Magnetic Azimuth Dials were first produced in London by Henry Sutton. Dials of his are dated as early as 1653. The Walter Hayes dial illustrated uses the Sutton printing plate where his name has been erased and 'Walter Hayes' put in its place. Careful examination of the print shows remnants of Sutton's signature beneath that of Hayes. He obviously acquired Sutton's plate about two years before his death in 1665.

THE EIGHTEENTH CENTURY

A considerable number of dials were produced in London during this period by a large number of instrument makers but very few of them made sundials alone. Their trade was widely spread throughout the field of scientific and mathematical instruments. It was usual for each instrument maker to have his own shop from which to sell his wares. In London, most were to be found in the area around Fleet Street. Evidence shown by the Trade Cards and Advertisements of the time indicates that most makers could supply virtually any instrument on demand. It is unlikely that each of them would actually manufacture all of the items offered and there must have been a considerable amount of trading between them. It is quite difficult to actually prove this point unless one particular maker had an individual style that could easily be identified. The vendor would, in nearly all cases, add his own signature to the instrument. Similar practices have been found amongst the clockmakers of the period. One case known to the author is of a bracket (or mantel) clock signed by Henry Jones but stylistically, it must be the work

CHAPTER 11   ENGLISH DIALS

10.2 CM DIA.

An exceptionally fine silver Compass Dial by Richard Glynn, London, c1710

of Joseph Knibb. Jones, appears to have merely completed the work by adding the finishing touches including the decorative engraving plus his own signature.

The fine Compass Dial illustrated by Richard Glynn(e) is typical of many of the London dials of

Decorative gnomon of the Richard Glynn dial

Centre of the compass bowl showing an engraved boar's head with smaller versions inside the four cardinal pointers

CHAPTER 11   ENGLISH DIALS

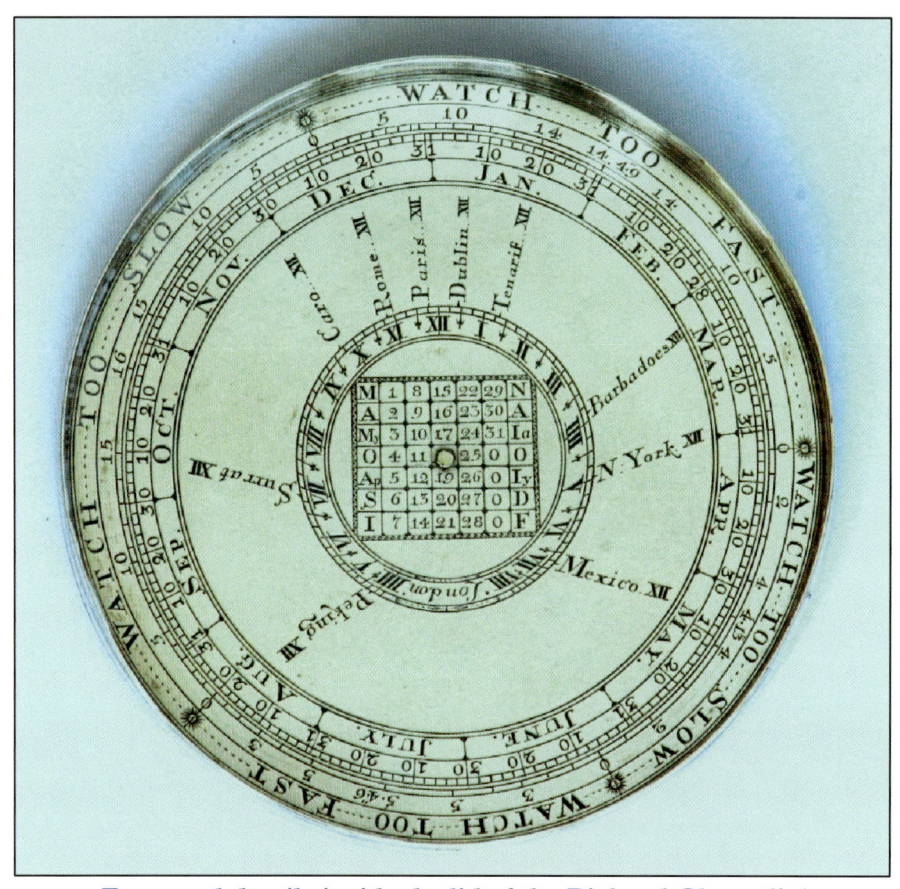

Engraved details inside the lid of the Richard Glynn dial

Both sides of the Glynn dial have protective leather discs

is engraved the Equation of Time for each two days of the calendar. Inside this are 10 cities around the World showing on a replica of the main chapter ring the time for noon at each place. In the very centre is a Perpetual Calendar. Refer to Chapter 25 for more details of their use.

Some dials are known signed by Masig, London but these are clearly the work of one or both of the Augsburg makers, Johann Martin and/or Johann Willebrand. It is believed that Masig was their local agent in London and that he also represented several other makers there. As far as we know there are no dials of Masig's own manufacture. [Zinner 1956 - p441]

The range of dials produced in London covered almost every type imaginable with a few notable exceptions. The most prominent exception is the Pillar Dial that was most commonly made in France and Italy but possibly never in London. Another type that is rarely seen from London makers is the Universal Equinoctial Mechanical Dial which is described in Chapter 21.

Several Butterfield style dials were made in London and these were described in Chapter 10. Like most English portable dials, these were usually of brass and were generally of much higher technical standard but less ornate than their French counterparts.

If any dials could be said to be typically London (or English) these would be the Universal Inclining Dial or the Universal Equinoctial Dial. Versions of both are illustrated, both made by Dollond. The only real difference between the two is that the gnomon of the former is at an angle

this period but it is certainly one of the finest of these known. It is larger than most being 4" (100mm) diameter, perhaps a little large for the average pocket. Its gilt gnomon is superb showing a swan-like bird sitting on a coronet and holding an arrow in its bill. In the centre of its compass bowl is engraved the head of a boar. Unusually the dial has red leather discs added to the lid and underneath its compass bowl, presumably as protection against being scratched. Inside its lid

Chapter 11 English Dials

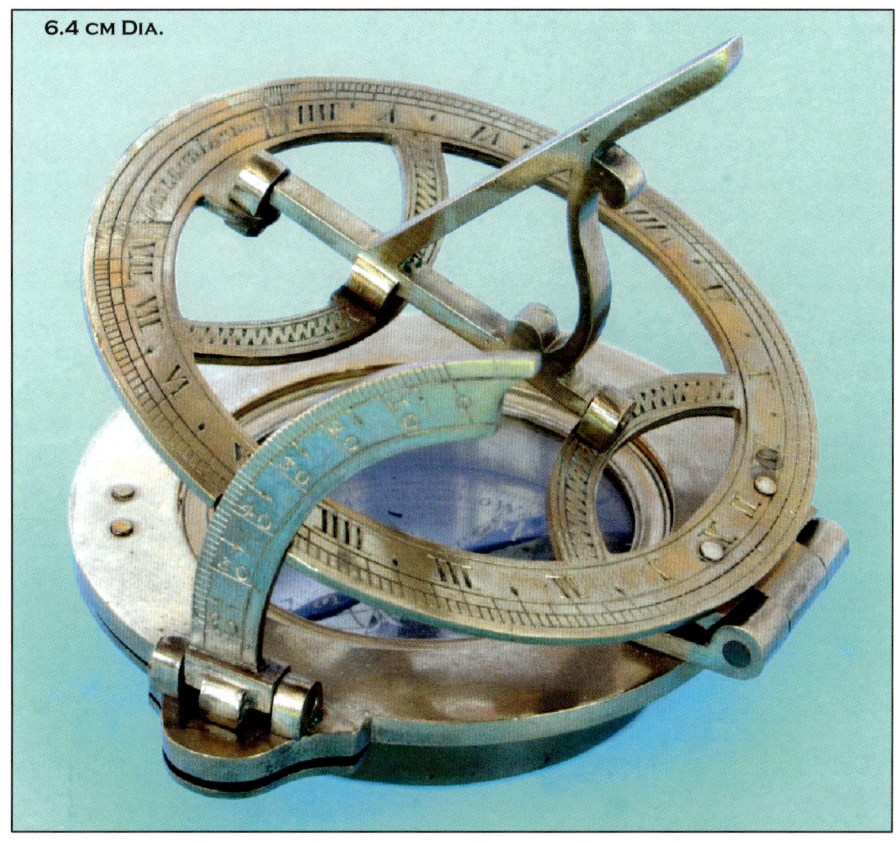

A typical eighteenth century Inclining Dial by Dollond (6.4 cm dia.)

A typical late eighteenth century Equatorial Dial by Dollond (8.1 cm dia.)

Note the layout of the chapter ring on some Inclining Dials with two arcs used to help support the gnomon. The material is thin enough to be flexible and one arc acts as the spring to keep the gnomon erect.

The Equatorial Dial is mounted over a large compass with a finely divided ring of degrees allowing readings to 1°. To allow for variations in Magnetic Declination the complete chapter ring assembly may be rotated within the compass housing to the desired figure.

The styles of London dials varied somewhat but they were nearly always heavily built and were made with a large compass. In use, they were capable of fairly accurate time recording. For further information about Inclining Dials, including those by English makers, see Chapter 16.

The 'Equation of Time' was sometimes engraved around the edge of English dials and a list of European towns with their latitudes underneath the dial. Some, designed for wider travel, included towns in the 'New Colonies' of the British Empire.

The inclusion on a dial of the Equation of Time or a Perpetual Calendar will often provide good evidence as to its date of manufacture. See Chapter 25. If it is an English dial, we know that the calendar was changed in 1752. A quick check on the date for the 'First Point of Aries' will give March 11th (or 10th after 1700) for the older Julian Calendar and March 21st for the

to the chapter ring, usually 60°, and in the latter it is perpendicular.

CHAPTER 11   ENGLISH DIALS

6.2 CM DIA.

Silver Compass Dial by James Simons of London, ca. 1770

It is engraved:- '***March begins on in the Year 1700 &***', '***Thurfday 70. 81. 92. 98.***' It is therefore probable that it was made in the year 1770 or soon afterwards. This form of calendar is attributed thus:- '***The Univerfal Time Table, S Kingdon inv.***' Many of the dials of this period were made so that the chapter ring was a push fit into the compass bowl. In this way the dial position could be adjusted over the compass to allow its owner to set it to the latest magnetic declination. When this dial was made the local rate of change of compass declination was at its maximum being around 1° for each 4 year period.

Similar Compass Dials to that by Simons were made by several other London makers. In many cases they did not sign their work but the other dial illustrated is by James Search. His dial is made of brass with the scales silvered. Overall it is of the highest quality and is placed over a large sized, and clearly readable, precision compass.

current Gregorian Calendar. Where the Zodiac signs are not used it may still be possible to check these dates by comparing the points on a calendar scale where the two scales cross. If the 21st March is opposite, or nearly opposite, to 23rd September it is Gregorian. If the 10/11th March was opposite 11th September it would be the earlier Julian calendar. A Perpetual Calendar would often indicate the years of its intended use, giving a good check against recorded dates for its maker.

The silver dial by J. Simons of London carries a Perpetual Calendar on its lid. It is possible to find the date of this dial from the calendar inscriptions.

THE NINETEENTH CENTURY

The portable sundial was being made in quite large quantities throughout the nineteenth century. It was essential to have some means of setting both clocks and watches. Ownership of mechanical timekeepers was now widespread and many gentlemen would own a pocket watch. With the invention of improved watch escapements and the use of temperature compensation for the watch's balance, accuracy and reliability of the watch had dramatically increased. They were now widely available at affordable prices, being made in large quantities, especially in parts of Lancashire. During the first half of the century the domestic clock would have been made in Britain with those of the highest quality coming generally from London. Mass production techniques were being applied in watch and clock manufacture by this time. In the second half of the century cheaper imports were flooding the market from from France, Germany and the ex-colony of America sending the British clockmaking trade into decline.

Underside of the dial by James Simons

Chapter 11 English Dials

8.7 CM DIA.

Compass Dial by James Search of London, ca. 1780

The precision compass of the dial by James Search

To set any clock to time is was necessary to refer to a sundial. This dial would normally be placed on a pedestal in the garden and at this date it would probably have been made in London. Portable dials were not generally thought to be exact enough for adjusting the relatively accurate pendulum clock and eventually they became obsolete as the watch took their places. For those without a Garden Dial the correct time was frequently available from the local church clock. This would have been set against a church sundial and would convey the time by its bells over a wide local area.

Most of the dials from the nineteenth century were mass produced. They were generally much simpler and utilitarian, but still capable of producing accurate results. Higher quality (and usually more accurate) dials continued to be made but could, as before, only be afforded by the richer members of society.

The Compass Dial similar to those of the eighteenth century continued. Many were like that illustrated in the Perpetual Calendar box on Page 96. The parts were usually simple castings quickly finished, being silvered where necessary. The compass card was often printed on paper and sometimes hand coloured giving quite an attractive appearance.

The other popular dials of the period were Magnetic Compass Dials and these are described later, in Chapter 19.

There were several other types of portable dial produced at this time. One of these is illustrated that is on the reverse side of a 6" bone rule. It is unsigned but the design was '**REGIST^D JUNE 28 1853**'. A small lid lifts to reveal a tiny compass and the

Chapter 11 English Dials

7.7 cm Dia.

4.4 × 8.3 cm

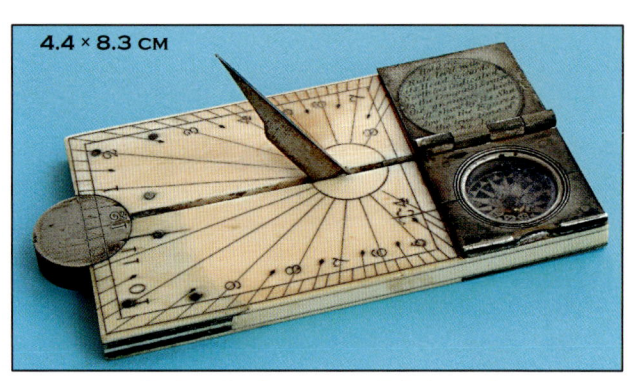

A simple Compass Dial on the reverse of a 6" bone rule

An unsigned simple Compass Dial, ca. 1797, fitted into a Perpetual Calendar box

gnomon is hinged between the two halves of the folded rule. Instructions for use are pasted to the inside of the compass lid. *'Hold the Rule level with its Head towards North (as indicated on the Compafs) and raise the gnomon which will show by its Shadow on the Figures the true time of the day.'*

With the introduction of Railway Time in the late nineteenth century it became necessary to have clocks and watches set to the same time throughout the Country. The railway telegraph then became the prime disseminator of the nation's timekeeping, and towards the close of the century the pocket sundial and most other types of sundial became redundant. It was still necessary to find the nation's time from the Sun, but this could now be done at the Royal Observatory in Greenwich from where it was transmitted throughout the nation, at first by telegraph and later by radio.

For details of other English made dials refer to the Chapters on specific types of dial.

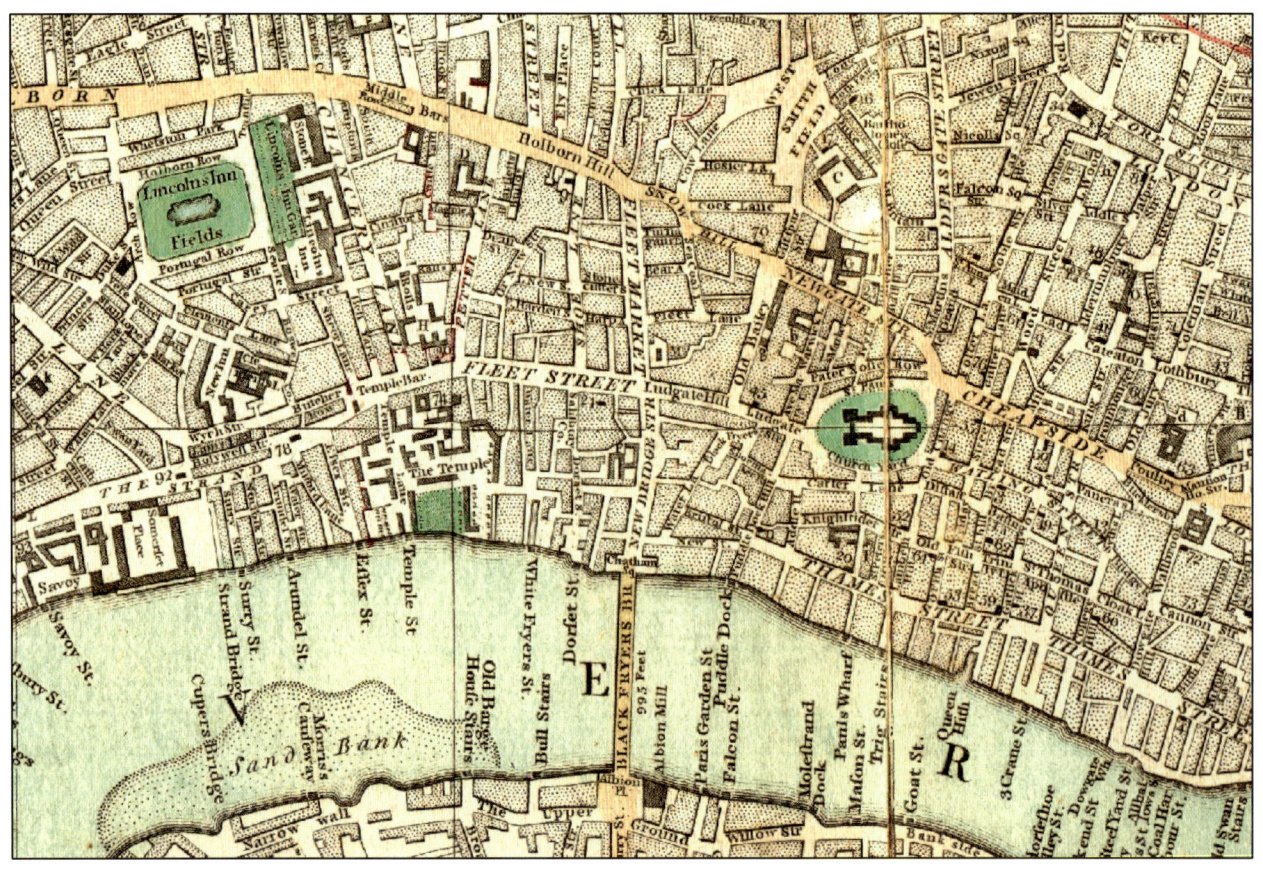

Map of the centre of London dated 1790 showing the area of the City where many instrument makers worked

CHAPTER 12 UNIVERSAL EQUINOCTIAL DIALS

The Universal Equinoctial or Equatorial Dial was made in many countries, but the most commonly found are those from Augsburg. See Chapter 15. The principle of the dial is that its chapter ring is parallel to the Equator of the Earth and its gnomon is aligned with its Polar Axis. A dial of this type can be used at any point of the Earth's surface by adjusting it to align with the Equator and the Pole. If used in the Southern Hemisphere the chapter ring may sometimes be turned over, but if not the hours must be read in reverse. In practice many of these dials were limited in their range of latitudes due to mechanical constraints.

6.1 CM DIA.

Equinoctial Dial by Johann Wilhelm Schultze of Kassell, dated 1688

Some were also limited due to the fact that their chapter rings could prevent the user from taking observations at and around noon and around the two Equinoxes. The Universal Equinoctial Ring Dial was one of the first to use the equinoctial principal. This type of dial has already been described in Chapter 4.

A quite early and unusual example of the Equinoctial Dial is shown by '***Johann Wilhelm Schultze***' of Kassel, and is dated 1688. This silvered brass dial folds flat into its turned wooden case for transit. Its lid has a fine thread to allow it to be screwed to the lower half of the case. When erected for use, the dial sits high above and to one side of its built-in

Equinoctial Dial by Schultze folded to fit into its case

97

CHAPTER 12 UNIVERSAL EQUINOCTIAL DIALS

6.9 × 7.6 CM

Universal Equinoctial Dial by N. Bion

compass, allowing both to be read without hindrance. Its semi-circular gnomon may be set to suit all northern latitudes. It is the straight edge of the shadow that is used for reading the time. This dial suffers from similar limitations to the Universal Equinoctial Ring Dial due to the fact that its chapter ring obscures the Sun's light for a few days each side of the Equinox.

The more common pattern of Equinoctial Dial, and similar to those from Augsburg, is illustrated in a dial from Nicolas Bion of Paris. French makers at this time concentrated mainly on the Butterfield Dial which was not truly universal having a very limited latitude range of around 20°. On occasion, the French makers also made Equinoctial Dials. This dial is unusual for a French dial being made of brass rather than silver. Due to the fact that it has a closed chapter ring this dial is fully universal but it suffers from the same limitations as the Schultze dial around the Equinox.

In order to overcome the problems with the chapter ring obscuring the time around the

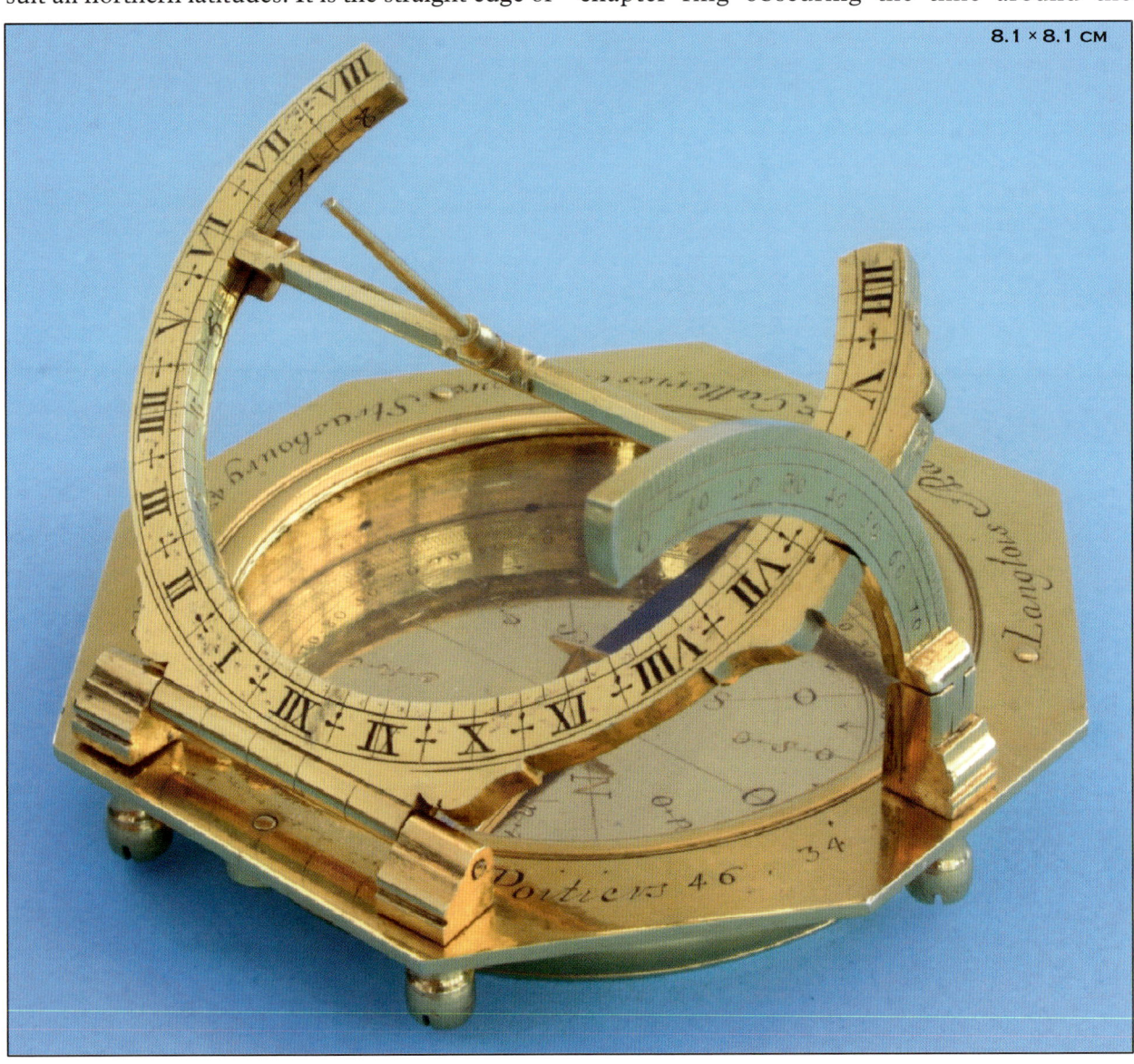

8.1 × 8.1 CM

Gilt Equinoctial Dial by 'Langlois AParis aux Galleries du Louvre'

98

CHAPTER 12   UNIVERSAL EQUINOCTIAL DIALS

ring is engraved with Roman numerals on top but with Arabic numerals on its inside edge.

Another French dial with a split chapter ring is on one half of a dual Butterfield and Equinoctial Dial. (This very unusual dial has already been described in Chapter 9.) Note its fine all-over engraving. This decoration seems to be rather excessive and was probably to a special commission by a rich client. Again, it is unusual for a French dial in that it is not made from silver and is unsigned.

A further Equinoctial Dial, not signed, is illustrated that was probably made in Austria. It is made of brass and has a gazetteer engraved on its

A nice feature on the Langlois dial with the fleur-de-lys ornamenting the cursor line

Equinox, some makers removed part of the chapter ring making it 'horseshoe' shaped. This act made the dials slightly less universal, but only insomuch as they could not be used more than about 16 hours in the day, i.e., at extreme Northern latitudes. The beautifully gilt dial by Langlois, ca. 1750, shows how this is done. It is a sturdily built dial and is inscribed with a total of 38 towns and their latitudes including **St Petersbourg 60** and **la Martinique 14.43'** (degree symbols not used), so truly designed for the travelling gentleman. Note how its chapter

Austrian dial with gnomon shown inverted as it would be used in the Winter months

underside in French with the towns in alphabetical order. The final town on the list is spread over two lines - **Viena de Austria: 48° 22'**. As an additional aid to setting it up it has a plummet fitted to a folding support on its southern side. Such plummets would get in the way of the Sun's rays especially in Winter months and would need to be folded flat across the compass when not needed. Its latitude setting arc is interestingly calibrated for latitudes, 0° - 60°, and for co-latitudes, 30° - 90°. One picture of the dial is used to

Dual 'Butterfield' and Equinoctial Dial

CHAPTER 12   UNIVERSAL EQUINOCTIAL DIALS

Gazeteer on the underside of the Austrian dial

illustrate the way in which these dials could be used during the Winter months of the year when the Sun is below the Equator. Here the gnomon is simply reversed so that its shadow will still be projected onto the inside of the chapter ring with a low positioned Sun. One complication does occur with such dials in that the gnomon is often too long for use at low latitudes as it comes into contact with the glass of the compass bowl.

The Equatorial Dial by Le Febvre is most unusual and is virtually a fixed version of the Universal Equinoctial Ring Dial. It is mounted on a square base and the dial is adjusted by the levelling screws so that the plummet is vertical. Its latitude is set against an arc calibrated from 30° to 90°, and a small 'finger' may be set at the current latitude to make repeated erections of the dial at the same latitude, simpler. The gnomon is in this

Universal Equinoctial Dial, unsigned but probably originating in Austria

100

CHAPTER 12 UNIVERSAL EQUINOCTIAL DIALS

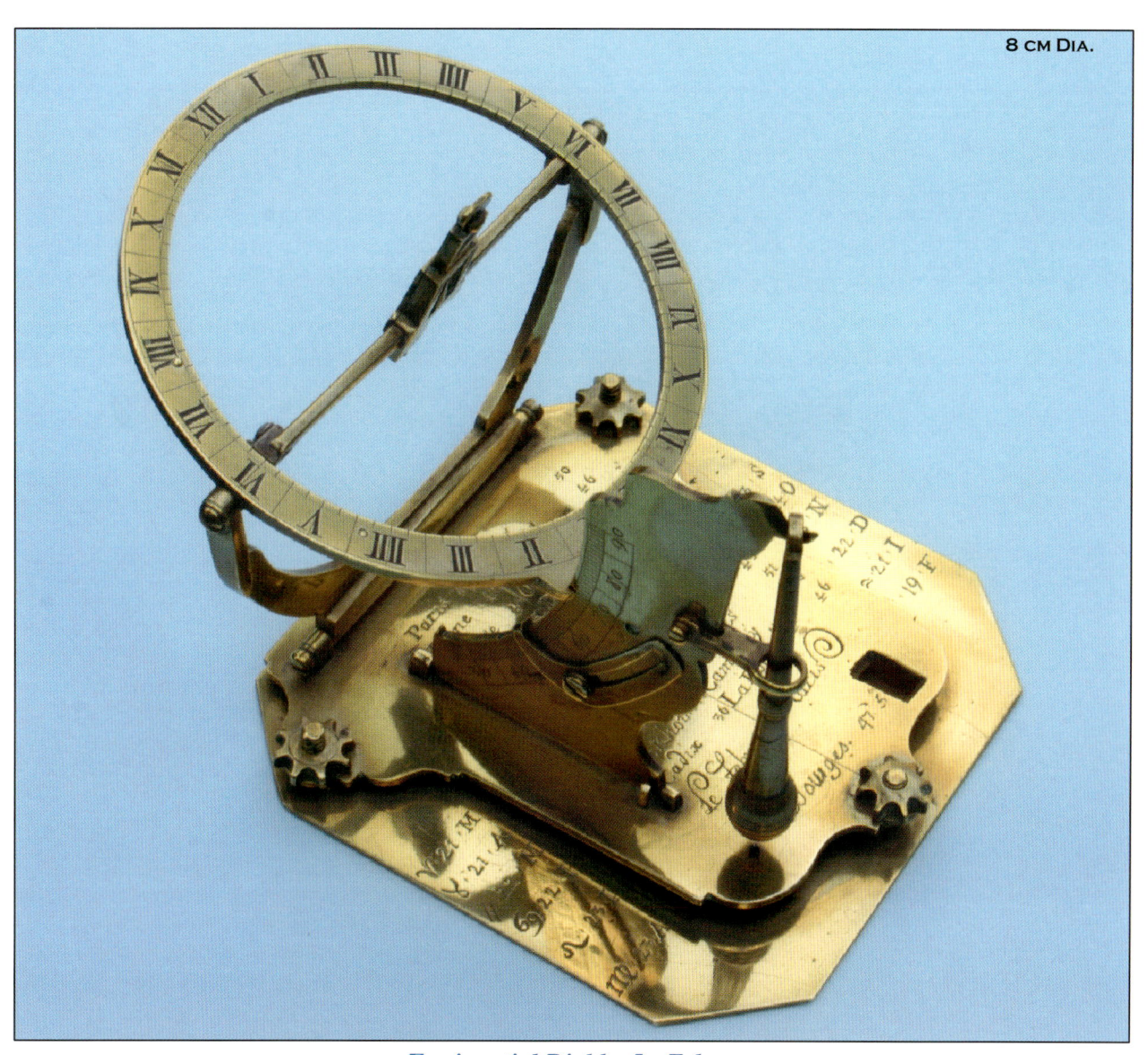

8 CM DIA.

Equinoctial Dial by Le Febvre

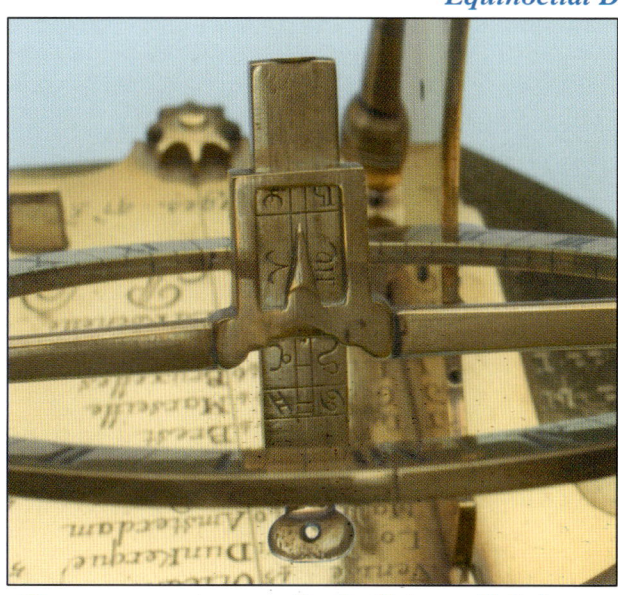

Gnomon aperture on the Le Febvre dial shown mounted below the chapter ring, as it would be for Winter use

case a small round aperture, which is at the end of a small brass strip. It is supported in a way so that the pointer indicates the current Zodiac date. In the Summer months it will be erected above the central bar when the Sun is above the Ecliptic and in the Winter it will be set below it. To enable conversion from Zodiac dates to regular dates, the day of the month for the entry into each of the signs is engraved on the upper side of the base plate.

Further Universal Equinoctial Dials are described in Chapter 15 describing Augsburg Dials.

CHAPTER 13

VERTICAL DIALS

The Vertical Dial is very seldom found as a Portable Dial but many types of Portable Dial have Vertical Dials as part of their structure, such as the back vertical face of an ivory Diptych Dial. The two dials described in this chapter, however, are purely Vertical Dials.

The first, from the late sixteenth century, is in the form of a square pillar carrying two Vertical Declining Dials on two of its faces. It is easy to confuse this dial with the Pillar Dials in Chapter 2, which are strictly Altitude Dials. This dial has spring loaded folding gnomons on two of its faces. All inscriptions are made with punches. One face is for morning hours, declining East, and is calibrated from, **IIII - XII - II** and the other for afternoon hours, declining West, **X - XII - VIII**. Both dials are set at angles of 45° with respect to South. To enable it to be set correctly, inside its top cap is a small magnetic compass which may be hinged out. It is calibrated such that the compass North - South line is set diagonally to the pillar. In order to set the dial perfectly vertically, there may have have been a plummet internally, but this is now missing.

The dial is almost certainly German but is unsigned. However, two others are known of this type, one in the Museum of the History of Science in Florence and the other in the British Museum, the latter being signed by Ulrich Schniep of Monaco (Munich), 1567.

The dials lower down the pillar operate from the tips of its two gnomons. The near vertical lines are Planetary Hours dividing the day (and night) into 12 equal portions irrespective of season. The more horizontal lines which are straight at the **AEQVATOR DIEI** (Equinox) are arranged to give the lengths of the day (in equal hours) for both **QVANTITAS DIEI** and **QVANTITAS NOC**

10.3 CM HIGH

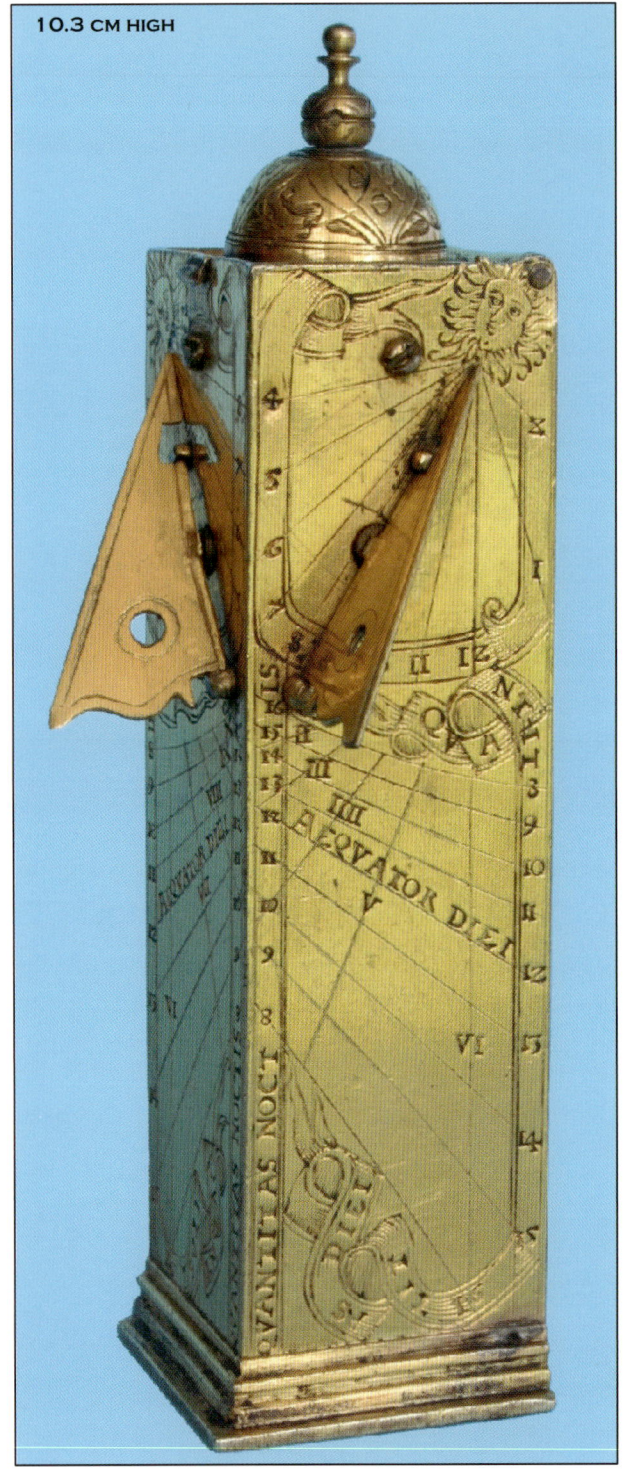

Pillar supporting two Vertical Declining Dials, probably by Ulrich Schniep, Munich, c1560

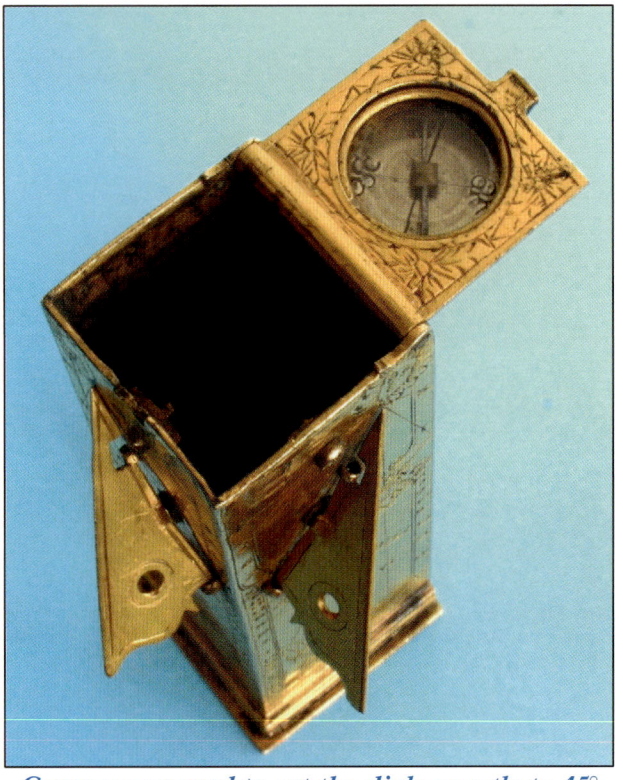

Compass opened to set the dials exactly to 45°

Chapter 13 Vertical Dials

Compass plate showing a magnetic declination marking of 12° towards the East

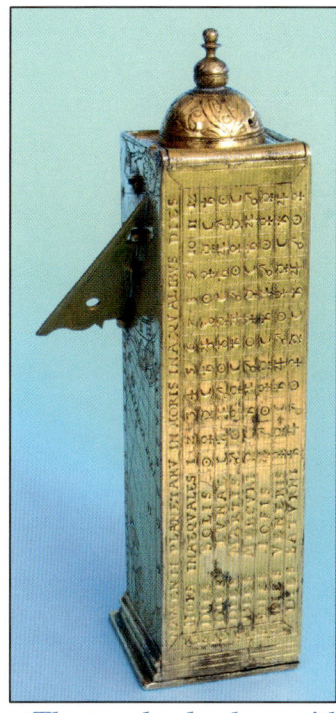

The two back edges with tables for Planetary Rulers for each hour of the day and night

(day and night). These vary between **8** and **16** hours each, depending on the season.

The compass is simple, with just the four Cardinal directions engraved on a silvered disc but it also has the current magnetic declination boldly inscribed. This has been accurately measured as 12° East, corresponding to a date of around 1550, but at this time a truly accurate figure was probably not known.

The rear two faces of the dial have tables for the Planetary Rulers for each hour during the course of a week. Each hour of each day, it was believed, was ruled by a different planet or god. The days of the week are named after the first Planetary Hour and these are clearly seen on the left of the tables. The hours then go in sequence, day and night: Sun, Venus, Mercury, Moon, Saturn, Jupiter, Mars and back to Sun at the eighth hour, repeating for the full 168 hours in the week.

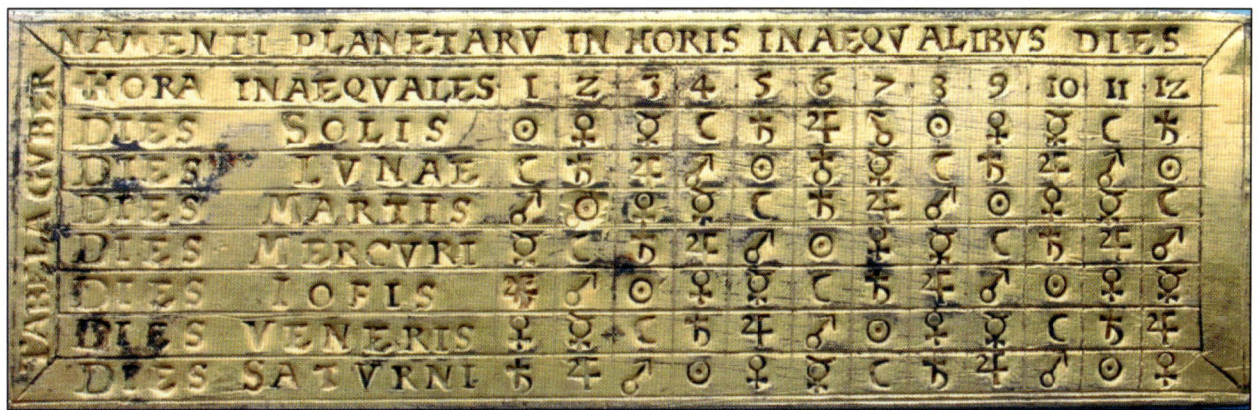

The table of Planetary Rulers for the day period

The table of Planetary Rulers for the night period

Chapter 13 Vertical Dials

Gilt Vertical Dial with adjustable string gnomon and calibrated chapter rings for latitudes from 41° to 53° in 3° steps

The second example is a rather attractive gilt Vertical Dial, using a string gnomon. It is also unsigned but probably German and dates from the mid seventeenth century. It has chapter rings for 41°, 44°, 47°, 50° and 53°. It is designed to fold flat so it was probably originally housed in a case with other instruments, including the compass, which it lacks. It has a spring device at the back to keep the gnomon taut and for each latitude, the gnomon may be set into a different notch on the lower gnomon support. There is also a plumb line at the back of the dial to set it absolutely vertical and two volvelles that function as a Perpetual Calendar. See Chapter 25. Its motto **VT VMBRA SIC VITA FVGIT** tells us that the shadow like life flies by.

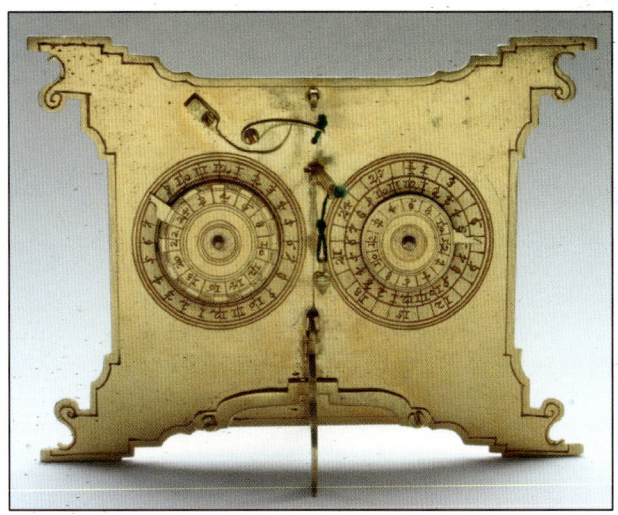

Reverse of the Vertical Dial showing the gnomon string support and levelling plummet

The lower gnomon support with the string hooked around the appropriately marked slot, here set to the latitude of 50°. (The extreme end of the arm is now missing)

CHAPTER 14 POLAR DIALS

Polar Dials function in a similar way to Equinoctial Dials but the dial plate is in the polar axis. Portable Polar Dials are not very common, the most frequently found being the Cruciform Dial. In use it has to be inclined so that its top is pointing directly South and towards the Ecliptic. To enable this to be set a small angle scale or quadrant is placed between the dial and its base to set its latitude. The dial will now function the same as it would at any other latitude. Its extremely small compass would severely limit its accuracy, perhaps only capable of showing the time to the nearest hour.

Although there are other types of Cruciform Dial the one illustrated here uses the

2.4 × 3.6 CM

Small Crucifix Dial in brass, with traces of original gilding

Top face with Christ on the cross

Underside with a serpent draped over the cross

105

Chapter 14 Polar Dials

Latitude setting quadrant on the Crucifix Dial

slightly flared top and ends of its arms to function as styles or gnomons. These throw their shadows onto six separate scales around its edges. The very top of the crucifix will show hours around noon along the horizontal cross bar. The styles formed by the lower edge of the cross bar will indicate the morning and afternoon hours on the sides of the main shaft. The styles formed by the upper edge of the cross bar will indicate hours before 6am and after 6pm in the Summer months on the top section of the vertical shaft.

The crucifix appears to be quite thick. The reason for this is that it has to be thick enough to show shadows of each style upon each hour scale throughout the year. If it had been made too thin the shadows would have fallen off the dial at times near to the two solstices. A version sometimes found includes declination lines.

Although unsigned and undated, this dial was

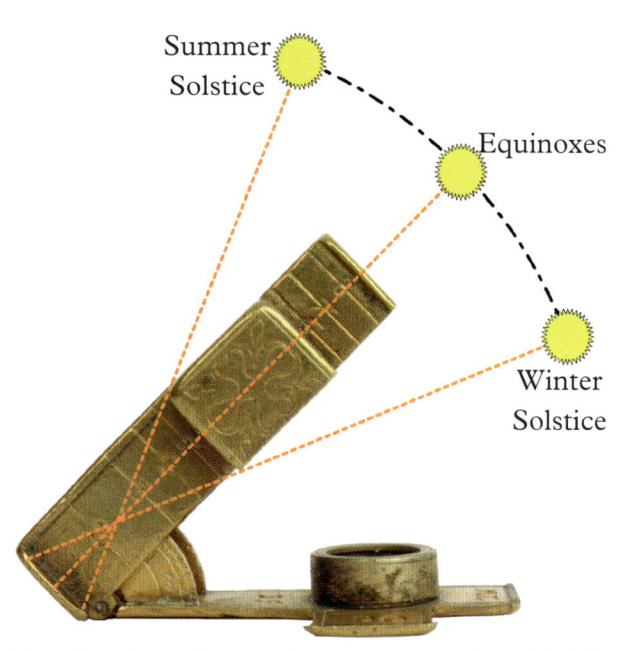

Showing how the shadows of the styles still fall on the body of the dial throughout the year

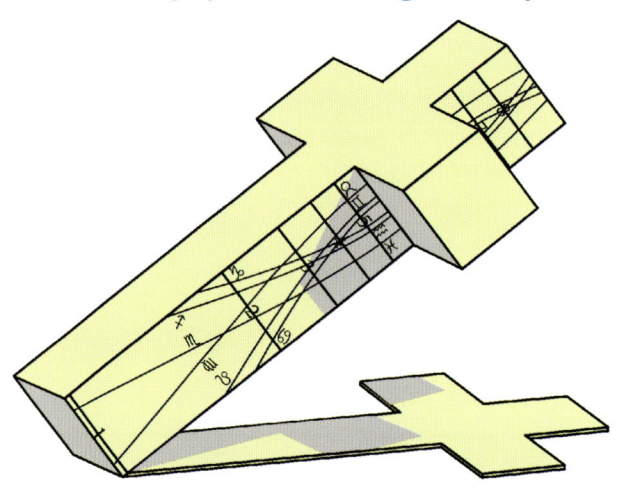

A version of the Crucifix Dial engraved with declination lines

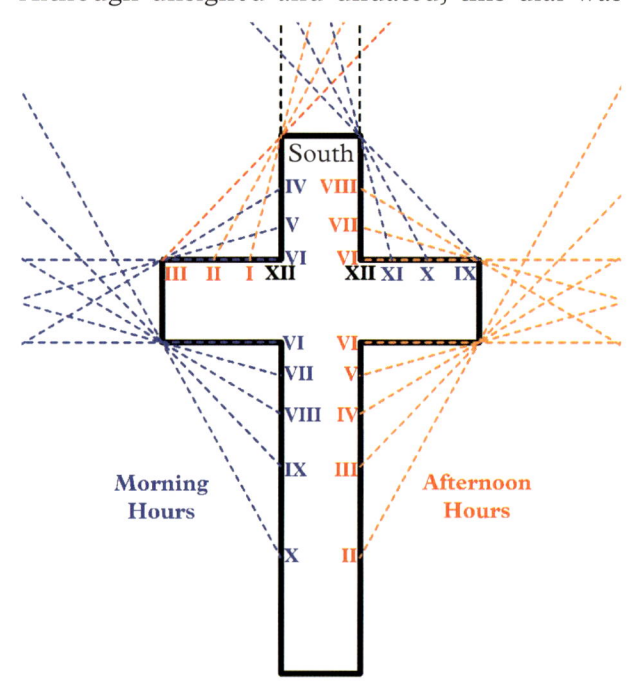

Sun rays from each of the six styles onto the six dial faces of a Crucifix Dial

probably made soon after 1600. On the other side of its latitude arc is a fixed line incised at 48°, suggesting that it was made for the latitude of Augsburg or Nuremberg. The dial is quite small, only 36 mm high, and would have hung from a chain or cord from around the neck of its owner. The supporting loop is missing but a hole can be seen at the top where this was originally fitted. To use the dial it would be best removed from its chain as the shadow from the chain could interfere with the shadows produced by the dial. Also, if it were used with the chain still around the owner's neck it would have been difficult to hold the dial far enough away to allow for proper alignment.

Many of these dials also contained holy relics in a special compartment inside. For a religious man therefore the Crucifix would perform two tasks, that of being a religious icon and the other a time teller.

106

CHAPTER 15 AUGSBURG DIALS

Augsburg is a relatively small town located in Southern Germany. Its position, to the South of Nuremberg puts it in an ideal position for trade, not only with Germany but also the surrounding countries of Bohemia (now part of the Czech Republic), Austria, Switzerland and its links to Italy. It was one of the most famous metalworking towns of Europe and became well known for its quality goods, particularly in gold and silver. Many of the items produced were very ornate reflecting the exceptional craftsmanship that was to be found there. In the sixteenth and seventeenth centuries it built up a reputation for its finely decorated and often complicated clocks. Many of these clock dials had astronomical scales occasionally in the form of an Astrolabe. It was not until the seventeenth century that sundials were made there in any quantity. It is probably from the earlier clockmakers and their descendants that the art of sundial making was first developed.

The earliest dials produced there were of high quality but were often somewhat complicated and usually quite ornate, somewhat like the clocks of the period. As dialmaking became well established, it became necessary to make dials at relatively low cost to sell them in any quantity, perhaps to compete with the large quantities coming from France. From around 1700 onwards, the majority of the dials produced in Augsburg were of a common pattern with only minor stylistic differences between them. They were mass produced, often quite simply, by a small number of workshops. There were, however, a few makers that specialised in the finer type of dial, often using silver as their main material and with some parts of their dials beautifully gilt.

Christoper Schissler (ca. 1544 -1609) was one of their earlier makers and perhaps the most famous. Although an Augsburg man he moved to Prague for some years, so some of his instruments are from that era.

The dial illustrated was made by him in 1604. It is neatly engraved around its periphery **CHRISTOPHORVS SCHISSLER SENIOR FACIEBAT AVGUSTAE AD 1604**. It is a standard horizontal Compass Dial in a round case. On its base is a Lunar volvelle for telling the time of the Moon and tides.

Dials are also known from his son, Hans Christoph who worked with him in Augsburg and Prague.

AUGSBURG STYLE DIALS

The commonest form of dial produced, and in considerable quantities, was the Universal Equinoctial Dial. In fact, it is this type of dial that

5.6 CM DIA

Compass Dial by Christopher Schissler (senior)

Signature around the edge of the Schissler dial

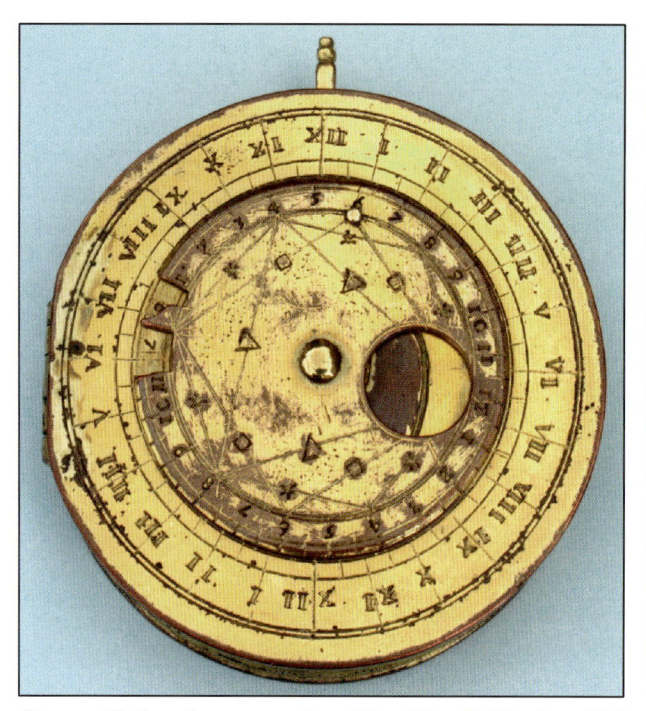

CHAPTER 15 AUGSBURG DIALS

Lunar Calendar on underside of the Schissler dial

The finely decorated lid of the Schissler dial

is most commonly found by those scouring antique shops or fairs for portable dials. It is universal because it could be used in most parts of the Northern Hemisphere, usually covering a range of latitudes from as low as 10° to 85° or more, and equinoctial because the hour divisions were of equal length, both Summer and Winter. The earlier and finer versions of these dials were made by two notable makers, Johann Willebrand and Johann Martin. These dials, made around 1700, were normally made in solid silver with some of the parts being mercurial gilt. The art of mercurial gilding was particularly dangerous and many of the workers employed to do this lived very short lives. The process involved mixing one part of gold to eight parts of mercury. This mix would then be heated until it united. The amalgam was then put into a chamois leather bag and the surplus mercury was squeezed out. The brass, copper or silver article to be coated, would then be rubbed with the amalgam until it adhered. It was then placed in a charcoal fire in order to evaporate the remaining mercury. This left a thin layer of gold on the surface that would then be burnished and polished. This gilding process was used quite commonly throughout Europe at this

5.4 × 5.8 CM

Typical silver dial from Augsburg made by Johann Willebrand, ca. 1700

108

Chapter 15   Augsburg Dials

Underside of the Willebrand dial with list of towns and their latitudes

attached inside the lid carrying an expanded list of towns and latitudes.

Later in the eighteenth century this design was taken up by several workers who turned out quite large quantities of the 'Augsburg Dials'. One of the simpler of these by Lorenz Grässl is shown in the Preface to this book. These dials, in common with most produced at this period, were constructed over a magnetic compass to allow correct alignment of the dial. Their compass bowls were normally marked with a line showing the local magnetic declination. See Appendix 4 for methods of dating these dials by compass declination. The dials were usually supplied in small leather cases for carrying safely in the pocket. Luckily, a few of these have survived and still protect the dials within them. To enable the dials to fit properly into their case, they were made so that each part, the chapter ring, its gnomon, the latitude arc and often a stand with a plummet could be folded flat against its body. For the travelling gentleman, the underside of the compass bowl was normally engraved with a short list of European towns with their latitudes. In addition to this list engraved on the dial, many dialmakers provided, within the dial's case, a

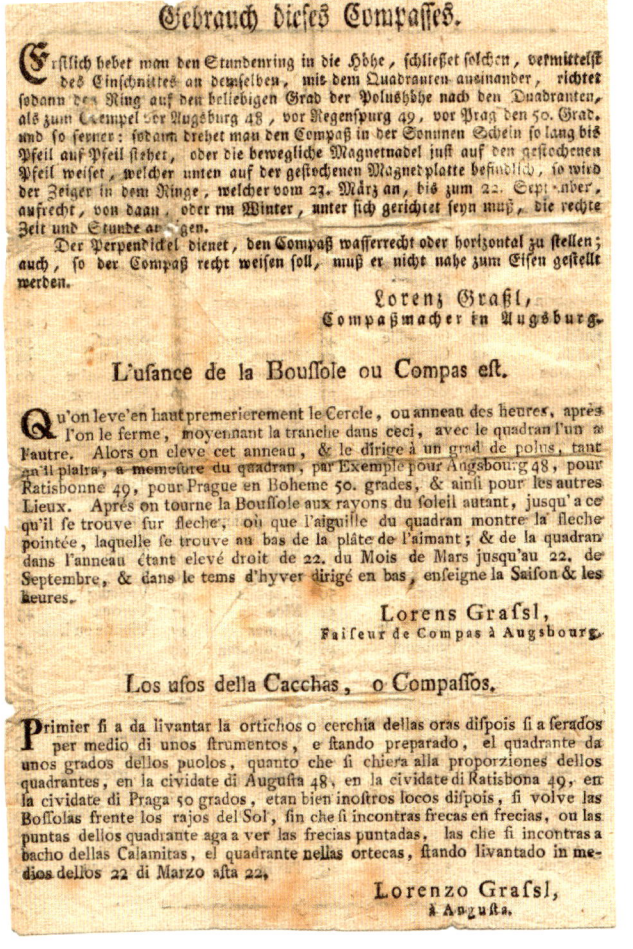

time. Augsburg was a centre famous for its many finely gilt products. The cases for these higher quality dials were normally made from leather and some had a silver or silvered brass disc

Printed sheet supplied with a dial by Lorenz Gräßl showing a list of towns with their latitudes. On the reverse are instructions for using the dial in German, French and Spanish

Chapter 15 Augsburg Dials

7.4 × 7.4 cm

Dial by Andreas Vogler with an attractive lyre-shaped Chapter Ring

Underside of the Vogler dial

fitted to enable these dials to be correctly levelled for use. Two of the three could be unscrewed by a small amount so that a precise setting could be achieved. In most instances, these dials would have simply been held in the hand giving their owners merely a rough indication of the time.

The main horizontal plate of most dials was made from a brass casting. It was then further decorated by engraving and sometimes by fretting. The compass bowl, the chapter ring, the latitude arc and the pin-like gnomon were usually silvered. This was a matt silvered finish that made the dials easier to read, being a good surface for showing the contrast of the shadow.

All of these later Augsburg style dials were relatively simple and were only intended to display the hours, unlike dials from many other parts of Europe that would often include both astronomical and astrological information.

Evidence given by file marks on many of these dials show that they were made in small batches. Such file marks would enable individual pieces of each dial to be identified during the printed paper sheet detailing the latitudes of many more towns and on its other side instructions for using the dial, often in three different languages, German, French and Spanish. Almost identical printed sheets were supplied by most of Augsburg's dial makers, the only real difference between them being the maker's name.

An interesting and attractive variant on the 'standard' Augsburg Dial was made by Andreas Vogler. Instead of using the commoner round chapter ring, he favoured a lyre shaped design.

Many of the Augsburg dials incorporate a simple plummet to aid precise levelling. This is suspended by a small folding frame at one end. Its small size precludes accurate alignment but it did provide some assistance to the owner when setting it up. Adjustable screw feet were often

Hinges of three Augsburg Dials showing the method of batch marking

110

CHAPTER 15   AUGSBURG DIALS

manufacturing process. From the marks seen on a selection of dials we can deduce that batch sizes would probably be between 5 and 20 at a time.

Most Equinoctial Dials are unusable for a few days on either side of each of the Equinoxes due to the fact that the chapter ring gets in the way, hiding the Sun's rays. During the Winter months when the Sun is low in the sky the shadow will only fall beneath the chapter ring. Consequently the gnomon must be erected in reverse so that it points downwards, although in practice this is not always possible at more southerly latitudes as it would probably hit the dial plate or compass glass.

In order to overcome the difficulties around the Equinox some makers removed part of the chapter ring. This would allow the Sun to reach the inside of the scale, at least for a few hours around noon. A dial of this pattern by Johann Martin is illustrated. It is of excellent workmanship being finely gilt and with silvering on the latitude arc, compass and the chapter ring giving a higher contrast for observing the gnomon's shadow. This dial is a snug fit into its leather case and has no towns engraved on its underside. This suggests that it was intended to be used whilst still

4.4 × 5 CM

An attractive silvered and gilt dial by Johann Martin

fitted into its case. A small list of towns with their latitudes has therefore been placed on its top plate.

A most unusual dial has been found that may be from an Augsburg workshop. Its general engraving and its compass are similar to those of many Augsburg Dials. Its body is finely gilt and the compass and gnomon are silvered. The gnomon can be raised and lowered, a little like that on Butterfield Dials. A limited latitude scale, 40° to 50°, is engraved on the gnomon, this being set against its gilt brass support. However, with only a single chapter ring, deviations from its design latitude, measured at 47.5°, will cause inaccuracies. From its magnetic declination marked in the compass bowl it is probably from between 1740 and 1760. The three levelling screws fitted to this dial make little sense without a plummet or spirit level and were possibly added later, because with these screws in place it is impossible to lay the gnomon flat for storage.

THE CRESCENT DIAL

This is a very interesting form of dial that was originated by Martin and Willebrand. These utilised two back-to-back crescents, although rarely one single crescent may also be found. The silvered double crescent arrangement is particularly attractive, the space between being

6.1 CM DIA.

An unusual dial attributed to Augsburg

CHAPTER 15 AUGSBURG DIALS

6.8 × 6.8 CM

Crescent Dial by Johann Martin

filled with ornate gilt scrolls. The easterly crescent was employed to show the scale of hours before noon and the westerly one for the afternoon. The gnomon, similar to a pair of horns, has sharp tips and is of minimum thickness to throw a fine shadow, especially at the 6am and 6pm points. It can moved up and down along its polar axis against a date scale so that the shadows produced by the fine tips of the gnomon would fall at the correct position. In use, once the date has been set, the dial would be rotated until the tip of one gnomon coincided exactly with the equatorial line of the hour scale. The design of this dial is similar to the Universal Equinoctial Ring Dial but here the ring has been divided into two halves. Therefore, it is a dial that does not use a compass for alignment and in consequence it is possible to take a reading from the wrong scale, especially around noon.

These dials are not common and most of those extant are to be found in museums. The pattern was occasionally copied by other dialmakers and examples are known from other areas of Europe, particularly France.

STRING GNOMON DIAL

This is another rarer form that was occasionally produced in Augsburg. Its style was quite individual and unlike other String Gnomon or Diptych Dials made in France or other parts of Europe. The string is attached to a folding arm, such that when erected the gnomon is taut and at the correct angle for the latitude. Unfortunately this String Gnomon Dial cannot be made truly universal, and in these Augsburg models there are several anchoring holes at the top of the folding arm to allow for a selection of closely related latitudes. In the silver and gilt example illustrated opposite by Johann Martin there is only one hour scale engraved, and this is for 48°, being the mid-point of the range of the possible string positions. This dial by Martin is housed in an octagonal non-magnetic metal case that is thought to be original. The narrow range of latitudes provided on this dial were hardly sufficient for the travelling gentleman and dials such as this were probably made for the more static members of the community.

The most important feature of this dial is its Lunar dial fitted inside the chapter ring. In use,

Chapter 15   Augsburg Dials

6.4 × 6.7 CM

String Gnomon Sun and Moon Dial by Johann Martin

Sun and Moon Dial by Johann Martin

Underside of the dial by Johann Martin

were quite inaccurate giving their users little more than the approximate time. Like most types of Lunar Dial, readings would only be possible in the bright moonlight produced a few days either side of Full Moon.

THEIR MAKERS

As already stated, there were only a few dialmakers recorded as working in Augsburg. Those makers producing the finest work were Johann Martin and Johann Willebrand. Dials of a similar quality and identical in style are sometimes found with the name Masig on them. This was not another Augsburg maker, but is thought to be a retailer of their products in London. [Zinner 1956 - p441] Johann Martin and Johann Willebrand were obviously making their dials without signature or with that of Masig on them for export. It is noteworthy this is rotated to the actual day of the Moon, found from an almanac, setting one of the **12** hour readings against it. The string's shadow from the moonlight falling on this scale will then give readings directly in solar time. Such dials that virtually all Augsburg Dials are signed. For this reason we may be reasonably certain that we know virtually all of the Augsburg makers. The same is not true of dials from many other parts of Europe.

CHAPTER 16

INCLINING DIALS

An Inclining Dial is any dial that is made for a fixed latitude but is capable of being adjusted to function at another latitude simply by tilting or inclining the complete dial (plate and gnomon). This technique has frequently been used so that an existing dial, usually a fixed Garden Dial, may be tilted to work at a different latitude. Certain makers used the same technique to make their portable dials universal, albeit over a relatively restricted range. This was normally done by providing the dial with a scale to enable this to be done simply. Such dials have the advantage that wherever they are placed on Earth they will

Engraving under the compass bowl

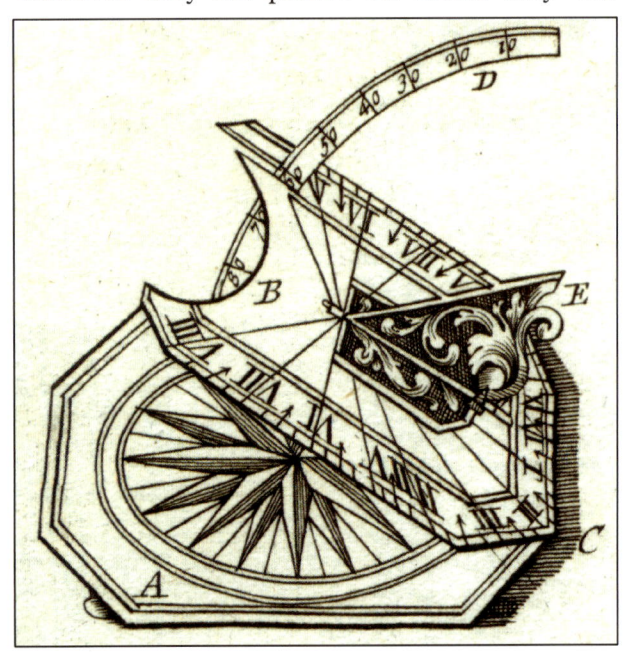

function exactly the same.

Most Inclining Dials were constructed for 60° North and would function as a 60° North dial at all latitudes, usually between the Equator and 60° North. However, there is no reason that the dials should not be constructed for any latitude and a dial by a Russian maker has been seen, delineated for 45° with its hinge at the opposite side of the plate giving a useful range of between 45° and 90° North.

Bion [Bion 1758 - Plate XXIV] illustrates an Inclining Dial in his book, but similar dials can be

An Inclining Dial as illustrated by Bion

Brass Inclining Dial by Edmund Culpeper

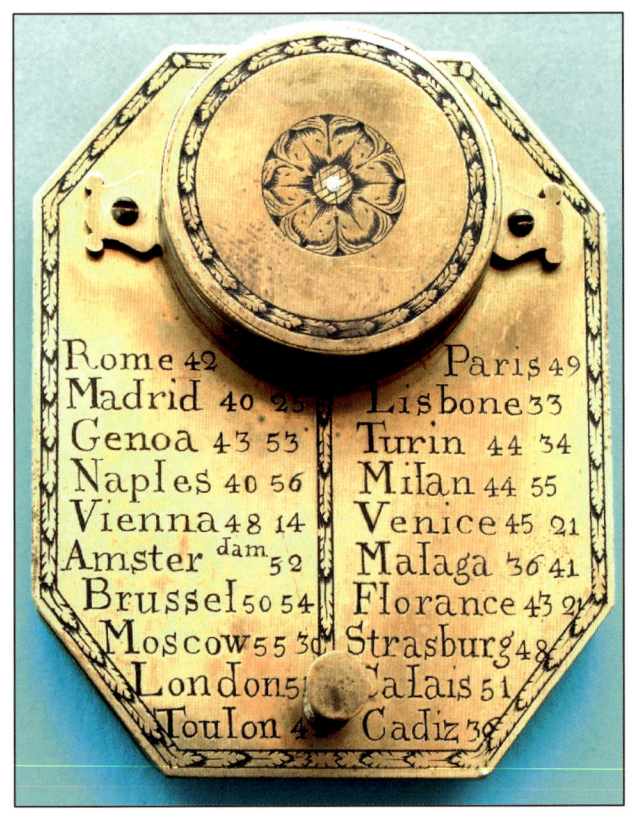

Underside of the Culpeper dial

114

CHAPTER 16 INCLINING DIALS

traced back to much earlier times. This type of dial was produced in both England and France. Although quite similar to the Butterfield Dial in its general styling, its function was much different. Edmund Culpeper is known to have made several such dials. His are in brass and of exceptional standard. Their accuracy was probably limited by the size of the compass used but such dials would probably indicate time to better than 10 minutes. Note his use of the English Rose on the base of the compass and the delicate 'wheat-ear' pattern around its edge to produce an attractive border.

Two other English dials of this type are illustrated. They are of a similar quality to those of Culpeper but are unsigned. From detailed studies of their engraving it is almost certain that both of these dials are from the same hand. Look particularly at the engraving on the spring for the latitude arc where the patterns are almost identical. The larger dial has an interesting mix of towns engraved on it suggesting that the owner lived in the Bewdley area and travelled to East Anglia. It is almost certain that this same maker was responsible for the two unsigned Butterfield Dials that were featured in Chapter 10.

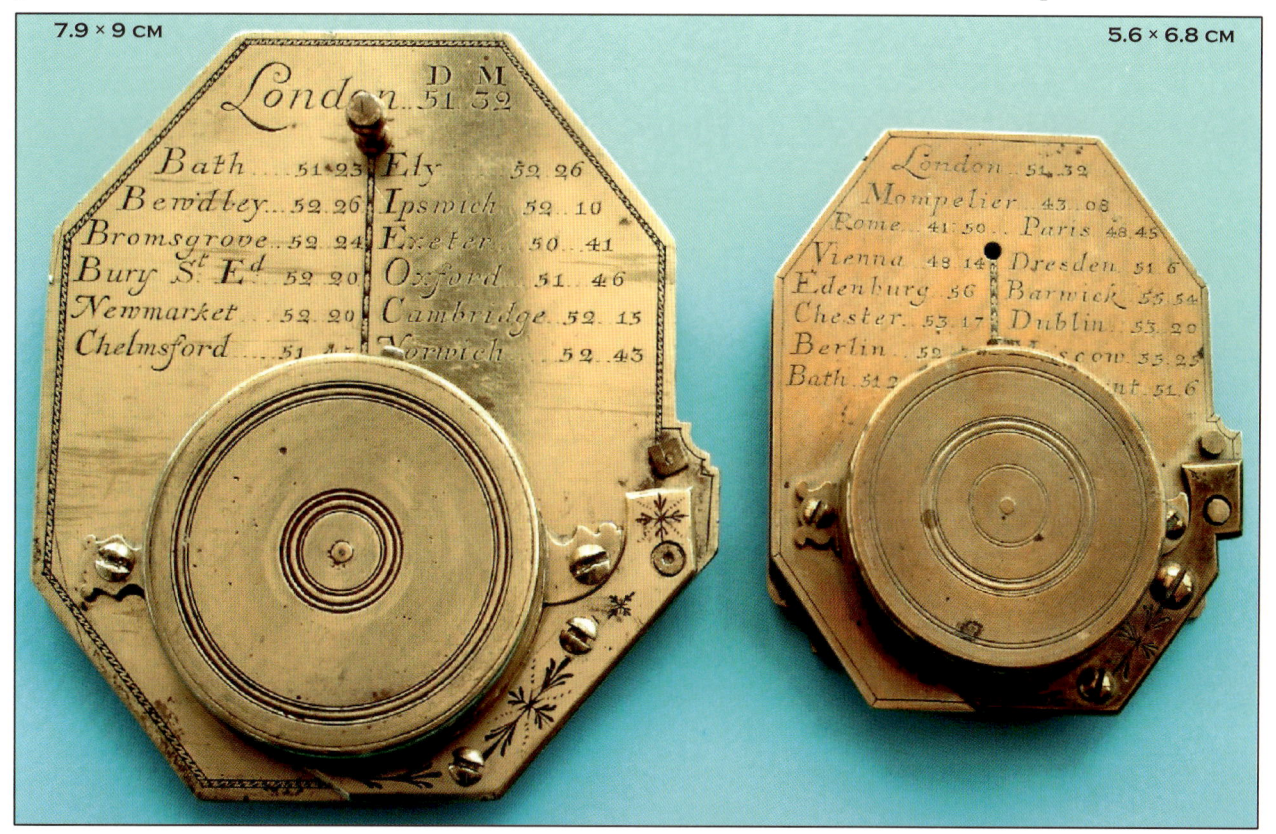

Two unsigned English Inclining Dials, both almost certainly by the same maker

English Inclining Dial

Silver Inclining Dial by Chapotot of Paris

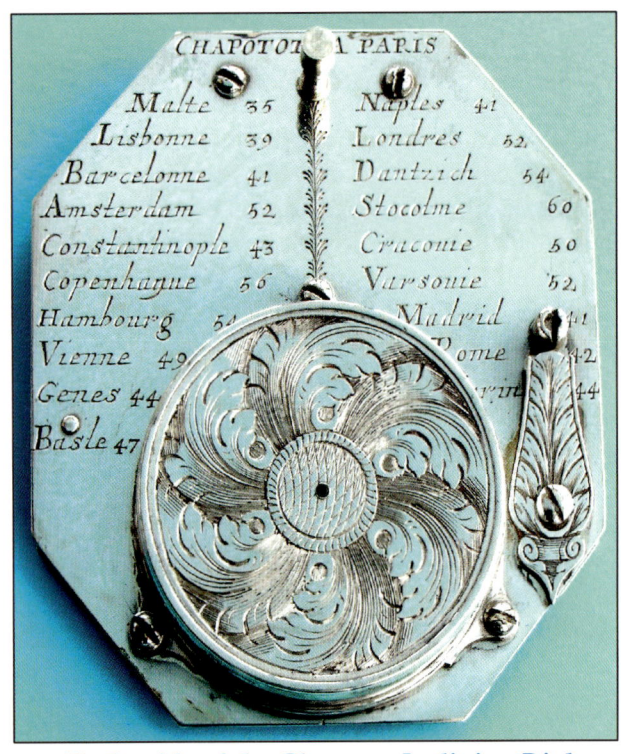

Chapter 16 Inclining Dials

Underside of the Chapotot Inclining Dial

Silver Inclining Dial by Macquart of Paris

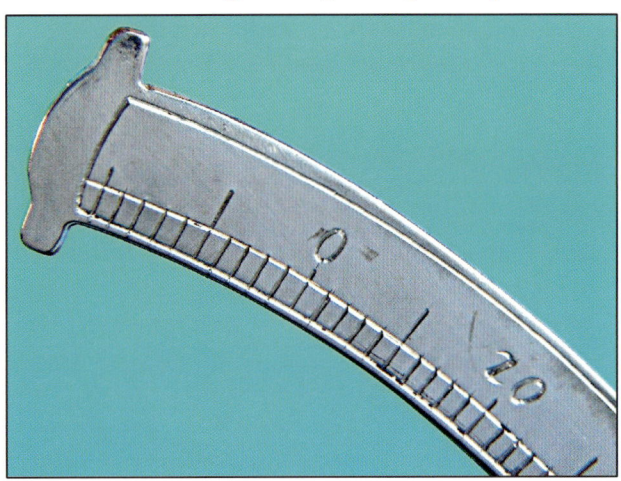

Extension of the latitude arc to include latitudes up to 10° south on the Macquart dial

English dials generally seem to be made of brass whereas their French counterparts were nearly always executed in silver. The decoration provided by French makers was much more flamboyant than the restrained style of their English counterparts. Two fine silver French dials are illustrated, one by Chapotot and the other by Macquart, both working in Paris. Note that the dial by Macquart can be adjusted beyond 0° latitude to cover a further 10° South of the Equator. This is achieved by making its latitude arm extend by these extra degrees. The only complication that this would cause is when used South of the Equator, it would restrict its usefulness in the times around sunrise and sunset. However, the extended latitude range available on this dial would be particularly useful as it could be used in French colonies, especially in Africa.

Note that Chapotot places the latitudes of the French towns prominently on the top plate whereas the foreign towns have been relegated to the underside.

The Inclining Dial was made later in London and took a completely different form. One example by Dolland was illustrated in Chapter 11 as it was typical of the many dials of this type made and

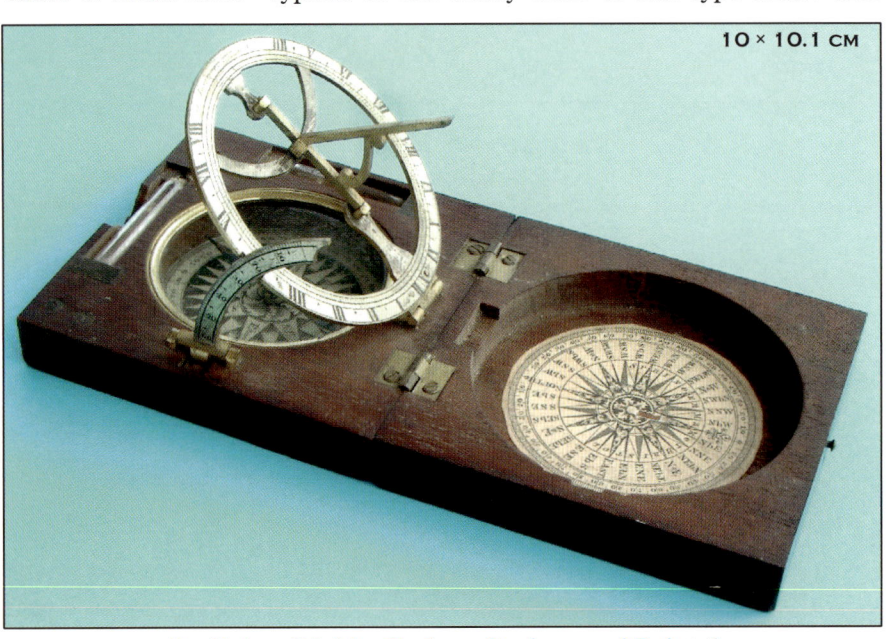

Inclining Dial by Joshua Springer of Bristol

116

Chapter 16 Inclining Dials

Compass of the Joshua Springer dial

signed **Springer BRISTOL** in the **E** and **W** compass points.

Another type of Inclining Dial is the Cube Dial. It is built for a fixed latitude but made adjustable by being mounted on a movable joint. Many of these were made in Germany between approximately 1720 and 1820. Polyhedral Dials too may be considered as Inclining Dials because many of these were mounted on a tilting joint to allow them to be set for an alternative latitude.

The Cube Dial illustrated is by David Beringer of Nuremberg. This dial was designed for a latitude of 45° North but is mounted on a hinged joint so that it can be used over a range of latitudes. It has five individual dials; direct South, direct East, direct West, direct North and a Horizontal Dial sitting on top. The dials are engraved on thin

these became almost a 'London' style for around 100 years. There is frequently some confusion between Inclining and Equinoctial Dials of this form. Several authors seem to mix the two. Although both appear to be Inclining Dials the Equinoctial Dial will have the gnomon at right angles to its chapter ring and will have the hours at equal 15° intervals, whereas the true Inclining Dial will have the gnomon at some angle, usually 60°, with unequal hour angles. Both the Inclining and Equinoctial Dials from London were frequently fitted with two transverse spirit levels to allow for accurate levelling.

Manufacture of Inclining Dials was not limited to London and eventually they were made throughout Britain for the local market, often by makers in seaports such as Bristol. A typical provincial dial, made around 1800 in Bristol, is by Joshua Springer. It is built into its own wooden box and can be erected quite simply with its lid opened. To improve the clarity of the shadow the chapter ring is silvered as on most English dials. In common with most dials of this period the compass has a paper scale and a separate compass rose is pasted into the box lid. Even its compass is

Silver Inclining Dial by J & W Watkins of Charing Cross, London

ivory plates glued to a wooden core. Cube Dials by Beringer are quite common and are normally made from a wooden cube but, unlike this model, they are usually fitted with paper scales, varnish protected. In most examples of Beringer dials, there is a plumb line hanging across either the East or West face so that the dial may be set at the correct angle against a latitude scale, but the dial illustrated does not have this scale. Its base has an inset compass for correct alignment.

Chapter 16   Inclining Dials

5.4 cm Cube

Cube Dial by David Beringer of Nuremberg made around 1750

CHAPTER 17 SCAPHE DIALS

The Scaphe Dial is relatively uncommon as a portable dial, probably because of its three-dimensional shape making it more bulky than other types of dial and therefore not very compact for the pocket. They were certainly used, and from very early times, as monumental dials, particularly by the Romans and Greeks.

The hollow form of dial is known as a Scaphe Dial from the Greek word skaphé, σκάφη, a bowl or a dug-out boat.

The Scaphe Dial featured here is made from brass. It is a full hemisphere with the spring loaded gnomon point set exactly at the centre of the sphere. It has to be spring loaded because the compass bowl pushes it backwards when the dial is closed. Once the dial is aligned with the compass, the shadow is formed inside the hemisphere to show the time on the vertical hour lines. This dial appears to be lacking its latitude arc with which to set the hemisphere at the correct angle, and there is evidence that this may have been fitted into the small slot on the compass plate and have been read from the right hand side of the hemisphere, where a small step may be seen. However, the dial will function quite satisfactorily without the latitude arc, and can be set such that the tip of the gnomon's shadow runs perfectly along the appropriate declination line, or at an intermediate point. When the dial is opened, the hemisphere drops below the level of the compass plate and it is not easy to support the dial on any flat surface, but it may quite easily be supported by the hand.

The compass too has some rather strange features. Around the edge of the plate are 32 'points', but these are not labelled. Inside this ring is a scale of hours, **I - IZ, I - IZ**, probably intended for use as a lunar conversion scale, but as such it is incomplete. The oddest feature is the scale to the left of the compass which is calibrated **90 - 0 - 90** to which a pointer on the side of the compass may be set. Similar scales were often used to allow the current magnetic declination to be set, but this never exceeded 26° in Central Europe, and that was over 200 years after this dial was made. It is possible that the maker had over-anticipated this feature. On the other hand, such a feature would have been

5.5 CM DIA.

Unsigned German Scaphe Dial in hemispherical case

CHAPTER 17 SCAPHE DIALS

Spring loaded gnomon inside the hemisphere

The compass with 32-points, a declination scale and a Lunar Dial?

Decoration of the outside of the hemisphere

Decoration of the underside of the dial

Another dial of a similar type is known that was made by Marcus Purmann of Munich, and that dial is dated 1588. The dial illustrated here may therefore be a little earlier, possibly as a trial piece but almost certainly from the workshop of Marcus Purmann. The engraving on the underside of the dial is very similar in quality to that on the lid of the Marcus Purmann dial shown on Page 130. The other Purmann Scaphe Dial shows a similar but shorter scale around the compass from **60° - 90° - 30°** and this is captioned **GRADVS DECLINACIO MAGNETIS**.

Scaphe dials are sometimes found on other types of dial, such as the ivory Diptych Dial. In this case, it is not a full hemisphere but merely a depression in the surface of the ivory. The dial illustrated below shows Italian Hours starting at sunset.

Scaphe Dial for Italian Hours, being part of an ivory Diptych Dial

useful to the (rare) traveller to Polar regions where variations could be of any angle, even showing a complete reversal in places. The dial is beautifully made, almost certainly in Germany. Its engraving on both outer faces is of the best quality.

Chapter 17 Scaphe Dials

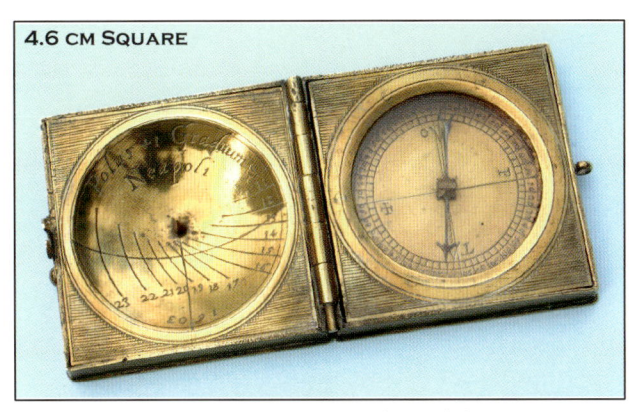

Unsigned Italian Scaphe Dial with compass, dated 1603

A similar dial in gilt brass is formed like a book. It has a scaphe in one half and the other half features a compass. The dial tells us that it was made for 41°, the latitude of Naples, and it is dated 1603. Like the last dial it is calibrated only in Italian Hours.

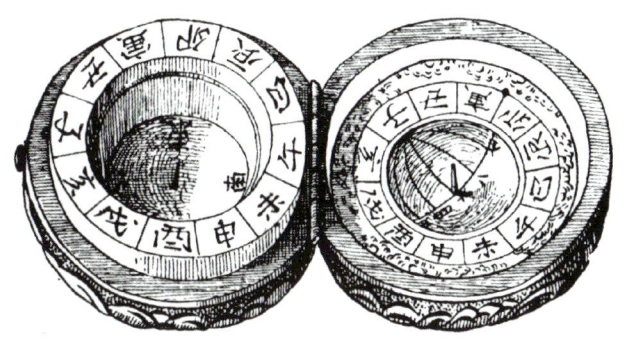

Silver Japanese Compass Dial

Other scaphe dials are often encountered on dials from China and Japan. The drawing of a Japanese dial shows it with a vertical pin gnomon. These are unequal hours with the day and night each divided into six 'Toki'. This system of time reckoning was used in Japan until 1 January 1873 when the European calendar and clock were finally adopted. For further details of markings and Japanese hour notation refer to Appendix 1.

Detail of the Italian Scaphe Dial

CHAPTER 18 ANALEMMATIC DIALS

The Analemmatic Dial is usually found in the form of a dual dial, being twinned with a Horizontal Dial on the same plate. The Horizontal Dial has its gnomon parallel to the Earth's axis and the Analemmatic Dial has a vertical gnomon adjusted to a position along a slot to agree with the current date. When both dials are mounted together on the same plate, an aligning compass is no longer required. The dial plate is simply turned on its horizontal axis until both dials read the same time. If both dials agree, then the time must be correct and the dial plate will automatically be set exactly North-South.

Bion illustrates a portable dial of this type [Bion 1758 - Plate XXIV] reproduced on the next page. Note that its style and decoration in many ways resemble that of a Butterfield Dial.

The Analemmatic Dial in this form is believed to be the invention of Thomas Tuttell (Tuttel) of Charing Cross in 1698. The gnomon for the Analemmatic section is sometimes a pin gnomon or sometimes in the form of a blade. Often the two dials are on two separate plates and are joined together by a hinge to allow for storage. This form of Analemmatic Dial, as with several other types of dial, notably the Ring Dial, does not give any indication as to whether the observed time is before or after noon. The user must use other clues to determine the correct setting or take two successive readings several minutes apart. Although these dials were necessarily made for use at one particular latitude they were frequently fitted with screw feet for levelling so that other near latitudes could be accommodated. In this case a small plummet will hang in the triangular

11.4 × 9.6 CM

Analemmatic Dial of the type made by Thomas Tuttell,
(its blade gnomon for the analemmatic section is missing)

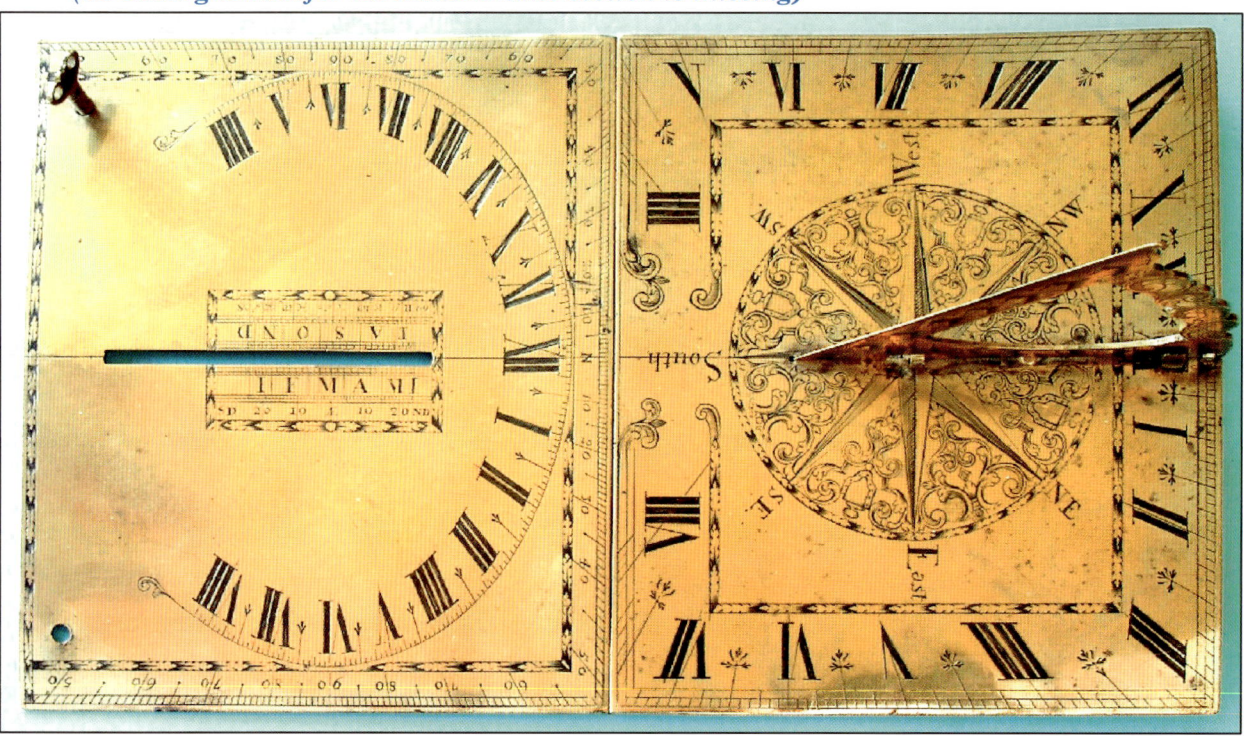

Analemmatic Dial, unsigned, but of the type made by Thomas Tuttell

122

Chapter 18   Analemmatic Dials

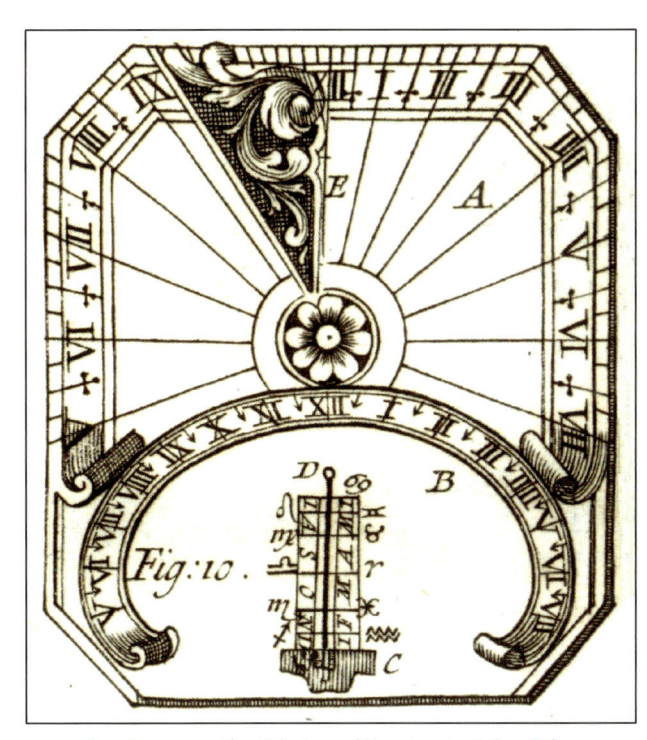

Analemmatic Dial as illustrated by Bion
[Bion 1758 - Plate XXIV]

cut-out section of the Horizontal Dial gnomon, its lower point indicating the angle of the plate

Analemmatic Dial by Gabriel Stoaks (Stokes) of Dublin

against the scale along its bottom edge. In practice latitudes of up to ±25° could be accommodated by tilting the dial. The sliding gnomon fitted to the analemmatic portion when set to the correct date can also indicates the angle of declination of the Sun and frequently it has a second scale showing the Zodiac degrees. On the reverse, where the gnomon protrudes through the plate is often a scale to show the hours of Sunrise and Sunset. These figures are, of course, only true for its manufactured latitude. Also on its reverse side there is frequently found a Perpetual

The oval analemmatic section of the dial by Gabriel Stoaks

123

Chapter 18   Analemmatic Dials

15.2 cm Wide

Substantial Analemmatic Dial by George Adams, London

Calendar showing Golden Numbers, etc. Further details of this part of these dials will be found in Chapter 25.

An Analemmatic Dial by **Gab Stoaks Dublin** is illustrated. It is similar to the Tuttell design but with no scales beneath. It is an attractive dial made by this uncommon Irish maker. It can be dated before 1752 because its calendar scale shows the Equinoxes as 11 March and 11 September. It also has corrections for the Equation of Time around the oval section of the dial. Note that its present analemmatic gnomon is a replacement.

The Analemmatic Dial by George Adams is a substantially made device with a normal Horizontal Dial on top that has a vertical back edge to the gnomon which acts as the analemmatic gnomon. This dial slides on top of the Analemmatic Dial to set this gnomon to the appropriate date. Inside the gnomon of the Horizontal Dial is a hinged spirit level (instead of a plummet) so that the dial may be tilted, using its levelling screws, to operate over a range of latitudes from 20° to 65°, and a further spirit level to set the dial level in the East-West axis. This dial still retains its original carrying case.

CHAPTER 19   MAGNETIC COMPASS DIALS

The Magnetic Compass Dial was introduced in the late eighteenth century, possibly in London. It consisted of a Horizontal Sundial for a fixed latitude mounted on a thin compass plate. The compass would automatically seek Magnetic North and the Sundial would immediately indicate the time without any adjustment being necessary by its owner. The dial plate was also self-levelling, being supported on a sharp pivot point. To protect the necessarily light and fragile assembly from wind deflection and finger damage, a domed glass cover was placed over the whole dial. These fragile glass covers are now frequently missing. The gnomon was still occasionally damaged against the domed glass cover through the action of inverting the dial. The dials also have the basic compass directions on the plate to give the direction as well as time, thereby having a dual function.

The dial by Fraser is a relatively early model of this type. It is substantially made and has clear scales. Performance was obviously expected to be good so its maker has included a detailed table for the Equation of Time around its edge. Similar dials by Fraser have been found, some with low angle gnomons made for tropical latitudes.

Although very simple to operate and virtually foolproof this type of dial had two major limitations. Firstly, it was made for a single latitude and was therefore unsuitable for long distance travel. Secondly, as the magnetic declination varied, the dial would need to have its compass adjusted. Fraser solved this problem by pivoting the compass magnet beneath the dial plate and providing a scale to set it by. A further long term problem for all compass devices was that with vibration in transit the dial plate would wear or even bend the pivot point. Fraser has also reduced these effects by providing a small lever that automatically lifts the dial plate off its pivot when the main cover is put on.

In the early nineteenth century this type of dial

Magnetic Compass Dial by Fraser, London, ca. 1800.
(Its domed glass cover has been removed for photography)

CHAPTER 19   MAGNETIC COMPASS DIALS

Top view of the Fraser dial with Equation of Time values around its edge

Magnetic needle showing method for adjusting the compass for varying magnetic declination

was being made by several makers including S. Porter and Essex & Co, who produced them in London around 1825.

One of the better dials by Porter in a turned ivory case is illustrated. This dial has lost its protective glass and the tip of its gnomon is broken off. The paper dial plate, mounted on card, is printed with the words '**S. Porter Fecit Feb^y, 16, 1824**' and '**Entered at Stationer's Hall.**' A label with similar wording is found pasted inside this dial's screw-on lid. The decoration around the dial plate is interesting showing a snake devouring its own tail and a sketch of Old Father Time with his scythe and hour glass.

Unlike the Fraser dial, magnetic declination is

5.2 CM DIA.

Ivory Magnetic Compass Dial by S. Porter, ca. 1824. (The top section of its gnomon is missing).

126

Printed dial plate of the Porter dial

Detail of Porter's signature and Old Father Time

Underside of the Porter dial plate showing the compass needle fixing

Porter label inside the dial's lid

Unsigned Magnetic Compass Dial, thought to be made for use in Rio de Janeiro

5.4 cm Dia.

fixed, the magnetic compass magnet being attached by gummed paper beneath the dial card. A very similar dial, this time unsigned, is illustrated. It is almost certainly of English manufacture but has a low angle gnomon for about 22½°. Notice that the hour numerals run anticlockwise. This indicates that this dial was made for the Southern Hemisphere, and its latitude suggests Rio de Janeiro where there was a fairly large British population at this time. Inside its lid is pasted a label with the Equation of Time. This type of Magnetic Compass Dial was also made in Germany but again most specimens are unsigned.

Chapter 19   Magnetic Compass Dials

Equation of Time pasted in the lid of the Rio dial

Underside of the Rio dial showing re-use of paper

11.2 × 10.9 CM

Magnetic Compass Dial with thermometer

Detail of the carved ivory dial and thermometer

Simple dials of this type found their way into several objects. One that has been seen is the model of a lighthouse with the dial at the top and with a thermometer vertically down its front face. Another version is illustrated where the dial is encased in a square mahogany box, mounted in the centre of an ivory plate. It is surrounded by a thermometer calibrated in degrees Réaumur and degrees Fahrenheit. Other markings are applied to the thermometer scale such as **F** for freezing, **SH** for summer heat, **BH** for blood heat and **FH** for fever heat. It too has the Equation of time pasted inside its lid.

CHAPTER 20 — STRING GNOMON DIALS

Several String Gnomon Dials have already been described in earlier chapters such as Ivory Diptych Dials and some Augsburg Dials.

A dial utilising a string gnomon is relatively simple, the gnomon being parallel to the Earth's axis. Such a dial is easy to fold and fit into the pocket requiring no special handling of fragile parts. The string gnomon will, in many cases, throw its shadow onto both horizontal and vertical faces.

The first dial illustrated is made of silver with a gilt case. Like most dials of this type it was made for one particular latitude. Although unsigned and undated it was probably made in the sixteenth century in Europe, possibly Southern Germany. Its string gnomon, now missing, throws its shadow onto both horizontal and vertical faces. Note that the vertical face has an attractive gilt Sun's image just below the gnomon fixing hole. The 28 mm diameter body of this dial is made from rock crystal, a particularly transparent type of quartz, resembling glass. Inside it is a simple compass with a paper scale showing only one mark; that of North. With its lid closed, the outside of the dial is gilt with a large ruby placed attractively at its apex. For carrying purposes the dial is housed in a beautifully tooled

2.6 × 2.8 CM

Small early dial with rock crystal body

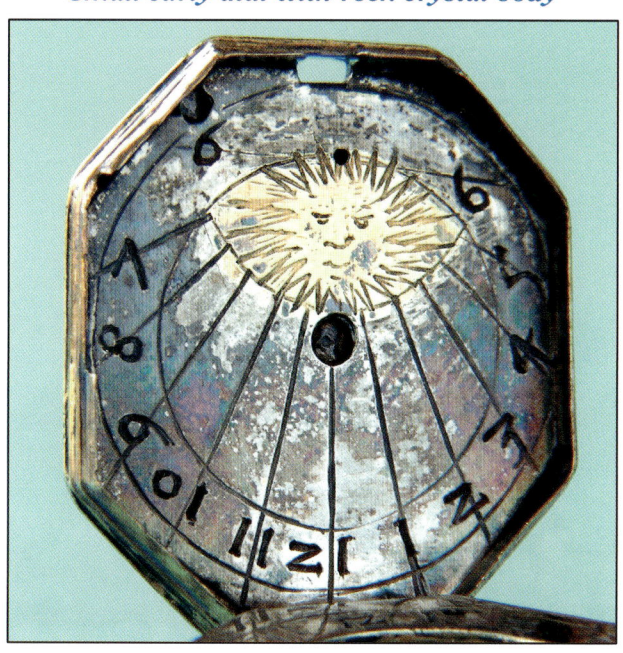

The gilt Sun's face on the rock crystal dial

Rock crystal dial with a ruby at its apex

Leather case for the rock crystal dial

Chapter 20 String Gnomon Dials

Top view of the dial by Marcus Purmann

3.8 × 5.2 cm

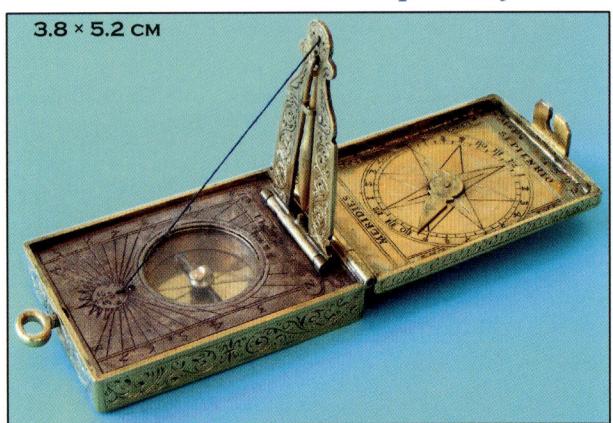

String Gnomon Dial by Marcus Purmann

leather case lined with green velvet. Around the lip of the box is some recycled paper with signs of red and green printing.

The dial by Marcus Purmann of Munich is signed simply inside the lid with his initials and date, ✸**M**✸**P**✸ **1593**. Its string gnomon is again only intended for a single latitude. The bracket holding the top end of the gnomon includes a long slender plummet for accurate levelling. Inside its lid is a twice **1** to **12** scale set around a compass rose with a central pointer. It could be used for recording wind directions or as a reminder of times of appointments etc. The brass case is mainly gilt with a silvered dial plate for better shadow contrast. The outside of the case is particularly well engraved with flowers, leaves

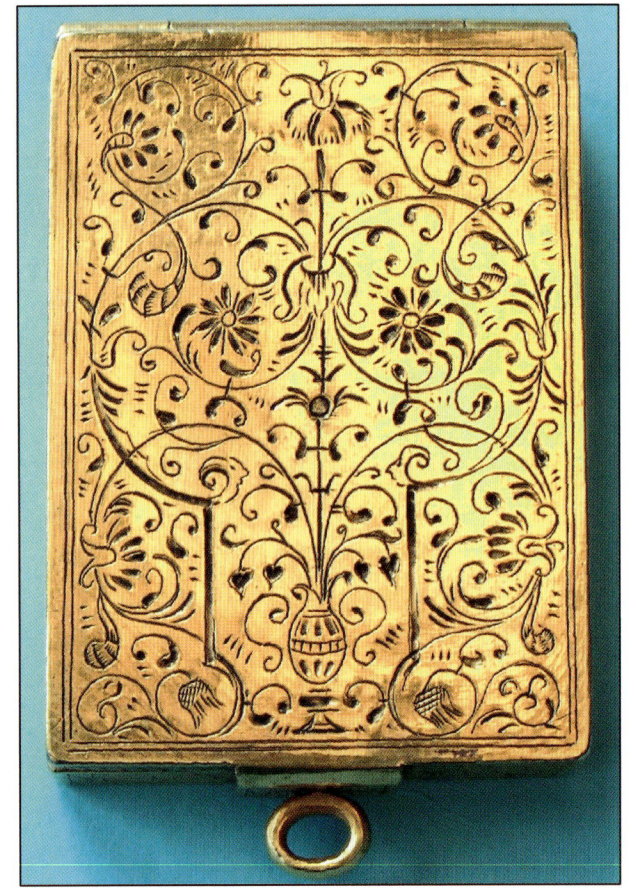

Lid of the Purmann dial showing engraving of a vase with flowers

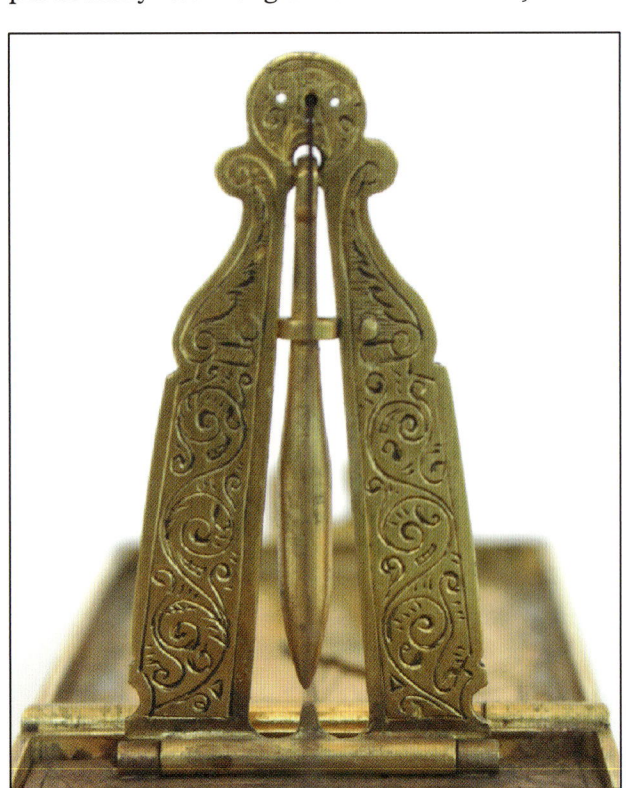

Gnomon support and plummet for the Marcus Purmann dial

130

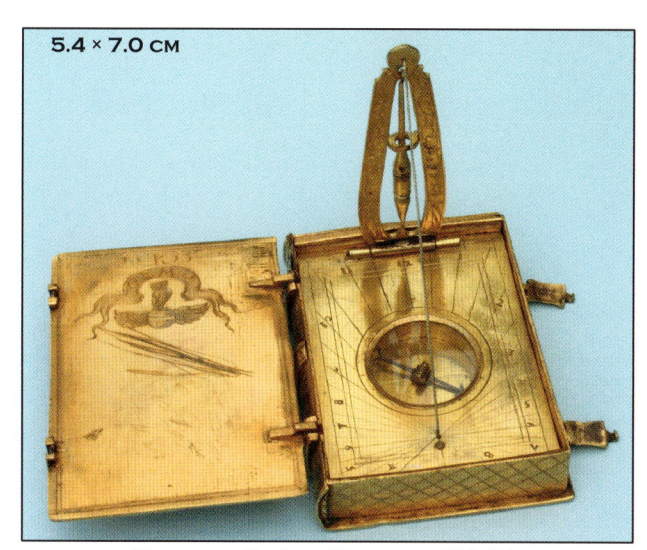

*German String Gnomon Dial in
the form of a book*

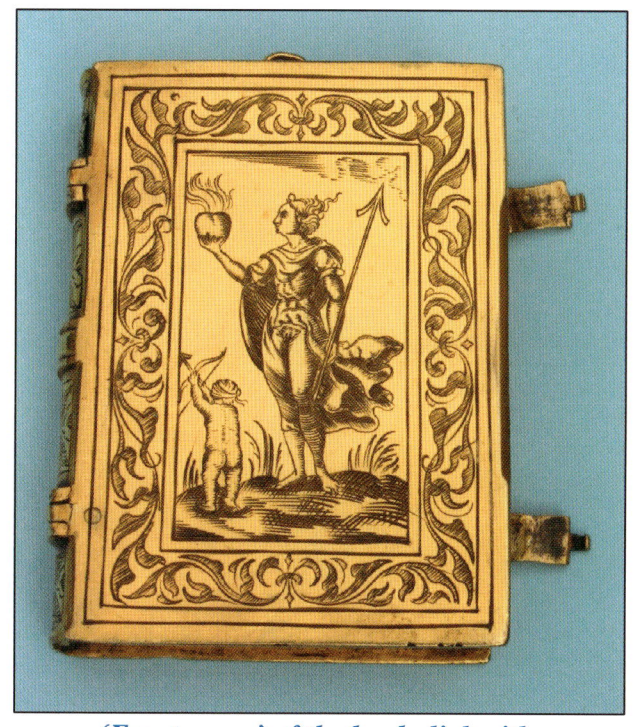

*'Front cover' of the book dial with
images of Venus and Cupid*

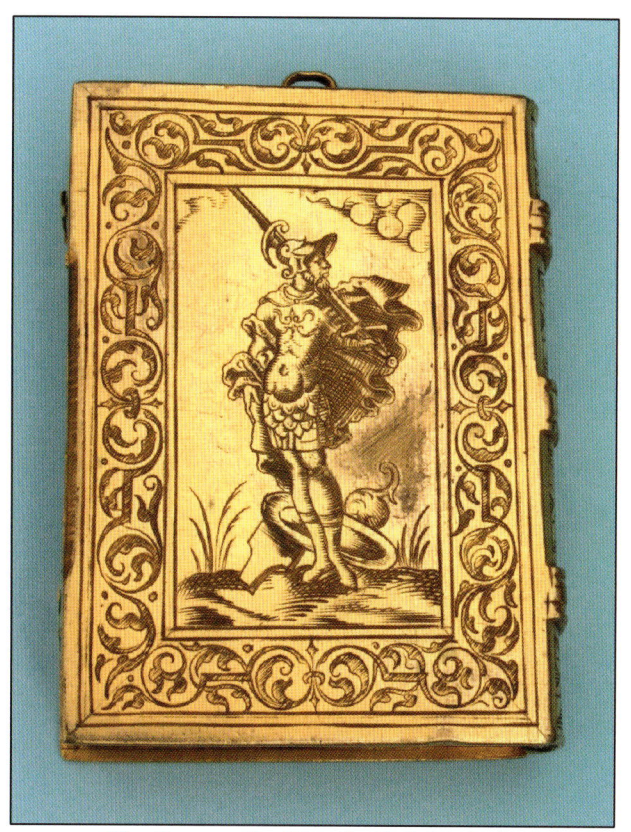

*'Back cover' of book dial depicting
Mars, the God of War*

and scrolls. Its lid is attractively engraved showing a vase containing flowers.

An unsigned String Gnomon Dial in the form of a book is obviously from the same region. It is dated **15 K 55**, the **K** possibly being the maker and it has further initials **GBMH** (probably those of its owner) inside the lid, above a hand and, what appears to be, a winged helmet. The outside of the case is particularly attractive showing Venus with a spear in her hand and a burning apple with cupid firing an arrow. On its back cover the figure portrayed is probably Mars, the God of War.

Occasionally a small String Gnomon Dial will be found on a Finger Ring. For use the lid is opened to reveal a very small magnetic compass and a tiny dial. It would be very inaccurate but probably a highly prized piece of personal jewellery. It would certainly be a useful gadget for the gentleman away from home and he would be sure to show such an object to all of his friends. With its lid closed it would look like any other ring.

A German dial simply signed **·S·A·V·Z·** and dated **Ao. 1643 KF** is illustrated. It has a beautifully gilt case with just the dial plate, decorative frets and plummet box silvered. It is particularly unusual in that it has a large plummet, something like the pendulum of a clock, contained in an upstanding box on the lid of the dial. Note the grotesque face on the plummet fret; probably that of the 'Green Man'.

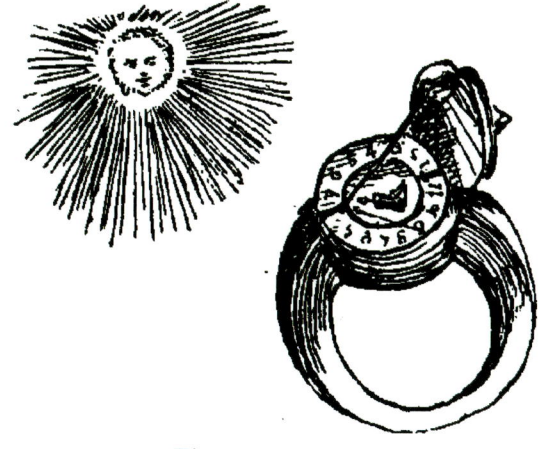

Finger Ring Dial

131

Chapter 20 String Gnomon Dials

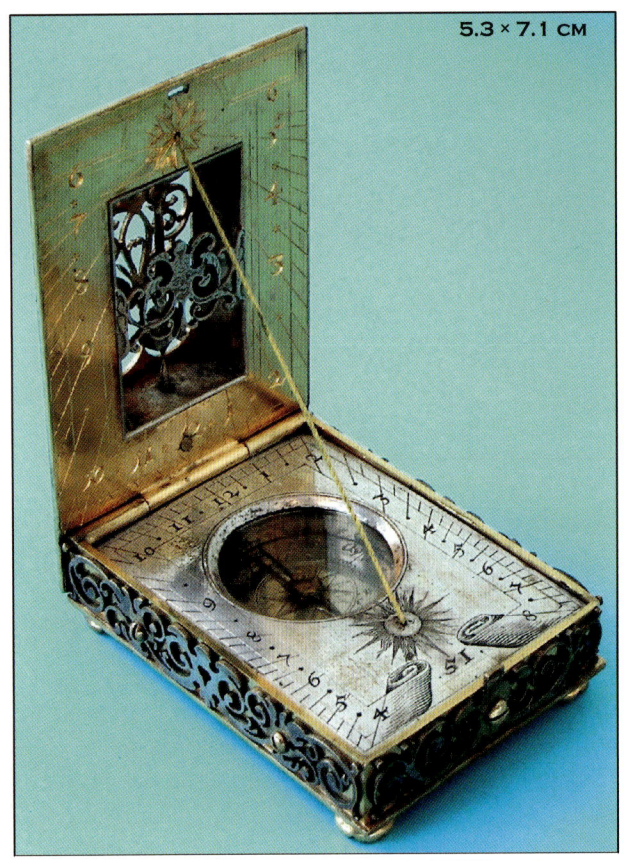

5.3 × 7.1 cm

Gilt German dial signed ·S·A·V·Z· 1643

Underside of the ·S·A·V·Z· dial showing the table for the length of day for each month

Overall the dial shows exceptional workmanship but its maker ·**S·A·V·Z**· has not been identified. Its underside is also rather interesting in that it shows a table for the lengths of the days and nights for each month and the times of Sunrise and Sunset.

The French oval silver dial shown is of an unusual construction. In many ways it resembles a Butterfield Dial but this one has a string gnomon supported by a spring loaded arm. The string is knotted at the top of the arm and is shortened by

Finely engraved and fretted outer case of the gilt German dial by ·S·A·V·Z·

132

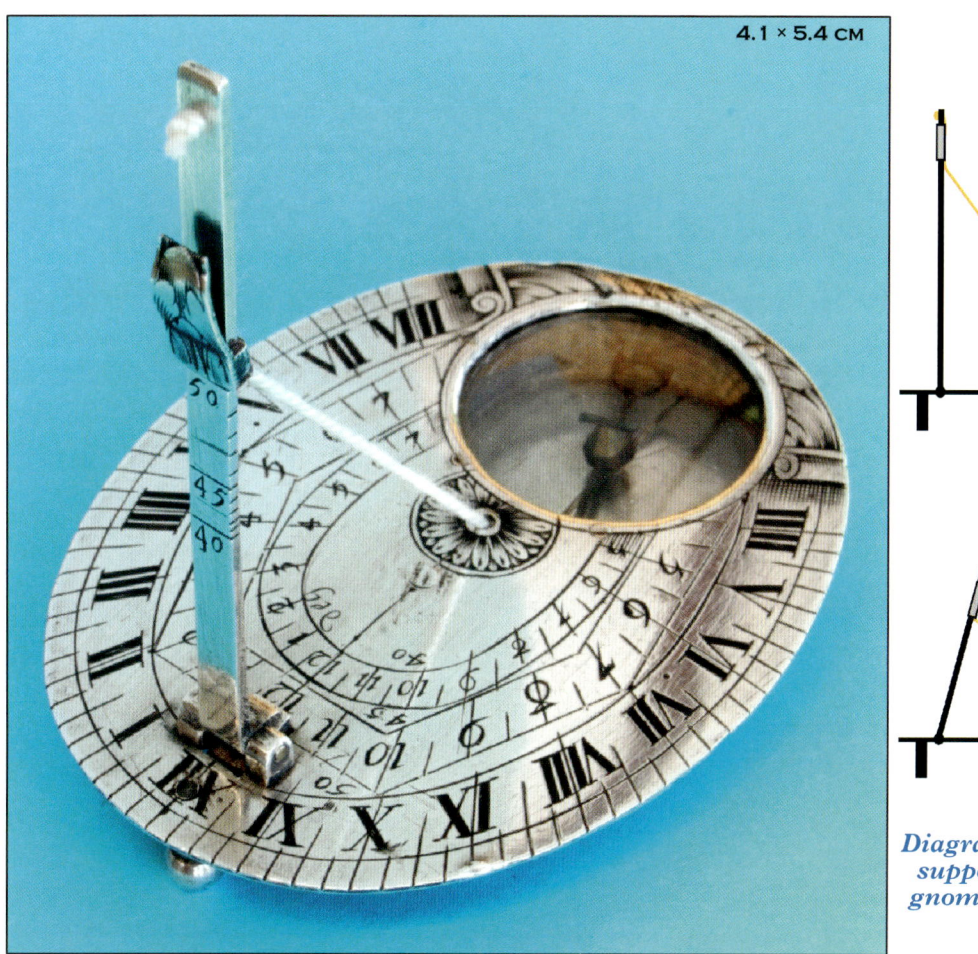

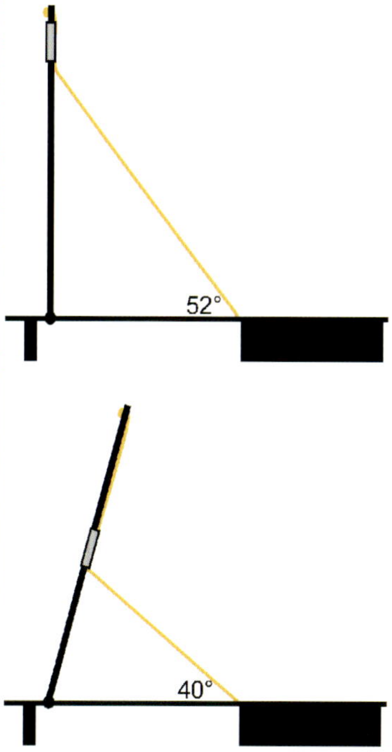

CHAPTER 20 STRING GNOMON DIALS

French oval silver dial with string gnomon set for a latitude of 50°

Diagrams showing how the support arm leans as the gnomon angle is changed

Oval silver dial set for a latitude of 40°

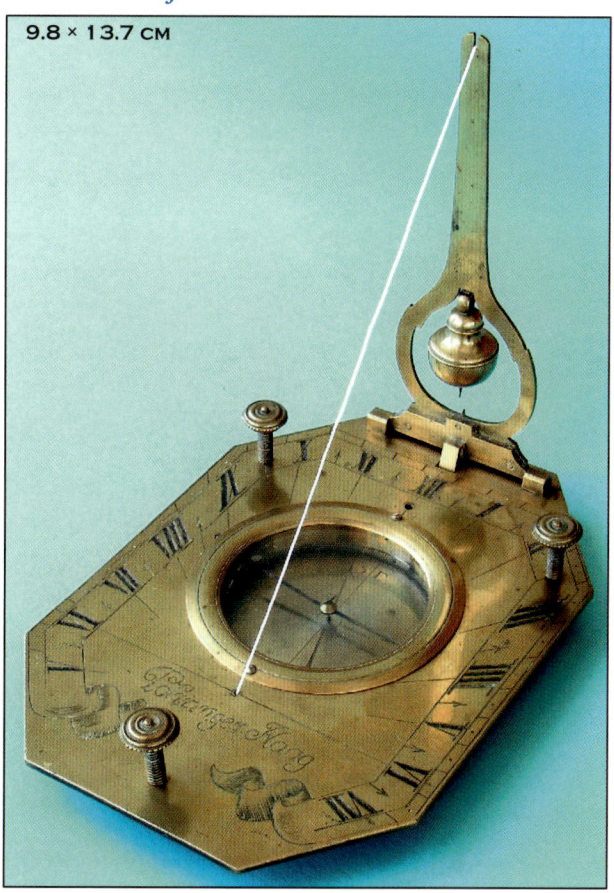

String Gnomon Dial signed Pohringer Haag

the sliding attachment when lower latitudes are required. Although a very convenient method of setting the dial for a range of latitudes, it depends for its accuracy on the correct length of string being fitted. Any stretching or shrinking of the

CHAPTER 20   STRING GNOMON DIALS

8.6 CM DIA.

Unsigned German dial with paper scales, mounted on card

Painted lid of the German card dial

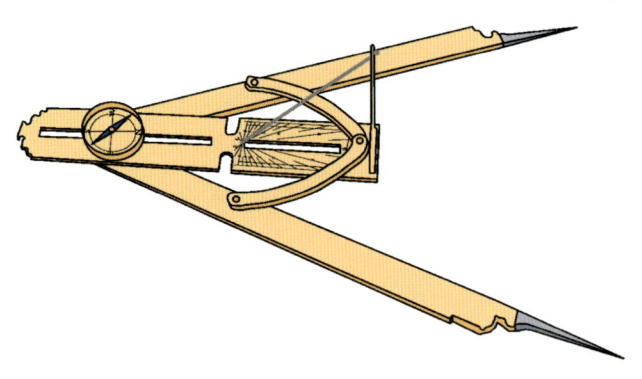

String Gnomon Dial on a pair of dividers

bob. For transit the bracket is folded down over the dial face and the plumb bob is screwed into a small tapped hole in the dial plate. The plumb bob and three levelling screws suggest that this dial should be capable of precise time recording, at least, when used at its intended latitude.

A German dial made principally of card with paper scales pasted on the surface is shown. It is a single latitude dial, and its vertical brass gnomon support needs to be inserted into a small wooden bush at **XII** o'clock before use. The decoration of the floating compass card is particularly attractive. The outer case is made from thin pieces of wood formed into a circle. Its lid is beautifully painted, almost in Chinese fashion, with a scene showing a sailing boat and a house.

Inside its lid is a card Perpetual Calendar. This is illustrated and explained in Chapter 25.

Dials will sometimes be found in most unlikely places. One by Habermel is sketched. It is on a pair of dividers with a folding support for a string gnomon. Several dials like this are known and the inclusion of a dial on a drawing instrument shows that it was made for surveying purposes; and was probably just one object from a box containing several instruments. Its rather small built-in compass would be used for dial alignment and for general surveying.

string will cause errors. It is difficult to calculate its length and this was almost certainly done empirically. Unusually for a French dial of this period (ca. 1700) the dial is not signed.

A brass String Gnomon Dial signed '*Pohringer Haag*' is illustrated. Its maker has yet to be traced but from its latitude and other features it is thought that the dial is of Scandinavian, possibly Swedish, origin. The string of the gnomon is draped over its top support, fitting into a small groove. It is held taut by the weight of the plumb

134

CHAPTER 21   TOWARDS PRECISION

Ever since the first sundial man has striven to improve the accuracy of his timekeeping. It has been shown in the earlier chapters how many types of dial have been invented, each subsequent type striving to improve on the former types either in its accuracy, lower cost or in its decorative appeal.

The Sun in the sky is a finite size subtending an angle of about ½° when seen from the Earth. This means that for every shadow produced there is an area of total shade (the umbra) and an area of partial shade (the penumbra). This area of indecision represents around 2 minutes on the average sundial scale. On the portable dial readings to this accuracy are seldom possible and as the dials get smaller the problem becomes even more acute. Various techniques have been tried to achieve an accuracy of closer than 2 minutes.

Naturally it is most important to know the exact latitude in order to set the dial correctly. The dial

How transversals can be used to read a dial with more precision

must also be set so that it is perfectly facing South, normally done by the use of a built-in compass. This is seldom accurate enough and a current magnetic declination figure must be used. The dial must also be set perfectly level, often achieved by the use of a built in plumb bob, or

Precision String Gnomon Dial by Franz Anton Knitl of Linz, ca. 1715   25.7 × 20.1 CM

135

Chapter 21   Towards Precision

Knitl Minute Dial.
The shadow of the string gnomon lies exactly along the central line marked on its arm

sometimes a spirit level. Finally the dial 'error' must be corrected by adding or subtracting the figure for the Equation of Time. With all of these points correctly set a way had to be found to improve on the basic two minutes of uncertainty.

One of the first techniques used was to add lines known as 'transversals' to the dial calibrations. These are essentially lines that go diagonally from one sub-division to the next, crossing an appropriate number of concentric circles in the process. The sketch on the previous page shows a dial sub-divided into quarter hours. The transversals have been added to each quarter, effectively dividing each of these by three allowing 5 minutes resolution without the clutter of extra lines.

The Knitl dial pointer reading a time of 8.08

Chapter 21 Towards Precision

7.9 CM DIA.

Universal Equinoctial Mechanical Dial by Thomas Wright, London. The time displayed is 12:09

relatively high intensity of sunlight against a shadow area, finding the mid point of a shadow edge is quite difficult.

A simple solution to this problem is to use a very thin gnomon, such as a string gnomon. With this it is relatively easy to bisect the now thin shadow and arrive at a fairly exact time. However, due to the fragility of a string gnomon very few precision dials used them. Another problem with such thin gnomons is that as the string slopes further away from the dial plate the shadow becomes less distinct.

An ingenious solution to this was found by Franz Anton Knitl who worked in Linz, Austria around 1715. He has used a string gnomon to throw its shadow onto a mechanical arm. The arm can be rotated such that the shadow of the string gnomon falls exactly onto a line inscribed on its surface. The other end of the arm is longer and effectively expands the scale by pointing to an hour scale on the opposite side of

Many makers took this process further and subdivided to 5 minutes with transversals indicating down to one minute. However, such a system is only as good as the observer who still has to estimate the mid point of the penumbra region of the shadow. In practice, with the

Large compass surrounded by a table for the Equation of Time on the Thomas Wright dial

Minute Dial display from the Mechanical Equinoctial Dial by Thomas Wright

137

Chapter 21 Towards Precision

The shadow of the gnomon near the fiducial line

also a small number of makers from Dublin. There are exceptions to every rule and a few dials of this type by Thomas Wright of London are known to exist. The details of this dial are worth description. Its base contains a large compass with a London magnetic variation of 14° West. Around the compass is engraved the Equation of Time and it is signed '**Made by T:Wright Inſtrumᵗ. maker to yᵉ KING**'. The chapter ring itself which is divided into the full 24 hours can be inclined for latitudes from 20° to 90°. Around the edge of the chapter ring are gear teeth that engage with a small pinion on the supplementary minute dial. Once the dial has been correctly aligned by the dial. The arm uses two pointers, one to indicate the hours and quarters and the other to point at two 2-minute scales, each displaced by one minute. The advantage of such calibration is that it is easier to resolve 30 divisions in an hour than 60. If the pointer lines up with a division line on one scale the minutes are even and the other line odd. This is probably the first type of dial capable of being read to an accuracy of one minute. It is not a pocket dial, due to its size, and was probably intended to be set up in a fixed position, just inside a window. It is certainly not suitable for mounting outside where it would be damaged by the weather. Knitl was a renowned maker of precision dials, many of them being Mechanical Minute Dials utilising gears driving a separate minute dial.

This type of dial is usually known as the Universal Equinoctial Mechanical Dial. It is not commonly found but when it is, it most often comes from the Central Europe. There were

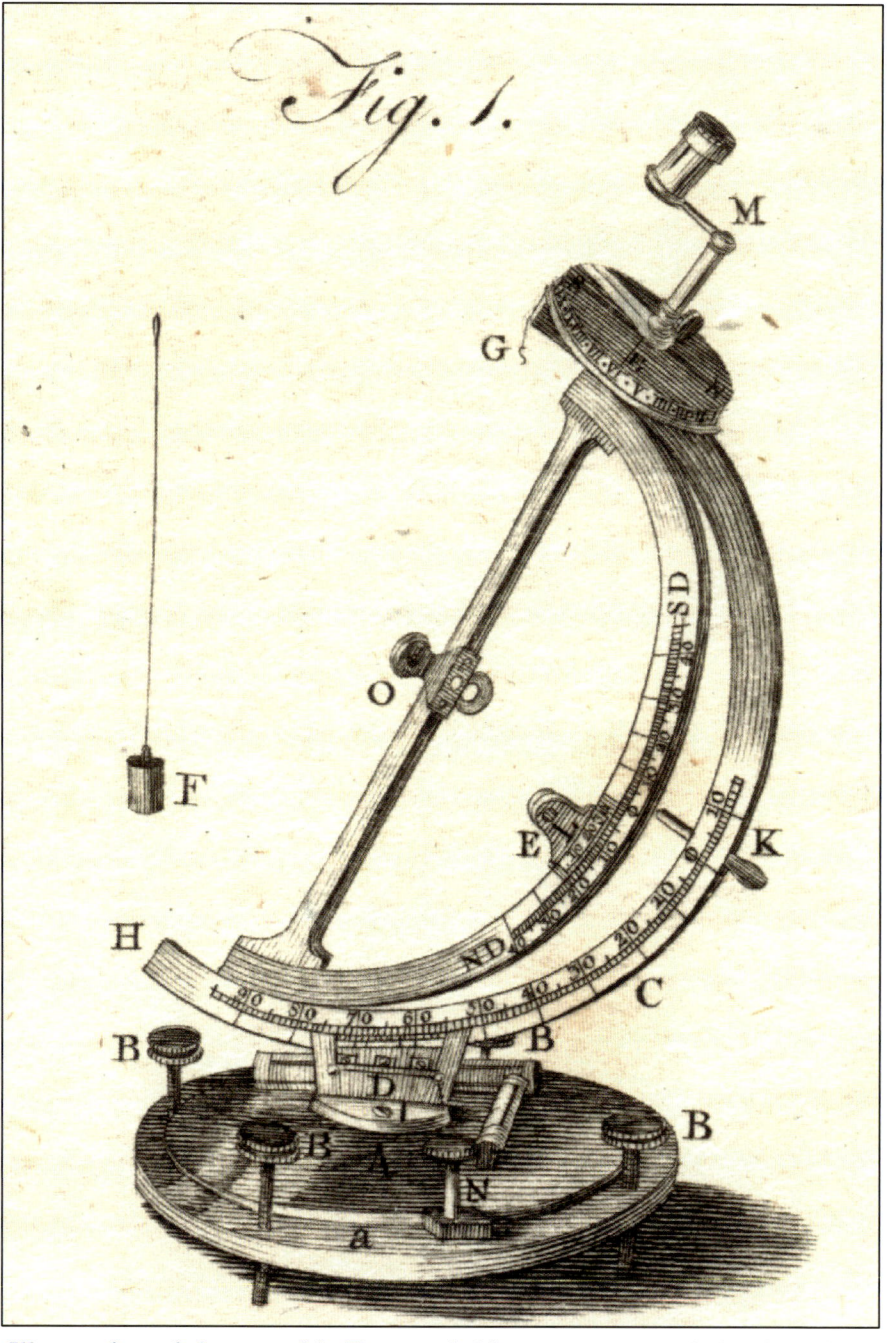

Illustration of the portable Equatorial Instrument made by G Wright

138

Chapter 21   Towards Precision

the compass to face South and with the correct latitude set, the small finger-like gnomon is erected. The minute dial assembly is then rotated around the periphery of the main chapter ring until the gonomon's shadow falls exactly on the line beneath the minute dial. The time is then read by combining the hour reading shown by the pointer on the main scale with the minute dial reading. Other dials of this kind have slightly different gnomon arrangements but their operation remains essentially the same.

A Portable Equatorial Instrument, or Universal Dial was invented by Gabriel Wright and was made by Benjamin Martin of London. It was described in a small booklet printed in 1781 which has detailed instructions for setting up the dial precisely for use. [Wright 1781] As a precision device it would not only tell the time to the nearest minute but could measure the user's latitude quite accurately. It could even be used for a range of surveying applications.

The overall view shows how the dial was made, with two

29.5 cm High

Portable Equatorial Instrument designed by Gabriel Wright, ca. 1781

Vernier scale for precise latitude adjustment

Detail of the four minute Vernier

139

Chapter 21   Towards Precision

Pivoted gnomon holes in the central bar

Hour scale on Wright's Equatorial Instrument

Use of the Dipleidoscope as illustrated in Dent's booklet

The Dipleidoscope as illustrated in Dent's booklet

large spirit levels, set at 90° to each other for precise levelling with its adjustable feet. Note that the pin, shown below, may be used for locking the two rings together when making latitude measurements. Unfortunately the sights on the fixed ring (for setting the Sun' altitude) are missing on this example as is the magnifier, shown on the drawing (looking like a handle on top) which assists with the reading of the hour vernier.

The time may be read from a relatively small dial set on the top of the instrument, with divisions at four minute intervals, but with the application of the vernier (or nonius) scale it can read to an accuracy of one minute.

The latitude scale too has its vernier allowing it to be set to five minutes of arc.

To use the instrument as a sundial it is set to the exact latitude and the meridian is found by observations of the Sun's altitude.

The booklet by Wright also gives tables for the Equation of Time for every day in the year in minutes and seconds. A further table is provided to correct for refraction, from ½° (in minutes and seconds or arc) to 90°, particularly important at low Sun altitudes. For example, with the Sun's altitude of ½° it needs a correction of 27' and at 1° it needs 24' 29".

There was little further improvement in solar timekeeping by portable dials until about 1840 when Edward John Dent introduced the 'Dipleidoscope'. His device was an accurate form of sundial that was capable of the measurement of the moment of noon to within seconds. It used prisms and formed two split images of the Sun that coincided exactly at noon as long as it was correctly set on the North - South axis. [Dent 1843] Although at first made by Dent it was later made by others under licence.

CHAPTER 22   MISCELLANEOUS DIALS

Several dials are shown in this chapter that do not conveniently fit into any of the former categories that have been discussed.

The dial shown here is constructed on the lid of a snuff box. Its numerals and decorations are punch marked and from its style and its fairly low gnomon angle, it possibly originates in Spain, although its numerals look Germanic. The small compass has a semi-circular lid for protection and its gnomon folds in one direction only. This would still leave it rather vulnerable to damage in a pocket. From its general style and numerals a date of late seventeenth century is suggested.

Snuff Box with a Horizontal Dial mounted on its lid

Polyhedral Dials are relatively rare, many of them originating in Italy. The drawing below shows a dial that is typical of these with multiple five sided dials. Most Polyhedral Dials did not have a compass so they were probably intended to be set

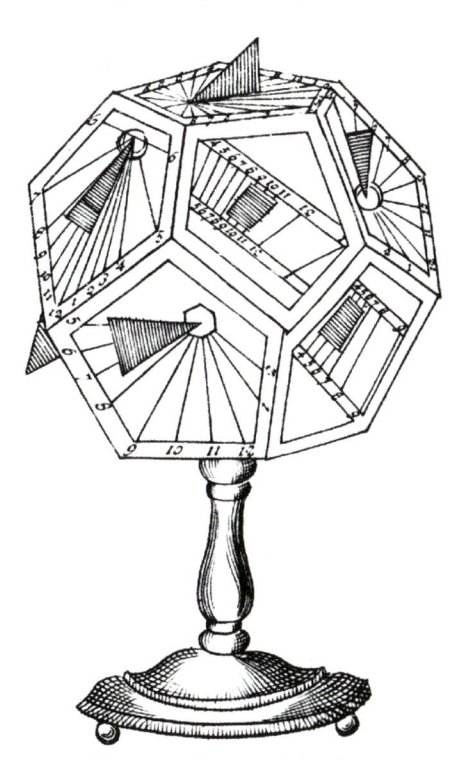

Typical Polyhedral Dial

A modern reproduction of a Polyhedral Dial

141

Chapter 22 Miscellaneous Dials

Typical French Noon Gun

Noon Gun as illustrated by Warrington Hogg[1]

up, semi-permanently, just inside a window. The inclusion of so many dials on one instrument was totally unnecessary and probably originated as a dialling exercise for their makers. However, they turned out an attractive item for their customers. Many of these dials were also made universal by placing a hinged joint on the supporting stem and a plumb line on one face or against a separate quadrant scale for latitude setting.

During the eighteenth century dials were produced that were mounted with a small gun or cannon. These were particularly popular in France. Above the cannon was a burning glass; its job was to ignite a small charge of gunpowder at the moment of noon to give an audible, as well as a visual, signal. These would have been great 'toys' for the gentleman and were seldom serious time telling devices.

The Pocket Time Indicator below was made in 1884. Its Instructions clearly state how the dial is to be used. **'Hold or place the card horizontally directed due north, raise the gnomon to a vertical position, and the shadow cast by the sun's rays will denote the correct solar time.'** It is printed on a folded sheet of card. Inside is a calendar for 1884. The remaining space carries some advertising so it was probably given away as a sales promotion

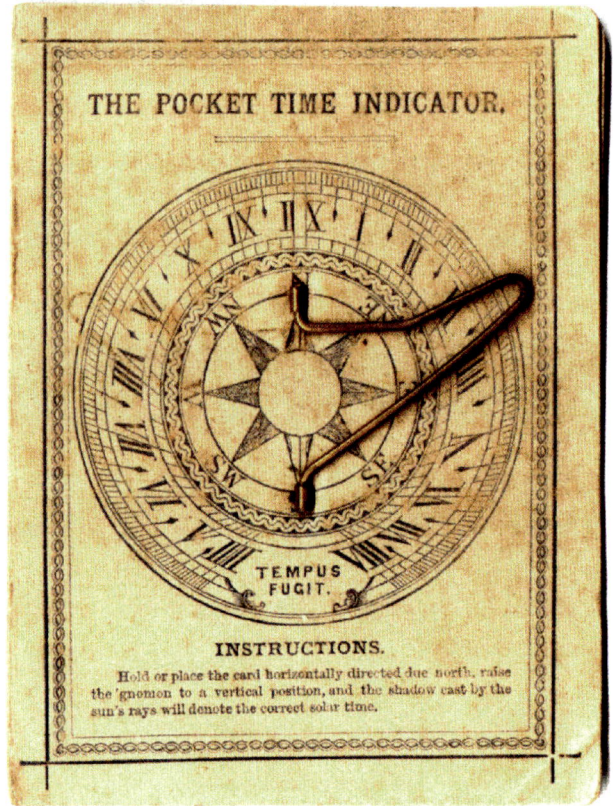

Simple card dial with folding gnomon

gimmick. This actual dial belonged to Eleanor Lloyd, co-author of Mrs. Gatty's later editions of 'The Book of Sun Dials'. [Gatty, 1901]

REFERENCES
1 Warrington-Hogg. The Book of Old Sundials and their Mottoes.

CHAPTER 23 — THE COMPENDIUM

Often called the Astronomical Compendium, these fine objects included several instruments in one case. They were usually they were made for the gentleman who wanted something really special with which to impress his friends. It is unlikely that many of these were used to their full extent, in some ways a little like the modern computer.

Most of the functions and scales included in a Compendium have already been discussed individually so, for complete details, reference should be made to each in turn.

known. The basic design of this type of Compendium was produced about 40 years earlier by Henry Sutton and it evolved over a period of years. Several of these Compendia by Whitwell are known and interestingly each are dated at two year intervals, starting 1600 and finishing in 1610. These other instruments, and some from other makers are illustrated in the book of Elizabethan Instrument Makers.
[G Turner, 2000]

The Whitwell Compendium itself is made of brass which has been finely fire gilt. Its central

Compendium by Charles Whitwell, 1608

The range of instruments included in a Compendium varied greatly from country to country and from maker to maker but the list below shows some of the more popular ones on English Compendia.

Equatorial Sundial	Magnetic Compass
Church Calendar	Tide Computer
Nocturnal	Latitude Tables

To illustrate the Compendium in this book, just one example has been used. It was made in London in 1608 by Charles Whitwell, a renowned and competent maker. He was trained as an engraver, and several plates by him are

instrument is an Equatorial Dial that is virtually self erecting as the Compendium is opened.

Face A. The lid has a Nocturnal, but this at first sight appears to be somewhat different to those normally found. In use, the pointer on the outer

Signature of Charles Whitwell on the underside of the chapter ring

Chapter 23   The Compendium

Top face of the Compendium showing the Nocturnal 'slot' for use with Ursa Minor

Face B. The underside of the lid has a Calendar for finding the date of Easter. This has two circles of numbers labelled **Epact** and **Prime**. Prime refers to the Golden Number for the year and Epact is the age of the Moon for that year. At the centre is the date with current Epact and Prime noted:

'1608 • E • 23 • P • 13 •'

Face C. When the Compendium is opened an Equatorial Dial erects itself above the hinge. The top side of its chapter ring is calibrated with the

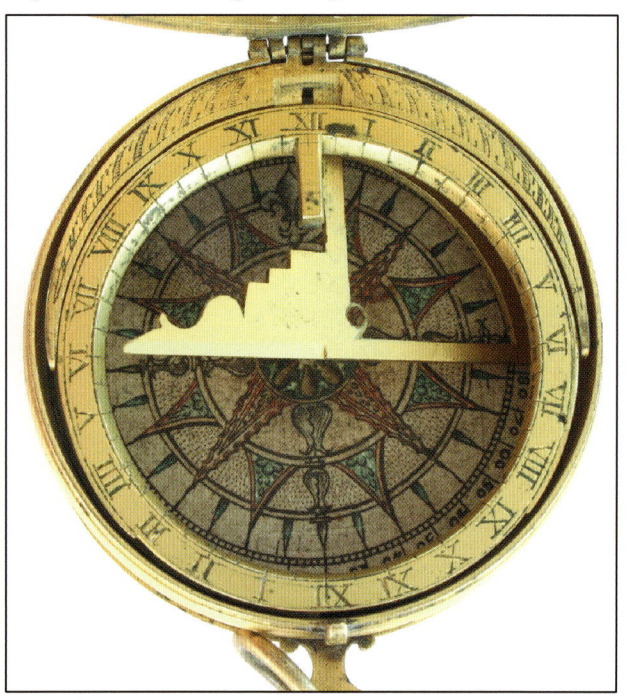

volvelle is set to the date on the outside scale. The lid is then opened and the stars are viewed through the slot, in the central section, that has enlarged holes at each end. In the centre hole will be Polaris (Pole Star) and then the volvelle is turned such that the outer hole will fit over the star Kochab in the Little Bear. The pointer will then show the time on the inner hour scale. Refer to Chapter 24 for details of Nocturnals.

Top of the chapter ring showing the 24-hour scale for the Summer hours

Underside of the lid with its calendar for finding the date of Easter

Underside of the chapter ring showing the Winter hours, VI - XII - VI

144

hours **I - XII, I - XII** covering a full 24 hours (Summer) and on its underside are just the hours **VI - XII - VI** (Winter). The full 24-hour calibration is necessary due to the fact that it is a Universal Dial which may be set to any latitude in the Northern Hemisphere. This is done at the lower edge of the gnomon which is furnished with a quadrant calibrated in degrees **0° - 90°**. Hanging from the centre of the dial is normally a plummet to be read against this scale, missing from this example. The lower tip of the plummet would point directly at the latitude angle and would also give a good indication that the user was holding the dial level. To prevent the quadrant rocking it is fitted neatly into a slot in the support ring, which incorporates a small brake pad, possibly made of leather, touching on its outer diameter. The chamfering of the ring at this point provides a clear indicator for setting the latitude.

The dial is mounted over a compass bowl (cover glass and needle now missing) with an outside scale of 360° divided into four quadrants. The card itself is marked with the 32 points of the compass. It is printed on paper from a plate engraved in Whitwell's hand and has been glued onto a backing card. It has been hand coloured in red and blue/green. Note the ornate ✠ on the east side indicating the direction to the Holy Land.

Face D. On the underside of the Compendium is a Tide Computer. With this it is possible to find the times of tides for any port. Sturmy explains its use and presents a working paper model of this computer in his book (see overleaf). (Sturmy 1679 - p7) The only difference between his model and the one by Whitwell is that the Moon's Age runs anticlockwise. This means that the two pointers need to be reversed. The setting of the Sturmy model illustrated is therefore: that on the 17th day of the Moon (*Luna* index) it will be roughly in the SE at 10 pm (*Sol* index). By knowing any two out of three of these facts, then

The latitude quadrant passing through the support ring, its outside edge pressing against a thin brake pad set into a slot below

Hand coloured compass card printed from an engraved plate by Charles Whitwell

Underside of the Compendium showing the Tide Computer

145

Tide Computer illustrated in Samuel Sturmy's Mariners Magazine of 1679

the third may easily be found. Furthermore, if the Tidal Constant for a place is known, its high tide may be computed. The Tidal Constant is either given in Hours or, as in earlier times, as a compass direction.

The small round window on the central volvelle of the Whitwell Tide Computer shows how the Moon would look at any time. It also has engraving for the 'Aspects' of Trine, Quartile and Sextile as described in Chapter 6.

CHAPTER 24 NOCTURNALS

A sundial may occasionally be used for telling the time at night. The famous dial at Queens' College, Cambridge has been provided with tables so that the shadow of the gnomon produced by the Moon's light can be converted to equinoctial hours. Many other dials, particularly portable dials, have additional lunar scales on them and may be used for time telling at night. One of these by Johann Martin is illustrated in Chapter 15.

However, there are several good reasons why telling the time at night by the Moon is not entirely satisfactory. The first is that the amount of sunlight reflected by the Moon's surface is only really sufficient to throw a visible shadow during the second and third lunar quarters, i.e., close to Full Moon. It is fruitless trying to take any readings for the remaining part of the lunar cycle. This problem is exacerbated in more recent times by light pollution from artificial sources.

The Moon's phases are normally divided, for convenience, into quarters. During the first quarter the Moon is nicely visible in the early evening. During the second quarter it is visible from sunset to early morning and in the third quarter it is visible from mid-evening to sunrise. In the fourth quarter it is only visible in the early morning hours. The Moon therefore is only of any practical use during its second quarter and for part of its third quarter for most people.

English fruitwood Nocturnal, ca. 1720

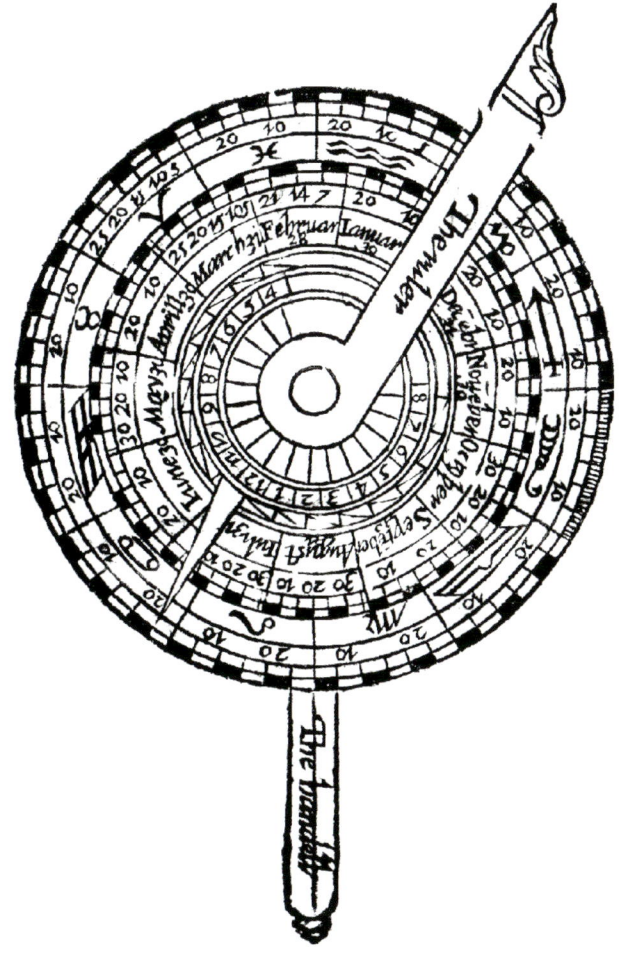

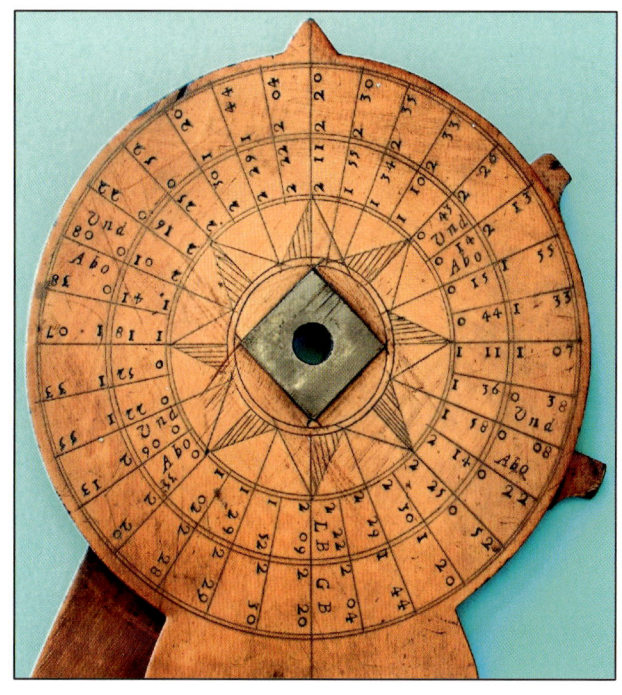

Nocturnal illustrated by Fale
[Fale 1652]

Reverse of fruitwood Nocturnal showing correction tables for GB and LB

Chapter 24 Nocturnals

Another complication arising is that the Moon's orbit varies over a period of about 19 years, being higher or lower in the sky depending on its position in its cycle. The Moon does not stay within the Ecliptic and therefore requires detailed correction tables if any real accuracy is desired. In the search for a means of finding longitude at sea, several astronomers tried to use the Moon, producing some very complex tables in the process. The Lunar Method, as we know, did not win the £20,000 prize originally offered by Queen Anne's government. This award was eventually given to John Harrison for his work on the development of his famous Chronometer.

The solution to finding the time at night was overcome by taking readings directly from the stars, a process simply achieved by the Nocturnal.

THE NOCTURNAL

This was a major step forward in time recording from objects unrelated to our Sun. Since early in man's history he will have noticed the stars moving each night, changing their positions to complete a full 360° rotation over a one year period. The stars could give us seasonal information, acting as a simple Calendar. The ancient Egyptians used the heliacal rising of Sirius as an indicator for the season of the Nile's flooding, telling them when to plant their crops. Basically the stars make an almost perfect clock, as they only rotate due to the Earth spinning on its own axis. The ellipticity of the Earth's orbit compared with the much vaster stellar distances is of no consequence, making corrections such as the Equation of Time unnecessary for stellar readings. The main problem is to find some point of reference from which to make any stellar observation. It seems that we on planet Earth are lucky to have one star, Polaris, which is currently positioned very close to our celestial North Pole. It is not exactly at North and its position is

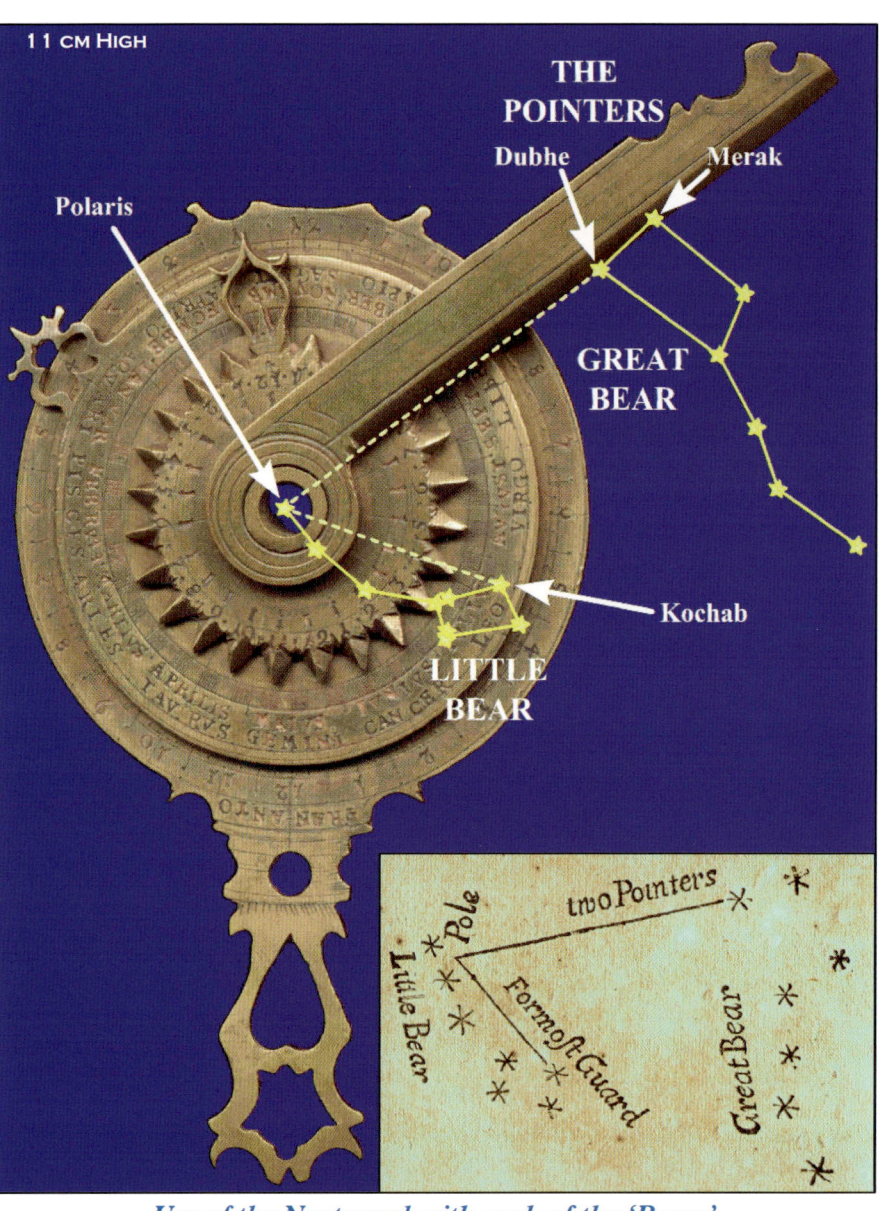

Use of the Nocturnal with each of the 'Bears'

changing slightly each year, but it has been conveniently close to this position for at least 1000 years. The Nocturnal makes use of Polaris for its basic reference. It is then necessary to find another star, away from Polaris, to give an indication of the Earth's nightly rotation. In practice two constellations are commonly used that have stars that are easily found and recognised. The first is the Great Bear (Plough or Big Dipper) with its two pointers, Duhbe and Merak. The other is the Little Bear (Little Dipper) with its bright star, Kochab. As the sky apparently rotates above the Earth once in every solar year, some method is necessary to apply a date correction to any reading. The Nocturnal solves all of these problems.

Many Nocturnals were made in the sixteenth and seventeenth centuries throughout Europe. Most of the English ones were made from wood (boxwood, yew, cherry, etc.) and as a

Chapter 24 Nocturnals

'Teeth' used to count the hours from the large pointer (midnight) by touch in the dark

Reverse of brass Nocturnal showing the Lunar Volvelle

'bear' has been chosen, the projection is set against a linear date scale on the main plate. A long arm is concentrically fitted that may be swung such that it lines up with the chosen 'bear' star(s). This arm is positioned directly over a 24-hour time scale enabling a time reading to be immediately taken. Normally, to read the device, some form of light is necessary. In the case of the fruitwood Nocturnal shown above, the scorch marks on its surface suggest that someone was rather careless with his light! To overcome necessity for illumination, on many of the metal Nocturnals, teeth or notches were used to mark the hours. These could be counted by touch away from the **XII** midnight tooth, which was often made longer or sometimes omitted. If more accurate readings were required, then a portable light was still necessary. Note that the Nocturnal chosen to illustrate its use is not dedicated to any particular stars. It may be used with virtually any convenient star by setting the pointer on the date volvelle to the Right Ascension for the star required. In the example shown (Page 148) RA has been set to 4 hours (left pointer) and the date at late November (top left pointer). The time may now be read (approximately 7:45 pm) from where the long arm crosses the teeth (top right). Note that the hour scale runs anti-clockwise because the observer has his back to the Ecliptic when viewing the Pole Star with a Nocturnal. An consequence relatively few have survived. Only a small number of these were signed, unless they were part of an Astronomical Compendium.

The Nocturnal usually consists of a main plate connected to a handle. In use, it is held vertically at arm's length, sighting Polaris through the hole in its centre. On its main plate is mounted a rotating volvelle, normally with two projections, one for each 'bear', 'GB' and 'LB'. Once the

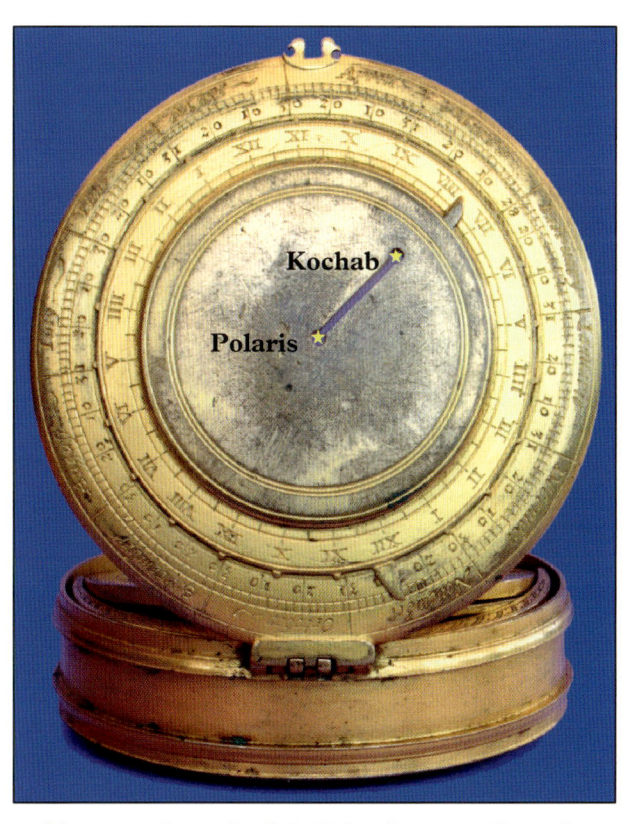

Nocturnal on the lid of the Compendium by Charles Whitwell used with Polaris and Kochab

149

Chapter 24 Nocturnals

Front of silver and gilt Nocturnal, German ca.1680

Reverse of silver and gilt Nocturnal, German ca.1680

interesting variant is seen in the Compendium by Charles Whitwell, 1608, described in Chapter 23. Instead of an arm to line up with the stars, he has chosen to use a slot with circles at each end. With the lid opened, the Pole Star fits into the central circle and the star Kochab of Ursa Minor at the other end of the slot.

The main sources of error from a Nocturnal are either due to the user not holding it quite vertically or from any error due to the position of Polaris. It seems that Nocturnals were never fitted with a plumb line or spirit level, but then it would be virtually impossible to see such a device in the dark. Other errors due to the wobble of the Earth's axis may be corrected by reference to a table sometimes found on the reverse of English Nocturnals.

The brass Nocturnal shown is signed simply **'FRAN ANTO'**. This was probably a monk, *Brother Anton*, working in some European monastery in the mid seventeenth century. On its reverse is a lunar volvelle. This allows time to be estimated from the shape of the Moon and, as can be imagined, accurate time measurement by this method was impossible. The Nocturnal was,

Early brass Nocturnal on the reverse of a Quadrant, probably for use with the star Alkaid

150

however, much more accurate and reliable than the Lunar Dial sometimes found on sundials.

A very attractive silver and gilt Nocturnal is illustrated. It was probably made in Germany a few years before 1700. This date can be ascertained from a small adjustment that allows a 10 day shift to be applied to the calendar scale. This setting depends on whether the older Julian or newer Gregorian Calendar was in use. The older Julian Calendar was finally superseded in Germany in 1700. (See Chapter 25)

An early brass Nocturnal, ca. 1600, is illustrated above that is found on the reverse of a Quadrant. (Its Quadrant side was illustrated in Chapter 5.) At first glance it seems virtually identical to other Nocturnals but on closer inspection it does not seem that it will function with either of the 'Bears'. A possible clue is on its central volvelle where **AL** is marked. This may refer to the star Alkaid, at the end of the tail of the Great Bear.

A Planispheric Nocturnal, rotated to match the position of the stars

THE PLANISPHERIC NOCTURNAL

A simpler form of nocturnal, often called a Planispheric Nocturnal, is sometimes found without the arm and it just has the common constellations marked on it. This is used quite simply by holding the star map up to the sky and rotating the volvelle until they both have their stars in the same position. As with other forms of Nocturnal, the most usual choice is to locate Polaris and the two pointers of the Great Bear. If this constellation is not visible due to cloud, then any other visible star can be used. The time is then read off from a date scale surrounding the volvelle.

The Planispheric Nocturnal is found on several types of instrument, most commonly the reverse of a Quadrant, but it is generally less accurate than the Nocturnal utilising the sighting arm.

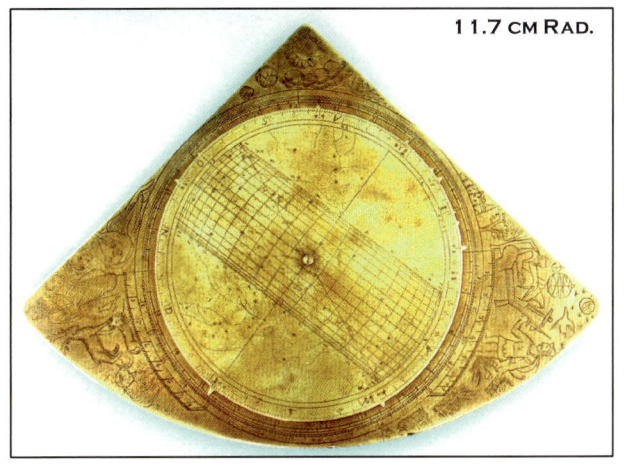

Reverse of a Quadrant by 'Nathanaell Heighemore' showing its Organum Ptolomaei incorporating a Planispheric Nocturnal

CHAPTER 25 PERPETUAL CALENDARS

Many pocket dials are found combined with Perpetual Calendars. The dial was therefore a combination of timekeeper and almanac. In order to understand fully the notation used for these Calendars it is first necessary to understand calendar systems.

The older Julian Calendar was introduced in 46 BC by Julius Caesar. His calendar system had small errors and in 325 A.D., Constantine I convened a council in Nicea to discuss, amongst other things, how the calendar could be corrected and to decide a fixed method for determining Easter. It had been realised for some time that the calendar was going astray and the beginning of the year was slowly getting out of synchronisation with the seasons. This was due to a small error that was corrected by changes to the times for inserting Leap Years.

By the year 1582 the calendar had again drifted by 10 days and Pope Gregory XIII introduced his new calendar which corrected for these errors. (His calendar is still in error by a small amount, being about 12 seconds longer than the Tropical Year, but this will only amount to an error of one day in 3323 years.) The Catholic countries immediately accepted the new Gregorian Calendar but, in Protestant lands, they were most unwilling to adopt anything that came out of Rome. For this reason many countries delayed accepting it until it became really necessary. Germany was a difficult case where each town or province could be either Catholic or Protestant. Therefore the two calendars had to run side by side for a long time. It was not until 1700 that the whole of Germany finally introduced the Gregorian Calendar. In Britain, we resisted the change much longer, until in 1752 by which time the error had increased to 11 days. When the change was made these 11 days were removed from the calendar and the day following September 2nd 1752 became September 14th. This caused widespread confusion and the population believed that they had been robbed of 11 days of their lives.

Before the change to New Style, the year in Britain began on 25 March (Lady Day), soon after the Vernal Equinox. It had already been realised that such a system caused confusion and therefore the year became reckoned in a slightly different way to satisfy both systems, i.e., those with the year beginning in January and those in March. As a result it is quite common to see dates in the early eighteenth century expressed in the form **1712/3** indicating that the event took place during the first part of the year of 1713.

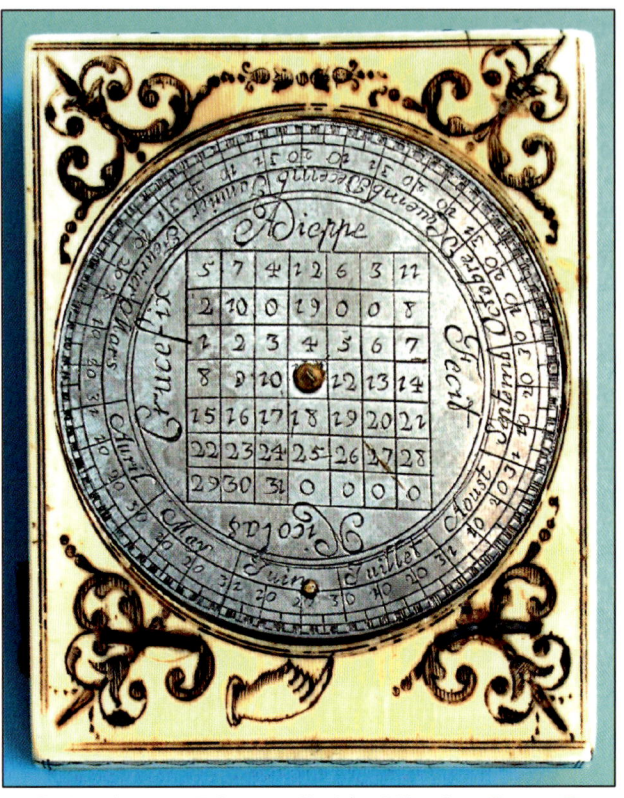

Calendar on Dieppe dial by Nicolas Crucefix

When looking at Perpetual Calendars we must first decide if they correspond to the older Julian system (Old Style) or the newer Gregorian system (New Style). It is also necessary to bear in mind the date for the start of the year.

One of the most important functions of any Perpetual Calendar was to predict the moveable feasts of the church, i.e., those relating to Easter. The calculation is quite complex but is related to the Moon. The basic rule for finding Easter is that it is the first Sunday following the first Full Moon after the Equinox, and if that day is a Sunday, then Easter is then deferred until the following Sunday.

A simple Perpetual Calendar is engraved on the date volvelle of many Magnetic Azimuth Dials from Dieppe. Similar calendars are to be seen on many other devices and these take a variety of forms, a few of which have already been illustrated. The table allows the user to find the day of the week for any day in a year.

There are seven lines of numerals, one for each day of the week. The first two lines of numerals represent the months of the year and the final five the actual date from 1 to 31. The first line starts with **5**, not May as in present reckoning but August (when the year starts in March, August is the fifth month). Therefore 7 is September, **8** October, **9** November and **10** December, exactly

152

Detail of Dieppe dial calendar

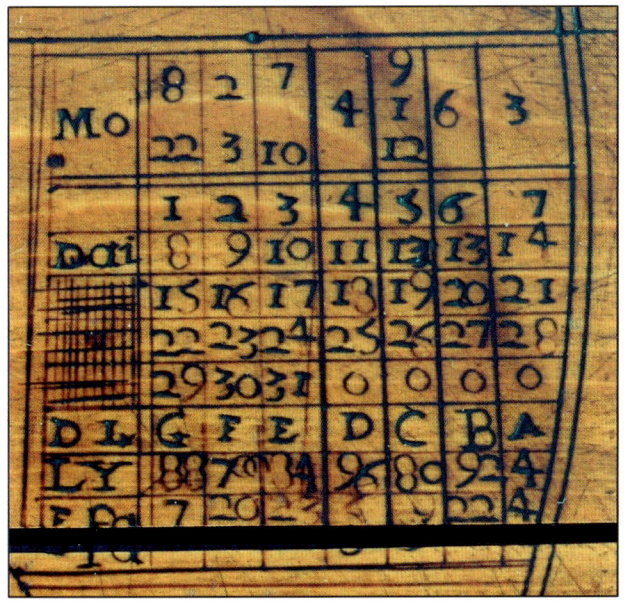

Calendar on wooden Quadrant, 1694

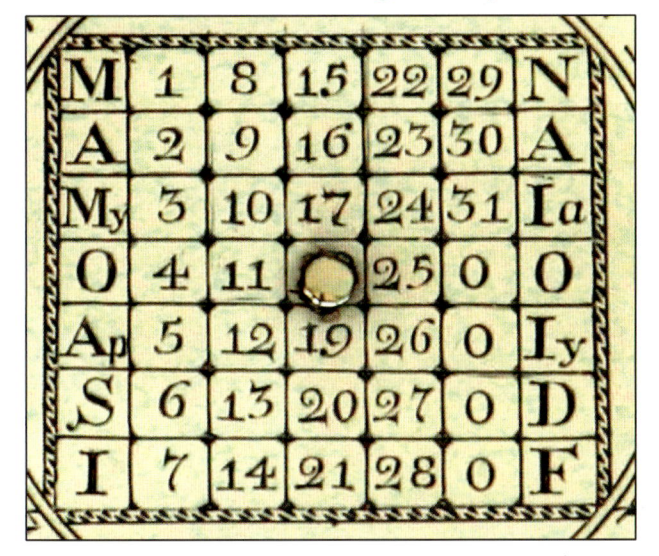

Calendar engraved inside the lid of the silver Compass Dial by Richard Glynn

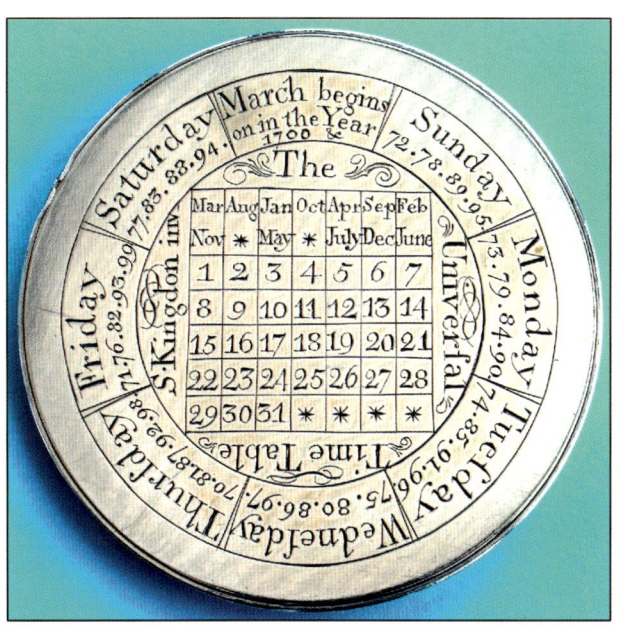

Calendar on lid of dial by J. Simons

as they ought to be from their Roman names. Confusion starts at month **19**. Actually it is not **19** but **1,9**. Both months, March and November, therefore start on the same day of the week.

Therefore once any day is known, any other day can be determined from it. Allowance for a Leap Year is of little consequence because it comes at the end of the last month, February. In the final line is a row of **0**s. These are just to fill unwanted squares but sometimes these spaces are used to show the year of manufacture or more rarely the maker's signature.

Other calendars are illustrated that use a similar Calendar Square. That on a Quadrant, dated 1694, has a couple of small errors. It has three extra lines of information **DL** = Dominical Letter, **LY** = Leap Years and **EPa** = Epact.

Perpetual Calendar that has been engraved on the reverse of a silver coin, 1715

Chapter 25 Perpetual Calendars

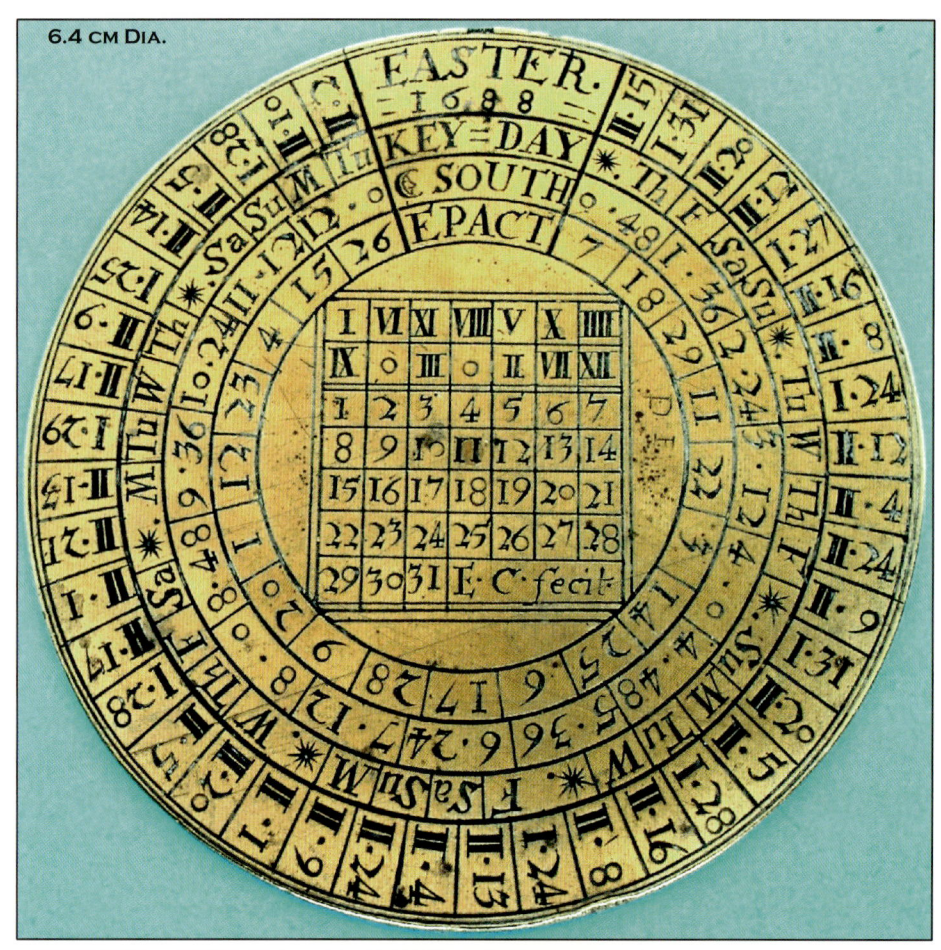

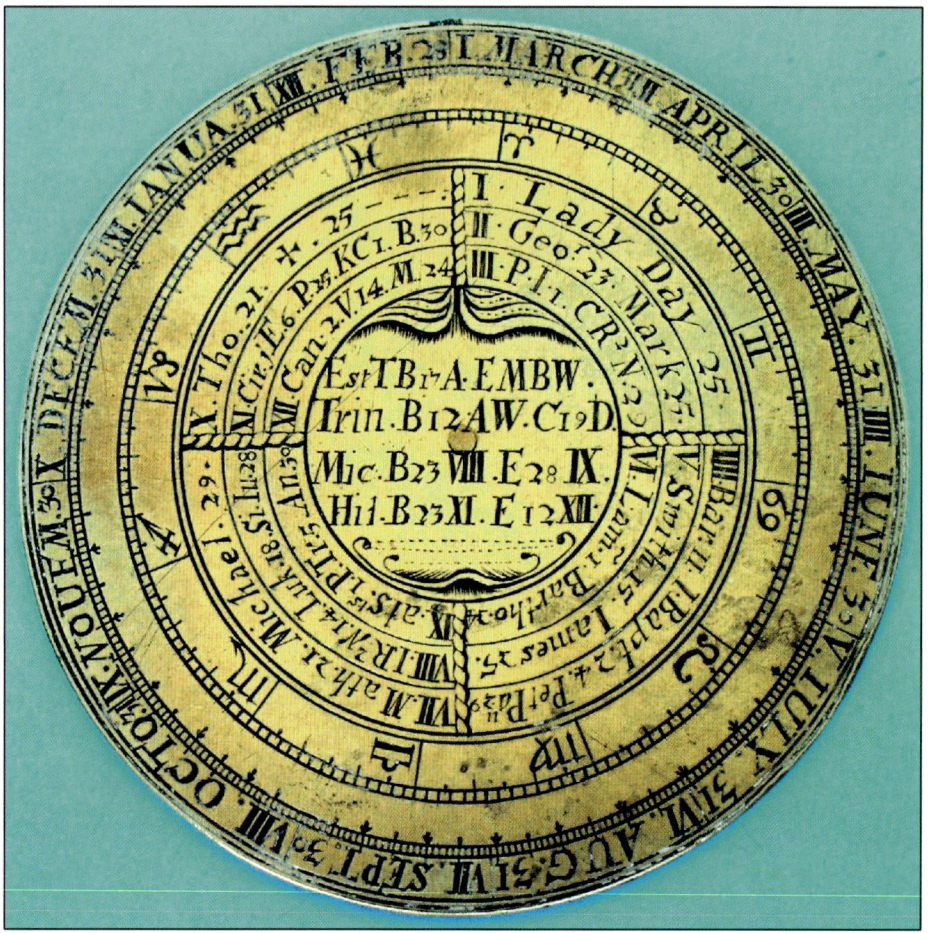

Two sides of the Perpetual Calendar by E·C·, dated 1688

Chapter 25 Perpetual Calendars

The calendar by Glynn is similar except the the initials of each month are given, with a second letter where necessary. For August and October, where only one line is required, for symmetry he has added the **A** and **O** at both ends of the line.

The calendar on the lid of the dial by J. Simons is dated 1770. It carries the information '**The Univerfal Time Table S Kingdon inv**'. Around its edge it has the information '**March begins on in the Year 1700 &**'. It then lists the days of the week and each year that March begins on that day up to 1799.

The brass Perpetual Calendar signed '***E·C· fecit***' (possibly Edmund Culpeper) is a quite complex and interesting device and deserves some explanation. In its centre is a calendar square like the others described except that the months are in Roman numerals. Around its edge is '**EASTER 1688**' with a ring of numbers that read clockwise showing the date of Easter for consecutive years. '**II 15**' refers to April (second month) 15th, 1688, and '**I 31**' refers to March (first month) 31st, 1689, etc.

The second ring '**KEY=DAY**' gives the day of the week for the year to start and uses '✱' to denote Leap Years. The next ring '☾ **SOUTH**' shows the time for the Moon's southing and the final ring '**EPACT**' gives the Epact for each year in turn.

The reverse side of this Perpetual Calendar carries even more information. Around its edge are the months numbered, '**I**' = '**MARCH**', with '**31**' days. Subdivisions are shown for every day of the year. Inside that is a scale with corresponding Zodiac degrees. The next three circles show important dates for each of the months. For example, '**I Lady Day 25**' = Lady Day on 25 March. More interesting dates are shown in other months like '**IX als^{ts}.1. P.Tr.5. An.30**' and '**XI Cir.j E.6 P25. KCI.B.30**'. The first translates as 'month 9 (or November) where All Saints festival is the 1st, Parliamentary Treason (i.e., Gunpowder Plot) is the 5th and St. Andrew is 30th'. The second is even more interesting. 'Month 11 (or January) where the Circumcision of Jesus and Epiphany fall on the 6th, the Conversion of Paul is celebrated on the 25th and on the 30th (a reminder of troubled times) when King Charles I was beheaded'. In the centre of the disc are some lines of letters where we can only guess the meaning. For example '**EstTB17A EMBW**' which probably translates as 'Easter Term Begins 17 April and Ends Monday before Whitsun'. The remaining entries here refer to the other Law Terms, which although still in use, now have somewhat different dates.

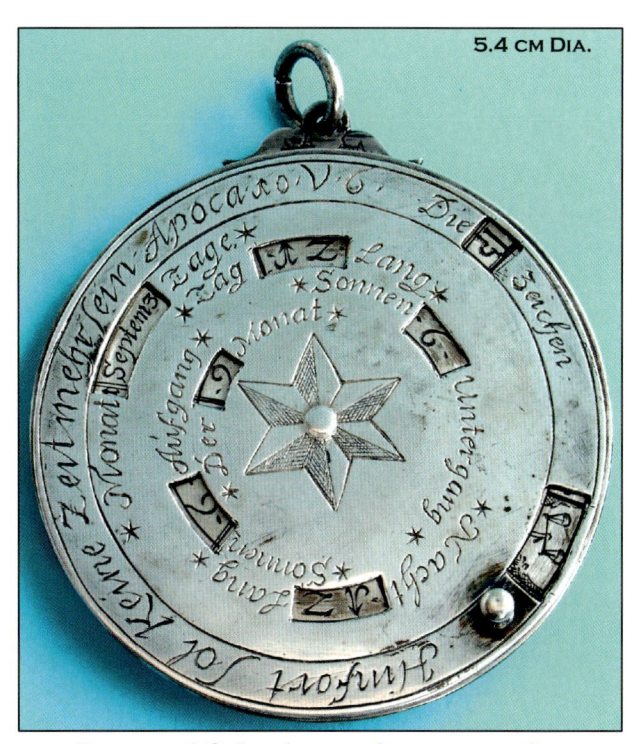

Perpetual Calendar on the reverse of an Altitude Dial — 5.4 cm Dia.

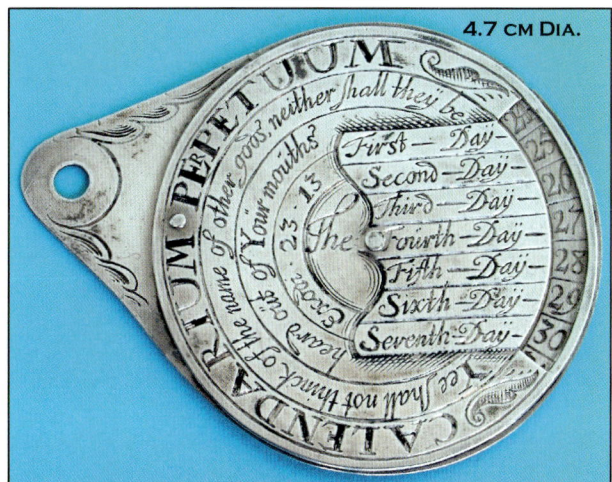

English Perpetual Calendar in silver — 4.7 cm Dia.

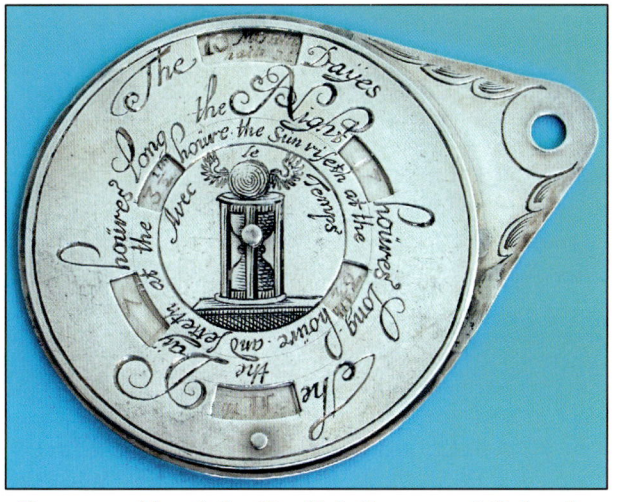

Reverse side of the English Perpetual Calendar

155

Chapter 25 Perpetual Calendars

A different type of Calendar is shown on the reverse of the silver Altitude Dial described in Chapter 2. The outer ring shows:

Die ♎ *Zeichen*

with its Zodiac sign, and its symbol ⚖.
The next ring inside that can be read:

✱*Monat* Septem 30 *Tage*✱

The Month of September has 30 Days.

✱*Tag* 12 *Lang*✱, ✱*Nacht* 12 *Lang*✱

Day 12 (hours) Long and Night 12 (hours) Long.

✱*Sonnen* -6- *Aufgang*✱
✱*Sonnen* -6- *Untergang*✱

Sunrise 6 (o'clock) and Sunset 6 (o'clock).
In its centre is:

✱*Der* -9- *Monat*✱

The 9th Month.

Calendars of this type are frequently found, usually of German or Low Countries origin but English ones are occasionally found. The silver '**CALENDARIUM PE^RPETUUM**' illustrated is English but very similar to the German one. In addition this one has the days of the week against which the dates can be set, e.g., as a reminder that if the '*First Daÿ* - **24**' then the '*Seventh Daÿ* - **30**'. Note how the engraver has missed the letter R in **PE^RPETUUM** and has inscribed it later between **E** and **P**.

A similar calendar from Germany has the days of

German Perpetual Calendar on the reverse of a Regiomontanus Dial

German Perpetual Calendar showing the days of the week in both Old and New Styles

the week showing in two places separated by 10 days. These are actually New and Old Styles, shown as '*Die Neüe Zeit*' and '*Die Alte Zeit*'.

The Regiomontanus Dial described in Chapter 2 also has a Perpetual Calendar on its reverse. This calendar is typical of many from Germany that are often found attached to other items such as sundials, ivory leaved notepads and snuff boxes.

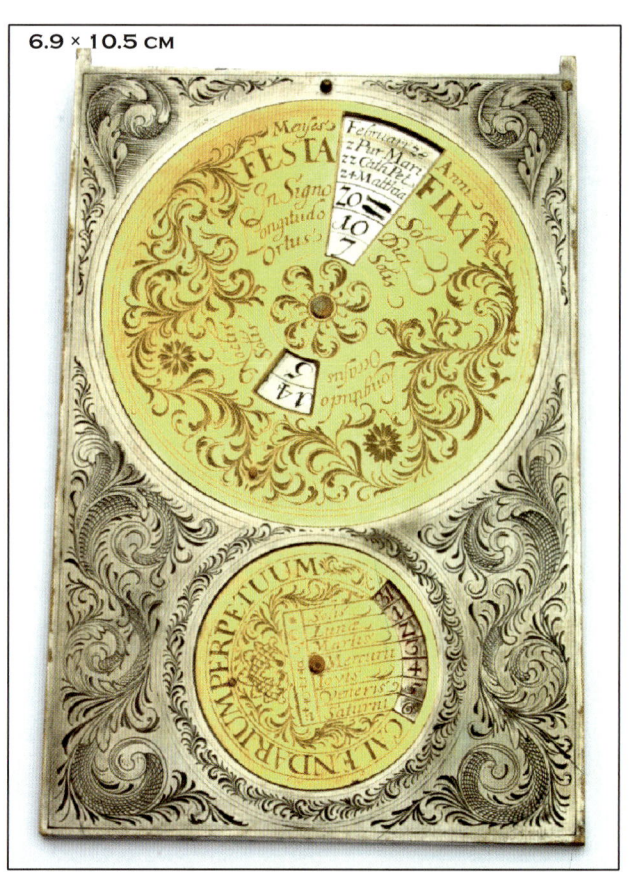

This one is particularly attractive having gilt volvelles mounted against its silver body. The lower dial is similar to that just described with the days of the week and their planetary symbols set against a scale of 1 - 31 days. In the illustration '☉ **Solis**' (Sunday) is set against '**31**' such that '♄ **Saturn**' (Saturday) is set against '**6**'. Its main dial is a little more complex. As illustrated it reads:-

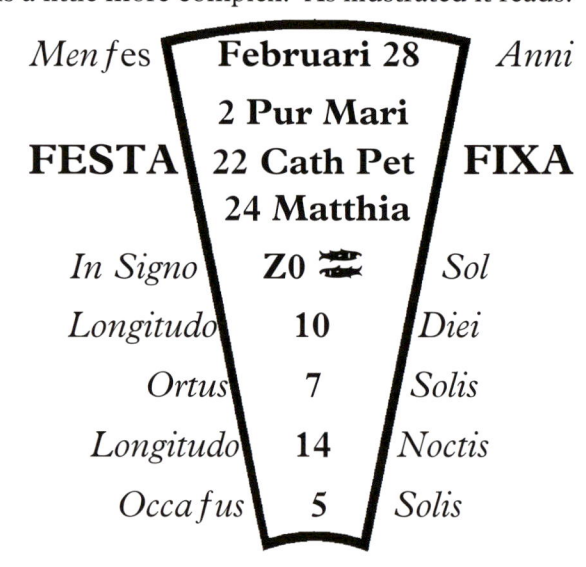

Menfes	**Februari 28**	*Anni*
	2 Pur Mari	
FESTA	22 Cath Pet	**FIXA**
	24 Matthia	
In Signo	Z0 ♒	*Sol*
Longitudo	10	*Diei*
Ortus	7	*Solis*
Longitudo	14	*Noctis*
Occafus	5	*Solis*

The approximate translation is 'The Month of the Year is February and has 28 Days. Feasts are Fixed as 2(Feb) Purification of Mary, 22 Chair of St. Peter, 24 St. Mathias. The Sign is entered on

CHAPTER 25 PERPETUAL CALENDARS

20th day of Pisces (♓), Length of Day 10 hours, Sunrise 7 o'clock, Length of Night 14 hours and Sunset 5 o'clock.'

The silver snuff box below has a similar calendar on its lid that is typical of many to be found from Germany. Dating of them is often assisted by the fact that both Old and New Calendars are catered for. The Catholics adopted the New Style in 1583 but the Protestants did not do so until 1700. Therefore a dual calendar signifies a date prior to 1700.

Perpetual Calendars were frequently found on Ivory Diptych Dials from Nuremburg. They were often of the form shown on the dial by Paul

German Perpetual Calendar on the lid of a Snuff Box

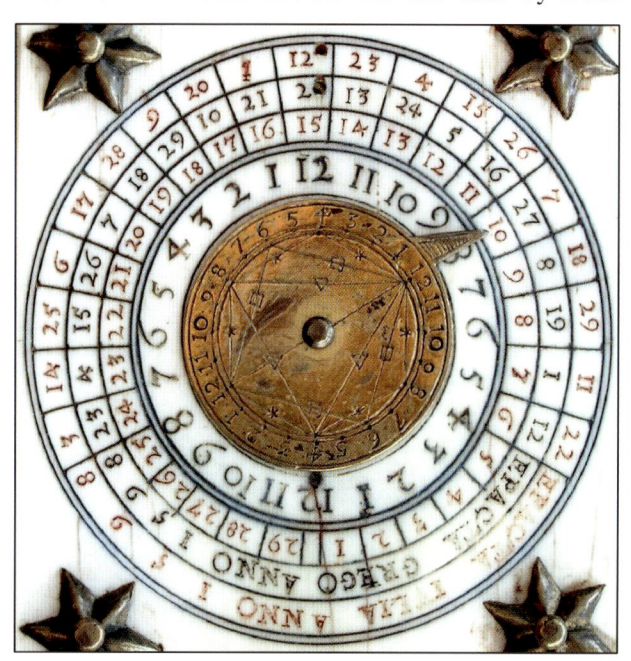

Calendar from Ivory Diptych Dial by Paul Reinman of Nuremberg, dated 1598

Detail of Snuff Box Calendar

Reverse of gilt Altitude Disc Sundial, ca. 1700

157

Chapter 25 Perpetual Calendars

Reinman, Chapter 6, clustered around a volvelle. The two outer rings are labelled:

EPACTA IVLIA ANNO 1598
and **EPACTA GREGO ANNO 1598**.

These are the Epacts for years from 1598, working clockwise around the dial for a total of 19 years, in both Julian and Gregorian reckoning. Both calendars were in use at this time and both forms were necessary. The additional rings and the rotating volvelle are to convert Lunar Dial readings to Solar time.

The reverse of a gilt Altitude Sundial, again from Germany, shows a similar layout to previous Perpetual Calendars. This one is interesting in that its construction is different and it had an arm hinged at the centre (now broken off) that

German Perpetual Calendar of coloured card inside the lid of a String Gnomon Dial

pointed to the date around its periphery.

A similar Perpetual Calendar built into the lid of a String Gnomon Dial is made from paper scales pasted onto card and is attractively coloured. It may be dated to no later than the mid eighteenth century and has survived in exceptional condition being protected by the sundial case.

A rather complex looking English Perpetual Calendar, ca. 1797, is illustrated. It uses paper scales pasted on the outside of a wooden box. Inside the box is a sundial (illustrated on Page 96). On the box lid are the following scales, working inwards:

a) Months with number of days in each. At the start of the four Quarters is a note about the seasons, such as *Spring Q^r. beg. 20.*

b) The next ring lists between three and five important events fear each month.

c) The Dominical Letters from 1792 to 1832.

d) Seven boxes with the months starting *MAY.*

7.7 CM DIA.

Perpetual Calendar on the outside of a box

Monday, AUGUST. Tuesday, FEB, MAR, NOV. Wednesday, etc.

e) The rotating volvelle is captioned **The Dominical Letters and Days of the Month.**

f) The outer ring has letters **A** to **G** with dates above them, e.g. **A** has 1, 8, 15, 22, 29.

On the underside of the box is a further calendar:

a) Date of the Sun entering each Zodiac sign, such as *Sun enters ♒ January 20.*

b) Times of sunrise and sunset in **H, M, H** for days 1, 8, 16 and 24.

c) *Easter Sunday is always the first Sunday after the first full Moon following the twenty first March except such full Moon happens on a Sunday in which Case it is the Sunday following.*

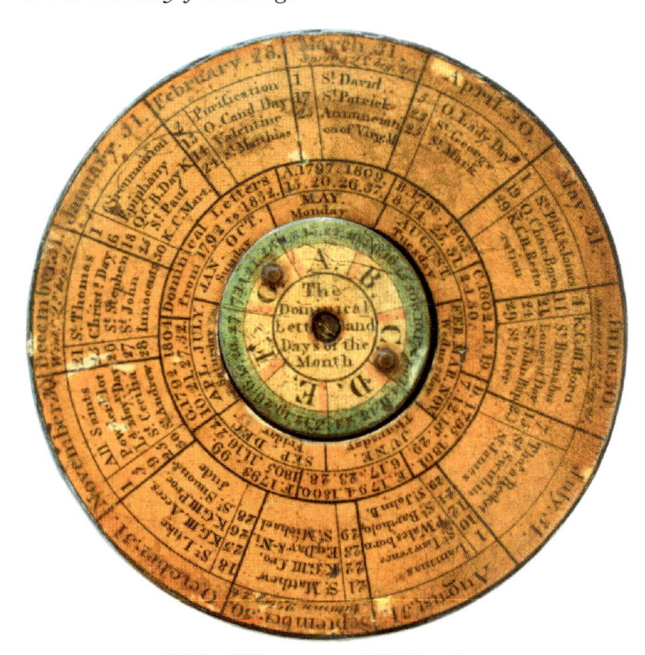

Lid of Perpetual Calendar

158

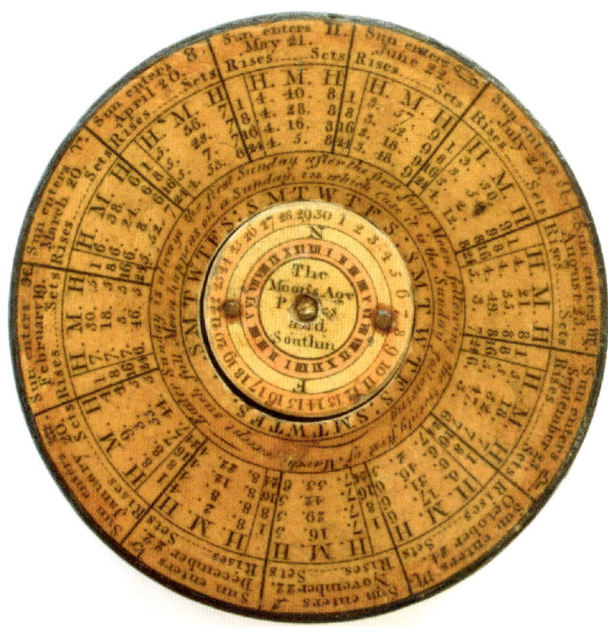

Chapter 25   Perpetual Calendars

Underside of Perpetual Calendar box

Detail from the edge of the Calendar box

d) Days repeated four times **S M T W T F S:**.

e) Volvelle labelled **The Moons Age, Phases and Southin.** (sic).

f) Around its edge 0 - 30 days.

g) **N** (New) against 29½ and **F** (Full) against 14¾.

h) 24 hour dial in Roman numerals.

Around the periphery of the box lid are hours **I - XII, I - XII** divided into halves, quarters and half-quarters. These are above the lower part of the box which lists a series of towns around the World. So if we set a time such as **XII** *Midnight* for London, it will tell us the time elsewhere. It also gives the directions and distance in miles from London.

Many other forms of calendar will be found on dials and other objects. The basic interpretations have been discussed and from these it should be possible to interpret the information on most of them.

MEDIEVAL QUADRANS NOVUS

The front side of this Quadrant was described in Chapter 5. On its reverse is a Calendar using an eagle with outstretched wings in the centre of two concentric scales.

Around the inner ring are the numbers '**1 - 19**' representing the years of the lunar cycle. The outer ring gives the date for the Easter Full Moon. The notation used here is unfamiliar to modern users in that it is laid

Medieval 'Quadrans Novus' with Roman Calendar

159

Chapter 25 Perpetual Calendars

out in terms of the Roman calendar (Ides, Nones and Calends) and not the days and months that we now use. The Roman Calendar for the months of March and April is shown as given by Wells. The system therefore works by counting down to these three points. Therefore, the 21 March is **XII** Calends of April.

The layout of the calendar circle is at first rather strange in that it does not follow in year order. However, it will be noticed that the eagle is pointing to **ƙᴀ 16** with its longest wing. The shorter wing points to **2Iᴀ 15** and the tail to **12ƙᴀ 17**. Therefore, the eagle is simultaneously showing the dates for the Easter Moon for the current year, the past year and the next year. This has been cleverly arranged by the maker who has separated the years in increments of six instead of sequentially. The picture shows the eagle pointing at **ƙᴀ** for year **16** in the cycle. **ƙ** is for Calends and **ᴀ** for April (or 1 April in modern notation).

One error has been noticed in this calendar and may be just a mistake by the engraver or of his information source. The year **19** clearly shows **14ƙⴟ**, which would be 19 March, but the required date is 29 March, being 11 days earlier than the previous year (9 April). Therefore, the correct figure should be **4ƙⴟ**, the leading **1** being erroneous.

The character engraved beneath the date for the third year in the Lunar Cycle is unclear. It should be an **A** but looks like a reversed **B**. This may be a poorly engraved character, but if a **B**, this could signify a bisextile (or leap) year.

For further information see 'Calendar Systems & Perpetual Calendars'. [Cowham 1999 - 2000]

The Roman Calendar for March and April from Edward Wells' book 'The Young Gentleman's Astronomy, Chronology and Dialling' published in London, 1725.

Year	Roman Date	Modern Date	Year	Roman Date	Modern Date	Year	Roman Date	Modern Date
1	**15ƙ**ⴟ	17 April	8	**3:ƙ**ᴀ	30 March	15	**2 I**ᴀ	12 April
2	**n:**ᴀ	5 April	9	**14:ƙ**ⴟ	18 April	16	**ƙ**ᴀ	1 April
3	**8:ƙ** (ᴀ?)	25 March	10	**7:I**ᴀ	7 April	17	**12:ƙ**ᴀ	21 March
4	**I:**ᴀ	13 April	11	**6:ƙ**ᴀ	27 March	18	**5:I**ᴀ	9 April
5	**4:n:**ᴀ	2 April	12	**17:ƙ**ⴟ	15 April	19	**(1)4ƙ**ⴟ	29 March
6	**11:ƙ**ᴀ	22 March	13	**2:n**ᴀ	4 April			
7	**4:I**ᴀ	10 April	14	**9:ƙ**ᴀ	24 March			

A comparison of the dates engraved on the volvelle giving the Easter Full Moon

CHAPTER 26   CARING FOR A COLLECTION

A collection of portable dials will usually include specimens of all ages and conditions. Some of the specimens will be less than perfect, being damaged, having missing parts or just plain dirty. It is sometimes a difficult decision to make, as to the amount of attention to give them. Over-cleaning a dial or incorrect repairs may severely damage it, thereby reducing its value. The aim of this chapter is to suggest remedies and solutions to the problems that may be encountered, but actual restoration, particularly of valuable dials, should always be left to the expert.

CLEANING

Many dials when acquired are in a filthy state, some having being untouched for centuries. There is no excuse for keeping a dirty object, and some form of cleaning ought be attempted as long as it can be done without damaging the dial or removing its patination.

In the case of brass, and some silver dials, previous owners have probably 'cleaned' them using metal polish. This is one of the greatest sins possible. The abrasive nature of most types of metal polish will remove the surface layer of the metal, obliterating the delicate patination of age, damaging delicate silvering or gilding and destroying the crispness of any engraving. In addition, residues of such 'cleaners' are usually left in the engraving, around screws and in holes as a white deposit. This is unsightly and may be damaging. There is little that we can do about a dial that has been cleaned in this way. Obviously, if it is too badly smoothed by repeated polishing, it is best avoided in the first place. Let someone else buy it. In practice, most dials that are found have these white deposits on them. These are best removed, as it is possible for corrosion to start where it remains, particularly if the dial is subjected to a high level of humidity, not uncommon in the British climate.

To remove all traces of metal polish, it is best to carefully dismantle the dial, taking care not to do any damage in the process, particularly to its screws. These may have been untouched for centuries and may be unwilling to move. Too much force on one of these may shear its head off or damage the thread in the dial plate. Always use a screwdriver with a blade that properly fits the screw slot. Many early screws had '**V**' shaped slots, and a modern screwdriver could damage them. If necessary, grind up the tip of an old screwdriver for this purpose. Much damage is done to screws by screwdrivers, particularly when the blade is too small for the screw. Make sure that the blade is as wide as the screw head.

Remember to keep the screws so that they will be fitted back into the same holes that they came out of. Old threads can vary, therefore the screws are seldom interchangeable. Also make a careful note of the position of each part so that you do not end up with some bits that won't fit. A close-up photograph taken of the dial before it is dismantled is often a useful aid. Alternatively lay the dial on a photocopier or scanner and increase the size of the print to fill the sheet of paper.

The cleaning process will depend on the material. In the case of a brass dial, warm soapy water is often

Residue of metal polish disfiguring a brass dial

Chapter 26 Caring for a Collection

An Augsburg Dial disassembled for cleaning

the best solution. The soap used can be a mild detergent such as Teepol or washing up liquid, but avoid those with fragrances such as 'lemon fragrance' just in case they contain harmful acids. Proprietary cleaners are available that are very effective without being too aggressive. Avoid cleaning the compass needle unless it is particularly soiled because the water could encourage rusting. The glass cover for the compass will certainly benefit from a wash. It will always have a dirty ring around its edge where proper in-situ cleaning was impossible. If the compass is covered by a mica window, just wipe its surface carefully with a damp cloth. Be careful not to crack or de-laminate the mica that may now be very fragile. The individual parts may be soaked for a few minutes, then may be gently rubbed with a piece of soft cloth. Be particularly careful of any filler in the engraving. Many waxes used as fillers may melt if the water is too hot. An ultrasonic cleaning bath is sometimes useful, but it should be used with special care. The metal parts of the dial should not contact the metal parts of the tank or its basket as this may cause local abrasion damage. A good protection is a layer of thin card or paper for the part to rest on. The agitation of an ultrasonic bath may also dislodge the filler from the engraving, may lift delicate gilding or silvering or remove loose paintwork, so it must be used with extreme caution, and usually only for a short time. Most

dirt will be seen coming from the part in the first few seconds. Once cleaned to a satisfactory state, the parts should be rinsed in clear water. From this time on, the parts should only be handled with gloved hands to prevent the oils and acids from the fingers being deposited on the now unprotected cleaned surface. A final rinse in distilled water is recommended. To dry the parts, use a warm (not hot) air supply, such as from a hair dryer to make certain that all moisture is removed from every crevice and particularly from screw threads. Take care when drying the screws, as the blast of air may send them in all directions. Put them into a vertical sided dish to prevent this. The parts, once cleaned, will be particularly vulnerable to any form of corrosion as any protective layers of grease or wax will have been removed.

One simple way of protecting the parts is to apply a thin coat of wax. One that is used and particularly recommended by most museums and professional restorers is Microcrystalline Wax, (marketed as 'Renaissance Wax').[1] It was introduced commercially in 1968, and has been approved by the British Museum. It is inert, with a neutral pH, and may be used on most materials including metals, wood, leather and even ivory. Apply the wax with a small piece of soft cloth or cotton wool. Avoid paper and wood based tissues as these will probably contain high levels of acid. Once thinly coated with the wax, use a clean soft

Severe damage done to a brass compass bowl due to acid from the fingers eating into the brass

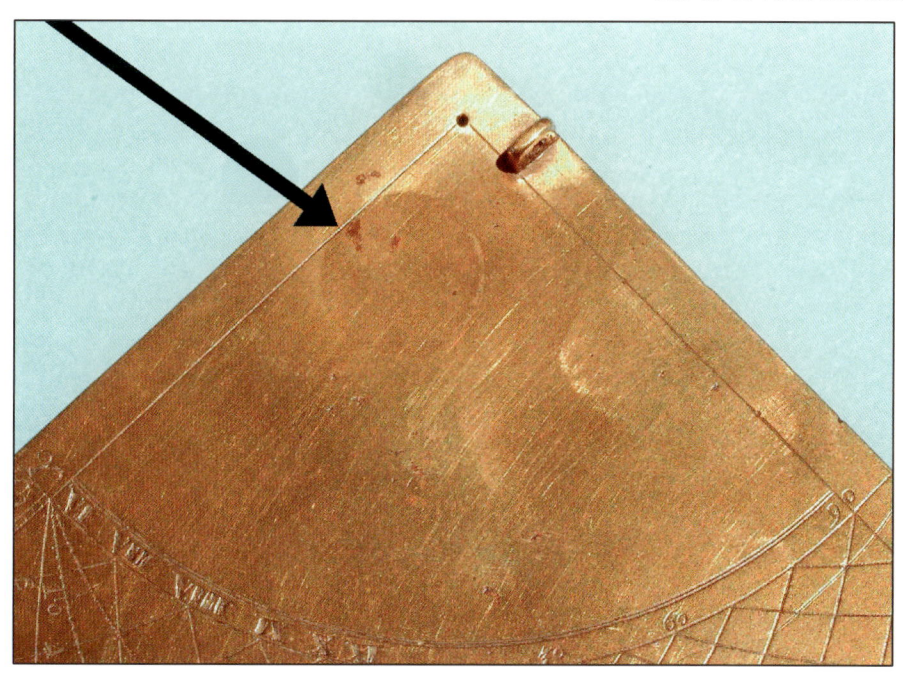

Mark on brass Quadrant where a self-adhesive label was once fixed

cloth to gently polish the part. If done correctly the wax will form a hard coating on the dial's surface, resistant to atmospheric pollution for some years.

An alternative to wax that may be considered is varnish. The choice is rather difficult, but whatever is used, it must be possible to remove it again, perhaps for further conservation. Most varnishes may be removed by acetone, but think what this may do to the wax filler in the engraving! Acrylic lacquers sprayed onto the items seem to be the best solution. However, if in doubt, don't do it!

Now is the time to re-assemble the dial. Do not hold any of the parts with un-gloved fingers. Cotton gloves are cheap and may be washed when soiled. Fit the screws carefully without over tightening them. Return the dial to its protective case, or place it in a suitable showcase.

If the cleaning has been carried out successfully, and the dial has been properly coated with wax or varnish, it should stay in this condition without further degradation for several years. Most museums do not expect to have to clean their artefacts more than once in perhaps 15 years, but most of their treasures are housed in climate controlled cabinets.

If the dial is showing signs of corrosion, particularly from a careless fingerprint left by a previous owner, it may be cleaned with a light abrasive cleaner, but this is only recommended in cases of severe damage and where the dial has previously been cleaned in this way. To fully remove corrosion damage left by the fingers, *metal has to be removed* from the object's surface. A dial in pristine condition apart from a corroded fingerprint is best left. There is little that can be done to rectify this type of damage and attempts should be made to remove the offending acid in the hopes of halting the decay process rather than completely removing the damage caused. Cleaning in warm soapy water is probably the best way to proceed, followed by a rinse and a coat of wax. To completely wash out all acids from the pores of the metal, it may be necessary to wash the parts several times in distilled water, leaving them to soak for a day or more each time. An elevated temperature will assist the process.

Another form of damage often found on all types of antique comes from the use of self-adhesive labels. These are still used by many salesrooms and dealers for identifying their stock. They should be banned from use anywhere near antique items. They always leave a sticky residue, often remove surface coatings and their former position will show if the rest of the surface has faded in light. The problem may also be due to the label *preventing* the formation of natural patination. The chemicals used in the adhesive may also be damaging. The same applies to other 'harmless' substances such as 'Blu-Tack'. This will certainly leave paper with an oily mark after just a few months.

Silver may be treated similarly to brass. However, silver may also have a blackened surface due to exposure from sulphur in the atmosphere. There is at least one museum in this Country that has a fine collection of blackened silver dials, so the problem is not unique to private collections. In most cases, this black layer will clean off with a soft cloth. In other cases gently rubbing with a finger will often remove the corrosion, but in this case the corrosive acids left by the fingers should then be removed. If this still does not remove the blackened layer, sparingly apply some proprietary silver polish (again an abrasive item, so take care) or use silver dip to remove the contamination. Leave the fluid to stand for a few minutes without rubbing the metal surface, then rinse it off. Most of the black corrosion should now have been removed from the surface. In the unlikely event that areas of corrosion are still persistent, try a very light rubbing with the cleaning fluid. If areas have severe pitting, cleaning of the cavities may be possible using a sharpened cocktail stick. Always rinse well in clean water following any chemical treatment because this may also be corrosive in the long term. Clean the parts as already described for brass dials, and apply the wax coating.

Silver is particularly prone to blackening. It may be noticed that certain pieces blacken quicker than others. This is either due to the grade of silver, its surface finish or its coating. The blackening comes mostly from sulphur. We all know not to eat a boiled egg with a silver spoon. Sulphur is present in the atmosphere from vehicle exhausts, fires and general industrial pollution. It is also present in the house in large quantities, coming from two main sources. The first is unavoidable, it is from the human body, and from our domestic animals. It comes from bodily waste and is even exuded by the skin. The second is also difficult to avoid, coming from the timber used in the house's construction, newspapers and even books, and what is more important, the furniture. The worst source of pollutants may be the display cabinet itself! The ideal display cabinet therefore will be made of glass and metal and be sealed well against the atmosphere. Wood will slowly breathe, giving out toxic gases, in particular sulphur, but generally by the time that it is around a century old its 'bad breath' is reckoned to have been dissipated and it is considered to be fairly safe to use. Modern 'woods' that are made from layers, such as plywood or chippings that are bonded together, may be even greater sources of dangerous gases. Humans and wood have to be lived with, but a good wax coating may protect the dial for a period of time.

If the dials are to be stored, wrap them only in acid free paper, then put them into polyethylene bags. Polyethylene bags are available from specialist plastics suppliers, and are well worth searching out. Standard plastic bags may be used for short times, but this material usually contains chlorine, and this is another major source of chemical damage.

Ivory dials need different treatment. Often they are quite dirty or even stained from years of handling and display. Most ivory dials did not have cases, so they are less likely to have been protected during their long lives. Do not try to take these apart. Clean them carefully with a damp cloth, with a little soft soap if necessary. Remember that the soap needs to be removed carefully afterwards. Do not expect all stains to be removed as these will probably be of a permanent nature, but most ivory dials certainly look whiter following a gentle cleaning. Another method that is generally successful for cleaning ivory or bone is to use isopropyl alcohol or even surgical spirit. Like all cleaning agents it must be used with extreme caution, and not too liberally. Apply it with a soft cloth rubbing it gently into the dirty areas. Be particularly careful of the wax filling in the lines and numerals. This wax may be dissolved by the alcohol. At the first sign of damage, stop and dry the dial with warm but not hot air.

Ivory needs special care and attention. In

Ivory Diptych Dial where the top leaf has split, probably due to storage at low humidity

particular it needs a fairly high humidity level, around 60% RH. Metals need a much lower level, 40% RH and below. It therefore makes it difficult to store or display both types of dial together. Two separate display cabinets are often the only sensible solution. For the display cabinet holding the ivory dials, a small dish of water should keep the humidity at the correct levels. A humidity meter is a good investment for such items. When ivory becomes too dry, it is prone to cracking, and many early dials from both Dieppe and Nuremberg are found severely cracked along their grain, or even split into two pieces.

CONSERVATION & RESTORATION

These two words often become confused. Conservation means the keeping of an object in its present state without it deteriorating further. In other words, it stabilises its present condition for the future. This is the primary priority for our valuable dials. Restoration is the process of re-creating the parts of an object so that it is in the same condition as it was when it was new, or the process of replacing missing parts. Obviously, this should not be attempted except under strict control. The most important point in both conservation and restoration is that whatever it is that is done to the object, it must be such that it is possible to return the object to its present state at any time in the future. In other words, it must not be damaged or modified by the processes that we use. Many museums have damaged the objects in their charge, particularly in the nineteenth century, by over-zealous acts of restoration. We are probably still doing similar damage today, inadvertently but to a much lesser extent. The most important task that we have now is to stabilise an object to prevent any further deterioration. At some time in the future, when restoration skills and methods have improved, it may be possible for the dial to be restored to its former glory.

REPAIRS & REPLACEMENTS

These two terms are really forms of restoration, but they will be considered separately.

Residue of solder on the back of an Astrolabe rete

If a dial is broken, should we repair it? This is often a most difficult decision. The best rule, as always, is that if in doubt leave it alone or at least obtain professional advice. A few examples will probably be the best way to illustrate possibilities?

If an ivory dial has been split due to misuse or to low humidity, should we attempt to join the two pieces together? If we decide to make a repair we should then consider how this might best be achieved. The obvious solution is to use a glue, but which one? It must be a type of glue that does not disfigure the dial. It must not stain or irrevocably damage the dial. It must always be a glue that can be removed in the future, leaving no deposits, so that a better repair may be attempted. Most common glues are clearly not suitable. An epoxy resin may be the best choice, if necessary with some white filler in it where it is required to fill a wide gap between the two parts. 'Super Glue' (usually known as cyanoacrylate) may also be considered as an option but is probably less stable than a good epoxy. It also emits a vapour which can leave a white smoky deposit around the joint. The parts to be joined should be lightly clamped together during the curing process and all flashes of glue must be removed. If the parts of the object are held too tightly together, especially where each has warped, when the epoxy sets, new strains will be placed on the object and leave open the possibility of further cracking of otherwise whole parts. Epoxy may subsequently be removed, if necessary, by careful chipping and peeling. The use of resin softening chemicals such as acetone or the much stronger dichloromethane should be used as a last resort, as these may leach the original oils from the ivory making it excessively brittle. They will also remove all traces of wax filling and any oil paint. The decision to repair is quite often a difficult one.

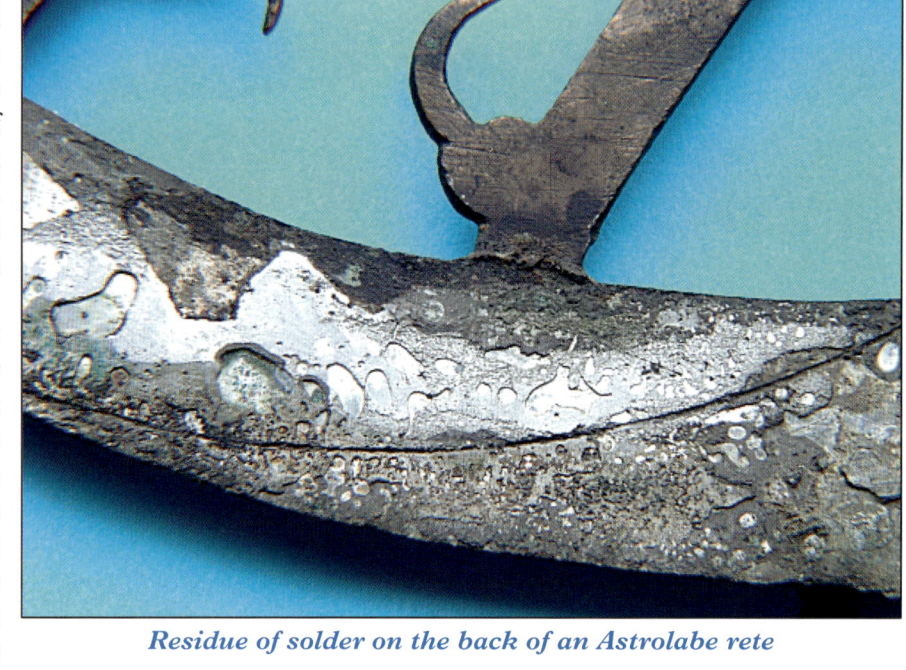

A metal dial may have a piece broken from it. Maybe an original casting has cracked. The solution here is similarly difficult. In many cases, epoxy will serve as a short to medium term solution. Its use is also reversible, especially on metals. If the pieces to be joined are part of an arm, the subsequent small joint will not be strong enough to hold them together for long. Solder may be considered to affect the join but with caution. Ordinary 60-40 lead-tin solder will join two pieces of brass, and often steel parts. Soldering should only be undertaken with considerable forethought, as solder forms an alloy with the metals joined and is extremely difficult, if not impossible, to remove in the future. There is the case of an early medieval Astrolabe where the rete became cracked in several places, and a previous owner decided to strengthen it with a thin sheet of brass soldered to its back surface. In time, due to corrosion, and because the soldering was not too well done, the thin sheet of brass lifted, and eventually fell off. The problem now is what to do. The back of the rete is covered in a thick layer of solder, and how can that be removed? This was a case of damaging restoration, and was probably done 100 or more years ago. Any process likely to remove the solder, is likely to damage the already weakened rete even more. If the decision is made to remove the solder, the only sensible way forward is to carefully scrape away all traces of it from the rete. This process will inevitably remove some of the original brass. There is then still the problem of bridging the cracks in the rete. With careful handling, it may be left in its present condition for someone in the future to find an acceptable solution. The object is in a relatively stable condition and is unlikely to deteriorate further if kept at low humidity. It can wait for future restoration when solder removal and new jointing materials become available. If a temporary repair is necessary to prevent the rete falling apart, a thin layer of rigid acrylic sheet could be applied to the rear face with a soft epoxy resin.

Another more permanent way of joining two pieces of brass or steel is by using silver solder. The joint produced will be almost as strong as the original material, so this seems to be the ideal method. The disadvantage is that the process of silver soldering needs a very high temperature, normally to red heat, and this may degrade and will certainly anneal the areas so joined. Any surface finish or patination will already have been lost at much lower temperatures.

Silver has its own special problems. Jewellers and silversmiths have used low melting point silver for centuries and many objects are found that have been almost invisibly joined. This process also needs considerable heat, often doing damage to the original parts. If the silver parts are gilt, as on many of the better portable dials, then most forms of soldering should not even be considered. The high temperatures involved will certainly melt any filler in engraved numerals etc.

A popular form of 'restoration' often used by clockmakers is to re-silver items. They frequently re-silver clock dials to make them look 'as new'. To do this, the original silvering is removed, and then the dial is polished, before the new silver is applied. They also use certain chemicals for cleaning the brass parts, such as the famous Horolene but we would never consider such products when used on precious instruments. A silvered sundial often has areas with the silvering worn away, particularly when it has been cleaned with an abrasive metal polish. These dials are best left alone. Resilvering may always be considered by a subsequent owner. Trying to patch the silvering normally leaves the part mottled and often looking worse than the original silver loss. We should again leave it alone. Resilvering will not significantly add to the dial's value, but in many cases may reduce its value to a prospective purchaser. If nothing else, he may become suspicious about what else may have been done to the dial.

Replacement parts of dials may be required so that they will still function as their maker intended. Where parts are missing, replacements should be made that are as close as possible to the originals. However, these parts must never be made such that a subsequent owner will be unable to tell them from the originals. When a new part is made, it is usually possible to mark it on an under surface with one's initials and the date. This is a way in which we can 'sign' part of the dial for ourselves.

A Quadrant Dial by Walter Hayes was found without its gnomon, which normally slides into a dovetail slot. It was therefore decided to make a replacement so that the sundial was complete. A similar dial by Culpeper is known in the Whipple Museum in Cambridge [Bryden 1988 - Item 285] so the new gnomon was made in a similar form. Modern brass was used. This is whiter than the yellow cast brass of around 1700, so it obviously does not look 100% original. Just in case it could be thought original this gnomon was stamped on the underside with its maker's initials and the date.

Many dials that are found have had replacement glass covers over their compasses. In some cases, the compass needle will have been lost and a replacement fitted. It is often simple to detect a new piece of glass, as the original would probably contain small bubbles and surface imperfections. Modern float glass is normally free from such features. Compass needles can be more difficult to spot, but they should be compared with others of the same period or region of manufacture. If a glass or the needle are missing on a dial, consider a replacement. Obviously, we would like the dial to function correctly. Try to mark the needle if possible to show that it is a replacement, but the glass will normally speak for itself.

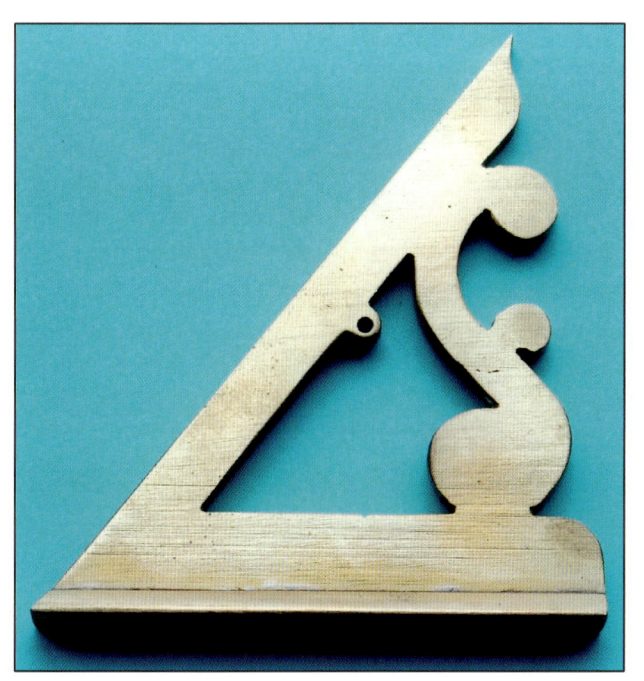

Restored gnomon for Walter Hayes dial, modelled on one by Culpeper

CHAPTER 26   CARING FOR A COLLECTION

HANDLING & STORAGE

Much has been said about the damage done to dials, and other valuable antiques, by handling them with naked hands. Human skin contains acids that will fairly quickly etch away brass and other metals. This is such an important point, that the author makes no apology for repeating the warning. Never handle these objects with the naked hands. Wear the best cotton gloves, nylon will do but this could leave abrasive marks on softer silver, or use a clean cloth. If the gloves become soiled, wash them well and rinse them in clear, preferably distilled, water to remove any residual detergent. When removing the gloves, remember that the second one to be removed will probably be pulled off with the other hand that is now naked. This contamination, although of a small risk, will still be there next time the gloves are used. Also avoid the possibility of the gloves being worn next time inside out. Similar remarks apply if a cloth is used instead of gloves.

Store the dials in their original cases, unless displayed. Whenever paper is used, make certain that it is acid free, but generally paper should be avoided for long term storage. If the dial is for display, choose a cabinet, if wooden, that is preferably at least 100 years old. If it is new, allow a gap in the door for ventilation. If the cabinet is 'safe', such as a metal framed one, then it is best sealed against airborne pollutants.

Be careful about lighting. Excess light and its associated heat may affect organic materials such as ivory, wood and paper. Fluorescent lighting is normally fairly safe, if unattractive, but look out for ultra violet radiation that may damage some items. Low voltage halogen lighting has become very popular due to its colour temperature and convenience. These lamps have been known to explode quite violently, so ensure that if such a thing were to happen, damage would be limited. These lamps are now produced with a glass cover to reduce the effects of UV radiation and to limit damage in the case of an explosion. In all cases, try to avoid sunlight if possible. A sundial without sunlight seems perverse! However, long term exposure to the Sun's radiation will severely damage most organic materials and even metals. For storage, use acid free materials and consider the use of polyethylene bags. These are available from specialist plastics dealers. They can be heat-sealed to make them airtight.

A red Marocco leather case for a Russian made 'Butterfield Dial' by Samoilov. Stored inside an original case a dial is likely to be well protected

CONCLUSIONS

A collection of dials is a very valuable asset. As with all antiques we are not the owners of them but merely their custodians. Therefore we must look after them to the best of our ability so that they will last for the benefit of future generations. To enjoy these dials to the full, they should be clean and preferably in good order. All visible dust and contamination ought to be removed. This is especially important, if by leaving it, further deterioration would take place. We must not damage these wonderful objects due to our ignorance.

Missing parts should be replaced where possible so that these dials remain functional.

A fine and well cared for collection is a treasure to be enjoyed by all. Display them safely and enjoy the beauty of their workmanship.

REFERENCE

1. Renaissance Wax Polish.
   Available from:-
   Picreator Enterprises Ltd.,
   44 Park View Gardens,
   Hendon,
   London NW4 2PN.

CHAPTER 27   REPRODUCTION & MODERN DIALS

The subject of Reproduction Dials is a difficult one. I have placed together Reproduction and Modern Dials as the two are often inseparable and are best discussed together.

Some dials are complete fakes or forgeries intended to deceive the unwary collector and to extract money from him. They may have been made in recent times or may be a century or more old. Dials have frequently been made as copies, some probably never intended to deceive anyone, just to make an attractive dial type available at a reasonable price. Certain dials are occasionally found that are contemporary copies where a well known signature on a dial would be more likely to sell it than the name of its real maker. Similar situations still exist with many High Street names having their goods copied and sold as originals.

In this chapter I am also including incompetent dials where the maker has perhaps not fully understood the principles of dialling.

It can sometimes be difficult to sort out the reproductions from the originals and even experts frequently disagree. It is important for the collector to know that such things exist and to be wary of any dial offered for sale. If the dial is from a reputable dealer it can always be returned for a refund. If it was obtained at auction, then it is sometimes possible to get a refund if it can be proved that the dial was actually made to deceive or if it was wrongly described.

FAKES

Dials made as fakes are often 'signed' by a well known maker. For instance if a dial is signed *Butterfield AParis* it is more likely to be a fake than one signed *Thourry AParis* because Butterfield is the one name that most people interested in dials will have heard of. Some of the more expensive scientific instruments can really be worth faking as a considerable amount of effort is often required to make a portable dial. Basically, the making of any fake has to be worth the exercise because a low value dial would not bring any returns. Fakes will normally be made singly or at least in very low number so mass production is not normally an option.

COPIES

Copies of dials are to be found in many places. In particular many museums will have copies for sale, frequently with a well-known signature on them. These dials are usually quite easy to separate from the real thing and very few collectors would be fooled.

A small Altitude Ring or Poke Dial was just an advertising gimmick for Piz Buin and they were sold by their thousands. Some of these are now being sold to collectors who believe them to be the real thing. The dial is signed '**H S THON**' and dated '**ANNO 1721**'. Several of these appear to have been sold through some of our major auction rooms in recent years. It seems incredible that they can be fooled by these cheap replicas.

At present there are quantities of reproduction scientific instruments and dials flooding into Europe, probably from India. They are generally quite good copies and are probably not intended to fool anyone. There are two models of Inclining Dial amongst them, and both are signed '**WEST London**'. These dials are brass castings and are mounted unashamedly in new wooden boxes with no attempt having been

A replica Poke Dial sold with Piz Buin products a few years ago

CHAPTER 27   REPRODUCTION AND MODERN DIALS

Modern reproduction of an Inclining Dial signed 'WEST London'

Signature from West dial

made to age them. The rough castings have been cleaned up on a polishing wheel leaving the edges, particularly of the chapter ring, rounded. The real thing would have crisp edges, especially to the chapter ring, which would originally have been silvered. Some of these dials too have found their way into good salerooms.

Copies were made of dials found on Henry VIII's ship 'The Mary Rose'. They have been sold through museums and elsewhere. It is unlikely that they will ever be mistaken for a real dial of this period, but only time will tell.

CONTEMPORARY FAKES

Contemporary Fakes can be more difficult to spot. As has already been said, these dials have been faked generally by a less competent maker so the workmanship involved is probably inferior to what we would normally expect. Having said that, most makers had various journeymen working for them, some of whom would be less competent than the rest, so their output could be seen as inferior. If the maker was particular with his checks on finished items he would not allow sub-standard products to leave his workshop, but due to commercial pressures it sometimes means that slight flaws are often overlooked. Furthermore, many makers would supply dials at different prices, the best constructed ones being the most expensive. Many of them had 'bargain price' dials for those who could not afford the best models. It is therefore very difficult to say conclusively that any particular dial is definitely a contemporary fake unless further evidence is available.

INCOMPETENT DIALS

The makers of these dials may be from the provinces and having seen dials, perhaps from London or Paris have tried to make their own versions of them. These dials may not have been correctly delineated, basically because they did not even appreciate that the art requires calculation or geometrical construction to get all the lines at the correct angles. There are many ways in which this incompetence could manifest itself but I have provided one example, which otherwise looks to be a nice product. This dial is an Ivory Diptych

A replica of dial based on those found in the wreck of the Mary Rose

170

Chapter 27 — Reproduction and Modern Dials

Dial, nicely engraved, if a little naively. My attention was first drawn to this dial because I could not fit it into any regular pattern. In some ways it looks like a Nuremberg Dial but it is clearly not from any of the regular workshops. Its age was difficult to judge but was probably nineteenth century rather than sixteenth or seventeenth century. The image of the Sun, with its tongue hanging out, is not a regular feature. The hinge between both tablets is a modern style of cabinet hinge whereas the originals used wire loops and hooks and had a recess for the top tablet to fit into the lower one. The engraving on the lid of the fish and trident looks great, and is full of interest. Its list of towns and their latitudes is correct except for Hamburg, but such mistakes were quite common. Its compass bowl is covered with a domed glass, just like those fitted to a

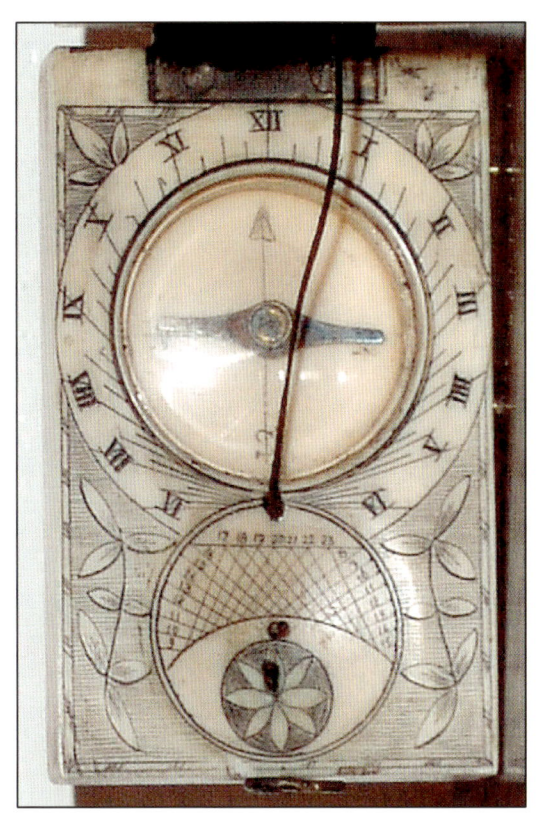

Incompetently made ivory dial
Photo: John Edgler

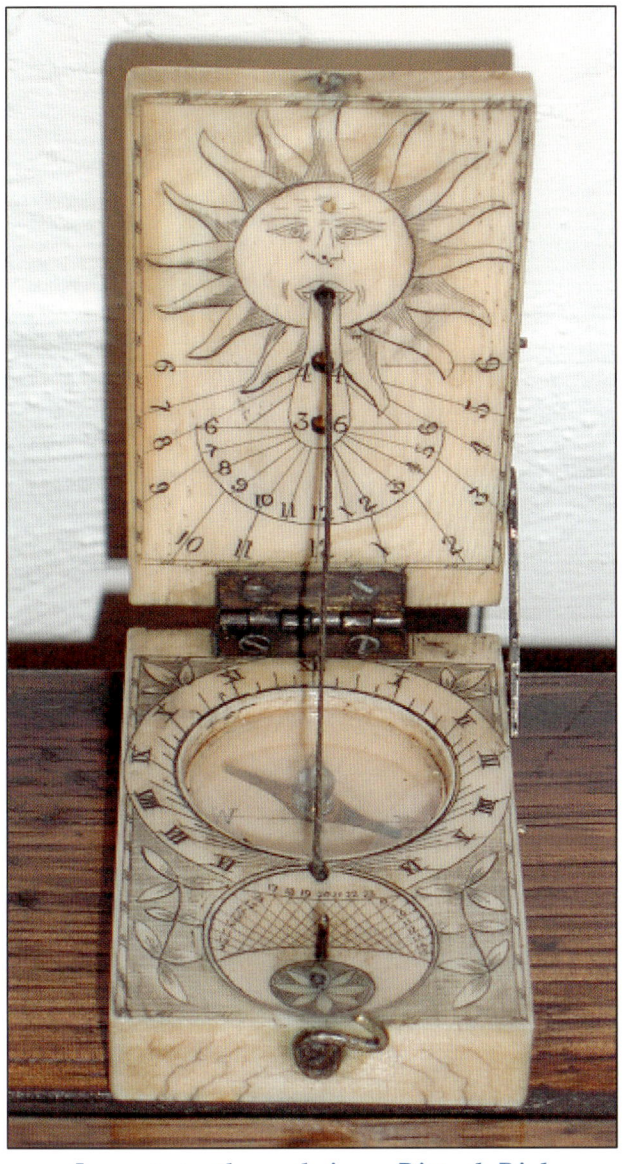

Incompetently made ivory Diptych Dial.
Photo: John Edgler

Lid with fish and trident on incompetently made ivory Diptych Dial
Photo: John Edgler

171

Chapter 27 — Reproduction and Modern Dials

List of towns on underside of incompetent dial
Photo: John Edgler

Two very small Horizontal Dials that were probably made as toys

watch, but again such features are quite common and show that it may have been replaced. Finally I looked more closely at its delineation and found that all of its hour lines were separated by precisely 15°, exactly as the hours would be on a clock face. On a sundial this can only be the case if it is an Equatorial Dial which this one is plainly not. The Scaphe Dial looks a bit strange too and checks on this have shown it to be incorrect.

Overall this dial looks good and is a great decorative object but don't expect it to tell the correct time.

Occasionally small 'Garden Dials' will will be found that really are too small for serious use. I have illustrated two of these that I believe were intended as toys. They are not correctly delineated and are somewhat crudely made. They may have been made in Victorian times to go with a dolls house.

MODERN DIALS

Pocket Dials are still being made, mainly as reproductions. These are often sold in museum shops as replicas. Probably the commonest type found is the Butterfield Dial as this is often regarded as the most attractive type.

A replica Ring Dial is being sold, made by Michael Kala in Austria. It is generally in the style

A replica of a Ring Dial made by Michael Kala

Reverse of Ring Dial made by Michael Kala

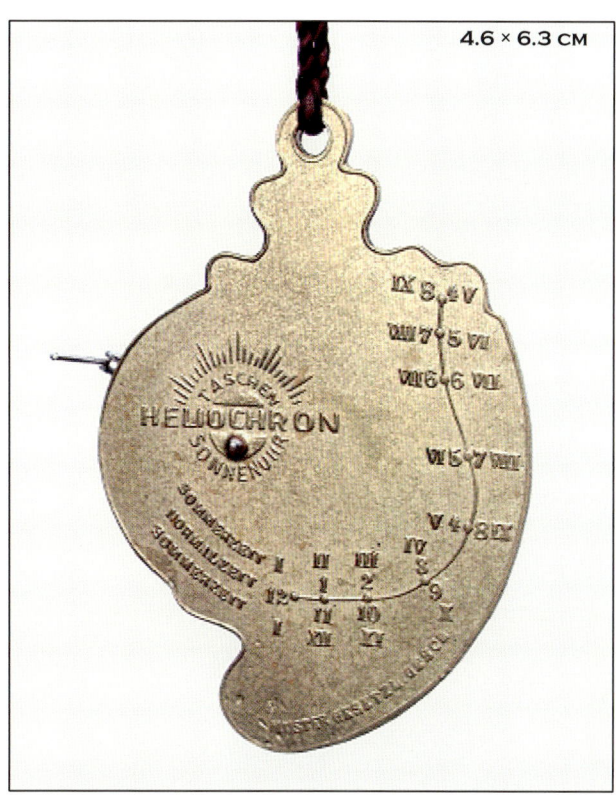

'Heliochron' Pocket Dial - a replica of a seventeenth century Vertical Disc Dial

Acrylic Refraction Dial made for the Zonnewijserkring 15th anniversary

of seventeenth or eighteenth century models but uses modern production methods and is unlikely to be confused with the real thing. One interesting feature is that it can be used in the Southern Hemisphere by setting the gnomon slider to an alternative scale on the opposite side of the bridge. This is contrary to period Ring Dials where the latitude arc is merely continued beyond 0° to minus 90°.

A Vertical Disc Dial known as the 'Heliochron' pocket dial is similar to dials from the late seventeenth century but is clearly made by modern production die-casting techniques.

Replica Pillar Dials too are often sold, some made from cardboard, but these still function quite nicely.

In recent years several new ideas have been worked on producing some new breeds of Pocket Dials. One such dial was produced in 20mm thick clear acrylic for the Dutch Zonnewijserkring in 1993 to mark their 15th anniversary. The round disc gnomon with its central speculum is similar to those

Chapter 27 Reproduction and Modern Dials

Modern replica dials on sale in a French tourist shop

7.6 × 9.1 CM

Modern replica of a 'Butterfield Dial' made by Villa-Alcor

allowing for the refractive index of acrylic. The dial does not have a compass so it is not really suitable for use as a Pocket Dial. It would probably be set up just inside a window either by using an external compass but more probably by setting it to the correct time taken from a watch!

Artisans, particularly in France and Italy, are making a wide range of pocket dials which are now being sold in tourist areas. The picture shows a display of some of these dials as seen in the old town of Carcassonne in France. Eventually some of these will become mistaken for 'the real thing' and some are already finding their way into auction sales. If they are thought to be genuine it is certain that some will find their ways into otherwise serious collections.

Sundial makers are still busily making dials of all types, some as jewellery and some as working replicas. Some of these are beginning to appear in the market but few of them can really be confused with older types.

It is therefore likely that the fine tradition of making Portable Sundials will continue for many years to come.

used on Noon Marks. It is screen printed in red on the dial's upper surface with its hour scale on its under surface. This scale has been calculated

CHAPTER 28

A FINAL GLANCE

In the foregoing chapters we have looked at many attractive dials and in some cases their decorative attributes have been detailed. Space has not always allowed the minutest detail to be shown so here are a few items that may have escaped proper attention. Many of these show aspects of the engraver's skill and often make the difference between a good functioning sundial and a true work of art.

Often, the way in which makers signed their works is an art form in itself. Over their period of work many developed very fancy signatures, not necessarily using them on all of their dials but

Particularly ornate signature of Michael Butterfield on a brass pocket dial

Fretted outer cover for plummet on dial by ·S·A·V·Z·

Fretted inner cover for the plummet on dial by ·S·A·V·Z·, with face of the 'Green Man'

reserving them just for special pieces. One excellent example of this is the brass dial by Butterfield where his signature is certainly much more decorative than his usual one. It is almost possible to imagine it growing.

Some makers excelled in their gnomon design, often with detailed fretting. Pictures of several of these have already been seen in Chapters 8, 9 & 10.

The String Gnomon dial signed ·S·A·V·Z·, Chapter 20, has a very attractive cover for its plummet. The outside half is beautifully fretted and gilt, but for me, the inside cover, with its small face, probably showing the 'Green Man' is outstanding, being delicately fretted and silvered, just revealing the bob of the plummet and its two aligning points.

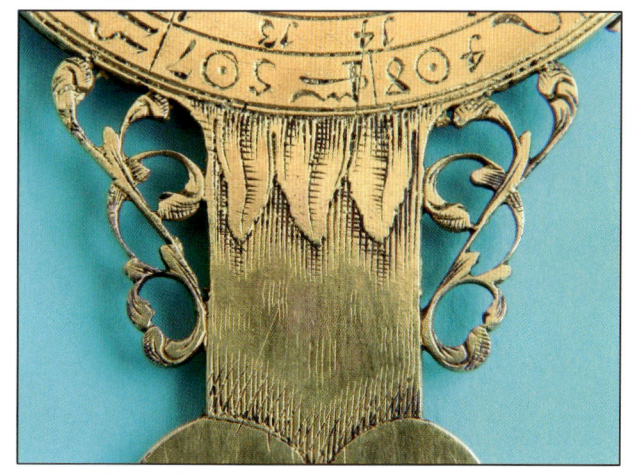

Fretted brackets between handle and disc of a German Nocturnal

175

Chapter 28   A Final Glance

Decorative fretting on handle of German Nocturnal

Five petalled rose design on ivory Diptych Dial by Charles Bloud, Dieppe

The silvered and gilt German Nocturnal, Chapter 24, is a very attractive item, particularly the fretted and engraved scrolls around the handle and where it is joined to the body.

Often engravers exercised their skills on just a small part of the dial such as a spring or on the reverse of a compass bowl. These are not the first things to be seen when using the dial so they must have come as a pleasant surprise to their owners when studying them closely.

The underside of compass bowl is an ideal place for the display of the engraver's skill and, if he has not used this area to extend his gazetteer, it is often decorated with a flower (frequently a Tudor Rose) or occasionally a picture as shown on the Butterfield Dial by Haye, Chapter 9.

The unsigned oval French dial, Chapter 8, permanently fitted into its silver case, could hardly be expected to be opened to reveal its reverse, but here we have a most beautiful floral engraving, still with its original wax filling on its tiny 14 mm diameter compass bowl.

Even the simplest and relatively inexpensive products could be enhanced with just a little effort.

Engraved floral pattern on underside of a compass bowl, just 14 mm diameter

Hand coloured compass rose on English Compass Dial

176

Chapter 28 A Final Glance

Detail from a compass bowl by Charles Bloud

The paper compass rose from the bowl of an English Compass Dial, Chapter 11, has had the points of the compass attractively hand coloured. Similarly, the compass bowl on the ivory Diptych Dial by Charles Bloud, Chapter 7, shows some fine detail including the dotted line showing true

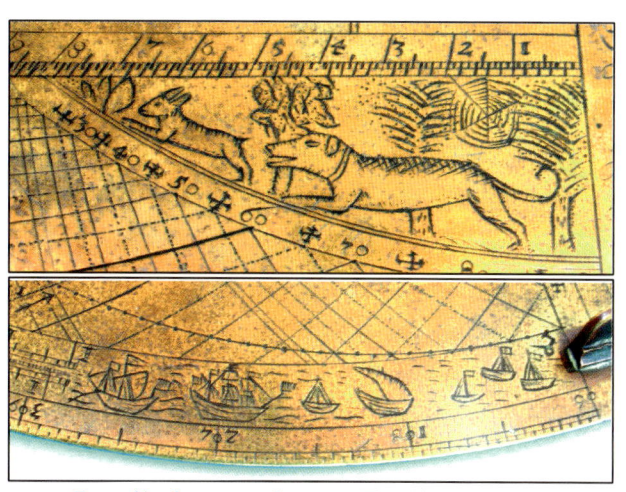

Detail of engraving on English Gunter Quadrant by Nathanaell Highemore

North with a Sun image at the lower end. Above this is a dish, probably a type of coaster used at table for supporting a wine bottle.

Many makers reserved their art for gnomon springs. The silver Butterfield Dial by John Rowley, Chapter 10, shows just one small aspect of his skill and artistry.

The Quadrant by Heighemore in Chapter 5 shows a dog chasing a stag, but the Quadrant also

Engraving of gnomon spring from a Butterfield Dial by John Rowley

Gnomon and plummet support on dial by Johann Martin, Augsburg

177

Chapter 28 A Final Glance

Above and left.
Engraved patterns on the gnomon springs of an unsigned English Inclining Dial

has a dog chasing a rabbit, a string of sailing ships and various other miniature pictures.

Other details to look out for are the decoration given to various springs and supports. The Gnomon and Plummet support by Johann Martin is finely chased. At the top it is even engraved with latitude settings for the thread fixing holes.

End of ornate spring on the dial by Timothée Collet

Detail of decoration from an Islamic Quadrant

178

Chapter 28   A Final Glance

Angel and figure in coffin (or is it a bed?) from a wooden Quadrant by P I Maynardie

The two English Inclining Dials, Chapter 16, have very attractive, if almost insignificant, patterns on their gnomon springs, but such embellishment is the true sign of an accomplished engraver.

This feature is almost taken to excess by Timothée Collet, Chapter 8, where his springs have been delicately fretted, engraved and gilt.

There were many other ways that makers would ornament their dials.

Wooden dials too would frequently be decorated. The Islamic Quadrant, Chapter 5, shows typical Arabic decoration in gold paint as well as the attractive use of Arabic characters in black and red ink to form patterns and tables.

The carved wooden Quadrant by P. I. Maynadie, in Chapter 5, is particularly interesting for its fine carved decoration. Its angel supporting the sights really adds to its interest, and who is the figure in the bed or coffin behind the angel? On its reverse is a drunken Bacchus with his dog beside its Lunar Volvelle.

It is these small details that really lift many of our Portable Dials to new heights of art and make them a joy to be:

A Dial in Your Poke.

A drunken Bacchus and his dog depicted on the reverse of the wooden Quadrant by P I Maynardie

179

APPENDIX 1 NUMERALS, LETTERS & SIGILS

NUMERALS

We are all familiar with markings on modern clocks and watches where the numerals are either Roman or Arabic. Most sundials too have used these same characters to indicate the hours. Roman numerals have been the most popular until relatively recently when the use of watches became widespread and the man in the street needed to read them with ease.

Care should be exercised with any old numerals, as there were many variations in the form of certain characters. Those on the accompanying chart should therefore be treated as a guide.

Arabic numerals have been used by us for many centuries. As their name suggests, they were derived from the numbers written by the Arabs, and many similarities can still be seen. Compare the two types, Modern European and Arab. To avoid confusion, the original Arabic numerals are here referred to as Arab numerals.

Before about 1500, the numerals used in Europe had some quite major differences to modern numerals. Occasionally, dials from this era will be found. Astrolabes, in particular, often carry the older numerals, and their study will show clearly the subtle changes made over the years as modern numerals were developed. A typical set of numerals from before 1450 are depicted as Early European. The numbers **4**, **5** and **7** are quite different to those used today. Note how easy it is to confuse the **5** with the **9**. Note also how the **7** is completely inverted compared with the Arab **7** and actually looks like the Arab **8**. During the following centuries, the **4** became rotated and straightened into the **4** that we know today. The loops on the **6** and **9** were closed, and the **7** was rotated clockwise to make our modern **7**. A number **7** more like **>** will sometimes be found. The rather sharp angled **2**, rather like our **Z** persisted longer, and was still in use in Germany until around 1700. The illustrations show some engraving from an Astrolabe of ca. 1300, where these older numerals are used. The Calendar scale shows the days in the month of January in increments of five (note that the **N** is reversed too, a common occurrence).

Many dials (and later mechanical clocks) were made in Europe from the late seventeenth century

Different types of numerals compared

Further numerals on Gothic Astrolabe

Letters and numerals on an early Gothic Astrolabe, ca. 1300

destined for Turkey and other Arabic states. The workers making these used stylised Arab numerals of the form illustrated. These characters were commonly used on clocks until the mid nineteenth century, and also on French-made pocket dials. A Butterfield Dial by Le Maire shown in Chapter 9 uses these numerals but on the underside of its dial plate the list of towns uses conventional Arab numerals. Note that although Arabic is

APPENDIX 1   NUMERALS, LETTERS & SIGILS

CHINESE AND JAPANESE NUMERALS

Hour	Numeral	Zodiac Sign	Animal
6 Sunset	六	酉	Cock
5	五	戌	Dog
4	四	亥	Boar
9 Midnight	九	子	Rat
8	八	丑	Bull
7	七	寅	Tiger
6 Sunrise	六	卯	Hare
5	五	辰	Dragon
4	四	巳	Serpent
9 Noon	九	午	Horse
8	八	未	Goat
7	七	申	Ape

ZODIAC SIGNS AND SIGILS

Capricorn		♑
Aquarius		♒
Pisces		♓
Aries		♈
Taurus		♉
Gemini		♊
Cancer		♋
Leo		♌
Virgo		♍
Libra		♎
Scorpio		♏
Sagittarius		♐

PLANETARY SYMBOLS

Monday	*Lunæ*	**Moon**	☾
Tuesday	*Martis*	**Mars**	♂
Wednesday	*Mercurii*	**Mercury**	☿
Thursday	*Iovis*	**Jupiter**	♃
Friday	*Veneris*	**Venus**	♀
Saturday	*Saturni*	**Saturn**	♄
Sunday	*Solis*	**Sun**	☀

written from right to left, their numerals are always written the same way round that we do. Chinese, Korean and Japanese numerals are a little more complex. Each 'hour' or 'Toki' of the day is given to a sign of the Chinese Zodiac. Their hours were counted downwards from the horse at midday (**9**), the cock at dusk (**6**), the rat at midnight (**9**) and the hare at dawn, (**6**). Later, conventional Japanese numerals were also used, but some clocks and dials carry both styles. Note that they did not use numerals **3, 2** or **1** in their timekeeping, as these are thought to have been reserved for temple use.

LETTERS
Letters have changed perhaps less than the numerals but several differences will be found. The most commonly found difference is the long **s**, more like a letter f but without its cross bar. Its use persisted, especially in handwriting until the end of the nineteenth century and will be found on sundials throughout most of that century. Normally it is found only where it occurs in the middle of the word and as the first one of a pair in the double s. The double s may also take the German form, (ß).

SIGILS
Sigils are the Zodiac symbols. Some instruments will use the Sigil and others the Zodiac image. Zodiac signs were used extensively, even more than months, in early calendar systems. Therefore they will be found, in one form or another, on many early instruments.

Also to be found are Sigils for the days of the week, actually the Planetary Symbols. The table shows the days in English and *Latin* with Planets and Symbols used.

APPENDIX 2   SAINTS DAYS ON CALENDARS

Perpetual Calendars often carry a large amount of information, but out of necessity much of this has to be abbreviated to fit onto a relatively small area. These abbreviations would have been quite obvious to their original owners but today many are somewhat elusive. The majority of the markings refer to Saints days and other fixed festivals.

Most calendars encountered are either English or German and the following tables show the markings found on a selection of them. Where possible a translation has been attached, but a few dates still remain a mystery. Naturally some dates have changed with these festivals now being celebrated on totally different days. A difference of 10 or 11 days is frequently found due to calendar changes from Old Style to New Style.

The list has been placed in calendar order starting in January.

On some English Perpetual Calendars important days may be noted with reference to the British monarchy. In particular the execution of Charles I (January 30) and the Gunpowder Treason (November 5) will be found. Some of the birthdays of our monarchs are also recorded on certain calendars.

Various important days displayed on an English Perpetual Calendar

Saints days displayed on a German Perpetual Calendar

Part of a Calendar as published in 'Practical Navigation' by John Seller, 1705

APPENDIX 2   SAINTS DAYS ON CALENDARS

DATE	ENGLISH	GERMAN
January 1	Cir.j / CIR / Circumcision = Circumcision of Jesus	Neu Jahr = New Year Beschneidung Christ / Cire Christ = Circumcision
January 6	E / EPI / Epiphany / Twelf-day = Epiphany	H3 König / Kinis / Epiphani = 3 Kings or Epiphany
January 13	Hill. = Hilary Term Begins, (Hilary of Poitiers. He was born c315. Invoked against insanity and snakebite)	
January 18	Q.C.B. Day K = Queen Caroline Birthday? Wife of George II or Queen Mother?	
January 20		Fab Seb = Fabian, Pope c236 & Sebastian, d c290 (Invoked against the plague)
January 25	P / St Paul / C.S.P. / Conv. Paul = Conversion of St Paul	Conv Pau / Paul:Bek = Conversion of St Paul
January 28		Carolu = Charlemagne
January 30	KCIB, K. Char. B. = King Charles I Beheaded 1649 K.C. Mart / K.C.M. = King Charles I martyred	
February 2	C Day / Can / Purification / Purif. Mary = Candlemas / Purification	Maria Leichtmes / Lichtme / Puriu. Mar / Mr. Rein = Mary's Purification
February 6	Dorothea (Invoked against fire, lightning and thieves)	
February 14	V / Valen / Valentine = St Valentine, c269 (Martyrdom of three different saints called Valentine is celebrated on this day)	
February 19		Susaña = Wife of Hilkiah? (Old Testament)
February 22		Cath Petr./Pet.Stulf = Chair of St Peter the Apostle (Now Jan 18)
February 24	M / S MAT / St Matthias / Matthew = Mathias, (since 1969 it is May 14), (The apostle who replaced Judas. He is invoked against alcoholism)	Mathiu / Mathias / Matthias = St Mathias
February 25	S. Matthias = St Mathias	
March 1	S Dav / St David / David = St David (Dewi) b c450	
March 5		Friedrich = Which Friedrich?
March 12		Gregori = Gregory I, (Gregory the Great, died March 12, 604)
March 15		Christop? (St Christopher is 25 July)
March 17	S. Patr. / St Patrick = Patrick, (Succat), of Welsh-Italian descent	Gertraut = Gertrude of Nivelles, (7th Century Belgian nun, invoked against rodents in Belgium)
March 19		Joseph / Iosephu = Joseph, husband of Mary
March 25	Lady Day / L DAY / An. Mary Annunciation of Virg: M = Annunciation of Mary	Maria Verkindi / Anu. Ma / Mr. Verk = Annunciation of Mary
April 1	A. F. = All Fools Day	

APPENDIX 2   SAINTS DAYS ON CALENDARS

DATE	ENGLISH	GERMAN
April 4	Ambro = St Ambrose	Aprosius = St Ambrose
April 5	O. Lady Day = Lady Day (New Calendar)	
April 10		Daniel = (Daniel the Stylite, Dec 11?)
April 12		Leo. Papp. = 13 Popes called Leo?
April 23	Geor / S Geo. / St George = George, Palestinian soldier in crusades (Invoked against plague, leprosy and syphilis)	Georgis / Georg = St George
April 25	Mark / S Mar / St Mark / Mark Ev. = St Mark the Evangelist (Invoked against fly bites)	Marcus Evange = St Mark the Evangelist
May 1	P.I / S.P & J. / St Philip & James / Phil. & Jac. = St Philip & St James	Phil:Jac / Philipi Jacobi = St Philip & St James
May 3	Inv. C. = Invention of the Cross	+Erfind/Inuinti + = Invention of the Cross
May 6	Io. Eua = possibly Ava from Brittany	
May 14		Christian = ?
May 19	Q. Char. Born / Q. Ch. B = Queen Charlotte Born	
May 25		Urban = One of 8 Popes called Urban?
May 26	August = St Augustine of Canterbury, Abp. (Should be May 27)	
May 28		Wilhe = Wilhelm?
May 29	CR2N / Carolus Rex II Natus / K. Charles II = Charles II Born 1630 K.C. Re / K.C.II Restoration = King Charles II Restored to the Throne 1660	
June 4	K.G3B / K.G. III Born = King George III Born 1738	
June 8		Medardus = Médardus. Bp of Tournai c600 (Invoked against rain and toothache)
June 11	Bar. / S. Bar. / St Barnabas = St Barnabas, Cypriot Jew	
June 13		Tobias = St Tobias?
June 15	Vitus = St Vitus	Veit / Vitus = St Vitus, Italian (Invoked in Germany for good health)
June 21	Longest Day / Lo. Day. = Longest Day	
June 24	I Bapt / S.I.B. / St John Bap = Birth of John the Baptist	Joh. Bat / Taufer / Tanf / Joh.Tauf = Birth of John the Baptist
June 29	Pet Pau / S.P & P / St Peter / Peter Ap. = St Peter & St Paul	Peto Paul / Pett et pa. / Petr:Paul = St Peter & St Paul
July 2	Visi Mar = Visitation of Mary	Mar Heims / Martheim = Visitation of Mary
July 4		Vlrich / Vlricus = St Ulrich (Swiss Bp canonised 993)
July 7	Thos à Becket = Murder of Thomas à Becket, Abp of Canterbury, - but this was 29 Dec 1170? (He was invoked against blindness)	
July 12		Heinric = Could be Henry HRE, Bavarian, 1014? Normally celebrated Jul 13
July 13	Margaretha?	

APPENDIX 2   SAINTS DAYS ON CALENDARS

DATE	ENGLISH	GERMAN
July 15	Swith / S. Swit. / St Swithin = St Swithin (Swithun) Bp of Winchester, d862	Apost Theil = ?
July 19	Dog Days begin (See also July 30) = Heliacal rising of Sirius (Old Style)	
July 22	Ma. Mag. = St Mary Magdalen	Mr. Magd = St Mary Magdalene
July 25	Iames / S. JAM. / St James / James Ap. = St James the Greater	Jacob / Jacobus = St James the Greater
July 26	Anna = Anne, Mother of Mary	Anna = Anne, Mother of Mary
July 30	Do. beg. = Dog Days Begin (New Style) (Heliacal rising of Sirius, Dog Star)	
August 1	Lam~ / Lam. D. / Lammas = Lammas Pet. Vin. = St Peter ad Vincula	Pet. Kettenf = St Peter in Chains
August 2		Gustavus = Gustav?
August 10	S. Lau. / St Lawrence / Laurence = St Lawrence, Spain, m257	Laurentius = Lawrence = St Lawrence
August 12	P. W. B. / P. Wales Born = Prince of Wales Born, (later George IV)	
August 15	Asc. Mariæ = Ascension of Mary	Mar.Him / Maria Himmelfart / Asc Maria = Ascension or Assumption of Mary
August 24	Bartho / S. BAT / St Bartholo / Barthol. A. = St Bartholomew, apostle (Invoked against nervous tics)	Bartholo = St Bartholomew
August 28	Dog Days End (Old Style)	
August 29	St John B. = Beheading of St John the Baptist	Joh:Ent = Beheading of St John the Baptist
September 1	Giles = St Giles, accidently shot by Charlemagne (Invoked against lameness leprosy and sterility)	Egidus = St Giles, late 8 Century
September 2	Lon. burnt 66 = Fire of London 1666	
September 7	Do. Da. E. = Dog Days End (New Style)	
September 8	Nat. Ma. / Lady Fair = Birth of Mary	Mar Geburt / Nat Maria = Birth of Mary
September 14		+Erhoh = Triumph of the Holy Cross
September 21	Math / S. MAT. / St Matthew / Matth. Ev. = St Mathew	Matheus / Matthaus = St Mathew
September 22	K.G. III Cro. = George III Crowned 1760	
September 23	Eq.Day & Ni. = Equal Day and Night	
September 24	Joh:Empf = St John the Baptist conceived	
September 29	Michael / S. MIC. / St Michael / Mich. Arch. = St Michael & All Angels	Michael = St Michael and All Angels
October 4		Fransiscus = St Francis of Assisi, b1181 or 1182, d 1226
October 13	Edw. = Translation of King Edward	
October 14	IR2N = James Rex II Natus 1633	
October 16		Gallÿ / Gallus = St Gall, Swiss, d645
October 18	Luk / S. LUK. / St Luke = St Luke the Evangelist	Lucas:E / LucEv = St Luke the Evangelist
October 21	Ursula = Ursula and 11,000 virgins martyred in Cologne (She is invoked against the plague)	

Appendix 2   Saints Days on Calendars

DATE	ENGLISH	GERMAN
October 25	K.G. III Acces = Accession of George III, 1760 Crispin = St Crispins Day, m286	
October 26	K.G. III Proc. = Proclamation of George III	
October 28	Si Iu / S.S. & J. / St Simon & Jude = St Simon & St Jude	Sim:Jud / SimIud = St Simon & St Jude
October 31		Wolfga = Wolfgang. Bp of Regensburg, d 994 (Invoked against stomach trouble and wolves)
November 1	alSts / A.Sai. / All Saints = All Saints	Aller Heili / Omni Sanct = All Saints
November 2	Om. Ani. = All Souls	
November 4	K. W. Nat. = King William III born (1650)	
November 5	P. Tr / Powder Tr = Powder Treason P. PLO. / Powder Plot / Pow. Plot. = Gunpowder Plot of 1604	
November 9	Ld Mayr Day = Lord Mayors Day (London)	
November 11	S. Mart. = St Martin = St Martin, Bp of Tours. b c315, d400	Martin / Martinus / Mart:Bisch = St Martin
November 19	Elizabetha (November 17?) (Invoked against the plague)	
November 21	Oblatio Mariæ = Presentation of Mary	Mar:Opf = Presentation of Mary
November 25	St Cecilia = Cecilia (now November 22) Catharina = Catherine of Alexandria, (Invoked against diseases of the tongue)	
November 30	An / S. AND. / St Andrew = St Andrew	Andreas = St Andrew
December 4	Barbara = daughter of Dioscurus of Heliopolis. (Invoked against explosions, fire, lightning and sudden death)	
December 6	Nicol. = St Nicholas	Nicolas / Nicolaus = St Nicholas (Santa Claus in Holland) Bp of Myra, Turkey, m305
December 8	Con. Ma. = The Immaculate Conception of Mary	Mar:Empf = The Immaculate Conception of Mary
December 13	Lucia = Lucy (meaning light) due to feast day falling on Winter Solstice, Old Style (Invoked against dysentery, eye disease, haemorrhage and throat disease)	
December 21	Tho / S. THO. / St Thomas = St Thomas	Thomas = St Thomas
December 25	+ / CHRIS / Christs Day / Nat. Do. / Nat. Christ = Christmas	Christa / H Christ / Nat Chri. / Christag = Christmas
December 26	S. STEP. / St Stephen = St Stephen First Martyr	
December 27	S. IOH. / St John = St John the Evangelist	
December 28	INNO / Innocents = Holy Innocents. Slaying of newly born in Bethlehem by Herod	Unsch:K = ?
December 29	Tho. = St Thomas à Becket	

Abbreviations used - Abp = Archbishop, b = born, Bp = Bishop, c = circa, d = died, HRE = Holy Roman Emperor, m = martyred.

APPENDIX 3 — BIBLIOGRAPHY

This Bibliography lists many of the books referred to in the course of the text. References will be indicated in the following form: -
e.g. [Bion 1758 - Plate XX] referring to:-
BION, N. (translated by STONE)
'The Construction and Principal Uses of Mathematical Instruments'. (1758) - Plate XX.

This Bibliography also lists many other works that will be useful in the study of Portable Dials. In addition to these books, other publications such as auction catalogues and journals of societies interested in sundials should be referred to.

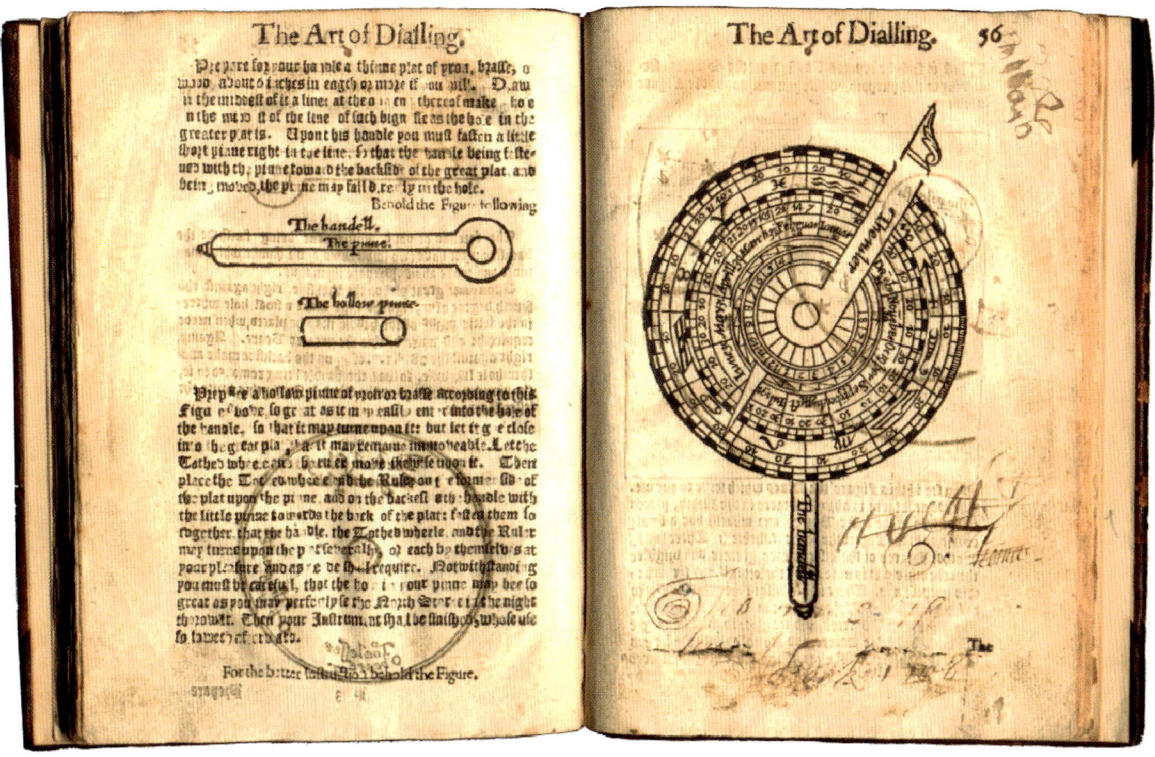

A Nocturnal illustrated in 'The Art of Dialling' by Thomas Fale, published in 1652

Ackermann, Silke
  'Sun, Moon and Stars', Antiquarian Horology, Vol. XXV, 31 - 46, 1999

Archinard, Margarida
  Les Cadrans Solaires Rectilignes. Nuncius, Museo di Storia della Scienza, Firenze, 1988

Bion, N (translated by Stone)
  The Construction and Principal Uses of Mathematical Instruments. London, 1758

Bonelli, M
  Il Museo di Storia della Scienza. Firenze, 1968

Brenni, Paolo et. al
  Orologi e strumenti della Collezione Beltrame. Museo di Storia della Scienza, Firenze, 1996

Brown, Joyce
  Mathematical Instrument-Makers in The Grocers' Company 1688 - 1800, Science Museum, London, 1979

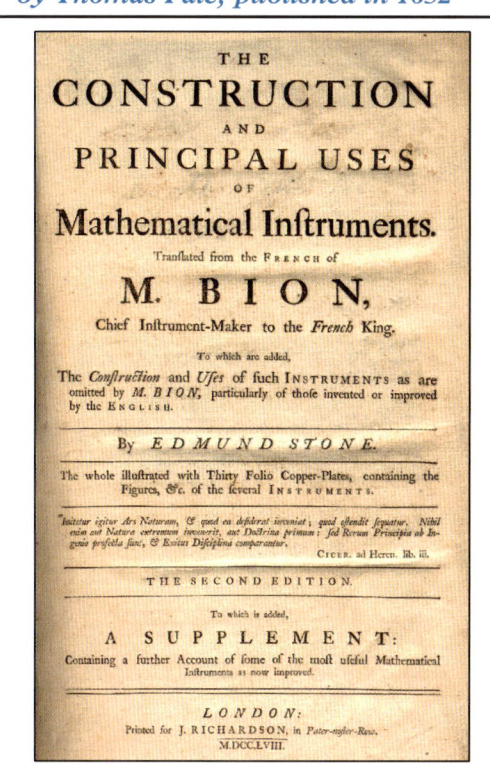

APPENDIX 3 BIBLIOGRAPHY

Bryden, David J
Sundials and Related Instruments. Whipple Museum Catalogue 6, Cambridge 1988

Chapiro A, Meslin-Perrier C and Turner A.
Catalogue de l'horologerie et des instruments de précision du début du XVIe au milieu du XVIIe siècle, Paris, 1989

Clifton, Gloria
Directory of British Scientific Instrument Makers 1550 - 1851. National Maritime Museum & Zwemmer, London 1995

Cousins, Frank W
Sundials. John Baker, London, 1969

Cowham, Mike
'Calendar Systems & Perpetual Calendars', Bulletin of The Scientific Instrument Society, 61, 62 & 64, 1999-2000

Cowham, Mike
A Study of Altitude Dials. Monograph No 4 of The British Sundial Society, 2008

Danblon, Paul
La Mesure du Temps dans les Collections Belges. Societé Generale de Banque, Bruxelles, 1984

Daumas, Maurice
Scientific Instruments of the 17th & 18th Centuries and their Makers. Batsford, London, 1972

Davis, John (Ed.)
BSS Sundial Glossary. British Sundial Society, Crowthorne, 2000

Dent, Edward J
The Dipleidoscope, London 1843

de Rijk, J. A. F
De Zon als Klok - Zonnewijzers. De Zonnewijzerkring, Utrecht, 1983

Eden, H.K.F & Lloyd, E
The Book of Sun-Dials. 4ed. Bell, London 1900

Fale, Thomas.
The Art of Dialling, London, 1652

Frémontier-Murphy, C
Les Instruments de Mathematiques XVIe - XVIIIe Siecle, Louvre, Paris, 2002

Gatty, Mrs Margaret
The Book of Sun-Dials, See Eden & Lloyd

Gouk, Penelope
The Ivory Sundials of Nuremberg, 1500 - 1700. Whipple Museum, Cambridge, 1988

Gouk, Lloyd & Turner
Ivory Diptych Sundials, 1570 - 1750. Harvard 1992

Grötzch, H & Karpinski, J
Dresden. Mathematisch-Physikalischer Salon. Seemann Verlag, Leipzig, 1978

Guye, Samuel & Michel, Henri
Time & Space. Measuring Instruments from the 15th to 19th Century. Pall Mall Press, London, 1970

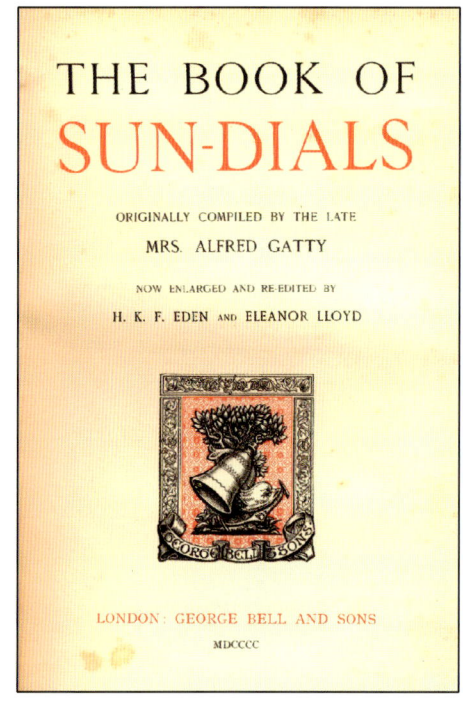

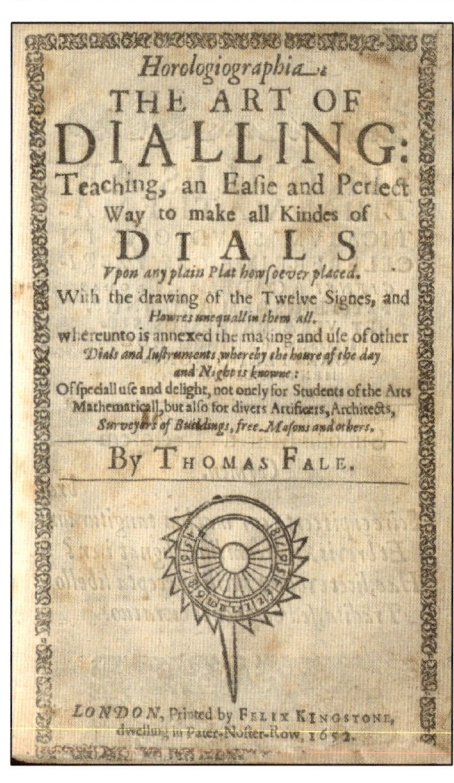

Hamel, Jürgen
Die Sonnenuhren des Museums für Astronomie und Technikgeshichte Kassel. Staatliche Museen Kassel, 2000

Hausmann, Tjark
Alte Uhren. Kunstgewerbemuseum, Berlin, 1979

Higton, Hester
Sundials. An Illustrated History of Portable Dials. Philip Wilson, London, 2001

Higton, Hester
Sundials at Greenwich. National Maritime Museum - Oxford University Press, 2002

Horský, Zdeněk & Škopová, Otilie
Astronomy Gnomonics, National Technical Museum, 1968

Husty, Peter.
Zeit & Mass - Sonnenuhren und Wissenschaftlichen Geräte. Salzburger Museum, 1994

Ickowicz, Pierre
Les Cadrans Solaires en Ivoire de Dieppe. Dieppe 2004

Laue, Georg
Scientifica - Kunstkammer Georg Laue, München 2004

Lenfeld, Jiří
Sluneční Hodiny ze sbírek UPM v Praze. Uměleckoprůmyslové Muzeum, Prague

Leybourn, William
Panorganon. London 1672

Lloyd, Steven A
Ivory Diptych Sundials 1570 - 1750. Harvard University Press, 1992

Marcelin, Franck
Dictionnaire des fabricants français d'instruments de mesure du XVe au XIXe siècle. Marcelin, Aix-en-Provence, 2004

Mattioli, Raffaele, Editor
Museo Poldo Pezzoli, Orologi - Oreficerie. Milan 1981

Meyrick, Richard
The John Gershom Parkington Memorial Collection of Time Measurement Instruments. St Edmundsbury Borough Council, Cowell, Ipswich, 1979

Michel, Henri
Catalogue des Cadrans Solaires du Musée de la vie Wallonne. Musée Wallon, Liège, 1974

Michel, Henri
Les Cadrans solaires de Max Elskamp. Musée Wallon, Liège, 1966

Michel, Henri
Scientific Instruments in Art and History. Barrie & Rockliff, London, 1966

Miniati, M
Museo di Storia della Scienza - Firenze. Catalogo, Firenze, 1991

Mollan, C
An Inventory of Historic Scientific Instruments in Institutional Collections. Dublin, 1990

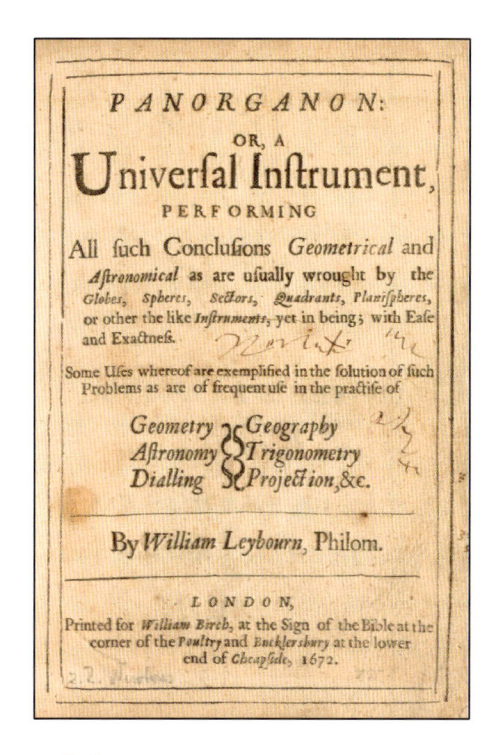

Moore, John
'Portable Dials'. Bulletin of The British Sundial Society. 92.2, 92.3, 93.3, 94.1, 94.2, 94.3, 95.1, 95.2, 95.3, 96.2, 96.3, 97.1, 97.2, 1992 - 1997

Pirovano, Carlo et. al
Museo Poldi Pezzoli - Orologi Oreficerie. Electra, Milano, 1981

Przypkowski, Piotr Maciej
Słoneczny Pomiar Czasu. Państwowe Muzeum, Jędrzejow

Rabenalt, P. Ansgar
Die Sonnenuhrensammlung der Sternwarte Kremsmünster. Berichte des Anselm Desing Vereins, Nr.33. Kremsmünster, 1996

Rohr, René R. J
Die Sonnenuhr. Geschichte, Theorie, Funktion. Callwey Verlag, München, 1982

Rohr, Rene R. J
Sundials. History, Theory and Practice. Dover, New York, 1970

Stott, Carole
Make-it-yourself Nocturnal. National Maritime Museum, London

Sturmy, Capt. Samuel
The Mariners Magazine. Second Edition, London 1679

Syndram, Dirk
Wissenschaftliche Instrumente und Sonnenuhren. Stadt Bielefeld, Callwey, 1989

Turner, A. J
Antiquités & Objets d'Art 36. Les Instruments Scientifiques. Fabbri, 1991

Turner, A. J
Time. Catalogue. Amsterdam, 1990

Turner, Anthony
Early Scientific Instruments, Europe 1400 - 1800. Sotheby's, London, 1987

Turner, Anthony J
Ritmi del Cielo e Misura del Tempo. Centro Internazionale A. Beltrame, Padova, 1985

Turner, Anthony J
Catalogue of Sun-dials, Nocturnals and Related Instruments. Instituto e Museo di Storia Della Scienze, Florence 2007

Turner, Gerard L'E
Elizabethan Instrument Makers. Oxford University Press, 2000

Turner, Gerard L'E
The Late-Mediæval Navicula. Trevor Philip & Sons Ltd, London, 1993

Van Damme, Jacques et al
Instrumentos Cientificos del Siglo XVI. Fundación Carlos de Amberes, Madrid, 1997

Wagner, Gerhard G
Sonnenuhren und Wissenschaftliche Instrumente aus den Sammlungen des Mainfränkischen Museums, Würzburg, 1997

Wagner, Gerhard and Fowler, Ian
Uhren aus vier Jahrhunderten. Augustinermuseum, Freiburg im Breizgau, 2006?

Ward, F. A. B
A Catalogue of Scientific Instruments ..... in the British Museum. British Museum, London, 1981

Ward, F
Time Measurement. Part 1: Historical Review. London 1958

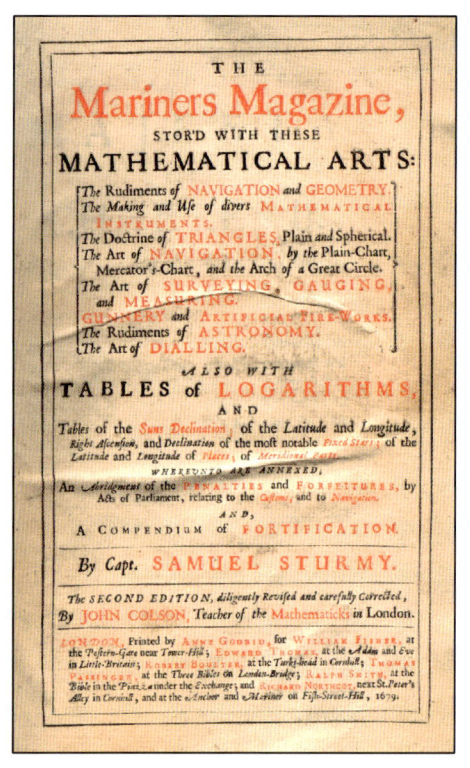

Ward, F
Time Measurement. Part 2: Descriptive Catalogue. London, 1955

Waterman, Trevor
A Measure of Time. 25th Anniversary of Trevor Philip & Sons Ltd. Trevor-Philip, London, 1997

Wilson, Jill
Biographical Index of British Sundial Makers from the Seventh Century to 1920. British Sundial Society, Crowthorne, 2003

Wright, G
The Description and use of a New Universal Dial or, Portable Equatorial Instrument. G. Wright, 1781

Wynne, Henry
The Description & Uses of the General Horological Ring or Universal Ring Dial. London, 1682

Wynter, Harriet
A Catalogue of Scientific Instruments. Vol 2, No. 1. March 1974. Sundials. Harriet Wynter, London, 1974

Wynter, H & Turner, A
Scientific Instruments. Studio Vista, London, 1975

Zinner, Ernst
Astronomische Instrumente. Beck'sche, München, 1956

APPENDIX 4   MAGNETIC DECLINATION

Magnetic Declination (or Deviation) has been recorded for at least 500 years. The Earth's magnetic poles do not coincide with the geographical poles and drift slowly in their positions. They are affected by many factors and the slow drift is probably due to the influence of other magnetic sources in the universe and even solar radiation.

In London the Magnetic North has changed from zero around 1660 to a maximum of 24° West in 1815 and is now slowly returning towards zero.

Historical records of Declination are reproduced on the chart below.

On many dials the built-in compass will show a Magnetic Declination line indicating the Declination at the time of its manufacture. If used carefully this Declination may enable the dial to be dated with some precision. However, the line may have been changed or re-cut at a later date so caution is necessary when using this method for dating.

Magnetic Declination line in compass bowl of unsigned Austrian dial, its 10°W declination suggesting a date of manufacture around 1710

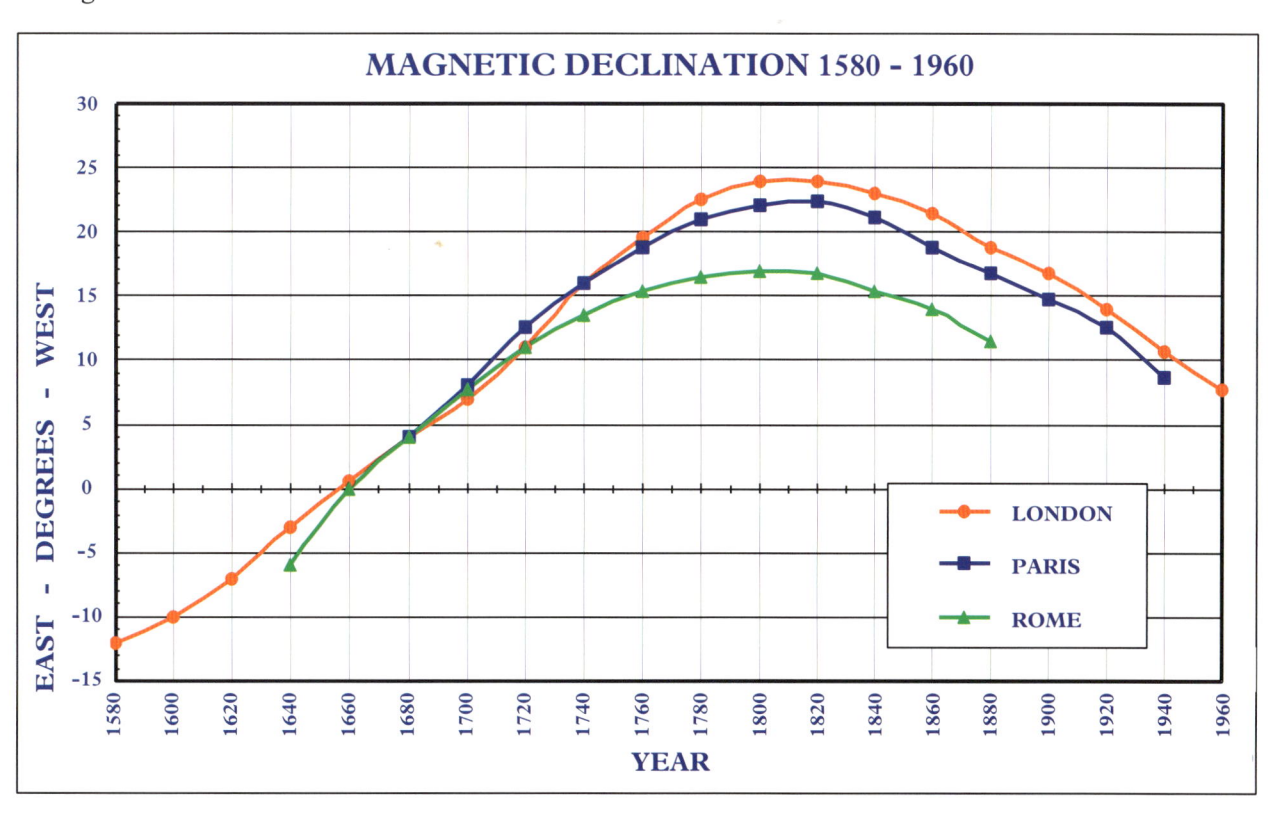

APPENDIX 5   ZODIAC & EQUATION OF TIME

When dealing with dials it is often necessary to use degrees of the Zodiac rather than the dates that we now use. The Zodiac was used for its convenience in dividing the year into 360 equal degrees, starting at the Vernal Equinox at the 'First Point of Aries', 21 March in the Gregorian Calendar (New Style). The chart below shows the correspondence between dates and Zodiac for this Calendar. For the Julian Calendar (Old Style) it will be necessary to deduct 10 or 11 days from the dates shown.

The Equation of Time is the variation between the Sun's time and that of a clock and it has been plotted inside the calendar scales. The Sun does not keep equal time due to the Earth's orbit being slightly elliptical and its axis being tilted. By adding or subtracting the amounts shown on the chart it is possible to convert Sun time to clock time.

Other representations of the Equation of Time, in the form of an analemma, like a figure '8', are often seen on public dials but not generally on portable ones.

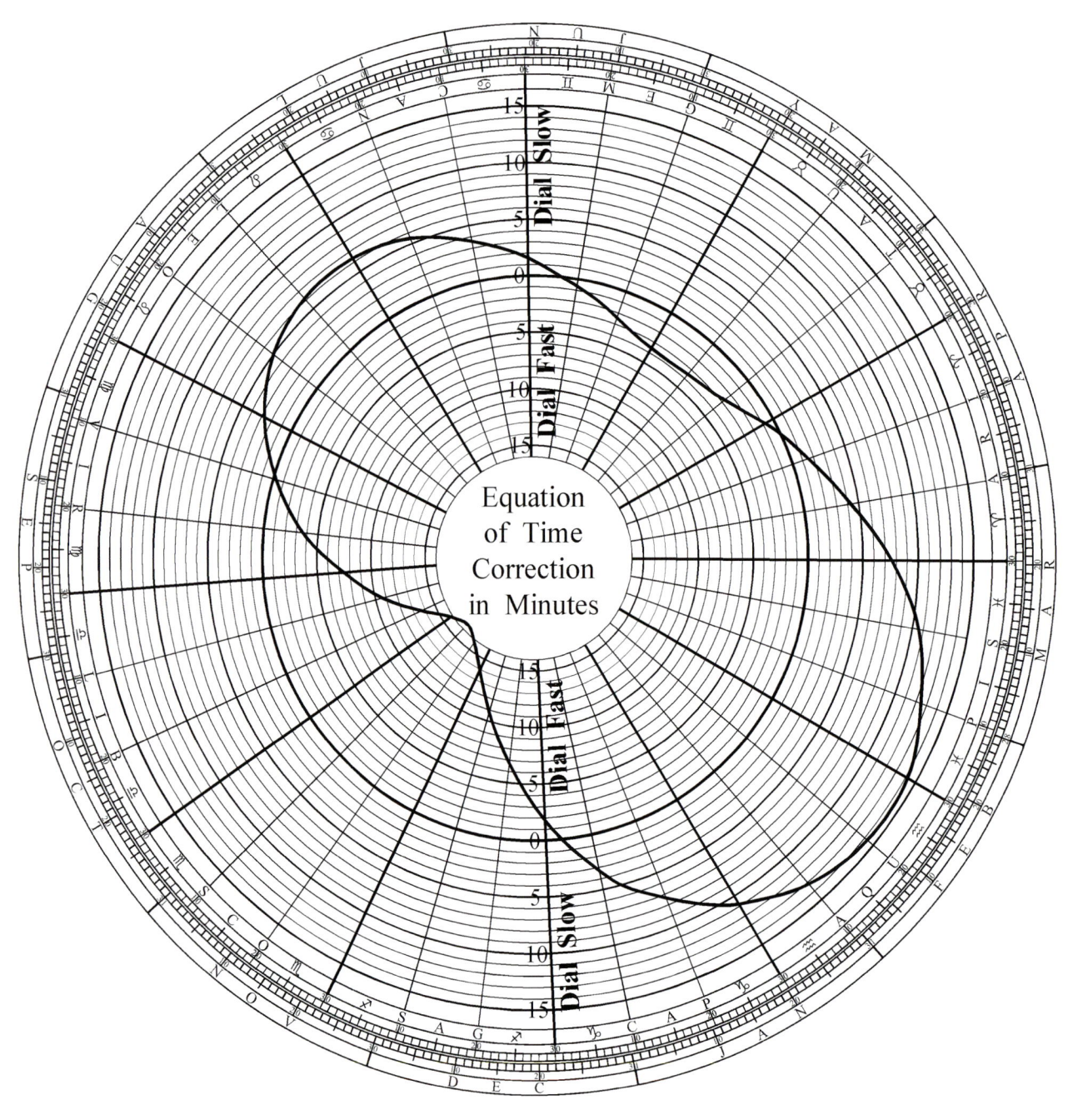

APPENDIX 5   ZODIAC AND EQUATION OF TIME

EXAMPLES OF EQUATION OF TIME

Some English dials were made to a high degree of accuracy and their makers would include Equation of Time details with their dials, either as a chart, sometimes pasted into the lid of a dial, or it would be engraved around the dial in calendar form.

It is also possible to tell from the table if the dial was made to Julian Calendar (pre-1752) or the later Gregorian Calendar. The dial by Glynn(e), of about 1710, has its figures about 10½ days earlier than that by Fraser, made about 1800.

Further examples will be found in various sections of the book.

Equation of Time pasted inside the lid of an unsigned Magnetic Compass Dial made for Rio

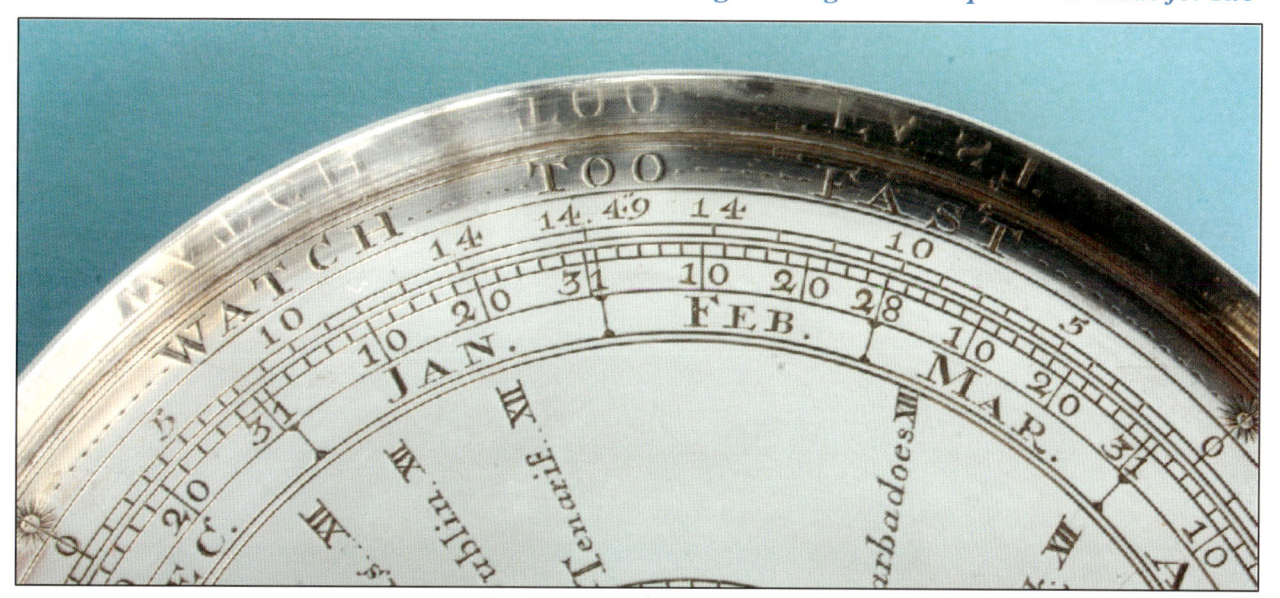

Equation of Time calendar inside lid of Compass Dial by Richard Glynn(e)

Magnetic Compass Dial by Fraser, London, showing one half of its Equation of Time calendar

193

APPENDIX 6   SUNDIAL COLLECTIONS

Portable dials may be found in collections all over the World. Most of these are in museums with a scientific bias, although some other museums occasionally have small collections. This list is not exhaustive, and the museums chosen are those known to the author where interesting collections can be seen. The museums listed are for convenience, separated alphabetically into countries. Certain galleries may close at various times, or the majority of their dials may be in store or in reserve collections. Where these details are known, they are listed. If a long journey is involved, it is recommended that the visitor contact the museum concerned to check on opening hours and availability of the collection.

The collecting of items is not a new habit. It has gone on ever since man started to treasure the things around him. The collecting of sundials too must have started very early - soon after the first dials appeared.

Most museum collections were started by private collectors which were then either bequeathed to or were bought by the museum.

The monastery at Kremsmünster

AUSTRIA
Kremsmünster
In the astronomical cabinet at the Observatory is a collection of over 90 sundials. These are catalogued and illustrated in a small booklet and on a CD.

BELGIUM
Brussels
Musée du Cinquantenaire.
The museum has a small collection of dials on display. These are mostly dials by Belgian and Low Countries makers.

Liège
Musée de la Vie Wallonne.
This museum houses a very large collection of portable dials, totalling around 400 items. The collection is not always available for viewing, so it is best to check with the curator before making a special journey.
The collection here was a bequest from Max Elskamp, born in Antwerp in 1862. He died in 1931 leaving his extensive collection to the museum. His collection of sundials was considered to be one of the most important in the world with 582 items. He was also a prolific writer and wrote some 150 papers on gnomonics. His studies gave an insight into the scientific thought, organisation of craftsmen and views of their social life. He was also a poet and was interested generally in folklore.

CZECH REPUBLIC
Prague
Národní Technické Muzeum (National Technical Museum).
An interesting collection of Dials and Astronomical Instruments described and illustrated in a catalogue of 1968.

Prague
Uměleckoprůmyslové Muzeum. (Museum of Decorative Arts).
The museum houses a large collection of sundials and scientific instruments. The sundials are well illustrated in their catalogue.

ENGLAND
Bury St. Edmunds, Suffolk
Moyses Hall Museum.
The collection was formerly housed in the Manor House Museum, sadly, now closed. Some of the collection is now on display in Moyses Hall and

the rest is in store at West Stow Museum, near to Bury St Edmunds. It is hoped that the whole collection will be displayed again soon.

They have an impressive collection of clocks, watches and sundials collected in the 1930's by the bandleader Frederic Gersholm Parkington, a native to Bury. He left his extensive collection in memory of his son John who had been killed in the Second World War. The collection is mostly of important clocks and watches but includes about 30 good quality sundials. A catalogue has been produced listing their collection with some photographs.

Whipple Museum, Cambridge

Cambridge
The Whipple Museum of the History of Science. Owned by the University and sometimes closed out of Term times. Open to the public weekday afternoons. The Whipple contains a great collection of portable dials as well as many other scientific instruments. A catalogue has been produced listing their entire sundial collection with many photographs. Most of the portable dials are conveniently displayed in drawer units which may be pulled out for close inspection.

The collection was started by R. S. Whipple who was formerly Managing Director and Chairman of the Cambridge Scientific Instrument Company. In 1944 he gave his extensive collection of instruments to Cambridge University. His collection represents about 30% of the dials now on display in the Whipple Museum. A further 30% have been placed there on permanent loan by the Fitzwilliam Museum, Cambridge.

Greenwich
The National Maritime Museum, Old Royal Observatory.

The Old Royal Observatory is the section of the Museum located at the top of the hill, overlooking the main National Maritime Museum. It contains a collection of astronomical and timekeeping instruments including sundials. There is a Students Room where the dials from the reserve collection may be viewed on application to the curator.

London
The British Museum.

This museum houses one of the best collections of early and important dials including two pocket dials by Thomas Tompion, one in gold and the other in silver. A few dials are on display, but to see the majority of the collection it is necessary to visit the Students Room. The collection is well catalogued by Dr F A B Ward. This book is available in the Students Room, and individual dials may be examined on request.

London
The Science Museum.

There are many portable dials to be seen in the Science Museum. A catalogue of Time Measurement lists the dials in the Time Measurement section but a further collection is to be found in the Astronomy department.

Oxford
The Museum of the History of Science.
Open Tuesday to Saturday afternoons.

The museum houses the most extensive collection of portable dials in the Country. Most of these were bequeathed by Lewis Evans. There are also extensive collections of scientific and medical instruments.

Museum of the Hisory of Science, Oxford

Lewis Evans, 1853 - 1930, had been trained as a chemist at University College, London, eventually becoming Chairman of the family paper making business, John Dickenson & Co. Ltd. His magnificent collection of Portable Dials was collected over a period of 50 years. He exhibited some of these at The Royal Society, The Society of Antiquaries and The White City between 1890 and 1911. His collection of Astrolabes and other mathematical instruments were to increase significantly in this period. In 1922 the collection was offered to the Ashmolean Museum in Oxford, being placed there in 1924. In 1935 these items were to form the nucleus of the Museum of the History of Science in the Old Ashmolean Building.

Lewis Evans wrote a chapter on Portable Dials for 'The Book of Sun-Dials' written by Mrs. Gatty, illustrating it with dials from his own collection.

FRANCE
Ecouen
Musée National de la Renaissance, Château d'Ecouen.
Major collection of Renaissance objects with one small room having a few sundials, clocks, watches and scientific instruments. However, this room is not always open to the public.

Paris
Musée des Arts et Métiers.
The museum houses a large collection of scientific instruments but many of these are held in their store at St. Denis.

Paris
The Louvre.
Landau Collection in Room 46.
The collection is housed in a pair of cabinets but is particularly strong in sundials, mostly of French origin.

GERMANY
Bielefeld
Kunstgewerbesammlung Stiftung Huelsmann.
The museum contains an impressive collection of portable dials that are well described and illustrated in the book by Syndram.
The collection was formed by Friedrich Karl August Huelsmann, 1904 - 1979. He worked as an art dealer and put together an impressive collection of fine art, including sundials. Following his death in 1979 and that of his widow in 1983 the collection was bequeathed to the town museum.

Mathematisch-Physicalischer Salon, Dresden

Dresden
Staatlischer Mathematisch-Physikalischer Salon, Zwinger.
The museum, which is part of the famous Zwinger, houses an impressive collection of instruments and clocks including an interesting but quite small sundial section. A well illustrated book, published in 1978, details and illustrates some of the fine articles in their collection.

Freiburg im Breizgau
Augustinermuseum.
A good collection of portable dials, clocks and other objects. Their horological collection is well illustrated in their catalogue 'Uhren aus vier Jahrhunderten'.

Hamburg
Museum für Kunst und Gewerbe.
This is a large museum of fine arts and has many beautiful objects. In particular it has a large collection of musical instruments. One room is devoted to its scientific instrument collection. It houses some impressive astrolabes and a quantity of good sundials.

Munich
Deutches Museum.
This is a large science museum with many interesting exhibits. A small quantity of dials are on display in the museum but many more are held in their reserve store.

Nuremberg
Germanishes Nationalmuseum.
This is a general museum displaying the arts and crafts of German artists. It concentrates on items from Nuremberg and the surrounding area. Its collection of portable dials includes some ivory dials made in Nuremburg, and other very rare and interesting dials.

APPENDIX 6   SUNDIAL COLLECTIONS

Museo Galileo, Florence

ITALY
Florence
Museo Galileo, (formerly Il Museo di Storia Della Scienza).
A science museum specialising in smaller artefacts. It has a very impressive collection of Portable Dials and Astrolabes, in particular those made in Italy. In common with many Italian museums it has produced several excellent catalogues of its collections.

Milan
Museo Poldi Pezzoli.
A fine arts museum with a large if not spectacular collection of dials. Again a well catalogued collection.

IRELAND
Dublin
National Museum of Ireland.
A general museum with many fine objects including a small collection of scientific instruments with some sundials. Most instruments are held in the store room. The museum now houses the well-known Eggestorff Collection.
Paul Egestorff put together a large collection of scientific instruments which he kept in his large Georgian house in Dublin. The collection grew so large that he and his wife retreated to live on the top floor. There were at least 200 instruments in the collection, even a car and at least one stationary steam engine, plus a few good quality sundials. In particular two Universal Equinoctial Mechanical Dials by T Mason of Dublin and some Nuremberg ivory dials.
Details of the many scientific instruments that are to be found in Irish collections are given by Charles Mollan.

NETHERLANDS
Leiden
Museum Boerhaave.
This is a science museum covering a wide spectrum of exhibits. They have a small collection of dials on display.

Large Vertical Dial over a shop near to the Przypkowski Museum, Jędrzejow

POLAND
Jędrzejow
Przypkowski Museum, (Panstwowe Museum).
This museum is based around a large collection of sundials that were put together by Felix Przypkowski. He was the local doctor in Jędrzejow, Poland where he worked from 1905 until his death in 1952. He was a keen amateur astronomer but his interests were wide, not confined to astronomy and dialling but also meteorology, photography and even gastronomy. It was in 1910 that he first exhibited his collection publicly. He keenly collected sundials and many of these are now to be seen in the Panstwowe Museum in Jędrzejow, (perhaps better known as the Przypkowski Museum). Many of his dials, nocturnals and quadrants were made by him, mostly in wood. Later he started collecting old dials and other time-measurement

devices. The house where he lived is now the museum, preserved with its furnishings and memorabilia as it would have looked in the early twentieth century. The main collection of sundials is housed in one large room in purpose-built display cases. A catalogue gives details and some photographs of the collection.

RUSSIA
St Petersburg
The Hermitage Museum.
A fine collection of scientific instruments including sundials but the collection is not on public display.

SCOTLAND
Edinburgh
The Royal Scottish Museum, Chambers Street.
The Museum has a collection of Scientific Instruments including a small collection of dials.

SPAIN
Madrid
Museo Naval.
A Maritime museum with a small dial and astrolabe collection.

SWITZERLAND
Basel
Kirschgartenmuseum.
A general museum in the centre of Basel. It has a large collection of portable dials which are well displayed. It also contains some fine early clocks.

Geneva
Musée de l'Histoire des Sciences.
A small museum housing an impressive collection of scientific instruments including some dials and a rare Navicula.

USA
Cambridge, Massachusets
Harvard University.
A very small museum with just one room open to the public for viewing. Its sundial collection is stored away and is only available by special application to the curator. Its collection of ivory dials is well documented in the book 'Ivory Diptych Sundials 1570 - 1750'.

The collection was formed by David P Wheatland who had graduated from Harvard University in 1922, initially entering his family's forestry business. Six years later he returned to Harvard as a research associate. He became interested in collecting scientific instruments and early books. At the end of the Second World War he collected many instruments discarded by Harvard. He put most of these items on display in 1949 as 'The Collection of Historic Scientific Instruments'. Wheatland then became curator of these instruments finding a permanent space for them within the University. He later obtained a large number of sundials from a private collector in 1949. He continued purchasing instruments, more particularly dials for the next 30 years. His collection numbered over 700 sundials with a similar number of books on dialling.

Washington, D.C.
Smithsonian Institute. National Museum of History and Technology.

Chicago, Illinois
The Adler Planetarium.
The collection also includes many of the dials from the former Time Museum collected by Seth Attwoood. He had become interested in astronomy and particularly the area related to horology. He began collecting clocks, watches, sundials and astrolabes about 50 years ago. He built his own museum, 'The Time Museum' at the Clock Tower Motel at Roquefort, Illinois. The museum has now been closed but many of its wonderful objects were taken into the Adler Planetarium in Chicago.

APPENDIX 7   SIGNATURES ON DIALS

Makers signatures from some of the dials pictured in this book are shown below.

Most makers had several signatures so expect variations of these to appear on some of their other dials. Signatures are generally in capitals, in an attractive cursive form or are marked using letter punches. All three types will be seen below.

David Beringer

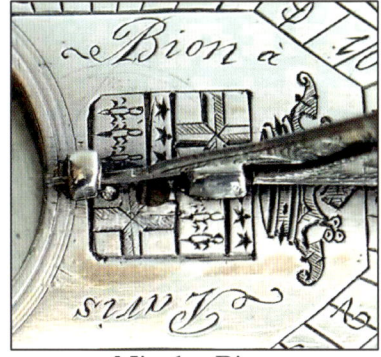

Nicolas Bion

J Bizot

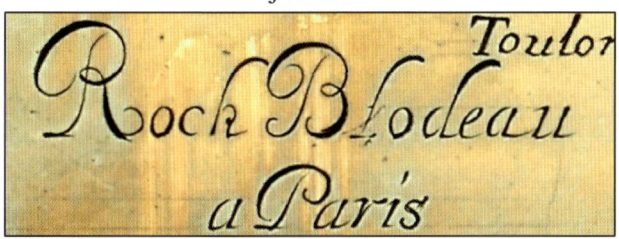

Roch Blondeau

Charles Bloud

Michael Butterfield

Michel Cadot

Jacques Canivet

Jean Chapotot

Chevalier

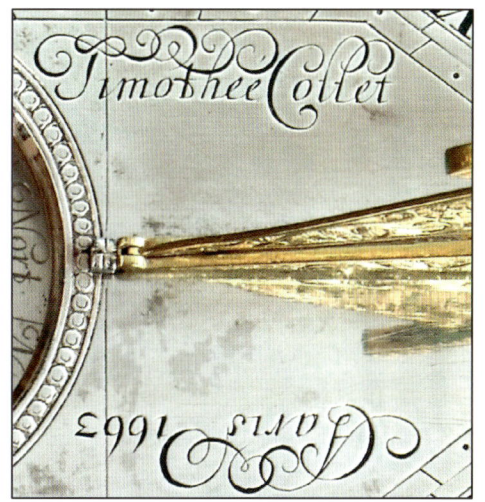

Timothée Collet

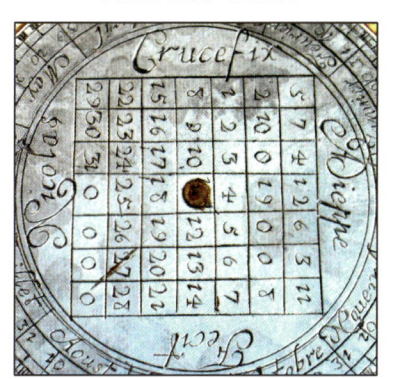

Nicolas Crucefix

Appendix 7   Signatures on Dials

Edmund Culpeper

Francoise de Laistre

Peter Dollond

E.C. *(Possibly Edmund Culpeper)*

Fran Anto

Fraser

Richard Glynne

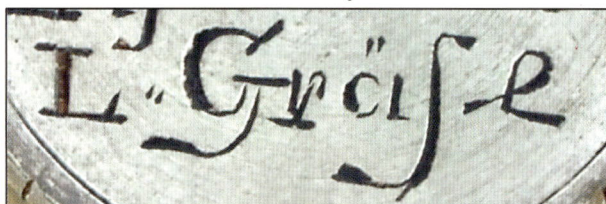

Lorenz Grassl

Thomas Haye

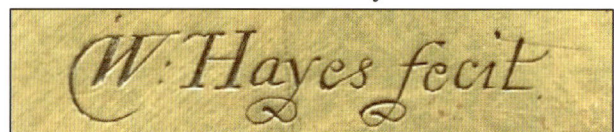

Walter Hayes

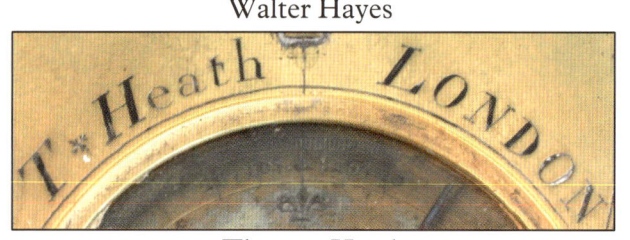

Thomas Heath

Nathanaell Heighemore

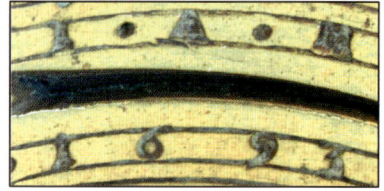

I. A. M. *unidentified maker of a Poke Dial*

Franz Antoni Knitl

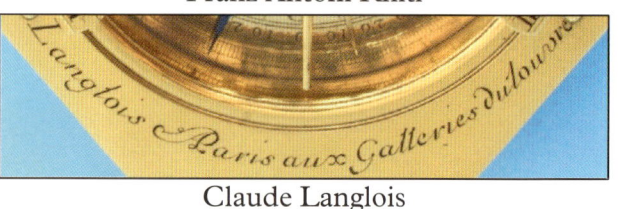

Claude Langlois

Le Febvre (Lefebvre)

Jacques le Maire et Fils

Pierre le Maire

Nicolas Lemaindre

Henry Macquart

APPENDIX 7 SIGNATURES ON DIALS

Manche

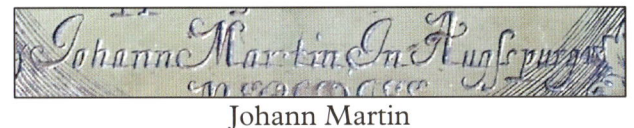

Johann Martin

P. I. Maynadie

Lienhart Miller

John Naish

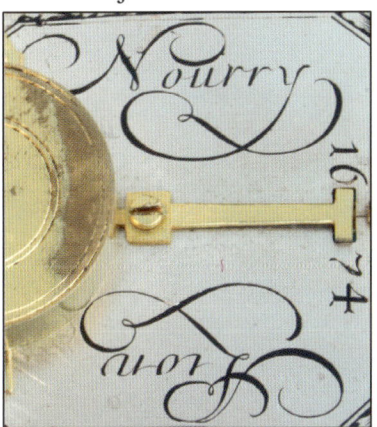

Jean Nourry

Pohringer Haag

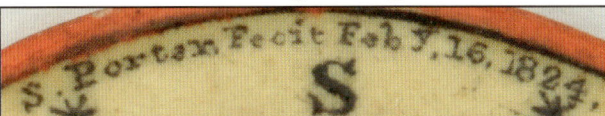

Samuel Porter

Marcus Purmann

Gottfried Reiff

Paul Reinman

R. F. *(unknown maker of French Ivory Dials)*

John Rowley

Samoilov *(from Izhora)*

Pierre Savtout-Choizy

S A V Z *(unidentified German? maker)*

Johann Wilhelm Schultze

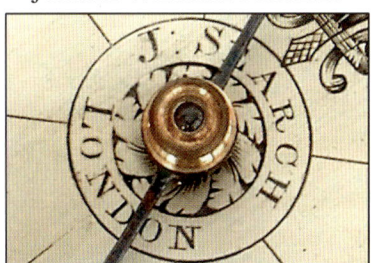

James Search

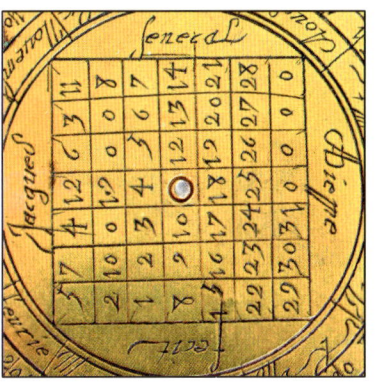

Jacques Senecal

201

APPENDIX 7   SIGNATURES ON DIALS

Pierre Sevin

James Simons

Joshua Springer

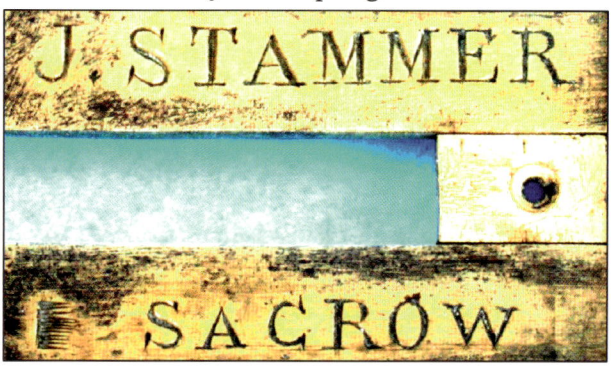

J Stammer (of Sacrow)

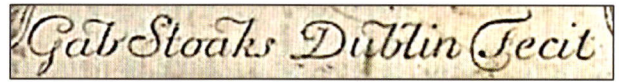

Gabriel Stokes (Stoaks)

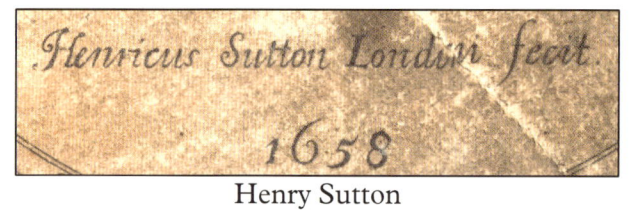

Henry Sutton

Hans Troschel

Hans Tucher

TW (unidentified maker of a Poke Dial)

Andreas Vogler

Jeremiah & Walter Watkins

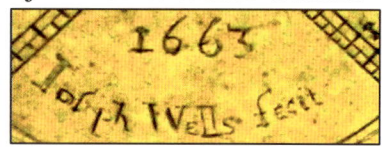

Joseph Wells

Richard Whitehead (Whithead)

Charles Whitwell

Johann Willebrand

John Worgan

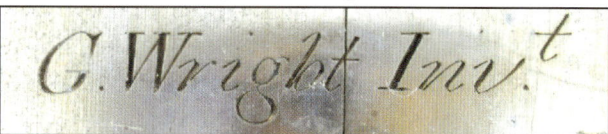

Gabriel Wright

Thomas Wright

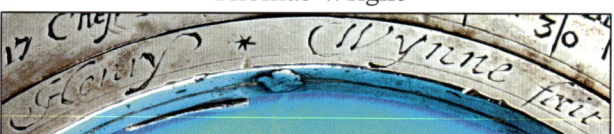

Henry Wynne

202

INDEX

KEY TO INDEX

Chapter Titles	**BOLD CAPITALS**
Chapter Sub Headings	CAPITALS, inset
Makers and People	SURNAME, Other Names
Illustrations	**bold numerals**
Notes	*italics*

All numbers shown are page numbers. Note that a page may have more than one illustration.

A

Abraham & Isaac   iv

ACKNOWLEDGEMENTS.   iv

ADAMS, George   **124**

AHAZ, Dial of   17

ALLEN, Elias   86, 87

ALTITUDE DIALS.
Chapter 2.   10 - 19
    THE PILLAR DIAL   11 - 12
    THE VERTICAL DISC DIAL   12 - 13
    VERTICAL PLATE DIALS   13 - 15
    RING & POKE DIALS   15
    THE REGIOMONTANUS DIAL   15
    THE CAPUCHIN DIAL   15 - 16
    THE NAVICULAR   16
    QUADRANTS   16 - 17
    SCAPHE DIALS   17 - 18
    NAVIGATIONAL INSTRUMENTS   18
    PLANISPHERIC ASTROLABE   18 - 19

Altitude Ring Dial   20

Anglo-Saxon Dial   **8**

ANALEMMATIC DIALS.
Chapter 18.   122 - 124

Arab Numerals   180

Aspects *astrological*   43, 44, **145**, 146

Astrolabe   18, **19**, 166, **180**

Astronomical Compendium   143 - 176

Astronomical Ring Dial   **30**

Augsburg Dials   vi, 4, **5**, 97, 107 - 113, **162**

AUGSBURG DIALS.
Chapter 15.   107 - 113
    AUGSBURG STYLE DIALS   107 - 111
    THE CRESCENT DIAL   111 - 112
    STRING GNOMON DIAL   112 - 113
    THEIR MAKERS   113

THE AUTHOR.   v

B

Babylonian Hours   43, 44, 45, 50

Babylonians   6

Backstaff   10, **18**

BARADELLE, Jacques   67

Bauernring   20

BECK, R & J   **50**

BEDOS DE CELLES, Dom Francois   67, 68, 70

BERINGER, David   117, **118**, *199*

BIBLIOGRAPHY.
Appendix 3.   187 - 190

BION, Nicolas   66, 67, 73, **98**, *199*

Bion/Stone Illustrations   **ix, 10, 20, 30, 32, 114, 123, 141, 187**

BIZOT, J   69, **71**, *199*

BLONDEAU, Roch   **14**, 65, 67, *199*

BLOUD, Charles   4, 51, 52, **54, 55, 176, 177**, *199*

Bohemian Hours   46

BUTTERFIELD, Michael   1, 4, 61, **62, 63**, 65, **68**, 69, 77, 78, **175**, *199*

Butterfield Dials   4, 59, 61, 65 - 77, 78 - 85, 92, **99**, 115

Brachiolus   15

C

CADOT, Michel   70, *199*

CANIVET, Jacques   **64**, 67, *199*

Capuchin Dials   **14**, 15, 16

CARING FOR A COLLECTION.
Chapter 26.   161 - 168
    CLEANING   161 - 165
    CONSERVATION & RESTORATION   165
    REPAIRS & REPLACEMENTS   165 - 167
    HANDLING & STORAGE   167 - 168
    CONCLUSIONS   168

Cases for Dials   3, 72, 73, 78, 81, 85, 168

Chapter Ring   5

Chalice Dial   **18**

CHAPOTOT, Jean   60, 67, **115, 116**, *199*

CHEVALIER   78, **79**, *199*

INDEX

Cleobury Mortimer Dial	9
Clockmakers Company	86
COGGS, John	79
COLE, Humphrey	86
COLLET, Timothée	**61, 178, 199**
Compass	**2, 5, 52, 56, 68, 76, 80, 89, 95, 176, 177, 191**
Compass Bowl	**2, 5, 95, 176, 177, 191**
Compass Card	**145, 176**
Compass Declination	**76, 80, 103, 191**
Compass Needle	5

THE COMPENDIUM.
Chapter 23. 143 - 146

Chinese Numerals	181
Conservation	165

CONTENTS. iii

Crescent Dials	110, **111**
Cross Staff	10, 18
CRUCEFIX, Nicolas	**55, 56, 152, 199**
Crucifix Dials	105, 106
Cube Dials	117, **118**
CULPEPER, Edmund I & II	**28, 29,** 86, 87, 88, **114,** 115, 155, **167, 200**
Cup Dials	17, **18**

D

DE LAISTRE, Francoise	**66, 200**
DENT, Edward John	140
Dial Plate	5
Dieppe	**4, 51 - 56,** 59
Dipleidoscope	140
Diptych Dials	**4, 40 - 50, 165,** 170, 171, 172, 176
DOLLOND, Peter	92, **93,** 116, **200**

E

E.C. *Perpetual Calendar by*	**154,** 155, **200**
Egyptian Shadow Stick	6

ENGLISH DIALS.
Chapter 11. 86 - 96
 THE SIXTEENTH CENTURY 86
 THE SEVENTEENTH CENTURY 86 - 90
 THE EIGHTEENTH CENTURY 90 - 94
 THE NINETEENTH CENTURY 94 - 96

English Rose	iv
Epact	**144, 154,** 155
Equatorial Dials	4, 53, 55, **93,** 143
Equation of Time	82, 92, **93,** 125, **128,** 137, **192, 193**

Equinoctial Dial	4

EQUINOCTIAL RING DIALS.
Chapter 4. 24 - 30
 UNIVERSAL EQUINOCTIAL
 RING DIAL 24 - 29
 STANDING RING DIAL 29 - 30
 ASTRONOMICAL RING DIAL 30

European Numerals	180

F

Fakes and Forgeries	50
FALE, *illustration by*	**147, 187**
Finger Ring Dial	**131**

THE FIRST PORTABLE DIALS.
Chapter 1. 6 - 9

A FINAL GLANCE.
Chapter 28. 175 - 179

FRAN ANTO	150, **151, 200**
FRASER	**125, 126, 192, 200**

FRENCH BUTTERFIELD DIALS.
Chapter 9. 65 - 77
 HISTORY OF THE
 BUTTERFIELD DESIGN 66 - 67
 HOW TO USE THE
 BUTTERFIELD DIAL 67 - 69
 DIAL BETAILS 69 - 70
 THE UNDERSIDE 70 - 72
 CARRYING CASES 72
 THE PRINCIPAL MAKERS AND
 THEIR WORKPLACES 72 - 75
 THE DECLINE OF THE
 BUTTERFIELD DIAL 75 - 76
 FAKES AND FORGERIES 76 - 77

FRENCH DIALS.
Chapter 8. 59 - 64
 BEFORE 1700 59 - 63
 AFTER 1700 63 - 64

FRENCH IVORY DIALS.
Chapter 7. 51 - 58
 DIEPPE IVORY DIALS 51 - 52
 MAGNETIC AZIMUTH DIAL 52 - 56
 OTHER FRENCH DIALS 56 - 58

FRISIUS, Gemma	24

G

Gazetteer	5, 43, 52, 53, 82, 109, 114, 115, 116
GLYNN, Richard	91, 92, **153,** 155, **192, 200**
Gnomon	5, 59, 60, 61, 63, 69, 76, 78, 81, 89, 91
Gnomon Decoration	59, 63, 91
GOATER, John	**18**
GRASSL, Lorenz	**vi,** 109, 110, **200**
Green Man	55, **132,** 175
Gregorian (New Style) Calendar	29, 47, 93, 94, 152, 158
Grocers Company	86

INDEX

Gunter's Quadrant	32 - 35

H

HABERMEL, Erasmus	13
Ham Dial	7
Hand Dial	7
Handling *of Dials*	168
HARTMANN, Georg	40
HAYE, Thomas	67, **71, 72**, 176, **200**
HAYES, Walter	**32, 35**, 86, **87, 88, 89, 90**, 167, **200**
HEATH, Thomas	**79, 80, 81, 85, 200**
HEIGHEMORE, Nathanaell	**34, 35, 151, 177, 200**
Heliochron	12, **13**, 173
Hemicyclium	7
Horodictical Quadrant	36, **37**

I

I. A. M. *unidentified maker of a Poke Dial*	22, **23, 200**
Inclining Dials	4, **93**, 114 - 118
INCLINING DIALS. **Chapter 16.**	114 - 118
INDEX.	203 - 207
INTRODUCTION.	1 - 5
Isaac	iv
Islamic Quadrant	39
Italian Hours	43, 44, **45**, 50, 120, **121**
Ivory Diptych Dials	4, 40 - 50, **165**, 170, 171, 172
IVORY DIPTYCH DIALS. **Chapter 6.**	40 - 50
OTHER DIPTYCH DIALS	49 - 50
FAKES AND FORGERIES	50

J

Jacobstaff	10
Japanese Numerals	181
JONES, Henry *clockmaker*	90
Julian Calendar	47, **93, 94**, 152, 158

K

KALA, Michael *modern dial*	172, **173**
KARNER, Albrecht	47, **48**
KINGDON, S. *Perpetual Calendar design*	**153**, 155
Kirkdale Priory Dial	8
KNIBB, Joseph *clockmaker*	91
KNITL, Franz Anton	**135, 136, 200**
KYNVYN	86

L

LANGLOIS, Claude	67, **98, 99, 200**
Latitude Arc	5
Latitude Tables	5, 143
LE FEBVRE (LEFEBVRE)	67, **69**, 100, **101, 200**
LE MAIRE, Jacques	**67, 68, 69, 200**
LE MAIRE, Pierre	71, **72, 200**
LEMAINDRE, Nicolas	**59, 200**
LEYBOURN, William	36, **88**
Lodestone	3
London Dials	4, 78 - 82, 86 - 96, 114, 117, **122, 124**, 125 - 127, 137 - 140, 143 - 146, **193**
London, Map of	96
Lunar Volvelle	44, 53, 57, **108**

M

MACQUART, Henry	**116, 200**
Magnetic Azimuth Dials	4, 51, **52 - 56**, **88, 89, 90**
Magnetic Compass Dials	95, 125 - 128
MAGNETIC COMPASS DIALS. **Chapter 19.**	125 - 128
Magnetic Declination	2, **103**, 126, **191**
MAGNETIC DECLINATION. **Appendix 4.**	191
MAIN PARTS OF A PORTABLE DIAL	5
MAIN PLACES FOR PRODUCTION OF PORTABLE DIALS	4
MANCHE	**64, 201**
Mariner's Astrolabe	10, 18
MARTIN, Johann	5, 92, 108, **111, 112, 113**, 177, 178, **201**
Mary Rose Dial	**9, 170**
MASIG *London agent for Augsburg Dials*	**92**, 113
MAYNADIE, P. I.	**37, 179, 201**
Meridian	64
Metal Polish	161
Microcrystalline Wax	162
MILLER, Lienhart	**40, 42, 43, 44, 45, 201**
Minute Dials	**135, 136, 137, 138**
MISCELLANEOUS DIALS. **Chapter 22.**	141 - 142

N

'n' Quality Symbol for Nuremberg	**46**, 47
NAISH, John	**24, 25, 201**
Nautical Quadrant	**26**

INDEX

Navicula	**15, 16**
N.H. *unidentified maker of Quadrant*	37
Nocturnals	57, 58, 143, **144**, 147 - 151, **176**

NOCTURNALS.
Chapter 24.	147 - 151
THE PLANISPHERIC NOCTURNAL	151
Noon Gun	**142**
Noon Mark	**64**
NOURRY, Jean	**59, 201**

NUMERALS, LETTERS & SIGILS.
Appendix 1.	180 - 181
NUMERALS	180 - 181
LETTERS	181
SIGILS	181
Nuremberg Dials	4, 40 - 49

O
Octant	10
Organum Ptolomei	35, **151**

OTHER BUTTERFIELD DIALS.
Chapter 10.	78 - 85
THE LONDON MAKERS	79 - 84
OTHER MAKERS	84
DIAL CASES	85
OUGHTRED, Rev. William	24

P
Panorganon	36
Paris	4, 59 - 64
Perpetual Calendars	42, 56, 92, 94, 95, 96, 152 - 160, **182**

PERPETUAL CALENDARS.
Chapter 25.	152 - 160
MEDIEVAL QUADRANS NOVUS	159 - 160
Pillar Dials	7, **10**, **11**
Plain Table (Plain Table)	**88**, 89
Planetary Hours	31, 102
Planetary Rulers	**102**
Planetery Symbols	181
Planispheric Astrolabes	10, **18**, **19**
Planispheric Nocturnal	35, **151**
POHRINGER HAAG	**133, 134, 201**
Poke Dial	20, **169**
Polar Dials	53, **105, 106**

POLAR DIALS.
Chapter 14.	105 - 106
Polyhedral Dials	**141**, 142
PORTER, S	**126, 127, 201**

PREFACE, HOW I BECAME INTERESTED IN PORTABLE DIALS.
	vi

PREFACE TO SECOND EDITION.	vii
Premier Cadran	**70**
Prime	144
Prophatius Quadrant	**39**
PRUJEAN, John	35
Punch Marking of Ivory	41
PURMANN, Marcus	120, **130, 201**

Q
Quai de l'Horloge, Paris *map of*	73
Quadrant	10, 16, **17**, **87**, **151**, **159**, **177**, **178**
Quadrans Novus	31, 32, **159**
Quadrans Vetus	31

QUADRANTS.
Chapter 5.	31 - 39
QUADRANS NOVUS	31 - 32
GUNTER'S QUADRANT	32 - 35
THE PANORGANON	36
HORODICTICAL QUADRANT	36 - 37
SUTTON'S QUADRANT	37 - 39
THE ISLAMIC QUADRANT	39
Quadrat	33
Quibla Indicator	8
Quintant	10

R
Regiomontanus Dials	14, 15, 73
REIFF, Gottfried	**11, 201**
REINMAN, Paul	**42, 46, 47, 157, 201**
Repairs	165 - 167
Replacements	165 - 167

REPRODUCTION & MODERN DIALS.
Chapter 27.	169 - 174
FAKES	169
COPIES	169 - 170
CONTEMPORARY FAKES	170
INCOMPETENT DIALS	170 - 172
MODERN DIALS	172 - 174
Restoration	165
R. F. *unknown maker of French Ivory Dials*	57, 58, **201**
Roman Calendar	**159**, 160
ROWLEY, John	79, **81, 82, 177, 201**

S

SAINTS DAYS ON CALENDARS.
Appendix 2.	182 - 186
SAMOILOV *from Izhora*	84, 85, **168, 201**
SAVTOUT-CHOISY, Pierre	**69, 201**
S A V Z *unidentified maker*	131, **132, 175, 201**
Scaphe Dials	17, **18**, **50**, 119 - 121

SCAPHE DIALS.
Chapter 17. 119 - 121

SCHISSLER, Christopher (senior) **107, 108**

SCHULTZE, Johann Wilhelm **97**, 98, **201**

Scientific Instrument Makers Company 86

SCHNIEP, Ulrich 102

SEARCH, James 93, **94, 201**

SENECAL, Jacques 52, **53, 201**

SEVIN, Pierre **28, 60, 202**

Sextant 10

Shadow Length 6

Shadow Square 15, **33, 34**

Shadow Stick 6

Shepherd's Dial 10

Signatures 199 - 202, 5

SIGNATURES ON DIALS.
Appendix 7. 199 - 202

SIMONS, James 79, **94, 153, 202**

SIMPLE RING DIALS.
Chapter 3. 20 - 23
    THE POKE DIAL 20 - 23

Spectacle Makers Company 86

SPRINGER, Joshua **116**, 117, **202**

STAMMER (of Sacrow) **26, 27, 29, 202**

Standing Ring Dial 30

Stepped Poke Dial 21, **22**

STOKES (STOAKS), Gabriel **123, 124, 202**

Storage *of Dials* 168

String Gnomon Dials 112, **113**, 129 - 134, **135, 136,**

STRING GNOMON DIALS.
Chapter 20. 129 - 134

SUNDIAL COLLECTIONS.
Appendix 6. 194 - 198

SUTTON, Henry 37, **38, 39**, 86, **90**, 143, **202**

Sutton's Quadrant 37, **38, 39**

Sun and Moon Dial 113

T
Table Dial 75, **76**

Temporary Hours 31

THON, H. S. **169**

TIBBON, Jacob ben Machir ibn 31

Tide Computer 143, **145, 146**

Toki *Japanese 'hour'* 121, 181

TOMPION, Thomas 86

TOWARDS PRECISION.
Chapter 21. 135 - 140

Towns and Latitudes 5

Transversals **135**

TROSCHEL, Hans **44, 45, 46, 202**

TUCHER, Hans **41, 42, 202**

TUTTELL, Thomas **122**, 124

TW *unidentified maker of a Poke Dial* **20, 21, 202**

U
UNIVERSAL EQUINOCTIAL DIALS.
Chapter 12. 97 - 101

Universal Equinoctial Ring Dial 7, 24 - 29, 97 - 101

V
Vernier **139**

VERTICAL DIALS.
Chapter 13. 102 - 104

Vertical Disc Dial **12**

Vertical Plate Dials 13, **14**, 15

VILLA-ALCOR *modern dials* **174**

VOGLER, Andreas 2, **110, 202**

W
WATKINS, J & W 117, **202**

WELLS, Joseph **36, 202**

Welsch Hours 46

WEST 169, **170**

WHITEHEAD, Richard 78, 79, **85, 202**

WHITWELL, Charles **86, 87, 143, 144, 145, 149, 202**

WILLEBRAND, Johann 92, **108, 109**, 113, **202**

Wind Rose 42

Wind Vane 42

WORGAN, John 86, 87, **88, 202**

WRIGHT, Gabriel **138, 139, 140, 202**

WRIGHT, Thomas 137, **138, 202**

WYNNE, Henry 24, **26**, 27, 78, 86, 88, **202**

Z
ZODIAC & EQUATION OF TIME.
Appendix 5. 192 - 193

Zodiac Sigils **29, 181**

ZUHDÎ, *Quadrant by* 39

OTHER BOOKS BY MIKE COWHAM

A DIAL IN YOUR POKE

First Edition 2004, hard cover, 224 pages in full colour, privately published. Now out of print but superseded by this revised and expanded Second Edition.

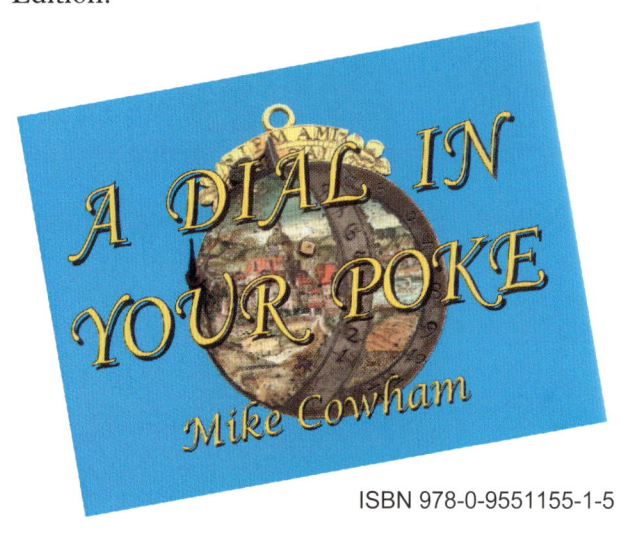

ISBN 978-0-9551155-1-5

A STUDY OF ALTITUDE DIALS

British Sundial Society Monograph No. 4., 2008, soft cover, 71 pages in colour, by Mike Cowham.

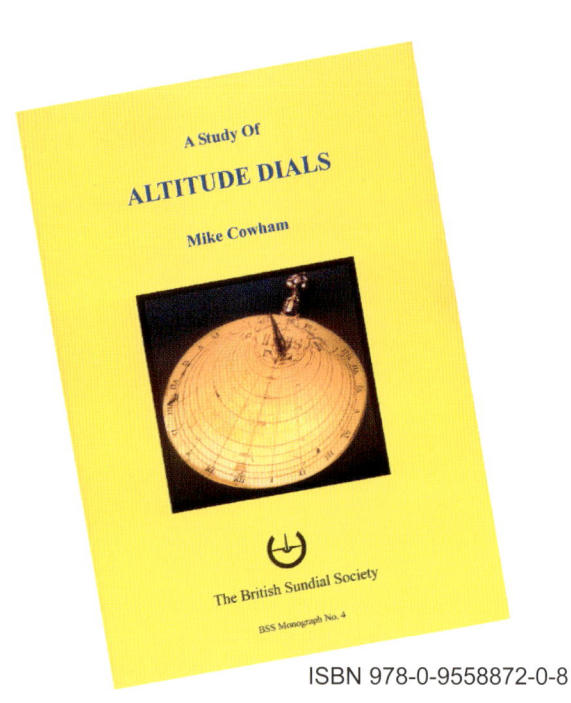

ISBN 978-0-9558872-0-8

SUNDIALS OF THE BRITISH ISLES

Privately published 2005, hard cover 272 pages. Edition limited to 600 numbered copies. This book was written by 27 authors covering the best sundials in their regions. Over 400 sundials are described and illustrated in full colour.

Compiled and Edited by Mike Cowham.

ISBN 978-0-9551155-0-9

TIME RECKONING IN THE MEDIEVAL WORLD

British Sundial Society Monograph No.8., 2010, soft cover, 145 pages in colour by David Scott and Mike Cowham.

Describes all known Anglo-Saxon and early Norman dials, so far discovered in Britain and shows a few of the Continental equivalents.

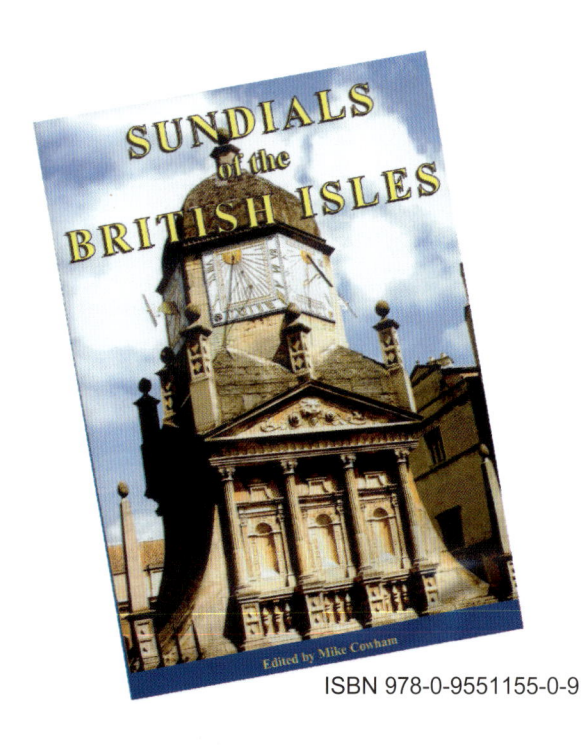

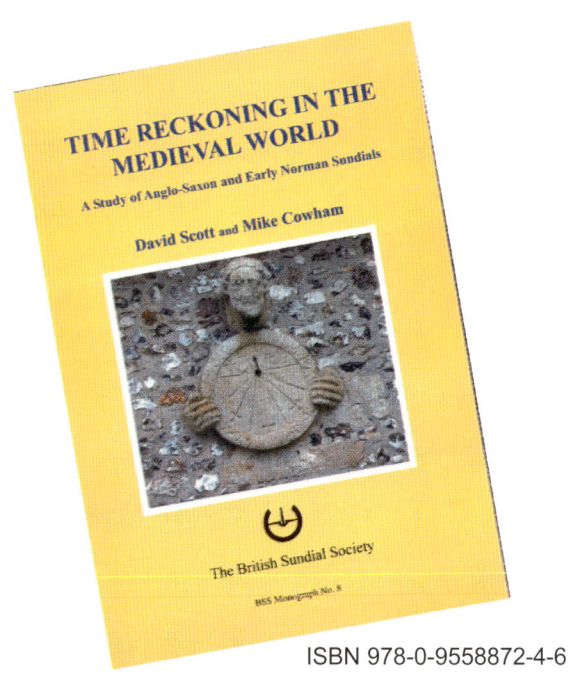

ISBN 978-0-9558872-4-6